# Mastering Salesforce Sales Cloud

You may also be interested in my other book, published by Apress:

**_Salesforce Developer I Certification: Learn the Basics of Apex, Lightning Web Components, and Flow, 2024_**

DOI: https://doi.org/10.1007/979-8-8688-0300-0

Apress®

# Mastering Salesforce Sales Cloud

## Building Your Sales Pipeline from Scratch

Konstantin Kapitanov

# Mastering Salesforce Sales Cloud:

## *Building Your Sales Pipeline from Scratch*

Konstantin Kapitanov

Borås, Sweden

First Edition, 2026



ISBN 978-91-531-6543-9 (Print)

ISBN 978-91-531-6544-6 (EPUB)

ISBN 978-91-531-6680-1 (PDF)

Visit https://libris.kb.se for more information.

ORCID™, the ORCID logo, and iD logo are trademarks of ORCID, Inc. and used herein with permission.

# Table of Contents


Preface.................................................................................................................ix

## PART I – Sales Cloud for Sales Managers and Sales Reps.................................................................1

### Chapter 1. Introduction to Salesforce Sales Cloud.............................3
1.1 Sales Cloud as a 360-Degree Solution.........................................3
1.2 Key Navigation Components..........................................................5
1.3 Objects and Relationships.............................................................8

### Chapter 2. Account and Contact Management............................11
2.1 Account Types and Structure.......................................................11
2.2 List View..........................................................................................19
2.3 Priority Level...................................................................................22
2.4 Contact Relationships...................................................................25

### Chapter 3. Building your Sales Pipeline......................................29
3.1 Create and Convert new Lead.....................................................29
3.2 Opportunity Stages........................................................................34
3.3 Products and Price Books............................................................36

### Chapter 4. Activities and Collaboration.....................................43
4.1 Opportunity Team...........................................................................43
4.2 Chatter..............................................................................................45
4.3 Activity Management......................................................................50
4.4 Campaigns.......................................................................................55

### Chapter 5. Reports..................................................................67
5.1 Standard Report Type...................................................................67
5.2 Custom Report Type......................................................................69
5.3 Tabular Reports..............................................................................73
5.4 Summary Reports...........................................................................80
5.5 Matrix Reports.................................................................................86
5.6 Joined Reports................................................................................89

5.7 Report Charts..........................................................................................93

## Chapter 6. Dashboards..........................................................................99
6.1 Standard Dashboards..............................................................................99
6.2 Dynamic dashboards.............................................................................105
6.3 Sharing dashboards.............................................................................106
6.4 Embedding Dashboards & Reports..............................................................108
6.5 Favorite Dashboards and Reports.............................................................115
6.6 Subscribe Option...............................................................................115

## Chapter 7. Salesforce Mobile App.......................................................117
7.1 Introduction....................................................................................117
7.2 Daily Tasks with Mobile App...................................................................119

# PART II – Sales Cloud for Product Owners, IT Managers, and Admins..........................................................................127

## Chapter 8. Settings and Customization.................................................129
8.1 Company Settings...............................................................................129
8.2 User Management................................................................................132
8.3 Business Processes.............................................................................135

## Chapter 9. Understanding Data Access and Security.............................147
9.1 Profiles and Permission Sets.................................................................147
9.2 Roles and Role Hierarchy......................................................................158
9.3 Data Management in Sales Cloud................................................................161
9.4 Data Import Wizard.............................................................................162
9.5 Data Export Tool...............................................................................167
9.6 Territory management...........................................................................171

## Chapter 10. Practice Lab with Example Data............................................183
10.1 Creating the Project Object..................................................................183
10.2 Creating the Project Expense Object.........................................................202
10.3 Creating the Junction Object.................................................................222
10.4 Building a Flow...............................................................................230
10.5 Testing.......................................................................................240
10.6 Summary.......................................................................................247

## Index...........................................................................................249

# About the Author

**Konstantin Kapitanov** https://orcid.org/0009-0001-6353-7978

Is a certified Salesforce professional based in Sweden with experience and a proven track record of delivering impactful Salesforce solutions and a commitment to innovation. Starting as a web developer, he later founded his consultancy firm, working on CRM projects across Austria, Germany, and Sweden ranging from startups to large enterprises. With a passion for Salesforce, he has successfully developed and implemented tailored solutions over a decade to meet unique business needs. This hands-on experience provided him with a comprehensive understanding of  Salesforce from various stakeholders' perspectives. Additionally, he has contributed to IT R&D projects, including open source tools and Progressive Web Application technology for educational materials.

# Preface

This guide is meant to be a useful, hands-on resource for sales managers who want to lead a high-performing team, sales reps who want to close more deals, and administrators who are in charge of setting up and maintaining the system. This book fills in the gaps between front-line sales work and back-end configuration, giving you the tools you need to get the most out of Salesforce Sales Cloud, no matter what your role or level of experience is.

Part I is where we start our journey. Sales managers and sales reps will find clear, useful advice on every part of the sales process. You will learn how to manage accounts and contacts, create and convert leads, build and monitor your sales pipeline, and use Salesforce's powerful collaboration tools through real-world workflows and best practices. This section is full of tips to help you work smarter and sell better, from learning how to use important features to using dashboards and reports to track performance.

Part II looks at things that happen behind the scenes. Here, product owners, project managers, and administrators will learn how to customize Sales Cloud to meet the specific needs of their businesses. We'll look at configuration options, security controls, user management, and process automation one step at a time. This section gives product owners and project managers a great chance to learn more about the technical landscape so they can have better, more informed conversations with IT teams and bridge the gap between business needs and technical implementation. It gives you the power to make better decisions, work well with technical stakeholders, and make sure that your Salesforce solution really helps your business reach its goals by making important ideas and processes easier to understand.

It will help you along the way, whether you're setting up your first sales pipeline, improving your current workflows, or running a large Salesforce environment. If you learn both the "How" and the "Why" of Sales Cloud, you'll not only get better sales results, but you'll also encourage teamwork in your company.

We encourage you to try out Sales Cloud and see how it can help you. Now is the time to start your journey to becoming a sales and CRM expert.

# PART I — SALES CLOUD FOR SALES MANAGERS AND SALES REPS

## Practical Workflows, Navigation, and Selling Best Practices

# Chapter 1. Introduction to Salesforce Sales Cloud

## 1.1 Sales Cloud as a 360-Degree Solution

In today's fast-paced business environment, effective customer relationship management (CRM) is crucial for organizations seeking to maintain a competitive edge. Salesforce Sales Cloud has emerged as a leading solution, offering a comprehensive platform that empowers businesses to streamline their sales processes, enhance customer interactions, and drive revenue growth. It centralizes customer information, automates sales tasks, and offers thorough analytics, all with the goal of improving customer engagement and accelerating the sales cycle. The platform is designed to support the entire sales lifecycle, from capturing leads to closing deals and maintaining long-term customer relationships.

For sales teams, managing interactions with customer projects is essential. Sales Cloud gives teams the tools to track leads, monitor opportunities, and close sales faster. One of the key purposes is to provide businesses with real-time visibility into their sales pipeline and performance, enabling data-driven decision-making. This transparency across teams helps align on goals, improve productivity, and increase revenue.

Perhaps one of the most significant advantages is its robust analytics and reporting capabilities. Real-time dashboards and customizable reports provide sales managers and executives with invaluable insights into team performance, pipeline health, and key performance indicators. This approach to sales management enables teams to identify trends, address bottlenecks, and continuously refine their sales strategies for optimal results.

Beyond core sales functions, it also supports quote proposals, order management, and territory planning. It seamlessly connects all aspects of the sales process, thereby reducing the risk of errors and enhancing overall efficiency.

By tackling these issues, Sales Cloud delivers tangible value to businesses of all sizes and across various industries. Small and medium-sized enterprises benefit from the ability to establish structured sales processes and scale operations efficiently. Larger organizations leverage its advanced features and customization capabilities to manage complex sales cycles and coordinate large teams across multiple territories.

As we study the features and benefits, it becomes clear that this platform represents more than just a technological solution. It embodies a comprehensive approach to sales management that aligns with modern business practices and customer expectations. By providing a centralized, intelligent, and user-friendly platform, it empowers sales teams to work smarter, collaborate more effectively, and ultimately drive sustainable revenue growth for their organizations.

Salesforce Lightning represents a significant evolution from the earlier Salesforce Classic interface. While Classic provided a functional platform for managing customer relationships, Lightning introduces a modern, user-friendly interface that enhances user experience and productivity.  It offers a streamlined layout, making it easier for users to navigate and access essential features.  This evolution reflects Salesforce's commitment to continuous improvement and innovation.

One of the standout features of Sales Cloud is its multi-device compatibility. Users can access the platform seamlessly across various devices, including desktops, tablets, and mobile phones. This flexibility is particularly beneficial for field sales teams who require access to real-time data while on the go. The Salesforce Mobile App enables sales representatives to manage leads, track opportunities, and collaborate with team members from anywhere, ensuring they remain productive regardless of their location. This mobile accessibility enhances efficiency and empowers sales teams to respond quickly to customer inquiries and capitalize on opportunities right from the start.

Sales Cloud is designed to integrate seamlessly with other Salesforce Clouds, such as Service Cloud, Marketing Cloud, Commerce Cloud, and others. This integration creates a comprehensive CRM solution that allows businesses to manage all aspects of customer interactions in one place. For instance, by connecting Sales Cloud with Service Cloud, organizations can ensure that sales and support teams have access to the same customer information, leading to more cohesive customer support. Similarly, integrating with Marketing Cloud enables sales teams to leverage marketing insights and campaigns to drive lead generation and conversion efforts. This interconnectedness boosts operational efficiency and delivers a unified, 360-degree view of customer relationships.

Further, Sales Cloud supports the integration of thousands of third-party apps from the Salesforce AppExchange marketplace. For more details see https://appexchange.salesforce.com. This allows businesses to extend the capabilities of Sales Cloud with additional tools.

# 1.2 Key Navigation Components

We begin by exploring the core navigation experience of the Sales Cloud, focusing on the Lightning Home Page. It serves as the central hub for users, providing quick access to critical tools, data, and insights needed for daily tasks. Upon logging in, users are greeted with customizable components that can display essential metrics like sales performance, upcoming tasks, and key deals.

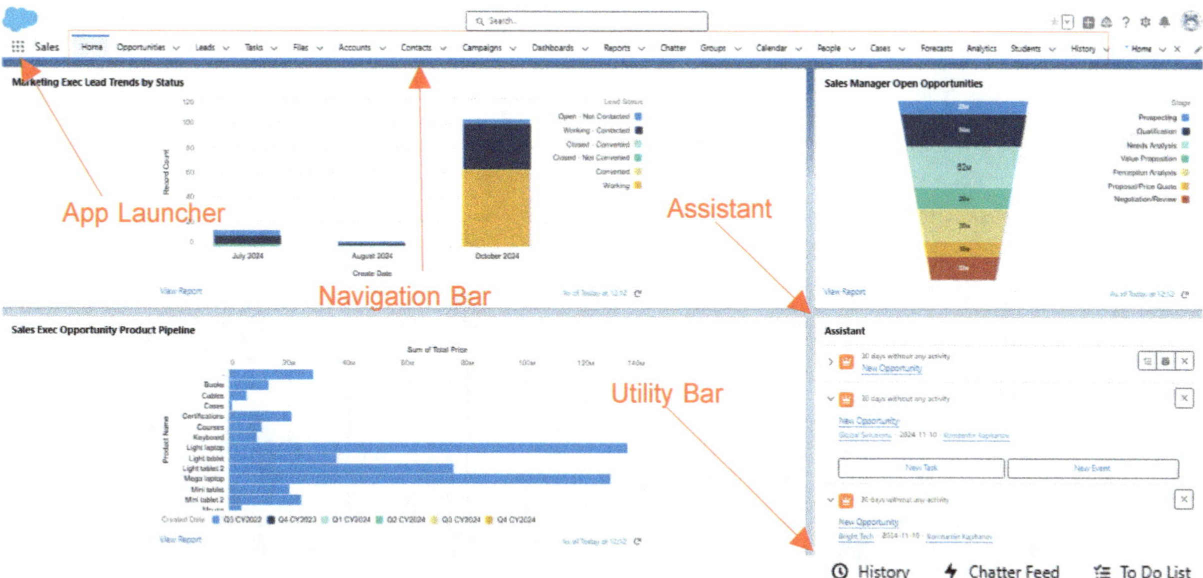


Figure 1.2-1 Lightning Home Page Components & Navigation

The Navigation Bar at the top of the screen includes a variety of tabs, such as Opportunities, Accounts, Contacts, and Leads, which provide direct entry points to key customer data. At the bottom of the page, the Utility Bar offers access to frequently used tools such as the To Do List, Chatter Feed, or History, making multitasking simple and efficient.

The Assistant component, for example, is a productivity feature that keeps users on top of urgent tasks or follow-ups. It highlights overdue activities and suggests next steps for deals that need attention.

The Lightning Home Page is fully customizable, empowering businesses to tailor the experience to their unique workflows. Widgets can be added or removed, ensuring each user sees the most relevant information as soon as they log in. It serves as the command center for users, offering a streamlined and personalized interface designed to boost productivity.

At the top of the page, the App Launcher provides a powerful, user-friendly interface for navigating apps. This menu consolidates all available tools into one place, reducing the need to toggle between different screens and ensuring that users can swiftly find what they need. It also allows customization, enabling administrators to tailor the available apps and layout for different user profiles. By prioritizing certain apps or creating custom ones, businesses can ensure that their users always have easy access to the tools they use most frequently. This level of customization helps streamline workflows and enhances productivity, making the App Launcher an essential tool for scaling operations within Sales Cloud.

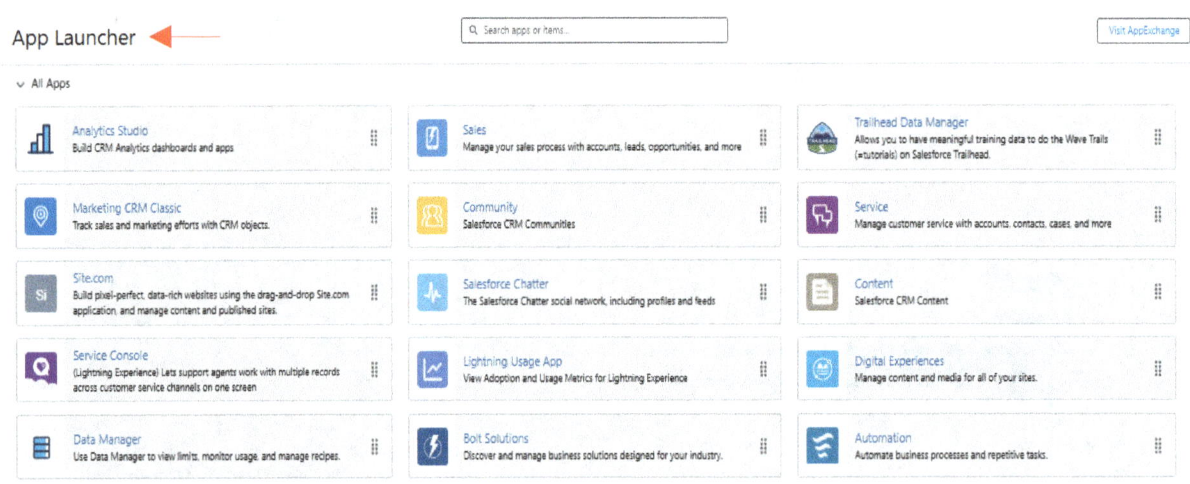

Figure 1.2-2 App Launcher

Global Actions are powerful features designed to enhance user productivity by enabling users to quickly execute frequent tasks from multiple locations. They allow users to perform various tasks like Log a Call or create New Task from different locations such as the Home page, Accounts, or Leads without needing to navigate to specific records or objects.

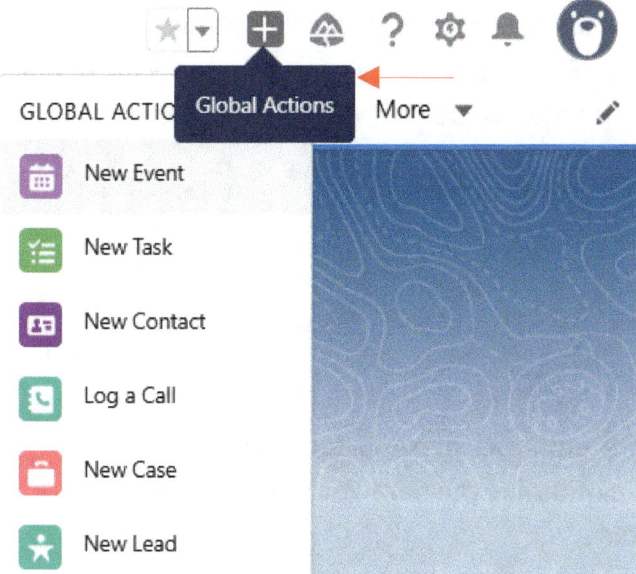

Figure 1.2-3 Global Actions

Global Search is a powerful, cross-functional search tool that allows users to search across the entire Sales Cloud platform for records, files, and data related to multiple objects from one central location. It enhances productivity by making it easy to locate relevant information without navigating to individual objects or specific record pages. It allows users to search for records in standard objects like Accounts, Contacts, Opportunities, Leads, and custom objects, and it pulls in results from any searchable data within the Salesforce org.

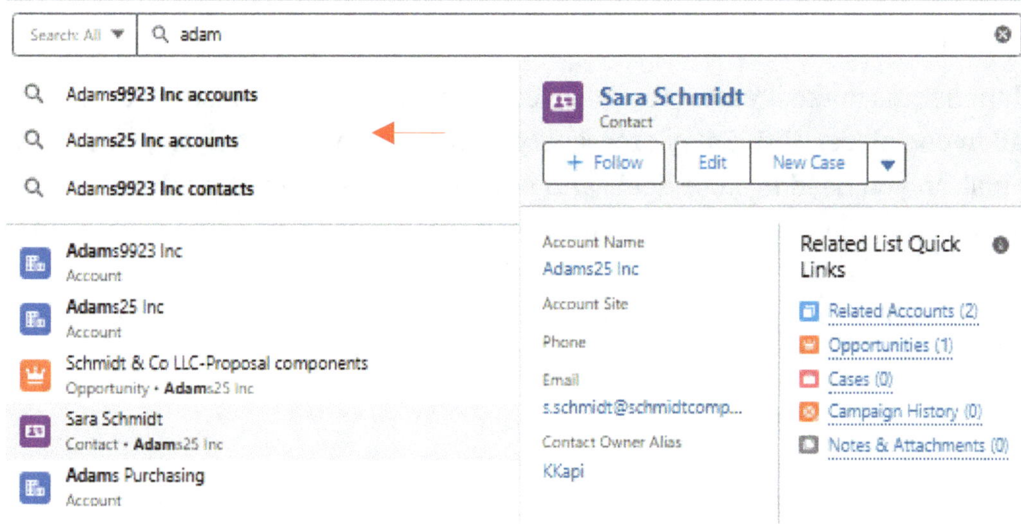

Figure 1.2-4 Global Search Bar

The records returned as a result of an activity or a search result can include various types of data depending on the search or activity performed. This collection is not the complete list, but it includes many of the standard objects provided in Sales Cloud. We will discuss the topic of objects in more detail in the next section.

# 1.3 Objects and Relationships

In Salesforce, objects are like folders that store different types of important business information. Think of them as categories that help organize the data your team needs to work with every day. There are two main types of objects.

**Standard objects** are built into Sales Cloud and represent the core data entities you'll interact with frequently, such as Accounts, Contacts, Opportunities, and Leads.

**Custom objects** can be created specifically for your organization to store additional data that's unique to your business processes.

Each object has fields, which are like the individual pieces of information inside the folder. For example, in the Account object, a field might be the account name or its industry.

Objects and Relationships in Salesforce are like connections between these different folders. They help link data so that you can easily see how things are related.  For example, you can link an account from a company to multiple contacts within that company. An opportunity, defined as a deal, is linked to its corresponding account, allowing you to track which deals are associated with each company.

These objects and relationships make it easier for salespeople to keep track of customers, contacts, and deals, all in one place. With Salesforce, everything is connected, helping you quickly find the information you need to close deals and manage customer relationships effectively.

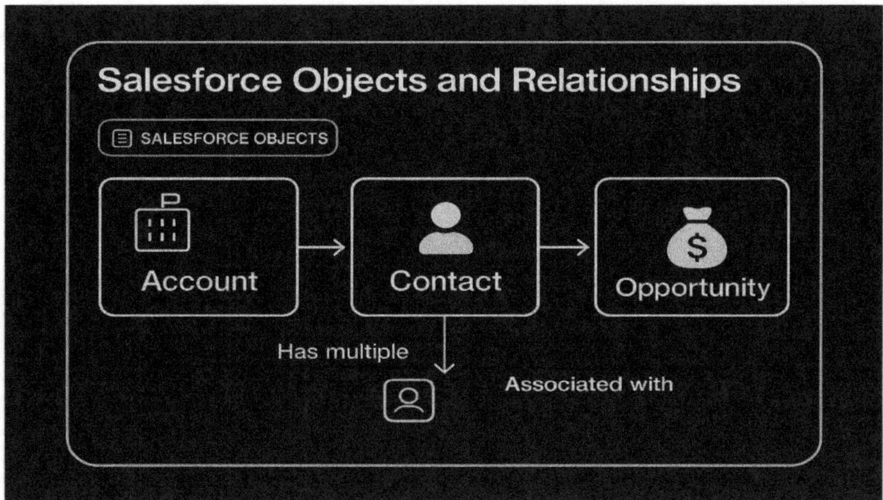


Figure 1.3-1 Objects and Relationships

# PART I — Sales Cloud for Sales Managers and Sales Reps

| Standard Objects | Description |
| --- | --- |
| Account | Represents a company or organization you do business with. Stores key information like industry, revenue, and account owner. |
| Lead | Potential customers who have shown interest but are not yet qualified. Lead records contain contact details and status. |
| Opportunity | Sales deals in progress, tracking potential revenue. Contains information such as stages, probability, and close dates. |
| Contact | Individuals associated with an Account or Opportunity. Contains personal details like name, email, and title. |
| Task | To do items or action steps assigned to users, often linked to other records like Leads or Opportunities. |
| Case | Customer support or service requests. Tracks the issue, its resolution, and any related follow-up tasks. |
| Order | Tracks customer orders related to products or services. Contains details like order status, products, and billing info. |
| Report | Custom views of Salesforce data that allow users to analyze metrics and track performance across different objects. |
| Dashboard | Visual representations of reports, displaying key performance indicators (KPIs) through charts and metrics. |
| Event | Scheduled meetings or calls. Events are linked to records like Contacts or Opportunities for tracking. |

Table 1.3-1 Objects and Records

# Chapter 2. Account and Contact Management

## 2.1 Account Types and Structure

The Account object is the backbone of most sales and relationship management activities in the system, as it represents the organizations or individuals your company interacts with. Understanding the different types of accounts and how to structure them is key to ensuring that your data is organized effectively and supports your sales processes.

Let's explore the types of accounts you can create in Sales Cloud, how to choose the right one for your situation, and how to manage more complex structures like parent-child accounts. When creating a new account, it's essential to choose the right type based on the relationship and context. Salesforce primarily offers two account types.

**Business Accounts** represent companies or organizations that your business deals with. For example, if you're selling products or services to other businesses, those businesses would be created as business accounts. They typically contain information like company name, industry, size, revenue, and more. This type of account is perfect for B2B relationships.

**Person Accounts** are used when dealing directly with individuals rather than businesses. They combine the functionality of both accounts and contacts into a single record, since the individual is both the company and the contact. B2C environments, like retail or individual service businesses, most commonly use these accounts. For example, if you run a real estate business, a home buyer would typically be represented as a person account.

When choosing between these two, it's important to consider whether your relationship is with a business entity or an individual. Business accounts are better suited for complex sales cycles involving multiple stakeholders, while person accounts streamline the process for consumer-focused sales.

**Note!** Person accounts are not automatically available in all Salesforce Orgs. They need to be enabled first, and once enabled, they cannot be turned off. Accounts representing individuals come with specific constraints not found in business accounts.

In our next examples, we will use only business accounts for simplicity. In many cases, your business may interact with large organizations or public institutions that have multiple divisions, subsidiaries, or units. These companies often have complex purchasing or organizational structures, and Sales Cloud allows you to mirror that complexity using parent-child account relationships.

**A Parent Account** is the top-level account, often representing a large corporate entity or a holding company. For instance, if you are dealing with a multinational corporation, the parent account could be the main headquarters or corporate office.

**Child Accounts** are the accounts associated with divisions, subsidiaries, or regional offices of that parent company. Despite having its own sales processes, contacts, and opportunities, each child account maintains its connection to the parent account.

This hierarchical structure helps you see the full scope of your relationship with large clients, including total revenue and opportunities across all linked accounts. In certain situations, such as when working with companies or public entities that have centralized purchasing processes, creating a separate account for a central purchasing organization can be beneficial. This scenario is particularly common in industries with complex procurement structures, such as manufacturing, government, or healthcare.

This setup can improve efficiency by centralizing communication, tracking all deals made through that purchasing department, and streamlining negotiations, while still maintaining a broader view of the entire company through the parent-child relationship.

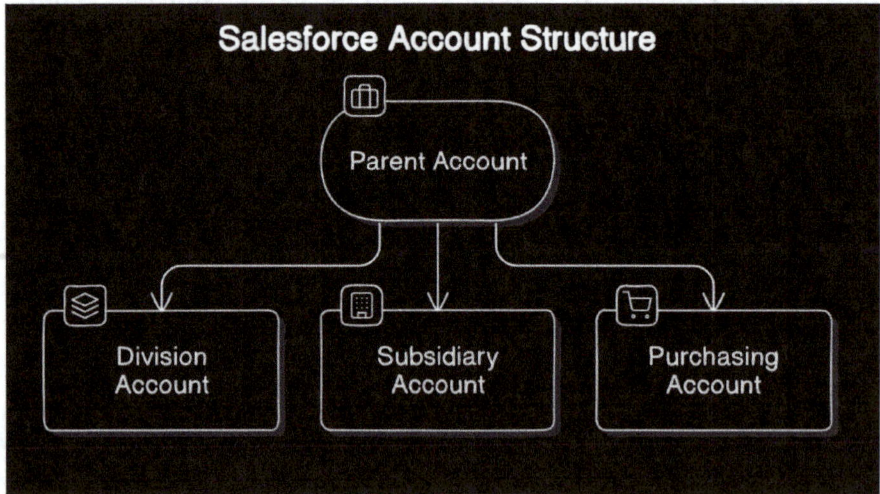


Figure 2.1-1 Account Structure

Now let us create a new child account that is connected to the parent account.

*On your top menu, click the Account tab. Then click the New button to create a new Account.*

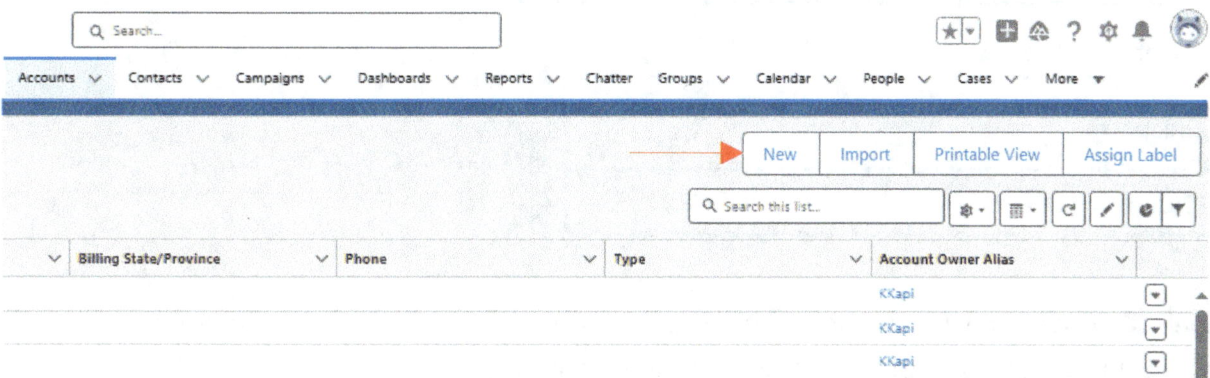

When creating a new account in Sales Cloud, one important step is selecting the right value in the Type field. This field helps categorize the account based on the type of relationship your company has with the organization.

**Account Types:**

**Prospect**: Represents a potential customer who hasn't yet purchased your products or services.

**Customer-Direct:** Represents a direct customer who buys from you.

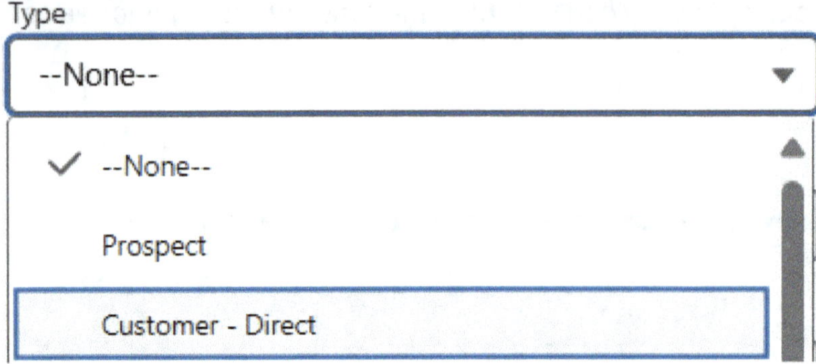


**Customer-Channel:** A customer that purchases through a channel, like a distributor or a centralized purchasing organization within a large company.

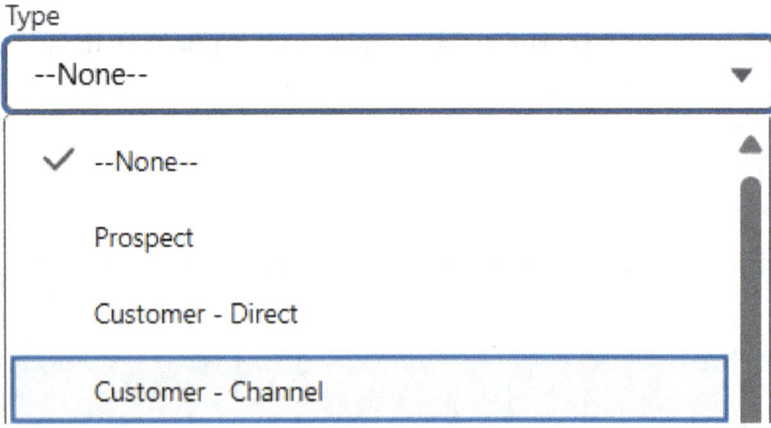

**Channel Partner/Reseller:** Represents a partner or reseller that sells your products or services on your behalf.

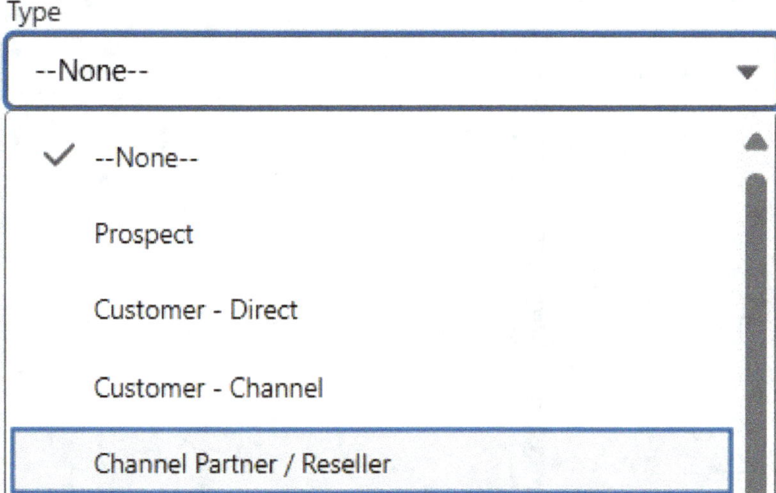

**Installation Partner:** Represents a partner that installs or sets up your product or services.

# PART I — Sales Cloud for Sales Managers and Sales Reps

**Technology Partner:** A partner that provides technology-related services or solutions.

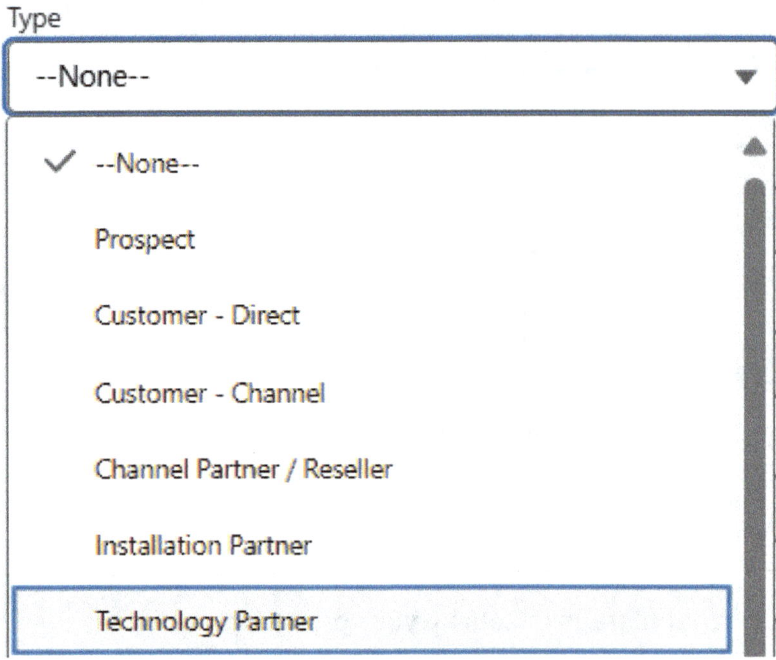

**Other:** Used for accounts that don't fit into any of the predefined categories.

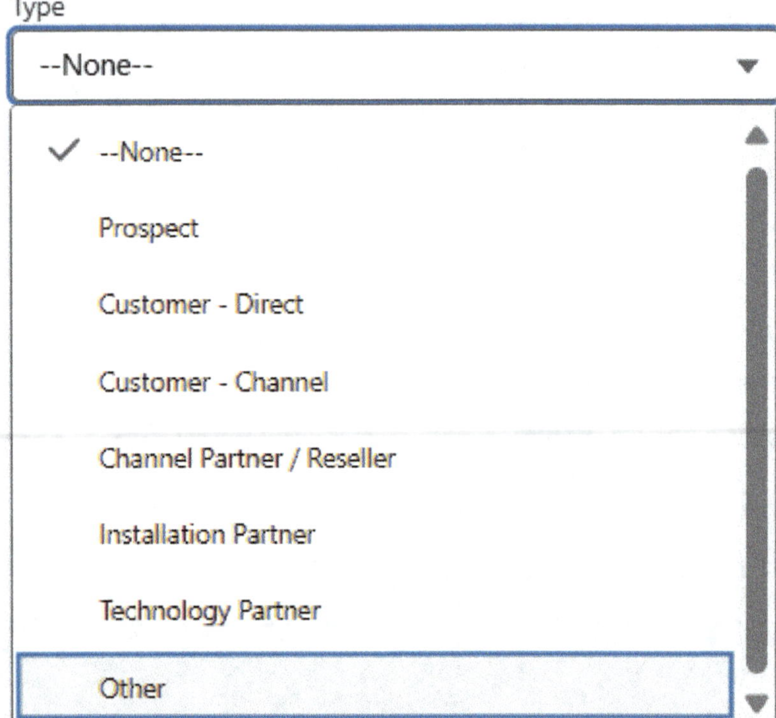

In this context, you're creating an account for a purchasing organization, which will be responsible for procurement, likely interacting directly with your business. Since the purchasing organization is your direct point of contact for sales, you would select Customer-Channel, indicating that this customer purchases through a specific channel or intermediary.

*Fill in the Account Information, select the Parent Account and click Save.*

New Account: Personal

* = Required Information

**Account Information**

Account Owner
Konstantin Kapitanov

Rating
Hot

* Account Name
Adams Purchasing

Phone

Parent Account
Adams25 Inc

Fax

Account Number

Website

Account Site

Ticker Symbol

Type
Customer - Channel

Ownership
Other

Cancel   Save & New   Save

*Our Purchasing Account is created now.*

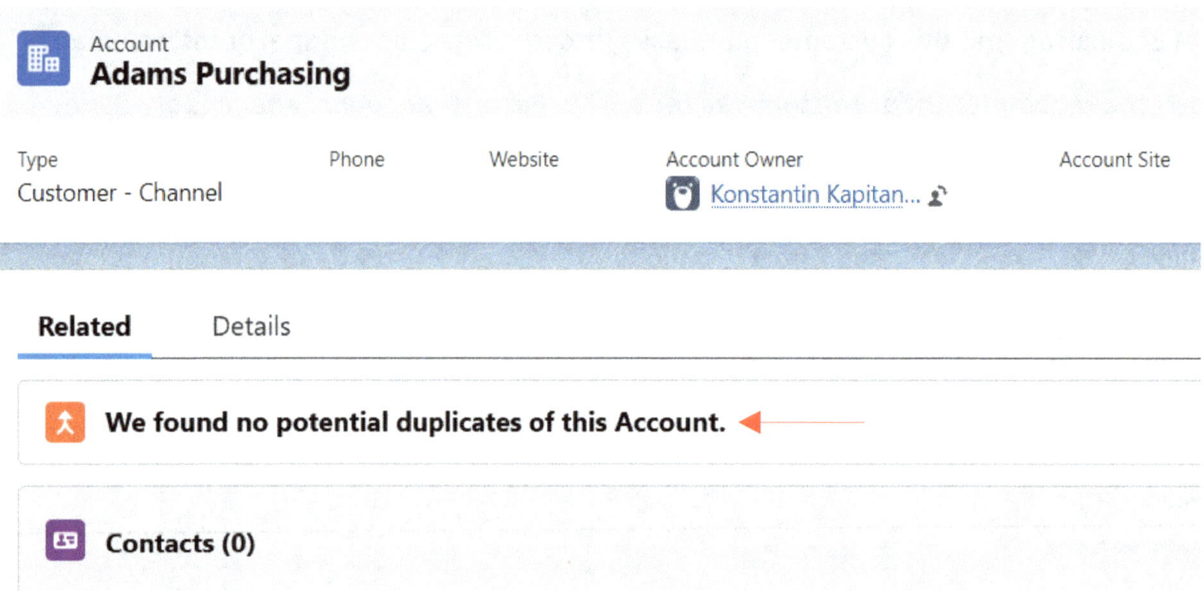

**Note!** It's important when creating a new account to ensure that no duplicates exist, because they can lead to confusion, inaccuracies in reporting, and inefficiencies in managing customer relationships. To avoid this, you can use duplicate management tools or perform a search beforehand to verify that the account you're about to create doesn't already exist.

When you create a new account, you will notice several related tabs, such as Opportunities, Contacts, and Cases. These tabs link to the account and facilitate the management of crucial information associated with it.

- Opportunities: These represent potential deals or sales tied to this account. You can track the progress of each opportunity here.

- Contacts: These are the individuals or key stakeholders associated with the account, such as decision-makers or points of contact within the company.

- Cases: These are support or service requests linked to the account, allowing you to manage any issues or inquiries the customer has.

Each of these tabs keeps the related data organized, so all interactions with the account are easily accessible and visible in one place.

*Go to the parent account you connected during creation and click the View Account Hierarchy button.*

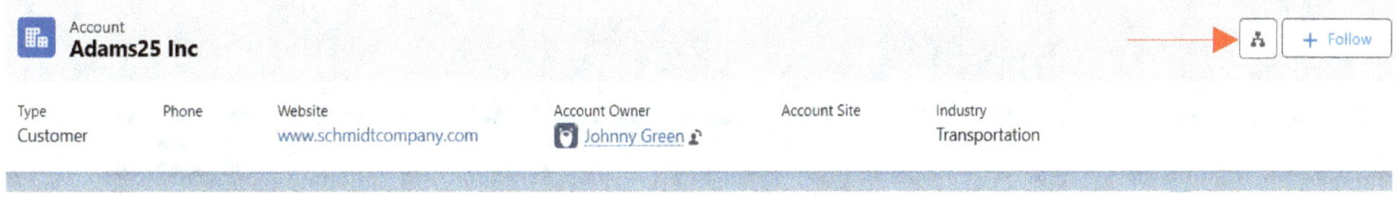

*You see your new account's hierarchy structure.*

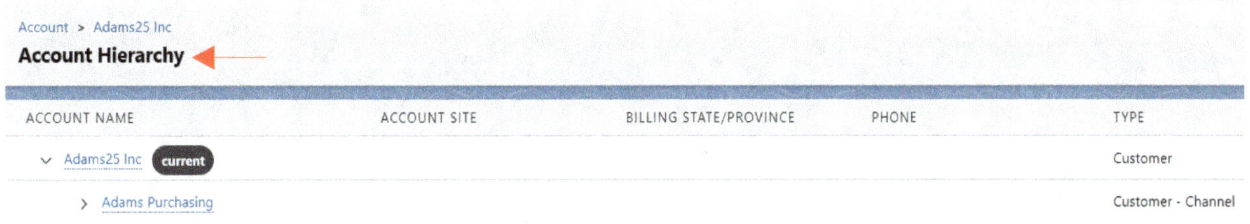

# 2.2 List View

A list view in Sales Cloud allows you to filter and organize account records based on specific criteria that matter to you or your team. For example, you might want to see a list of only your active accounts created in the last month or by a specific type, like Customer-Direct. Custom list views help you focus on the accounts that are most relevant, making your daily tasks more efficient.

# PART I — Sales Cloud for Sales Managers and Sales Reps

*Now, let us create our own Account List View. Click the Accounts tab on your top navigation bar, then select New.*

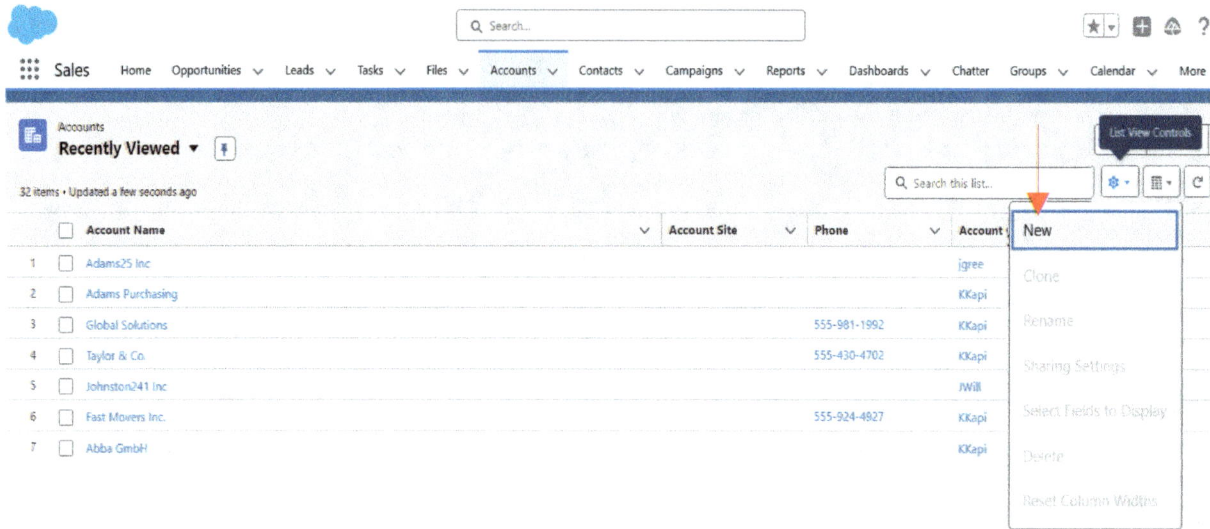

When creating a custom list view for accounts the "Who sees this list view?" setting allows you to control the visibility of the list view. There are three options to choose from, depending on who you want to share the list with:

**Only I can see this list view**, making it private and visible solely to me. It's ideal when you want to create a personal view for your own work or analysis without sharing it with others.

**All users can see this list view,** which makes it public and accessible to everyone. Anyone with access to the Accounts object will be able to see and use this list view.

**Share list view with groups of users** allows you to share the list view with specific groups, roles, or users. You can tailor who has access, making it visible only to certain teams or individuals.

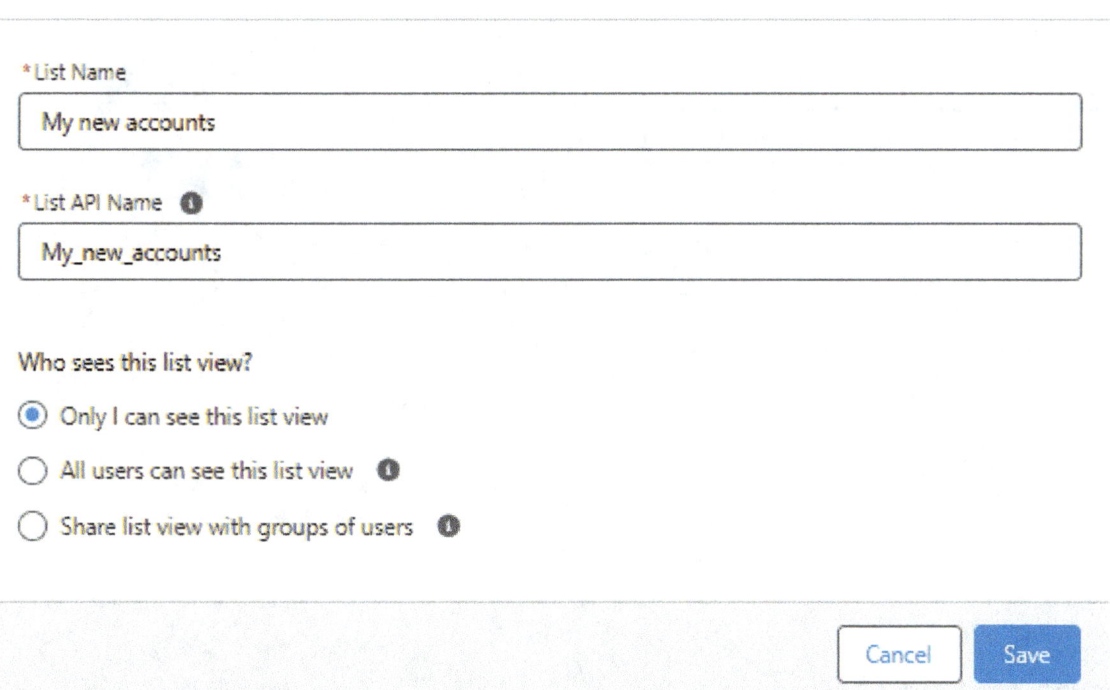

After saving your New List View click Add Filter to choose specific fields
and values.

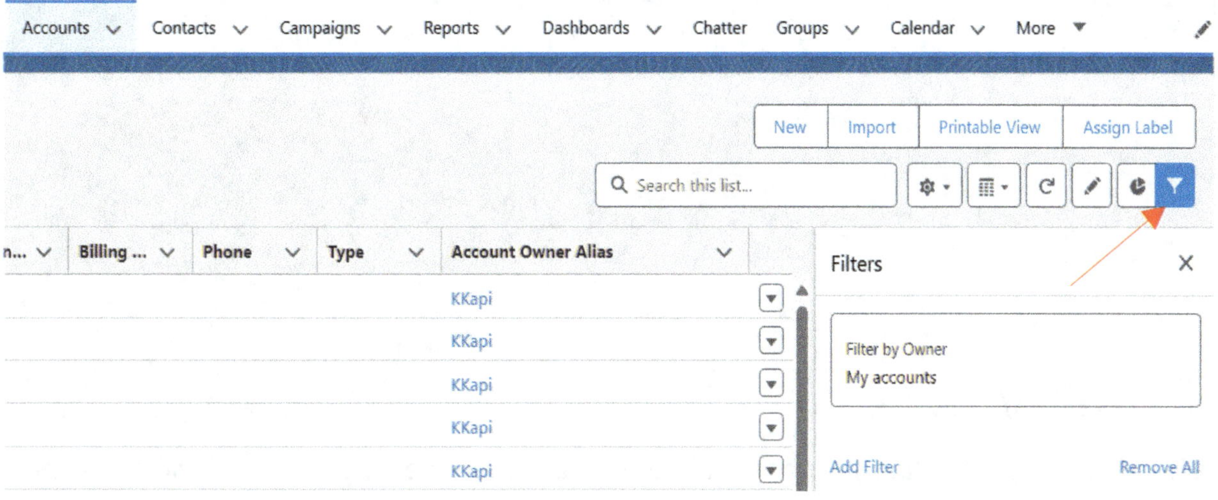

*Now, we can select the fields, apply values to those fields and click Save.*

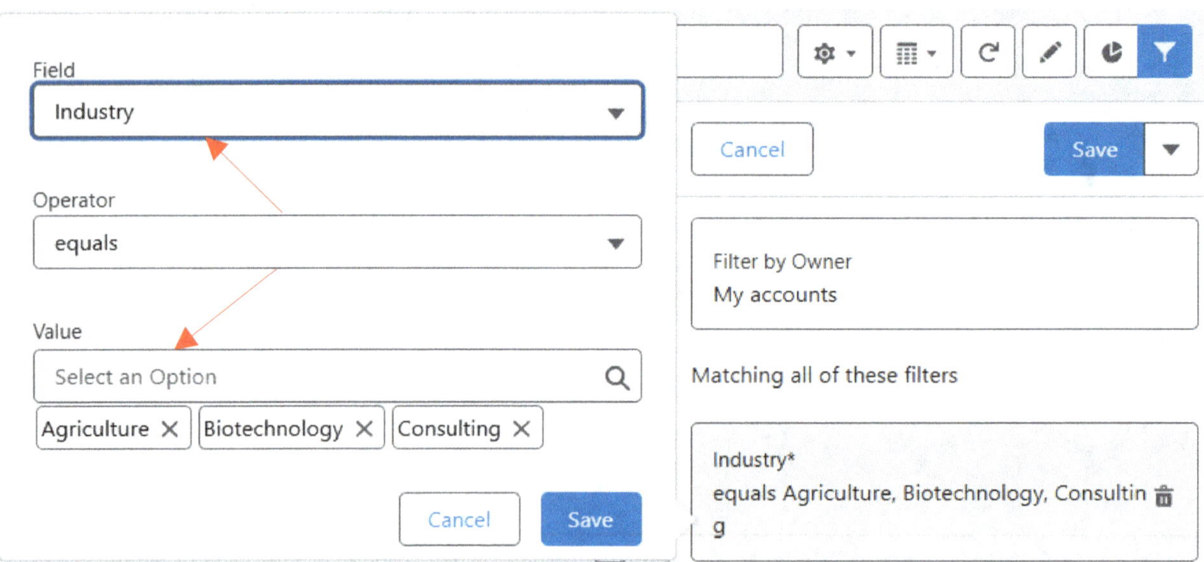

*The new Account List is created.*

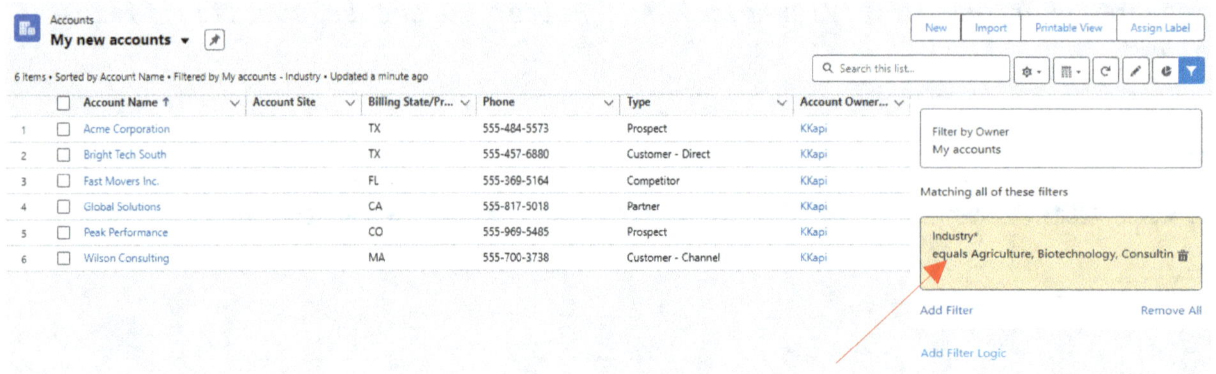

# 2.3 Priority Level

Service Level Agreements (SLAs) are crucial in managing customer expectations and ensuring that service delivery meets agreed-upon standards. SLAs help define the level of service a customer can expect, which can significantly impact customer satisfaction and retention. When working with SLAs, you will encounter several important fields on the Account object.

**Customer Priority** categorizes customers based on their importance to your business. Prioritizing customers helps in allocating resources effectively and ensuring that high-priority customers receive timely support.

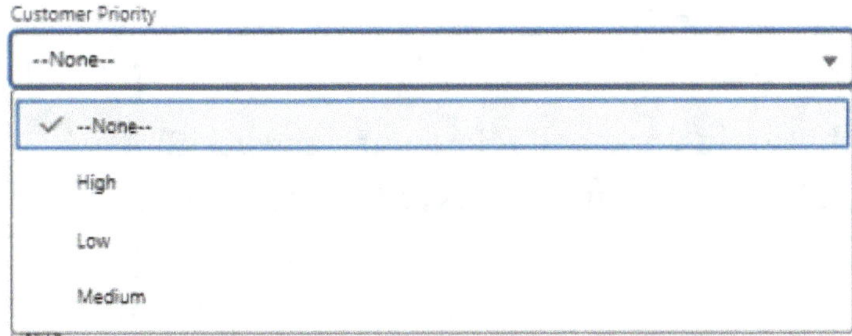

**SLA** typically contains values like Gold, Silver, Platinum, and Bronze, representing different service tiers. Each tier is associated with specific service levels and response times.

**SLA Tiers Comparison** (Tiers could be different for your organization)

| Tier | Response Time | Support Hours | Features |
|------|---------------|---------------|----------|
| Platinum | 1 hour | 24/7 | Dedicated support |
| Gold | 4 hours | Business hours | Priority queue |
| Silver | 8 hours | Business hours | Standard support |
| Bronze | 24 hours | Business hours | Email support only |

Table 2.3-1 SLA Tiers Comparison

# PART I — Sales Cloud for Sales Managers and Sales Reps

**SLA Expiration Date** tracks when the SLA agreement is set to expire. Monitoring this date is essential for renewing agreements and maintaining service continuity.

**SLA Serial Number** as a unique identifier helps in tracking and referencing specific SLA agreements, making it easier to manage multiple agreements across different accounts.

**Number of Locations** indicates how many locations the SLA covers. This is particularly useful for businesses with multiple branches or service points.

**Upsell Opportunity** identifies potential opportunities to sell additional services or products to the customer, which can be associated with SLA they are currently on.

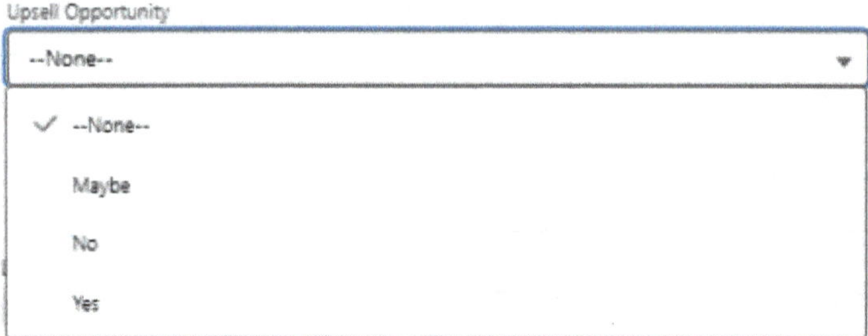

**An Active** checkbox indicates whether the SLA is currently active. Keeping this updated ensures that your team is aware of which agreements are in effect.

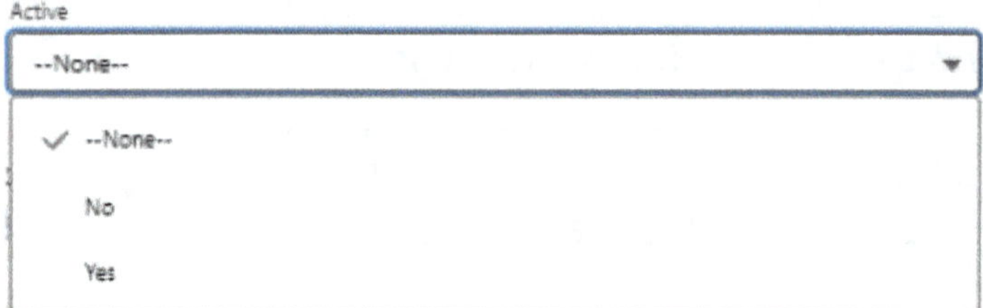

By effectively utilizing these SLA-related fields and features in Sales Cloud, you can ensure consistent service delivery, improve customer satisfaction, and identify opportunities for account growth and retention.

# 2.4 Contact Relationships

Sales Cloud enables you to define Primary and Secondary contact relationships for accounts, allowing you to specify the strength of each relationship.

**The Primary Contact** is the main point of contact for an account, often the key decision-maker or someone with significant influence. This contact has the strongest and most relevant relationship with the account.

**Secondary Contacts** are other contacts who may also interact with the account but have less direct or influential roles compared to the primary contact.

By default, contacts in Sales Cloud are associated with a single primary account, but you can enable Account-Contact Relationships to link a contact with multiple accounts, which is crucial for managing secondary account relationships. Ask your system administrator about this setting in your organization.

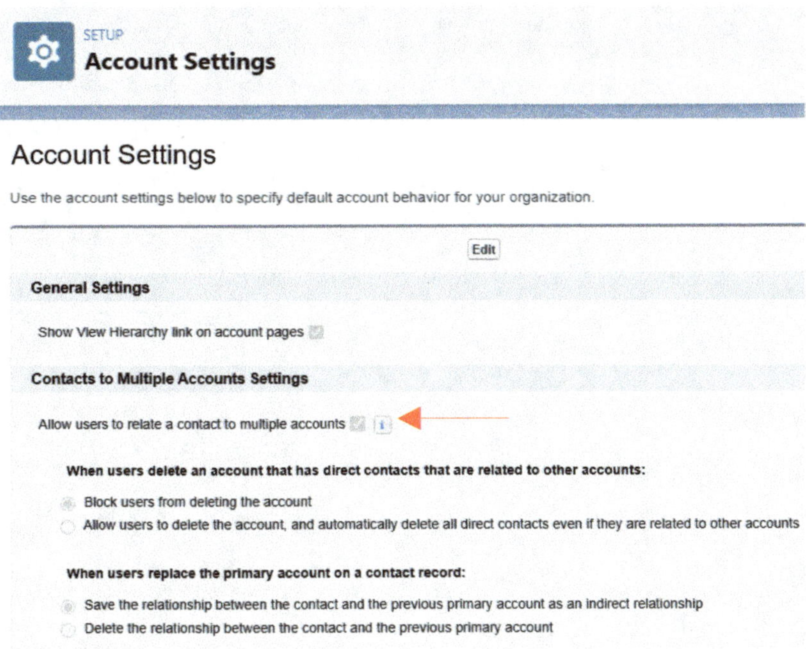

# PART I — Sales Cloud for Sales Managers and Sales Reps

*To add a new Account-Contact Relationship, click the Add Relationship button.*

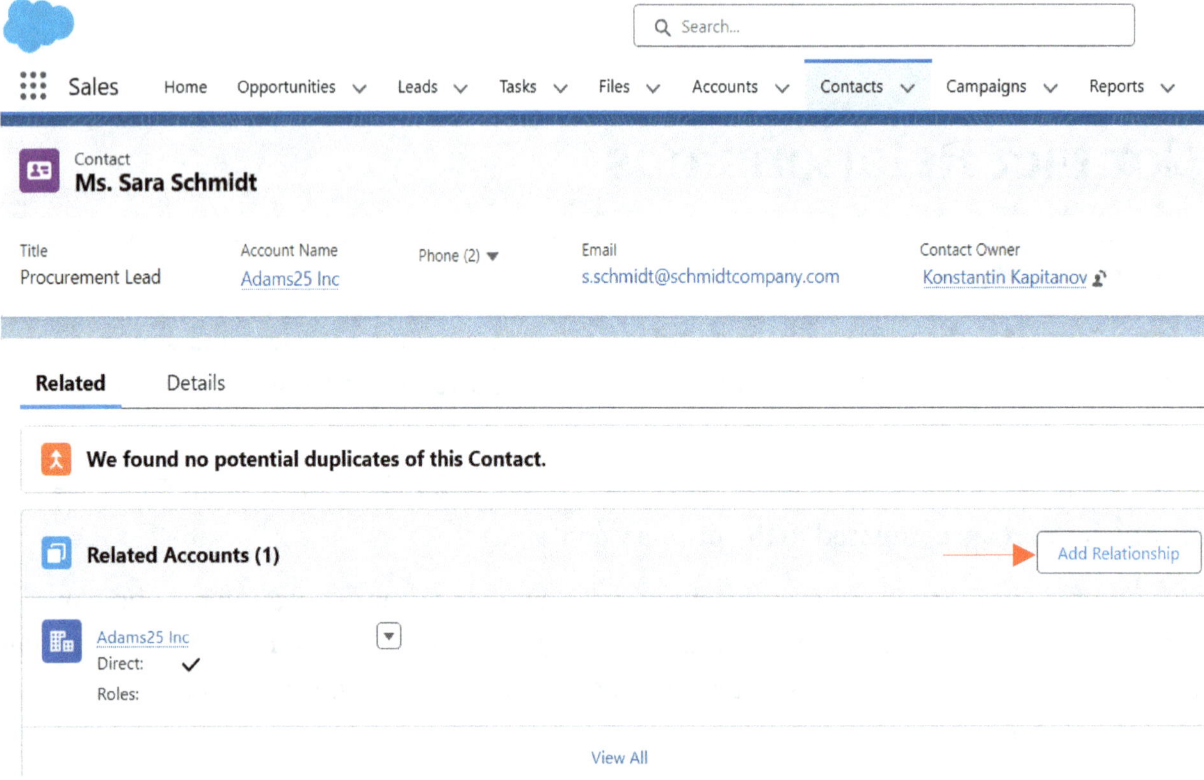

*Then, select the additional account and click Save.*

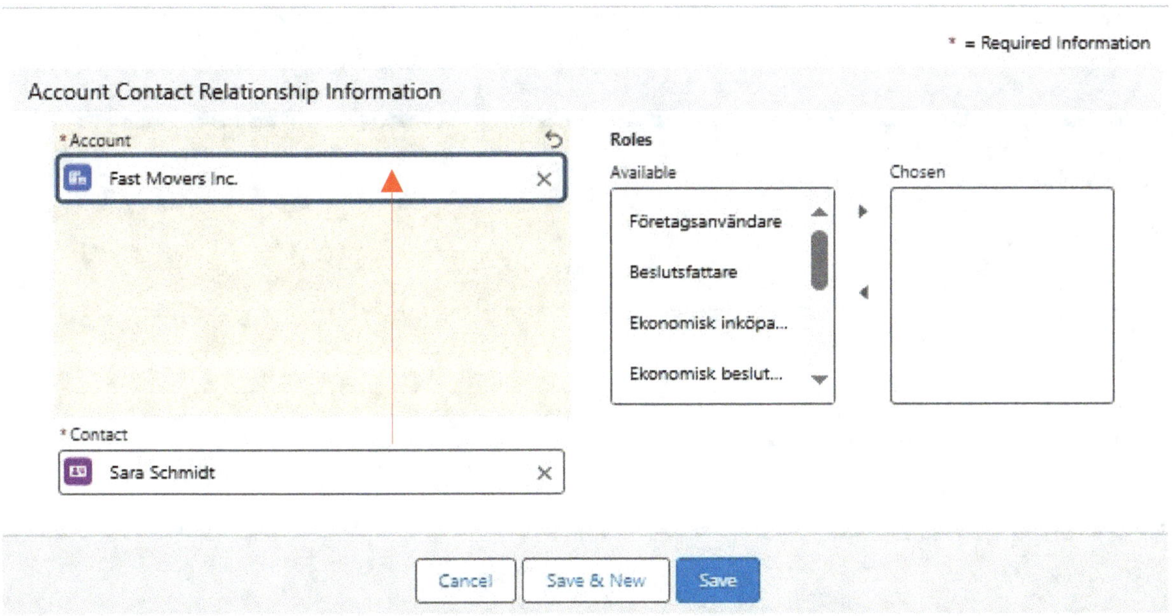

*The second account connection has now been created.*

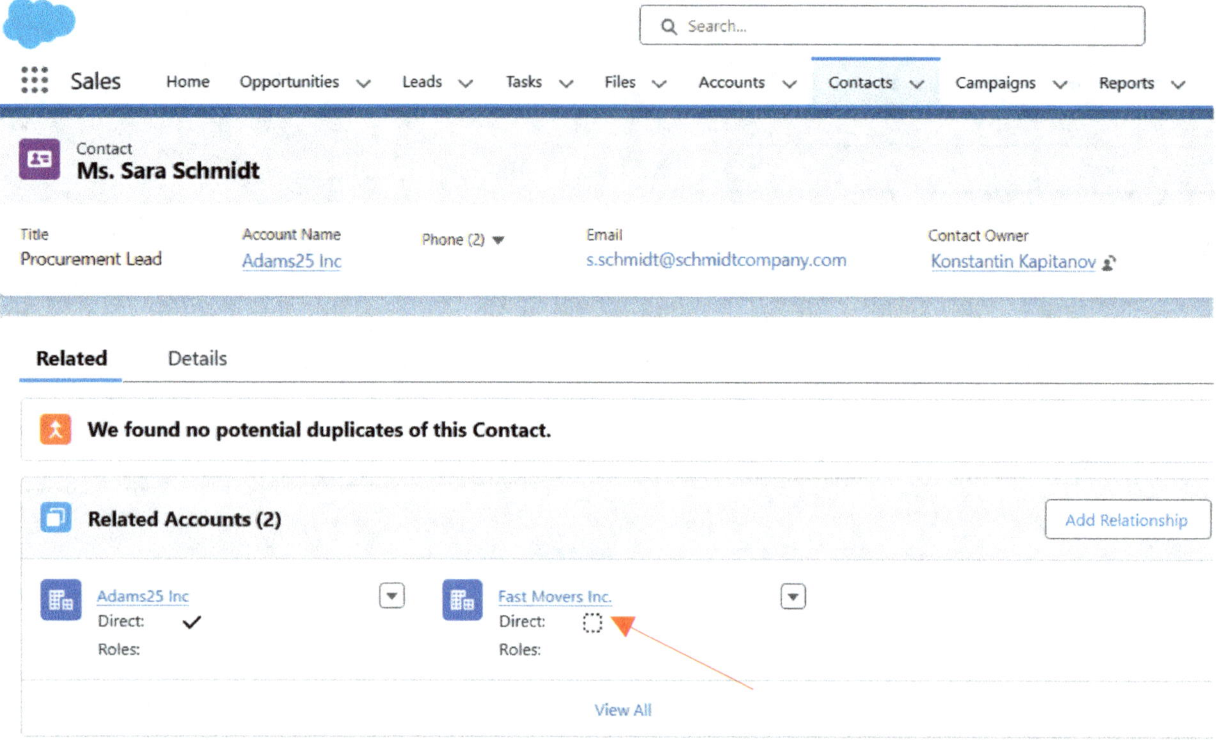

# Chapter 3. Building your Sales Pipeline

## 3.1 Create and Convert new Lead

Building a sales pipeline in Sales Cloud means tracking every step of the customer journey from the first interaction with a potential lead to closing a deal as an opportunity. The pipeline gives you a clear picture of where each prospect stands in the sales process. It helps you visualize sales opportunities and estimate future revenue.

As a first step, leads are potential customers who have expressed interest in your product or service but have not yet received qualification. Creating new leads is essential to ensure that no potential sales are missed and that you can track them from the very beginning of the journey.

We convert qualified leads into actual business opportunities, contacts, and accounts. This conversion plays a crucial role in advancing these prospects in the pipeline and estimating their potential revenue.

Opportunities represent sales deals. Qualifying a lead transforms it into an opportunity, enabling you to track it through various stages, from negotiation to final closure. Managing opportunities properly allows you to forecast revenue, track deal stages, and identify which ones need the most attention to close. Now, let's dive into the technical steps.

# PART I — Sales Cloud for Sales Managers and Sales Reps

*Go to the Leads Tab on the top of your screen, or if it's not visible, click the App Launcher and search for Leads.*

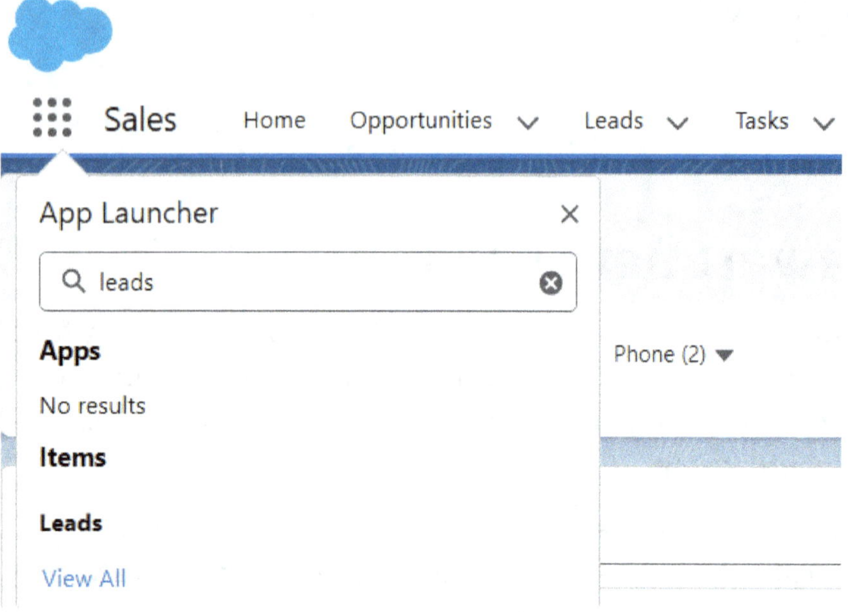


*Then you'll see a button labeled New click it.*

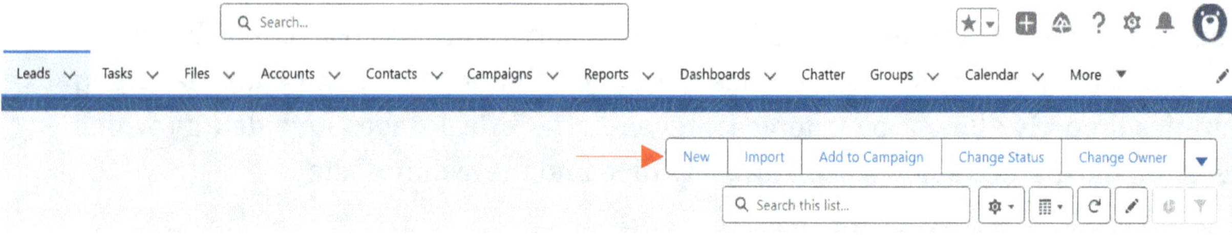

*Fill in Lead Information such as First Name, Last Name, Company, Mobile, Email, Lead Source, and any other relevant information before clicking Save.*

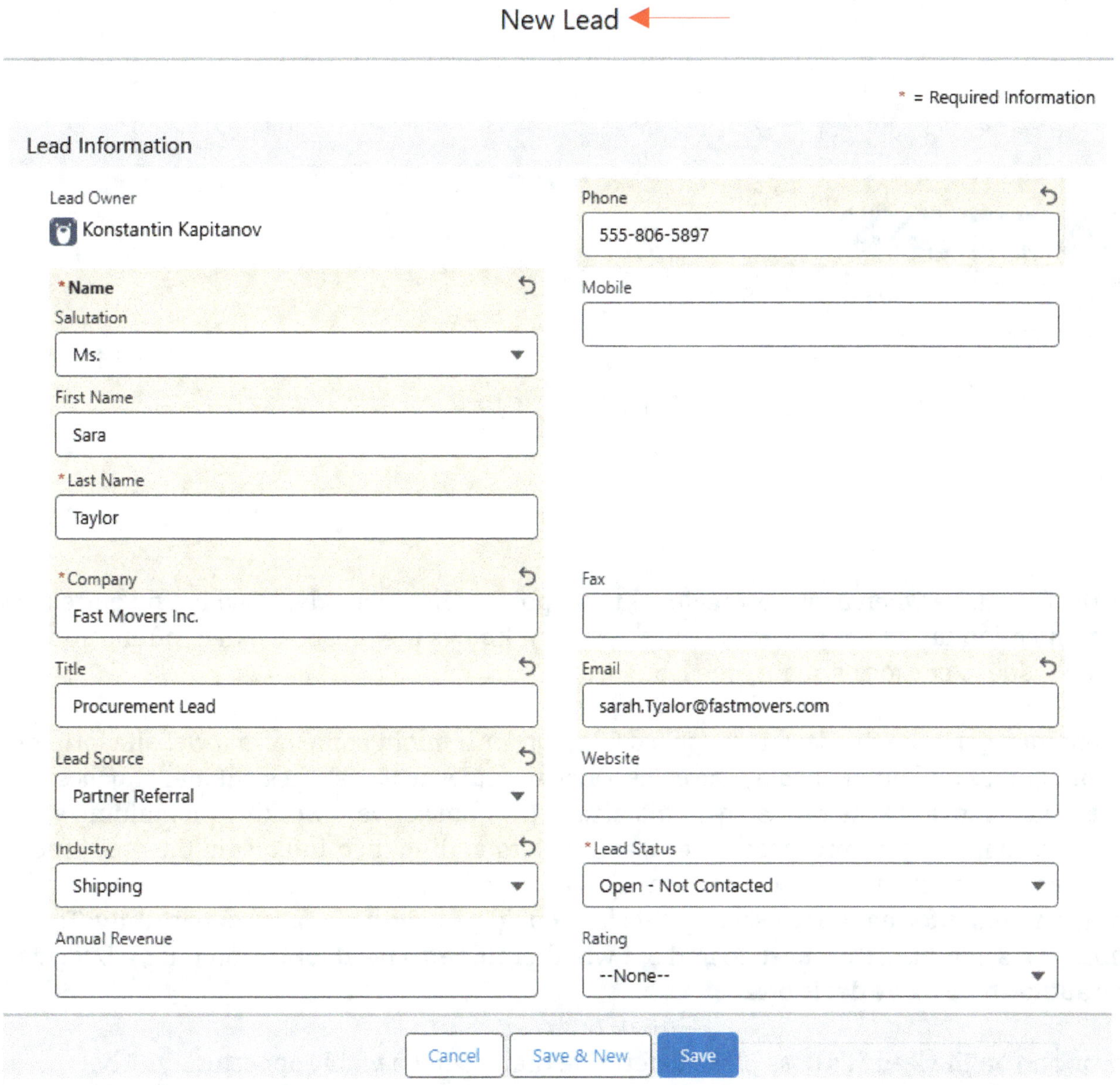

New Lead ←

* = Required Information

## Lead Information

Lead Owner
Konstantin Kapitanov

Phone
555-806-5897

***Name**

Salutation
Ms.

Mobile

First Name
Sara

*Last Name
Taylor

*Company
Fast Movers Inc.

Fax

Title
Procurement Lead

Email
sarah.Tyalor@fastmovers.com

Lead Source
Partner Referral

Website

Industry
Shipping

*Lead Status
Open - Not Contacted

Annual Revenue

Rating
--None--

Cancel | Save & New | Save

*After clicking the Save button your new lead has been created.*

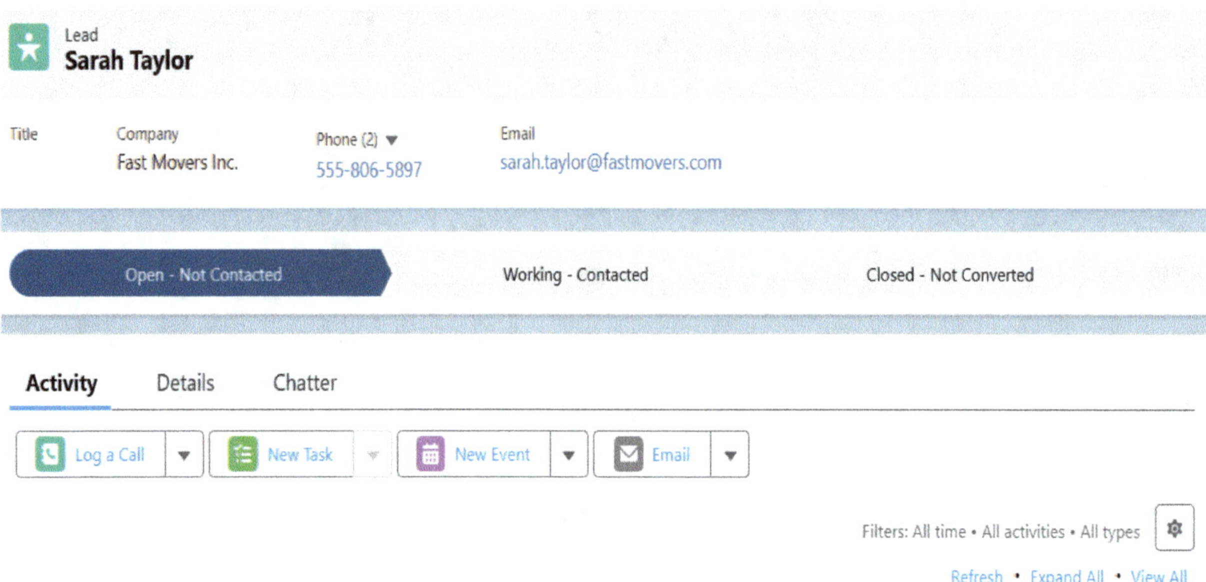

This is the first stage when a lead is created. At this point, it has been identified but no outreach or communication has taken place yet. The sales team knows the prospect exists, but no efforts have been made to engage or qualify the lead.

Marketing may generate this lead through a campaign, or it might come from a website form or list import, but it's still untouched by the sales. Once the sales team reaches out and engages with the lead, it moves to the next stage. This means they are actively working on building a relationship, qualifying the prospect's needs, and understanding their interest in the product or service. Communication may occur through an email, a call, or a meeting.
They're gathering information to assess if this lead could become a potential opportunity. To determine if it's qualified, they need to find out whether there's a need for the product, a budget, and the authority to make decisions.

After working on the lead, it's possible to determine that it's not a viable opportunity.  The situation could be due to a lack of interest, an absence of immediate need, or the lead being outside the target audience.

If the lead is deemed qualified, it is converted into an opportunity. At this stage, the information is used to create an account, contact, and opportunity, enabling the sales team to move forward in the process.

*Now we are starting to convert our lead by clicking the Convert button.*

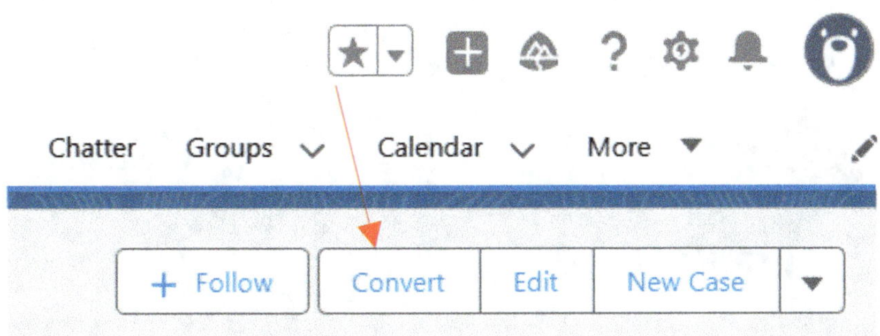

After clicking the Convert button, a conversion screen will open where you can confirm the details for the Account, Contact, and Opportunity. If the lead is associated with a company or organization, Sales Cloud will automatically populate the Account Name based on the lead's details or allow you to link it to an existing account. Otherwise, a new Account will be created. When this person already exists as a contact, you can merge the information with the existing record or create a new one. Check the box to create a new Opportunity if you want to track the sales potential further. In our example below, we decided to use the existing account by creating a new contact and opportunity.

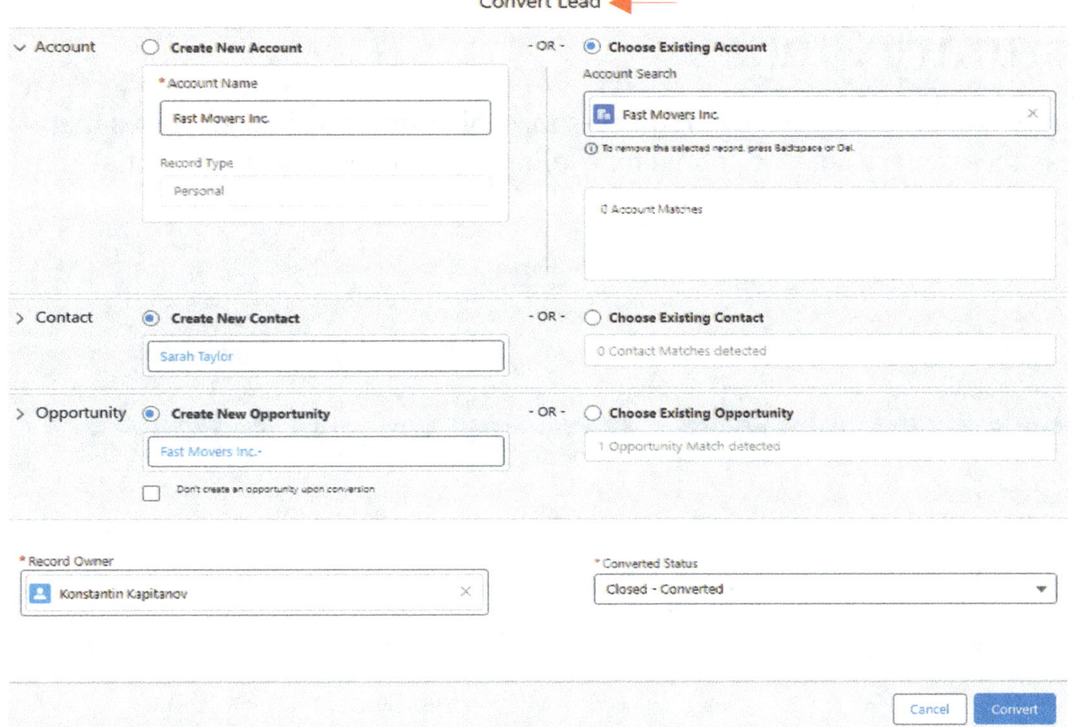

*Our lead is converted, and a new contact and opportunity have been created.*

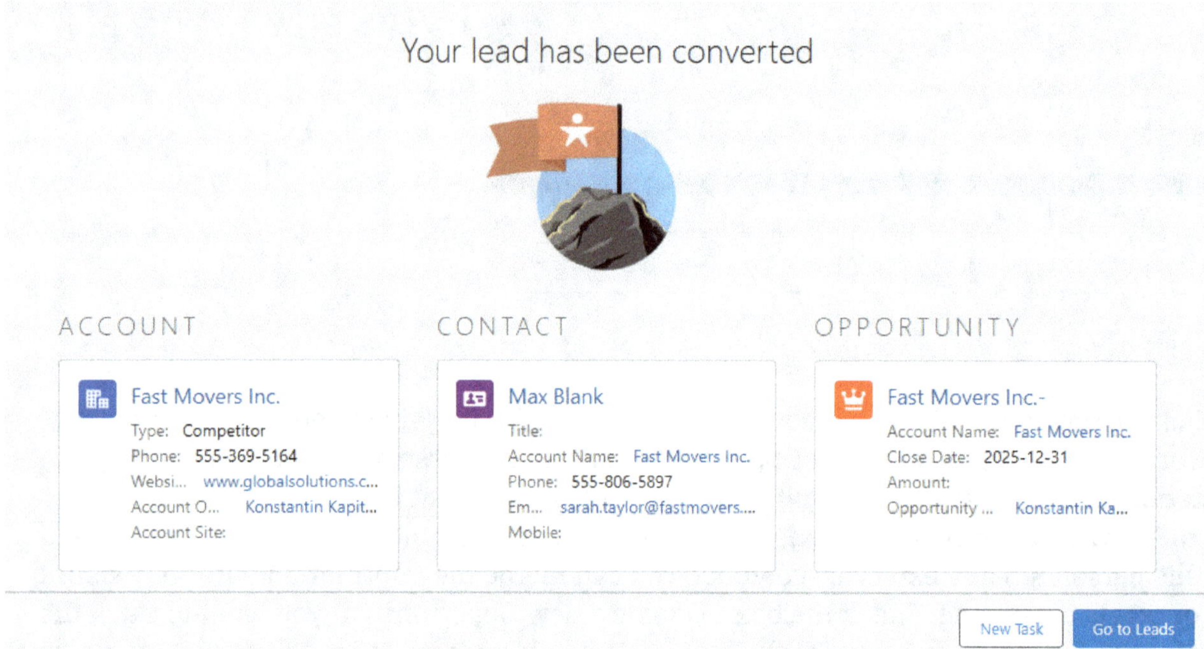


# 3.2 Opportunity Stages

When an opportunity is created, it typically progresses through a series of defined stages that represent the sales process. Each stage is crucial for evaluating the opportunity's potential and moving it forward.

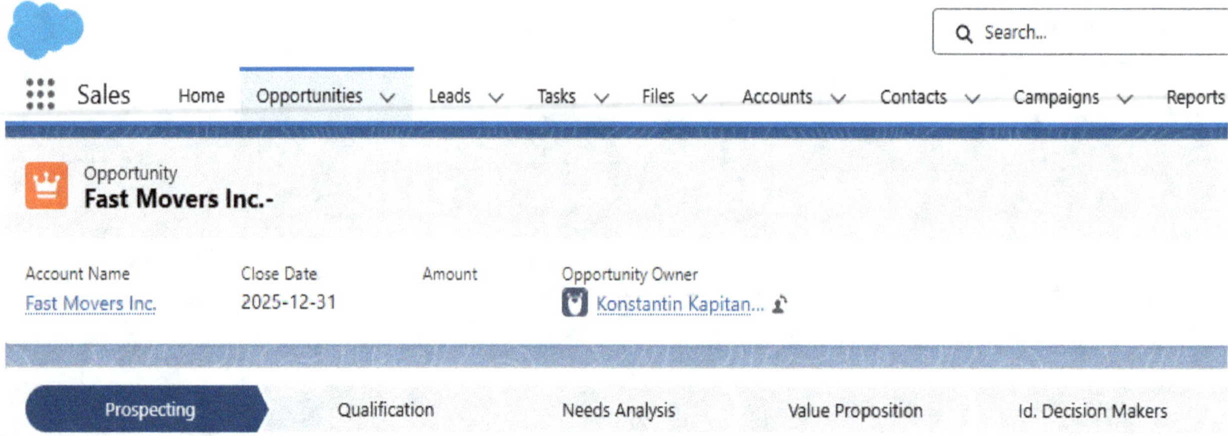

Prospecting is the initial stage where the sales team identifies potential customers and starts engaging with them. The focus is on generating interest and gathering information about the prospect's needs. Qualification stage evaluates whether the prospect fits the ideal customer profile and determines if the opportunity is worth pursuing.

Needs Analysis involves a deeper understanding of the prospect's requirements and challenges. The sales engage in discussions to clarify the specific needs of the prospect.

By moving to the Value Proposition stage, sales presents a tailored solution that addresses the prospect's identified needs. The aim is to demonstrate the unique value of the product or service.

In the next Identify Decision Makers stage, it is important to identify all the key stakeholders involved in the decision-making process. Understanding who has the authority to approve the purchase is critical.

Perception Analysis stage focuses on gauging the prospect's perceptions and attitudes toward the proposed solution. It's important to address any objections or concerns that may arise.

The Proposal/Price Quote stage visualizes the offer by providing a detailed proposal and price quote. This document delineates the conditions of the agreement and the offered value.

Negotiation/Review stage involves negotiating the terms and conditions of the proposal to reach a mutually beneficial agreement. It's a critical phase for discussing potential adjustments needed to finalize the deal.

The final Closed stage indicates whether the opportunity has been won or lost. If won, the opportunity is marked as closed, and the sales process transitions to order fulfillment and customer onboarding. If lost, the reasons are documented for future reference.

On the Kanban board, all opportunities are organized by stage. This layout provides a clear view of where each opportunity stands in the sales process. To access it, click the Opportunities tab at the top and select the Kanban view from the list.

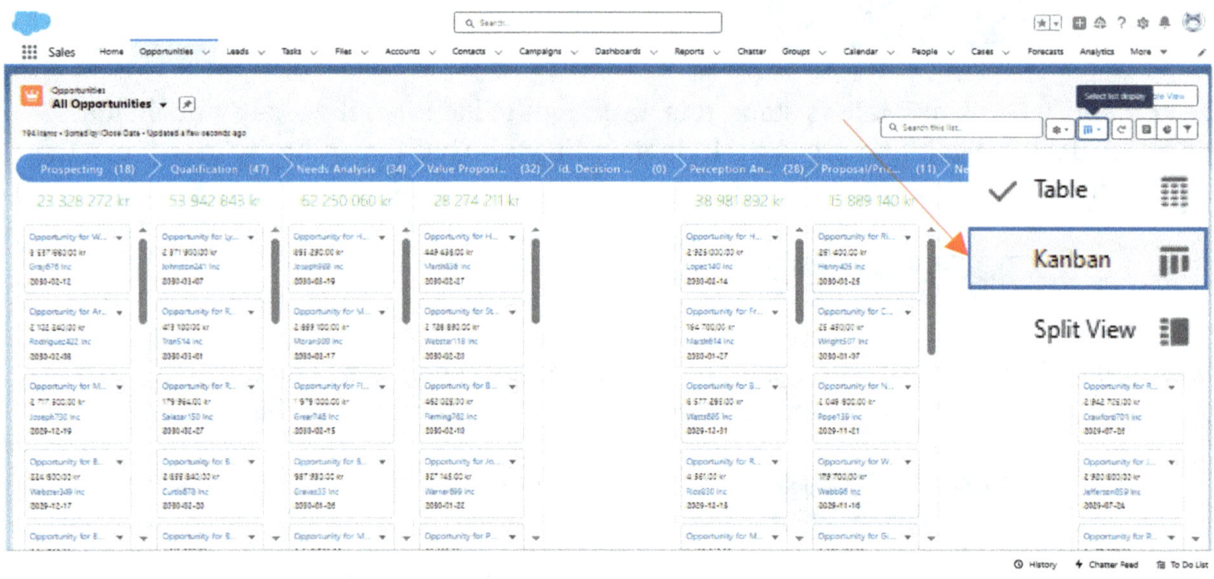

# 3.3 Products and Price Books

Products in Sales Cloud represent the goods or services of your company. Each product contains specific information, such as its name, description, and price. Price Books, on the other hand, are collections of products that can have different prices depending on the customer segment or sales strategy. For example, you may have a Standard Price Book for regular customers and a Discounted Price Book for special promotions or select customers.

To add a product to our opportunity, we will first create a product item and connect it to a price book.

*Click the App Launcher and type "product", then select Products from the search results.*

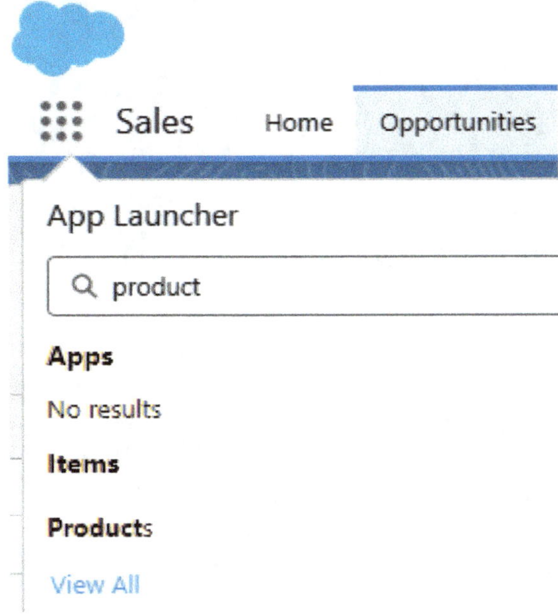

*Click the New button to create a new product.*

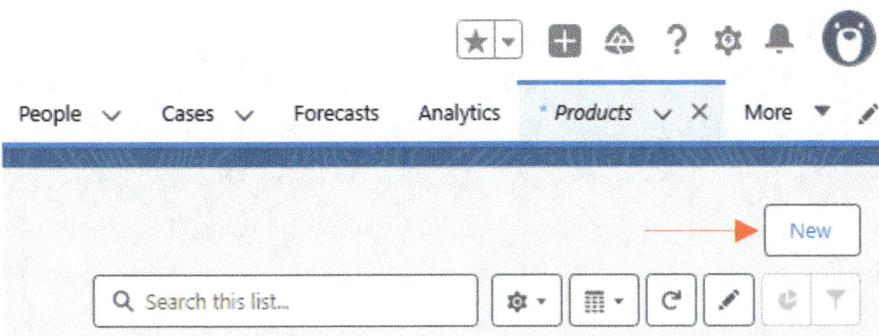

*Fill in the product details, such as the Product Name, Product Code with other relevant fields. Set the product as Active so it can be used in Opportunities, and click Save.*

# PART I — Sales Cloud for Sales Managers and Sales Reps

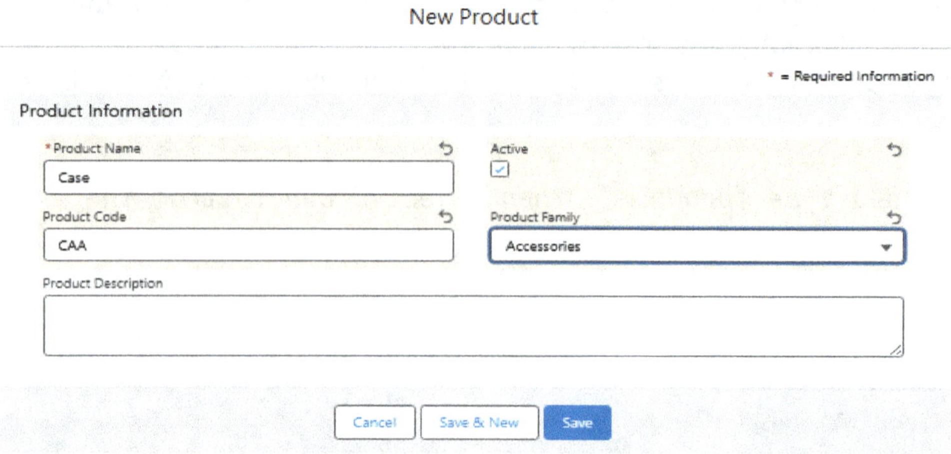

Go to the Related tab and click the Add Standard Price button.

Please add the List Price field and save.

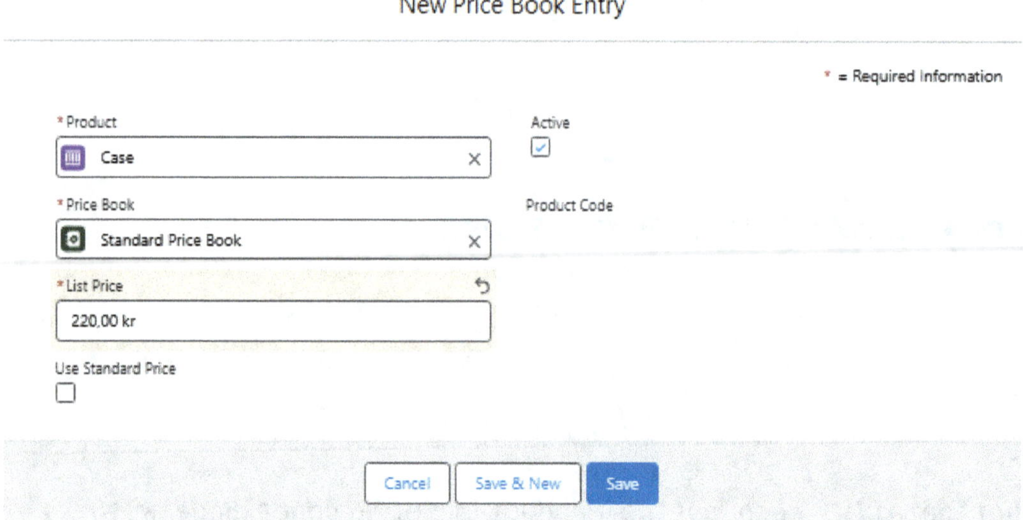

*Click the App Launcher and type "price", then select Price Books from the search results.*

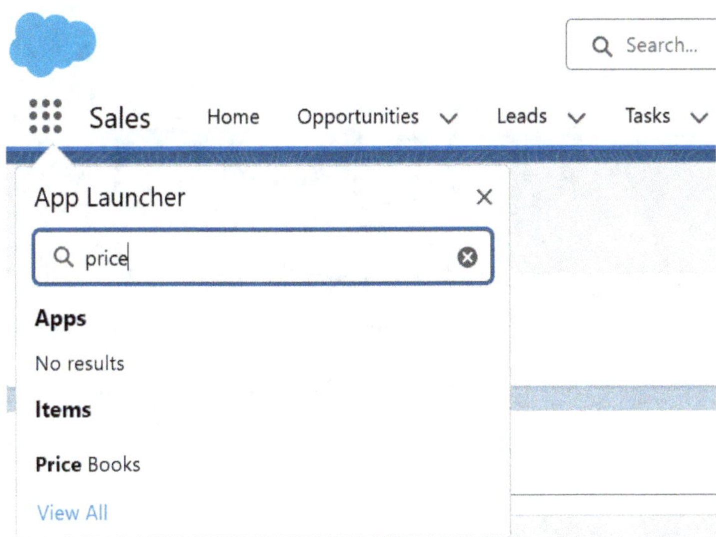

*Open the Standard Price Book and click the Related Tab to view the product you added. However, be aware that the settings for the Standard Price Book may vary depending on your Salesforce org.*

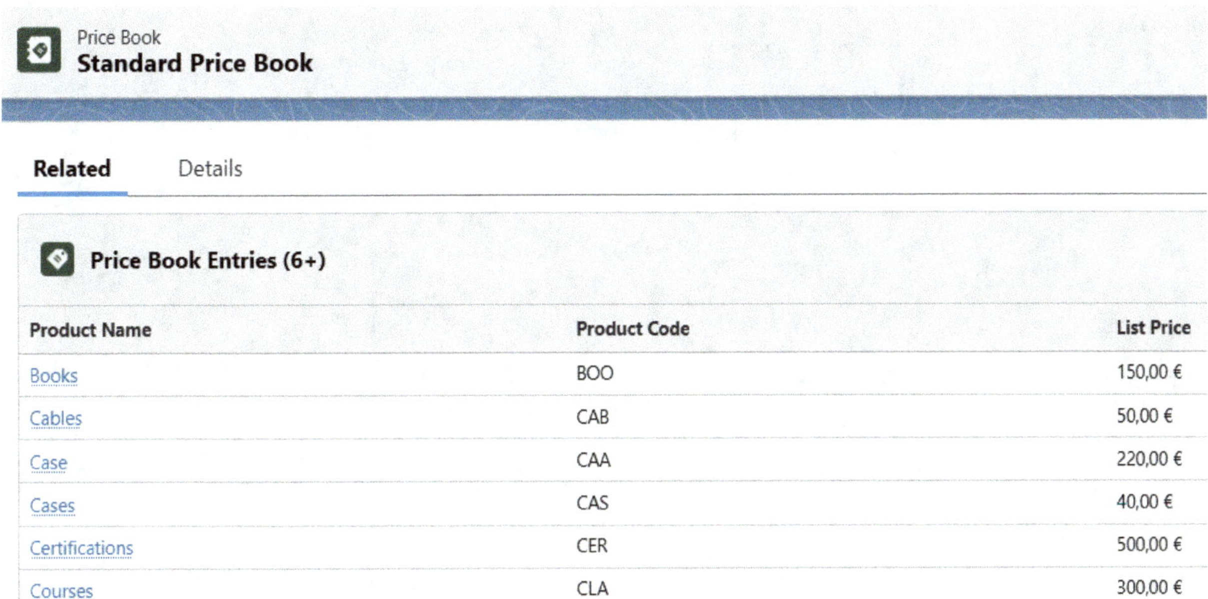

| Product Name | Product Code | List Price |
|---|---|---|
| Books | BOO | 150,00 € |
| Cables | CAB | 50,00 € |
| Case | CAA | 220,00 € |
| Cases | CAS | 40,00 € |
| Certifications | CER | 500,00 € |
| Courses | CLA | 300,00 € |

*By returning to our opportunity, select our price book by clicking on Choose Price Book.*

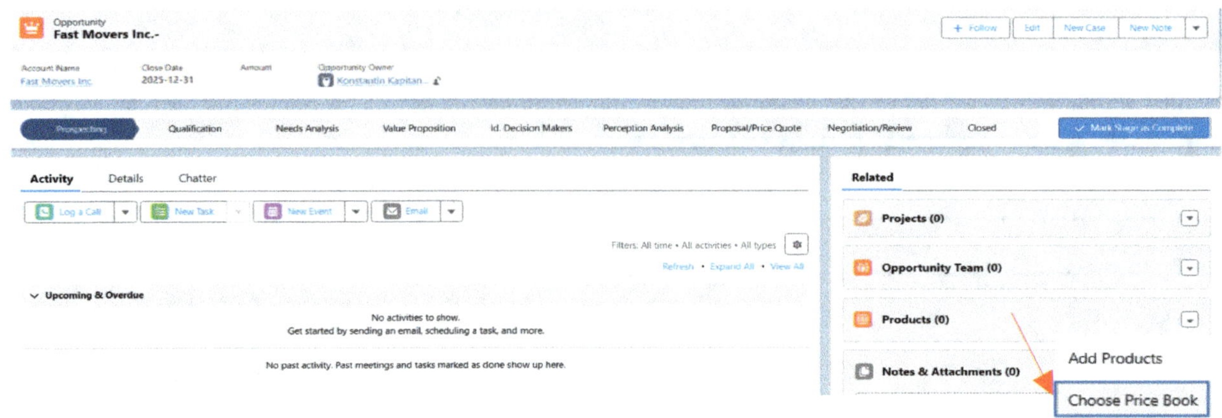

*After choosing Price Book click Save.*

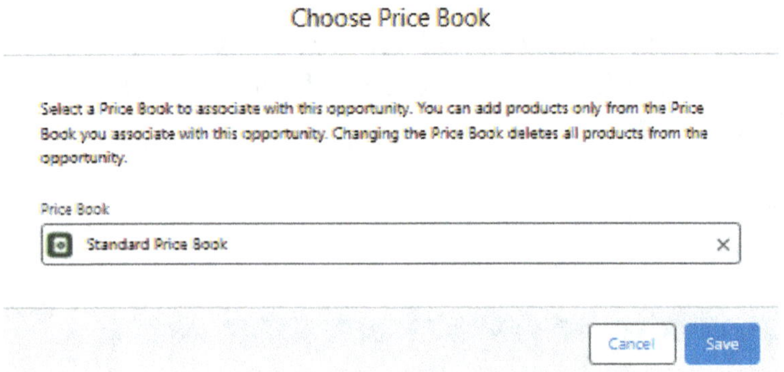

*Then you will add newly created product items to our opportunity and click Add Products.*

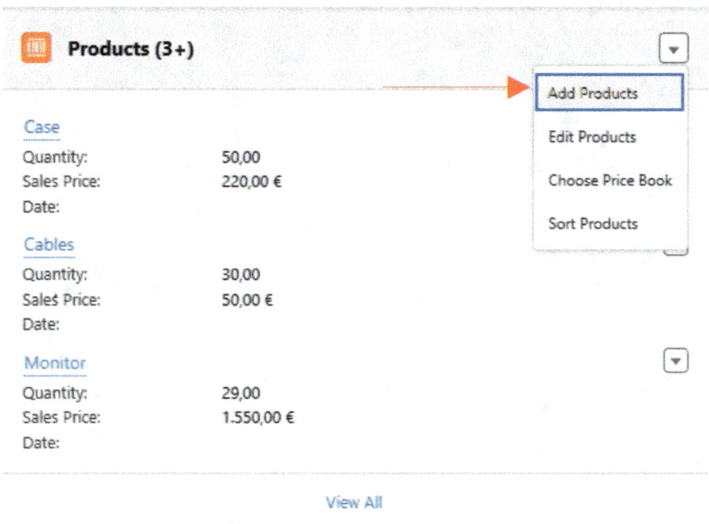

*Select the items you want to add, and then click Next.*

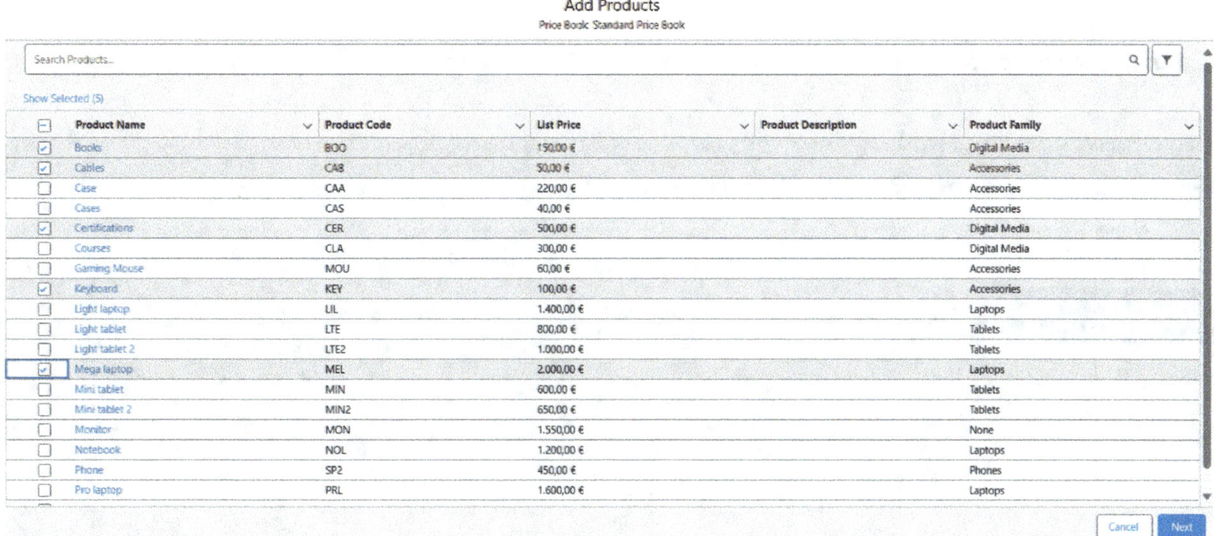

# PART I – Sales Cloud for Sales Managers and Sales Reps

*Now you can add the quantity of the selected item, adjust any other relevant fields and click Save.*

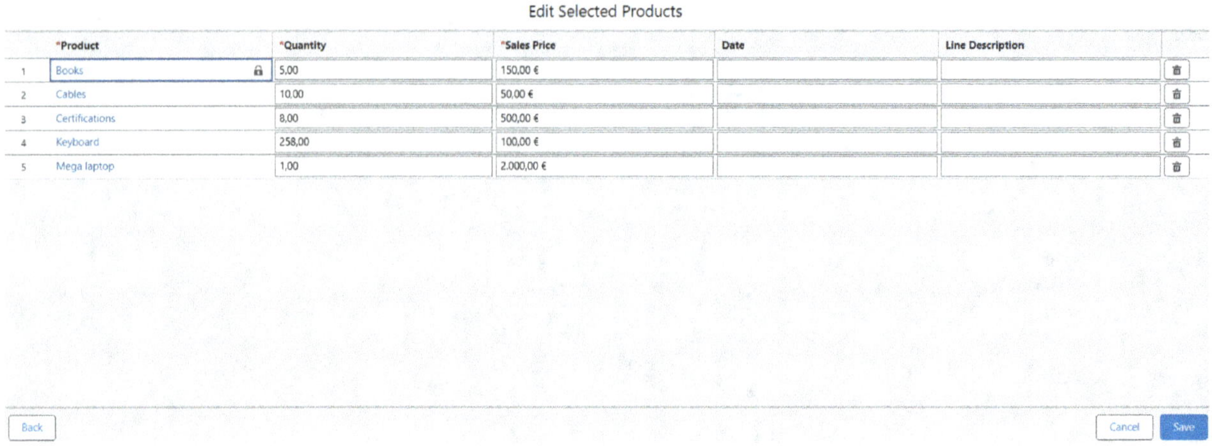

*The newly added product items have now changed the total amount of your opportunity.*

# Chapter 4. Activities and Collaboration

## 4.1 Opportunity Team

In larger or more complex deals, multiple people may need to collaborate to close an opportunity. The Opportunity Team feature helps ensure that each person has access to the information they need. It facilitates teamwork by defining roles for those involved in closing a specific opportunity. This ensures clarity around responsibilities, maintains a single source of truth for deal progress, and improves communication and accountability among team members. Clearly defining roles and access also enables management to track individual contributions, supporting a streamlined sales process. Ask your system administrator about enabling this feature in your organization. Let us create the new Opportunity team together.

*Navigate to the Opportunity Team Related List on the opportunity record page to Add Opportunity Team Members.*

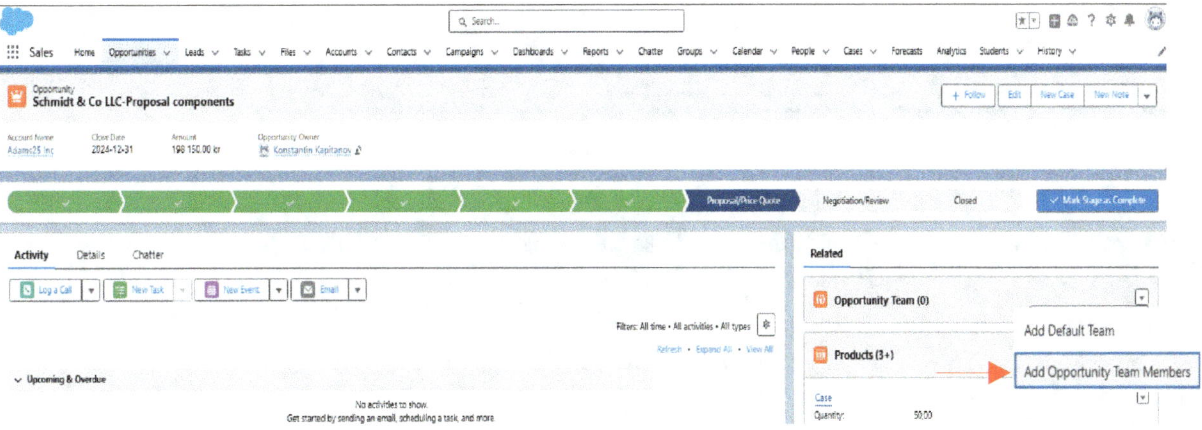

# PART I — Sales Cloud for Sales Managers and Sales Reps

*Now choose the members of your Opportunity Team and Save.*

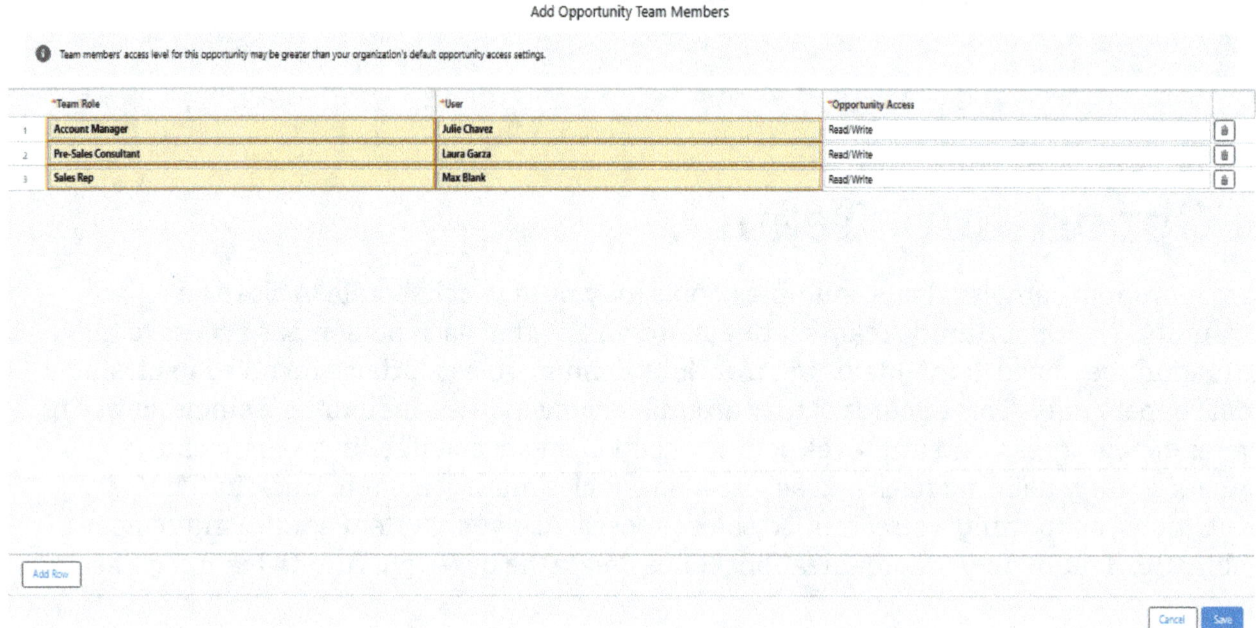

*Your Opportunity Team has been created now.*

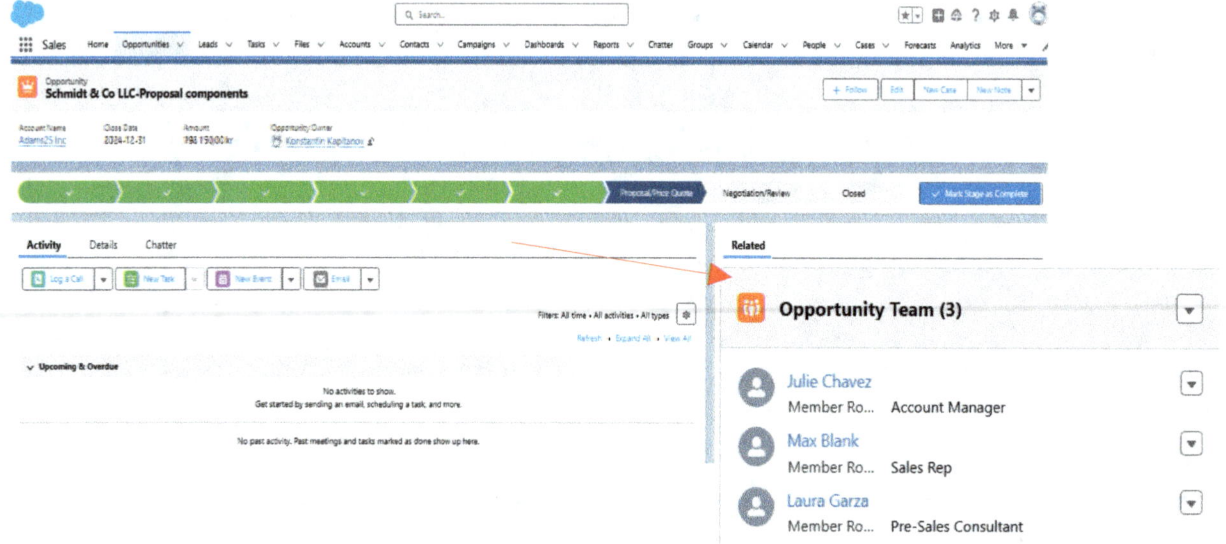

# 4.2 Chatter

Using Chatter within your opportunity team brings real-time collaboration, allowing team members to discuss deal details, ask questions, and share updates seamlessly. Chatter offers several built-in features such as Post, Poll, and Question, that help keep everyone in sync and encourage open communication throughout the opportunity.

Use the Post feature to share updates, observations, or files with the team. This format is ideal for general communication, sharing insights, or mentioning team members to get their attention on specific points. Posts are also searchable within Chatter, making it easy to look up past discussions at this opportunity.

**Note!** Keep posts concise, focusing on significant updates, quick feedback, or reminders for the team.

*Open your Post tab and insert your message there, tag your team member using @ to ensure they receive a notification, then click Share.*

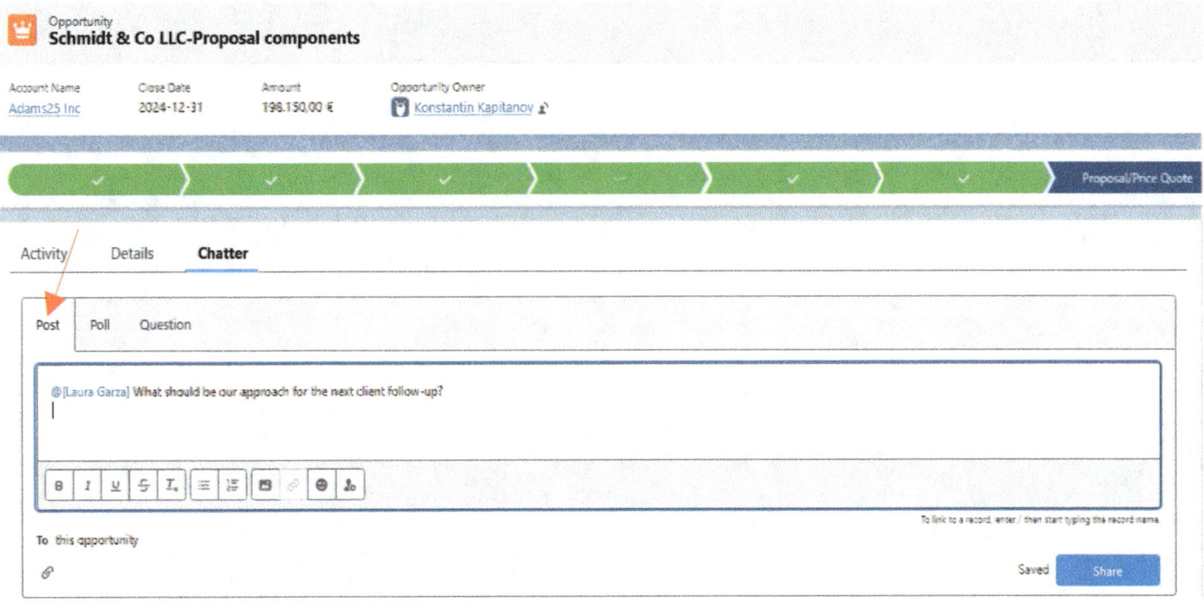


Polls are helpful for quick team decisions by gathering input without lengthy discussions. For example, if the team needs to choose between options for the next meeting time, polls provide a simple way to reach consensus. Use Polls for straightforward decisions, limiting options to avoid confusion. Polls help keep the team aligned and avoid lengthy back-and-forth communications.  Let's create a poll to determine the schedule for the upcoming presentation meeting.

*Open your Poll tab and add your choice options there, then click Ask.*

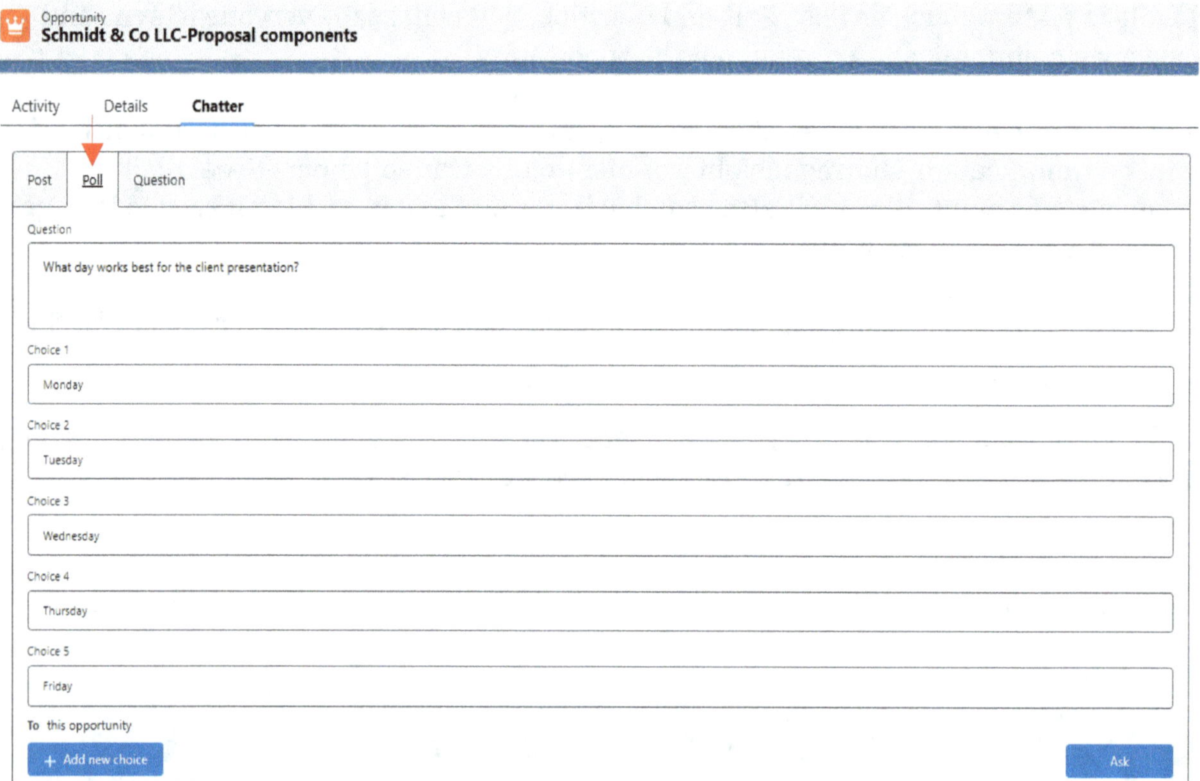

*Your poll has now been created.*

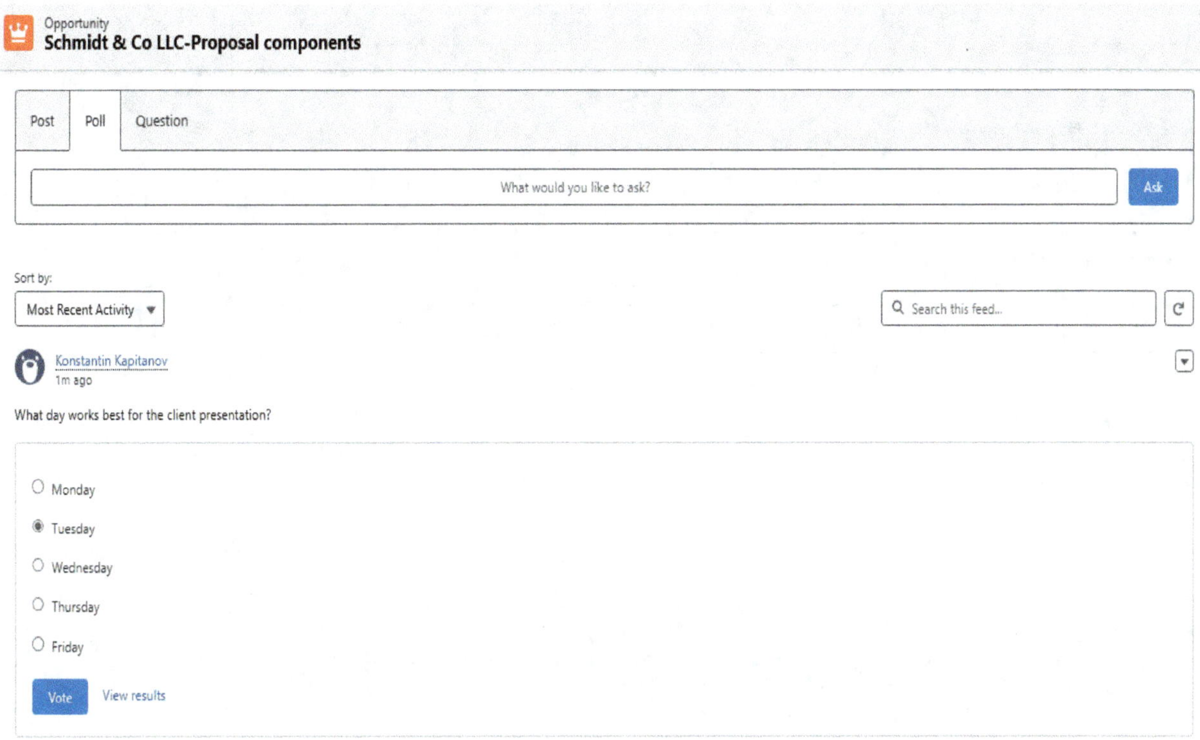

# PART I —  Sales Cloud for Sales Managers and Sales Reps

*Then you can see the votes for the options and make a decision.*

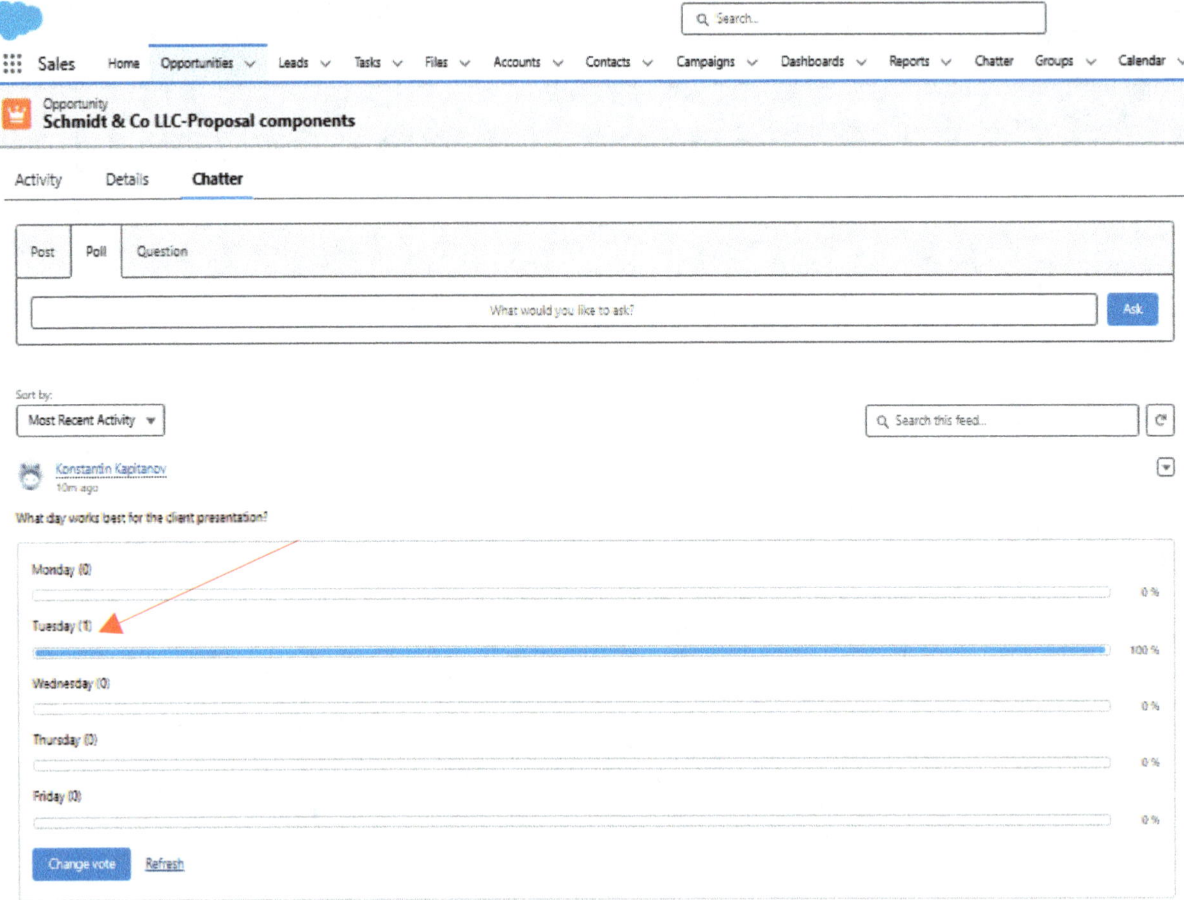

The Question is perfect for obtaining specific answers, clarifying doubts, or seeking advice from team members. Unlike Posts, Questions allow users to select a best answer, making it easy to resolve inquiries and provide clear direction. Use Questions to request guidance, confirm details, or clarify complex points. Marking a Best Answer helps everyone find the final decision or key information later on.

*Go to the Question tab, type your question, and click Ask.*

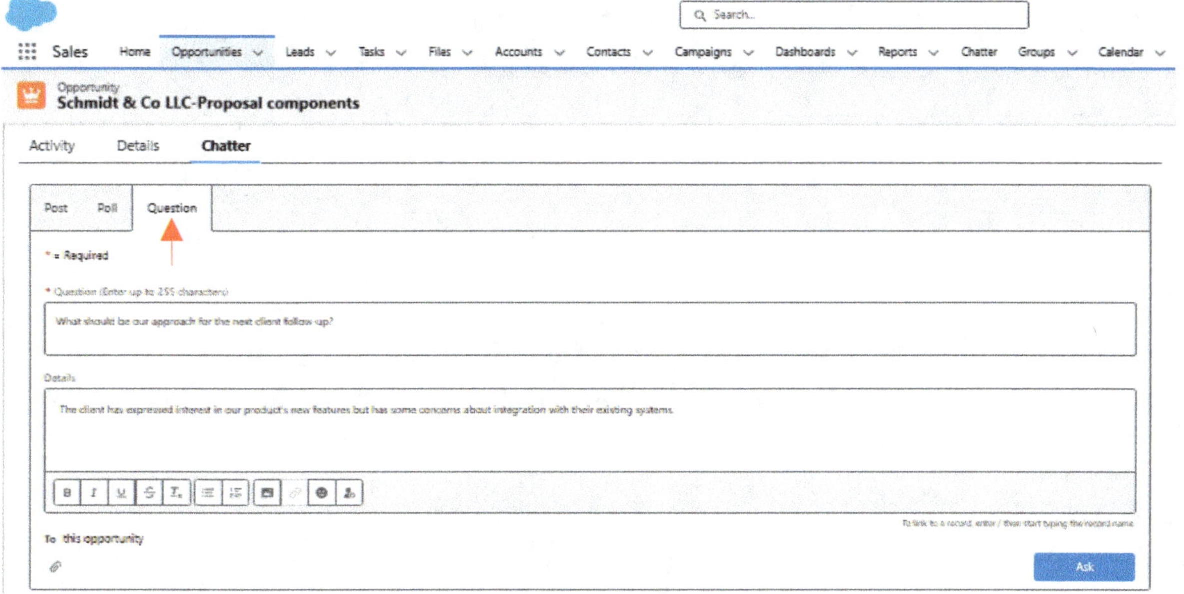

*The question form has now been created and can be used to collect feedback.*

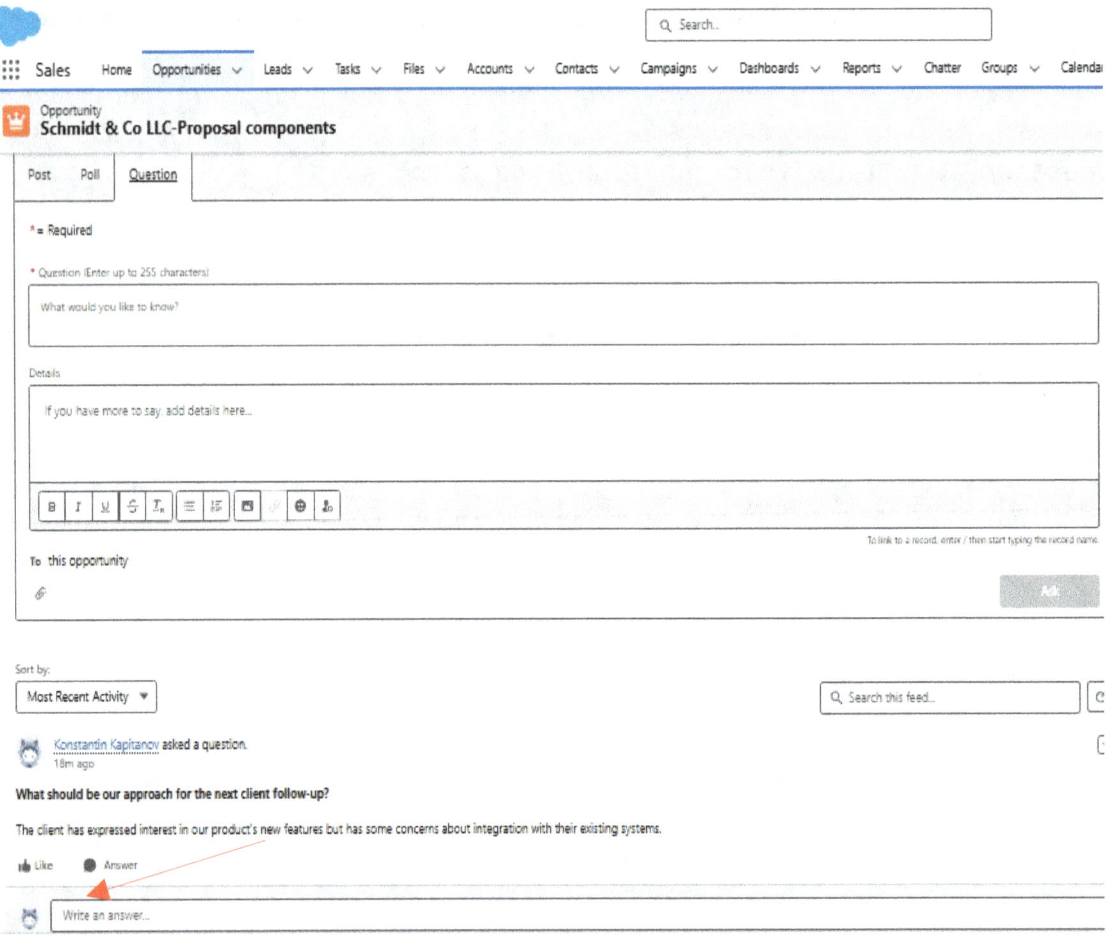

# 4.3 Activity Management

Activity features are essential tools for managing customer interactions, tracking tasks, and maintaining a comprehensive record of all engagements related to accounts, contacts, and opportunities. These features help sales teams stay organized, improve collaboration, and offer useful information about customer relationships. By using it consistently, teams can maintain a comprehensive view of all customer interactions, improve collaboration, and make data-driven decisions. They are available within every Account and Contact view and provide a chronological timeline of interactions, allowing users to quickly understand the history and current status of each record.

**Note!** The exact layout and options may vary depending on your Salesforce configuration and edition. It's always a good idea to customize these features to fit your organization's specific needs and processes.

Now, let's dive into each Activity feature and how to use. We begin with creating a new task on the Activity Timeline. Use this feature to create to-do tasks that you or other team members need to complete for the account. For example, following up with a customer or preparing documents for a meeting.

*Go to the Account record where you want to add the task, click the New Task button, fill in the details and click Save.*

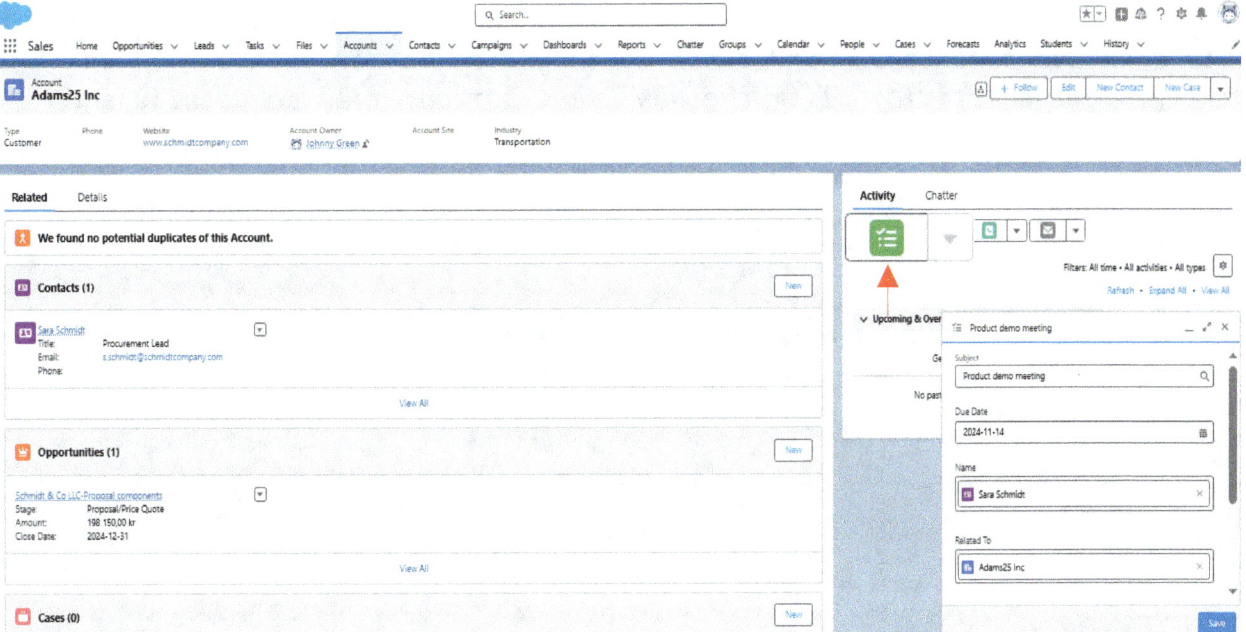

*The New Task has been created now.*

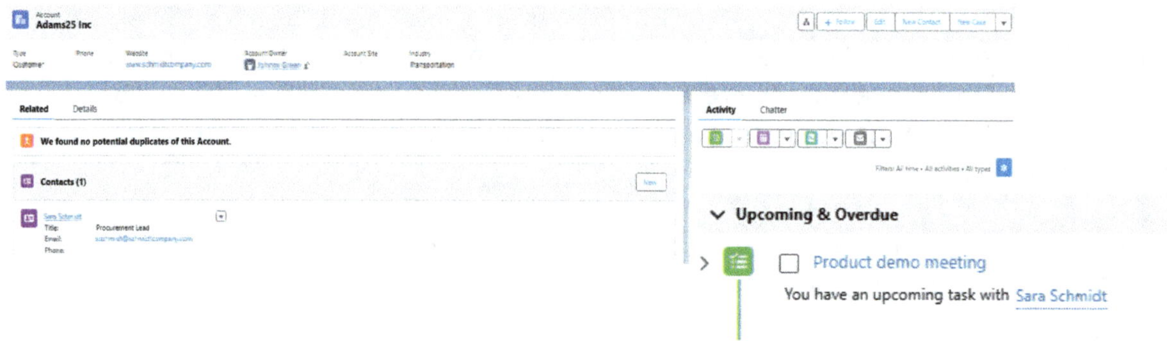

*Events are used to schedule and track meetings, calls, or any time-based activity. In the Activity click the New Event button, fill in details and click Save.*

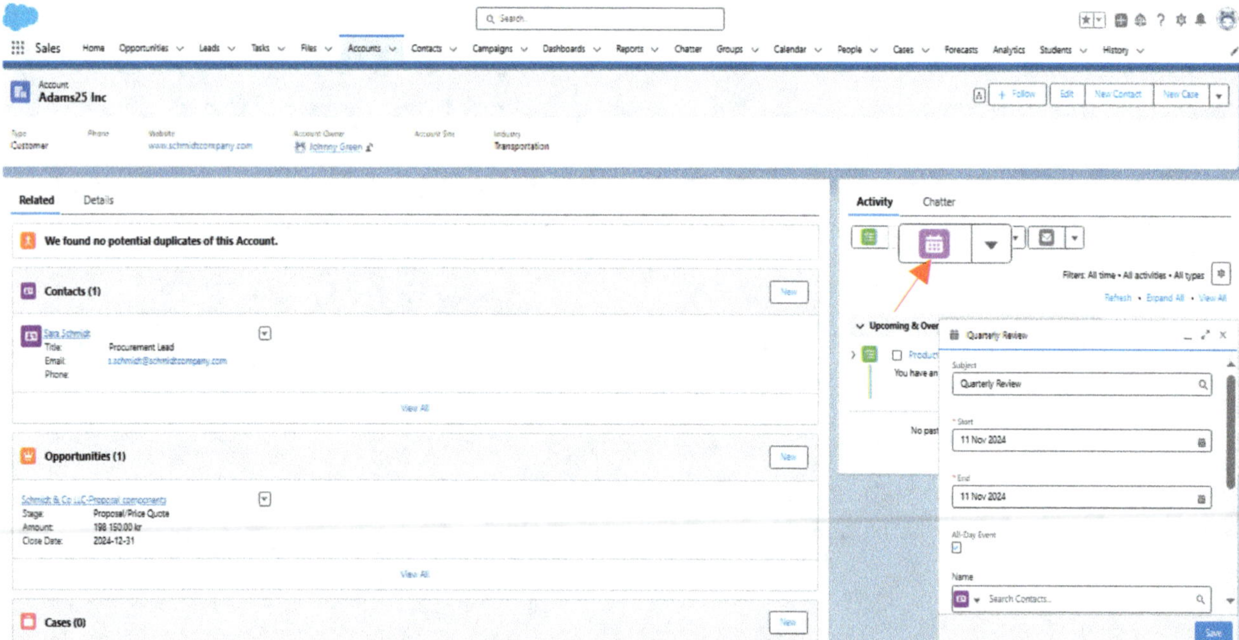

*The New Event has been created now.*

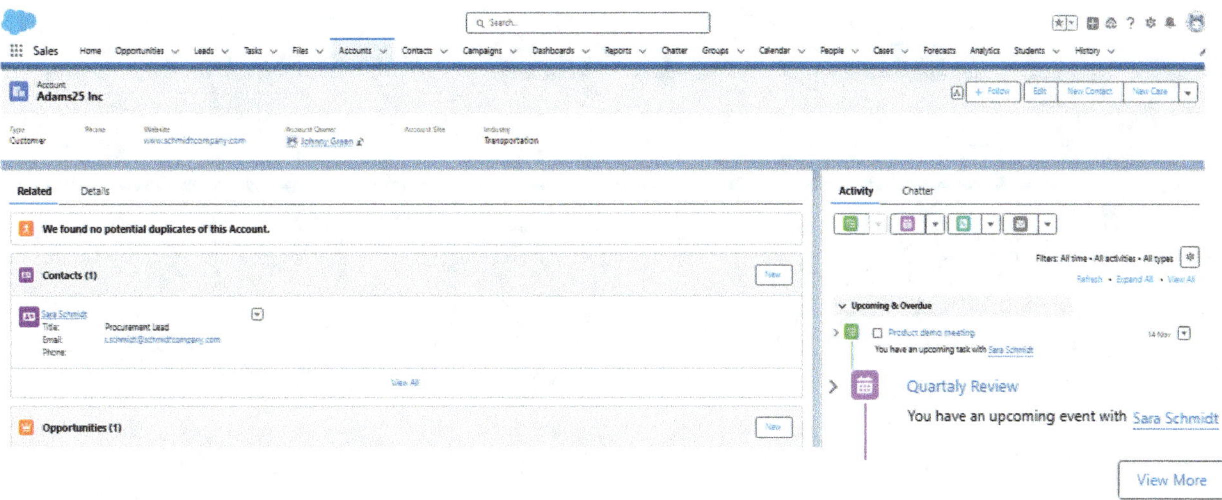

Log a Call is used to record details of a call conversation after it has taken place. This helps in keeping a historical record of discussions, which can be useful for maintaining a complete history of customer communications.

*In the Activity click the Log a Call button fill in details and click Save.*

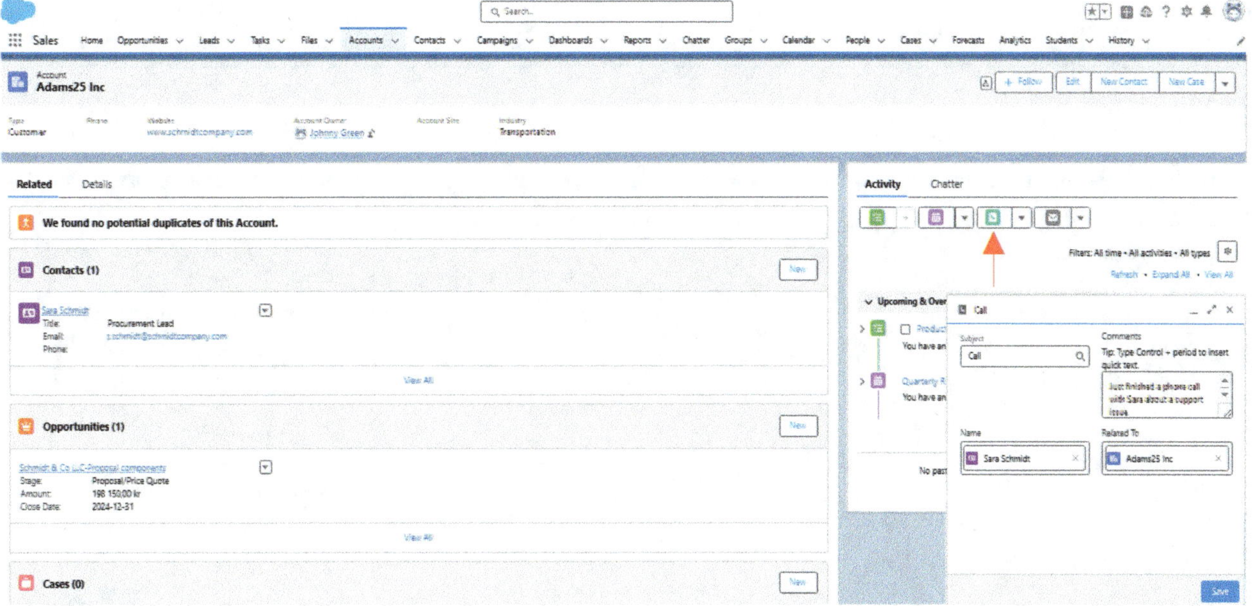

*The new Log a Call record has been created now.*

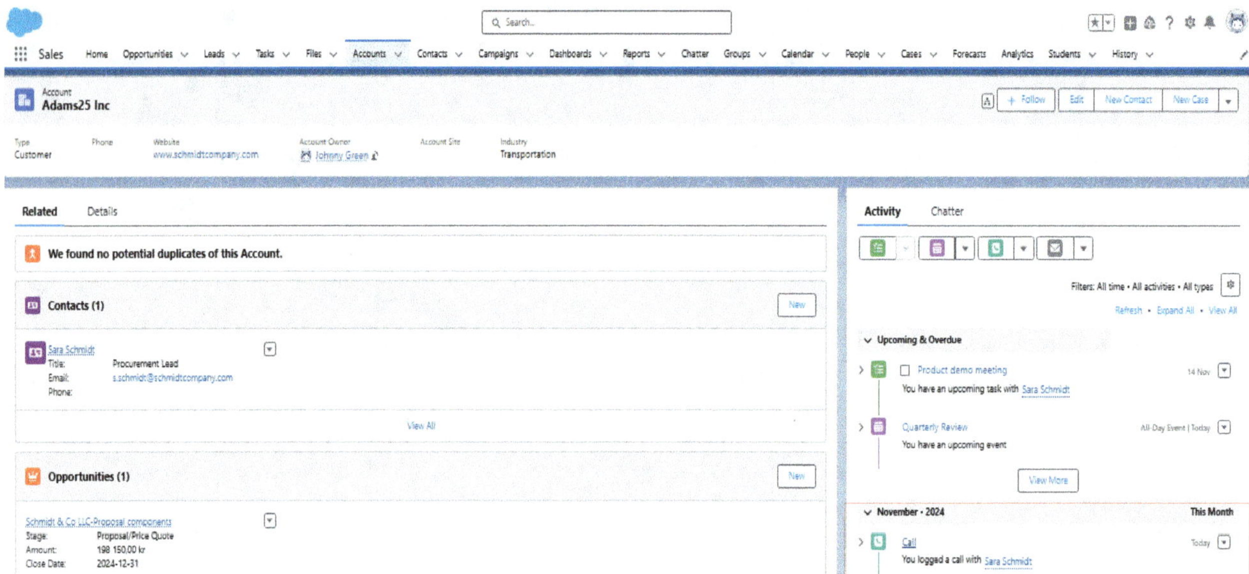

Use the Email feature to send and track emails directly from Sales Cloud. Any email sent from the Account page will automatically log to the account, giving you a record of all email communications.

*In the Activity click the Email button, write your email and click Send.*

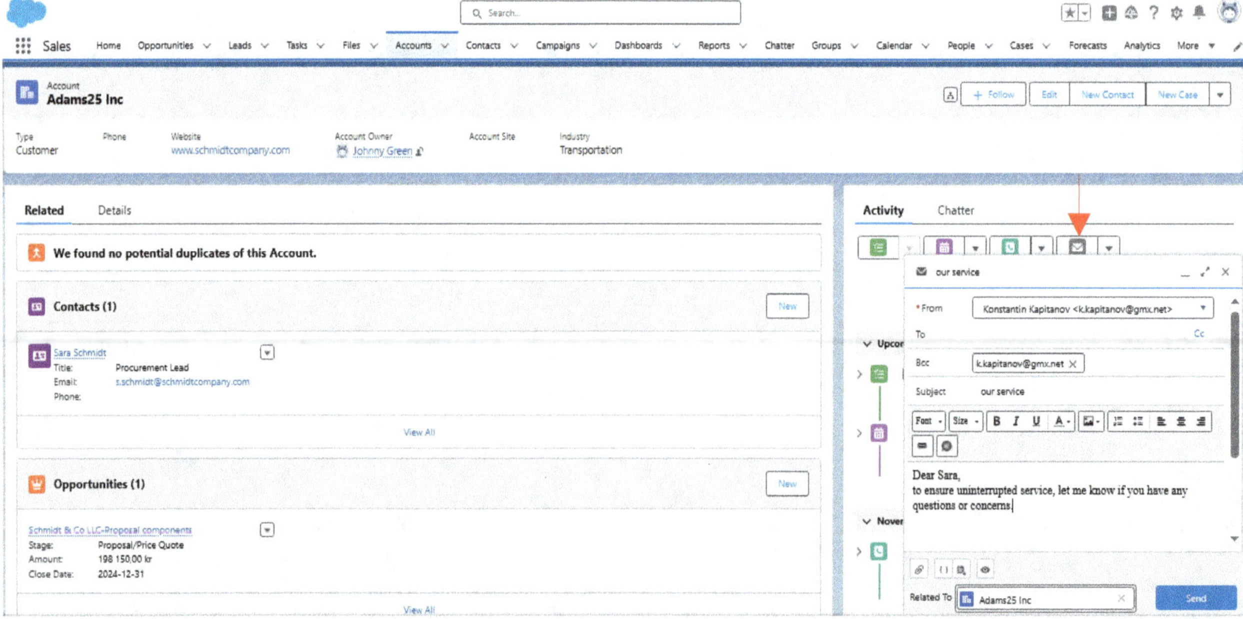

*The Email will be sent and automatically logged in the Activity.*

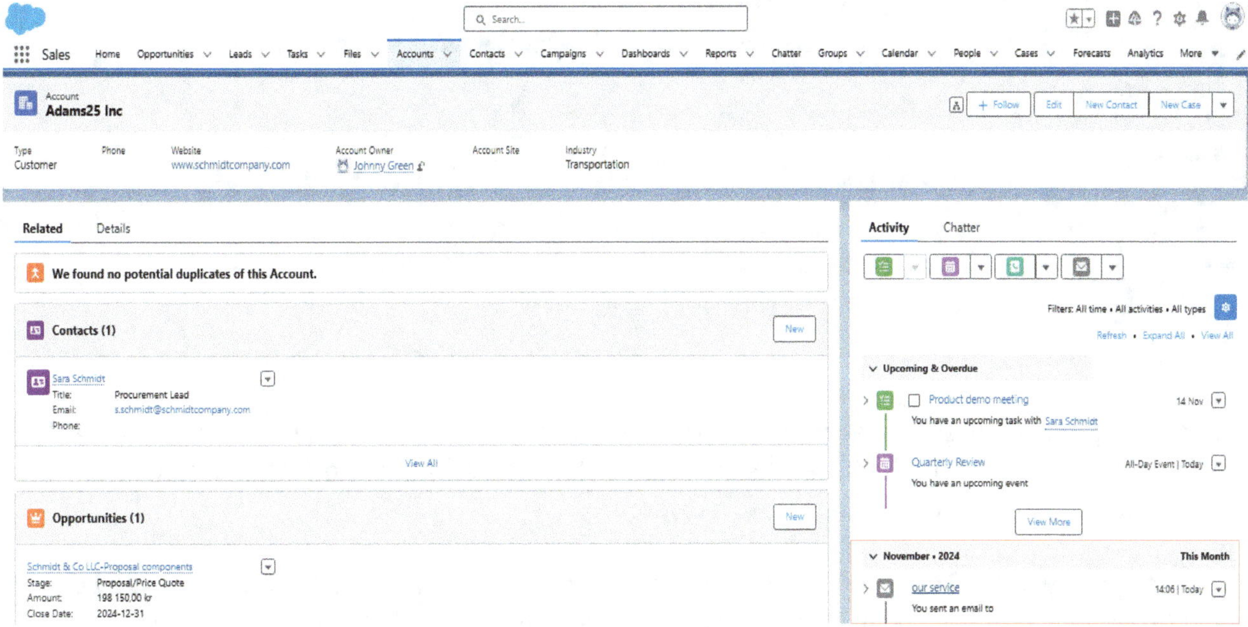

# 4.4 Campaigns

By linking marketing efforts to specific leads, contacts, and opportunities, campaigns help track and measure their success. They enable businesses to evaluate the effectiveness of marketing activities, such as email campaigns, webinars, or events, in generating and nurturing leads. The core purpose is to provide visibility into how marketing campaigns influence revenue and pipeline growth by linking specific leads and opportunities to the campaigns that engaged them.

Accounts can also be included in Campaigns if the relevant setting is enabled. This feature, called Accounts as Campaign Members, allows you to associate entire accounts with campaigns instead of just individual leads or contacts.

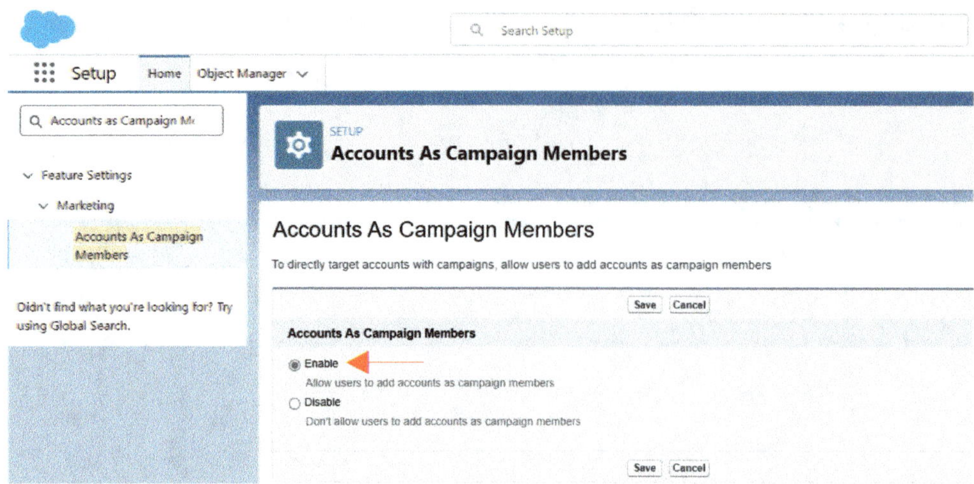

Campaigns can be set up in hierarchies using the Parent Campaign field. For example, a yearly marketing strategy could be the parent campaign, with quarterly or monthly campaigns as child campaigns. Now, let us create a new campaign.

*Go to the Campaigns Tab on the top of your screen, or if it's not visible, click the App Launcher and search for campaigns.*

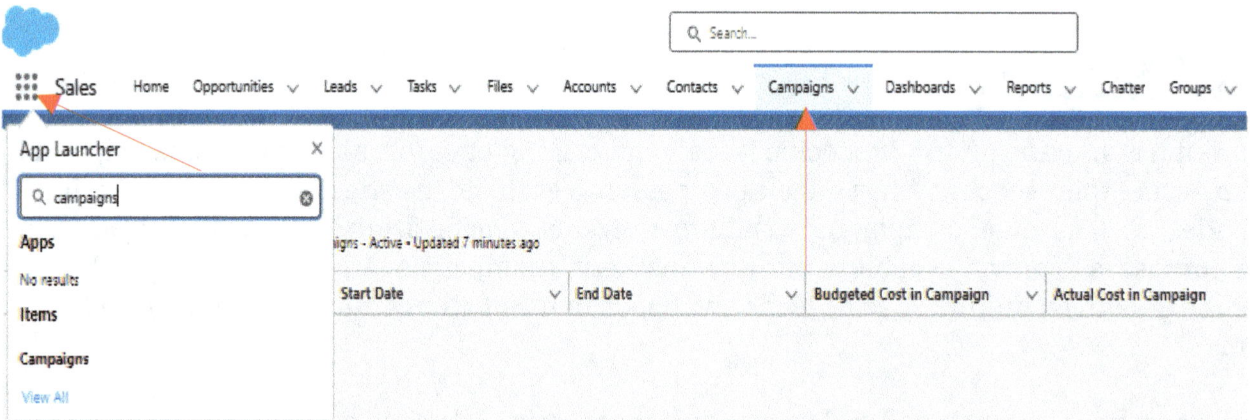

*Then you'll see a button labeled New near the top right corner, click it.*

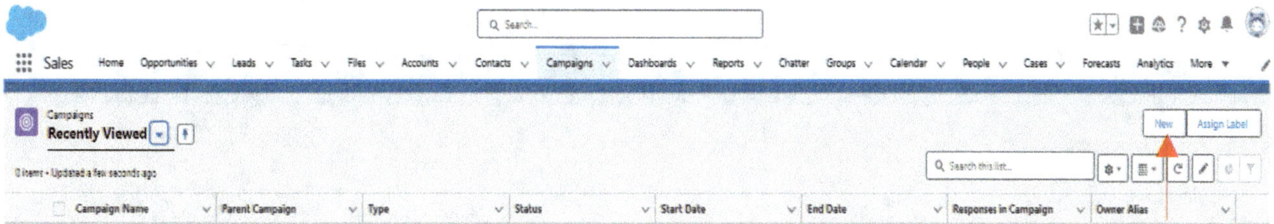

*Fill in Campaign Information such as Campaign Name, Status, Start Date, End Date, Expected Revenue, Budgeted Cost, and any other relevant information before clicking the Save button.*

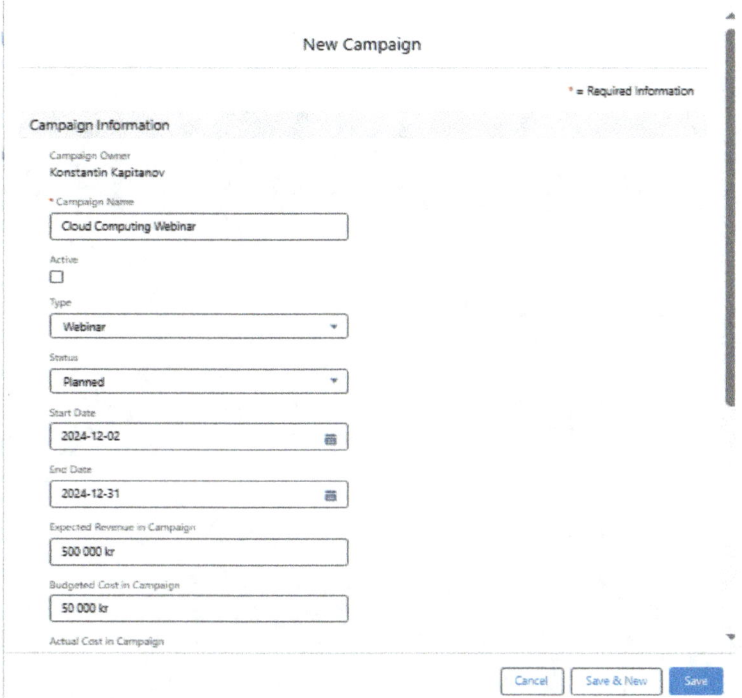

# PART I — Sales Cloud for Sales Managers and Sales Reps

*Your campaign has been successfully created.*

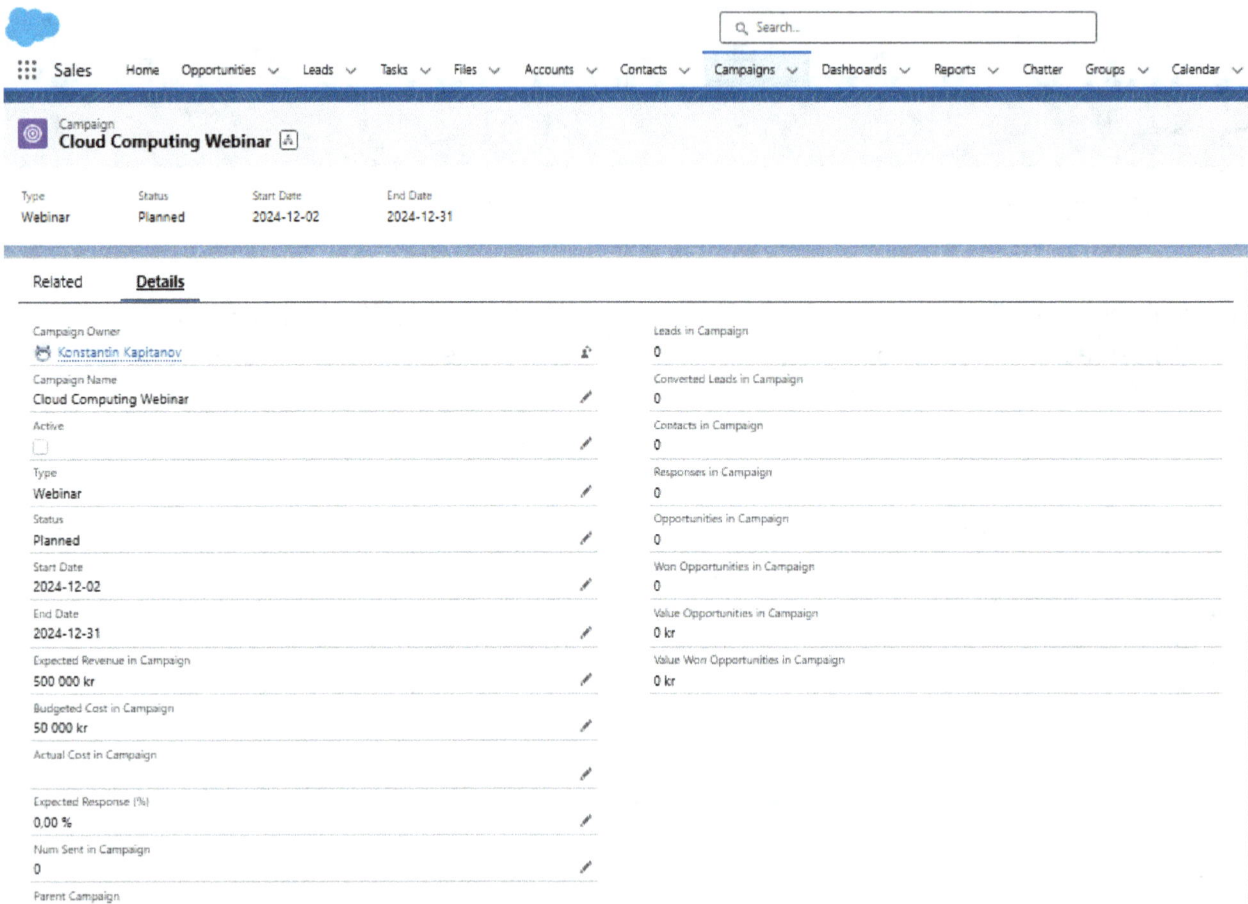

*We can add leads or contacts to the newly created campaign.*

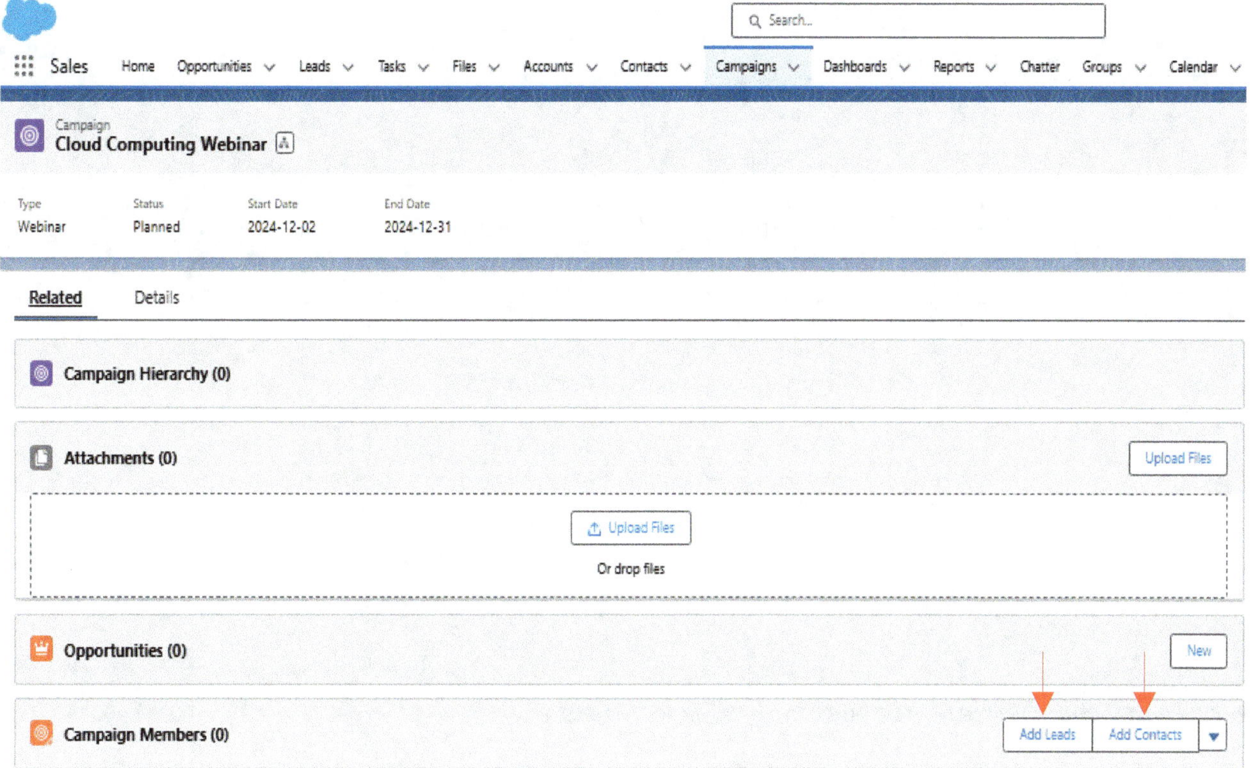

# PART I — Sales Cloud for Sales Managers and Sales Reps

*Click Add Leads button, select some leads and click next.*

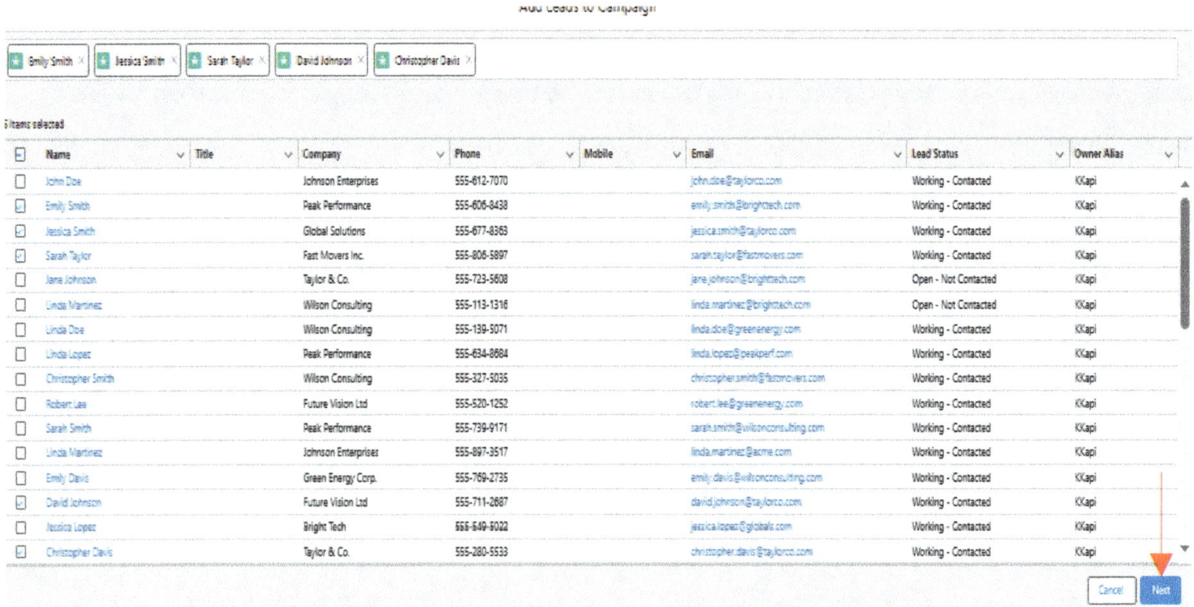

*Now select the member status and click Submit.*

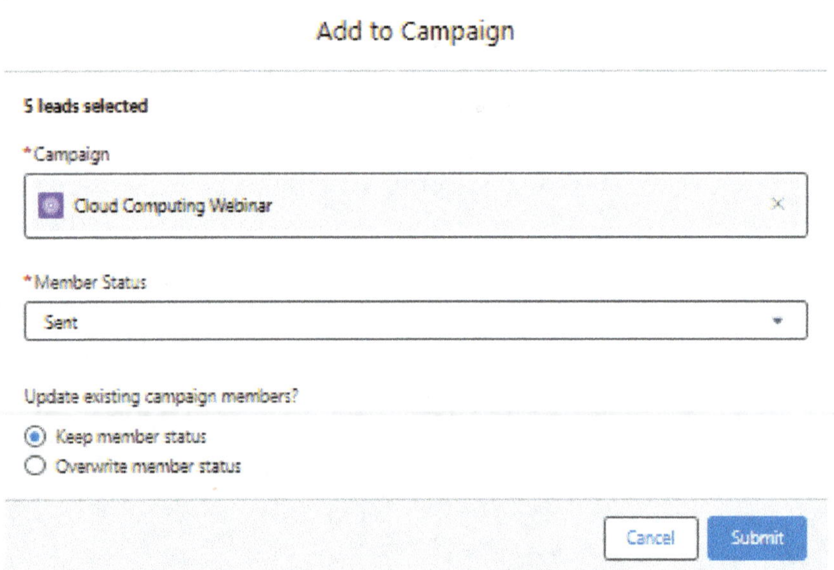

*After refreshing the page, you can see the newly added leads in your campaign.*

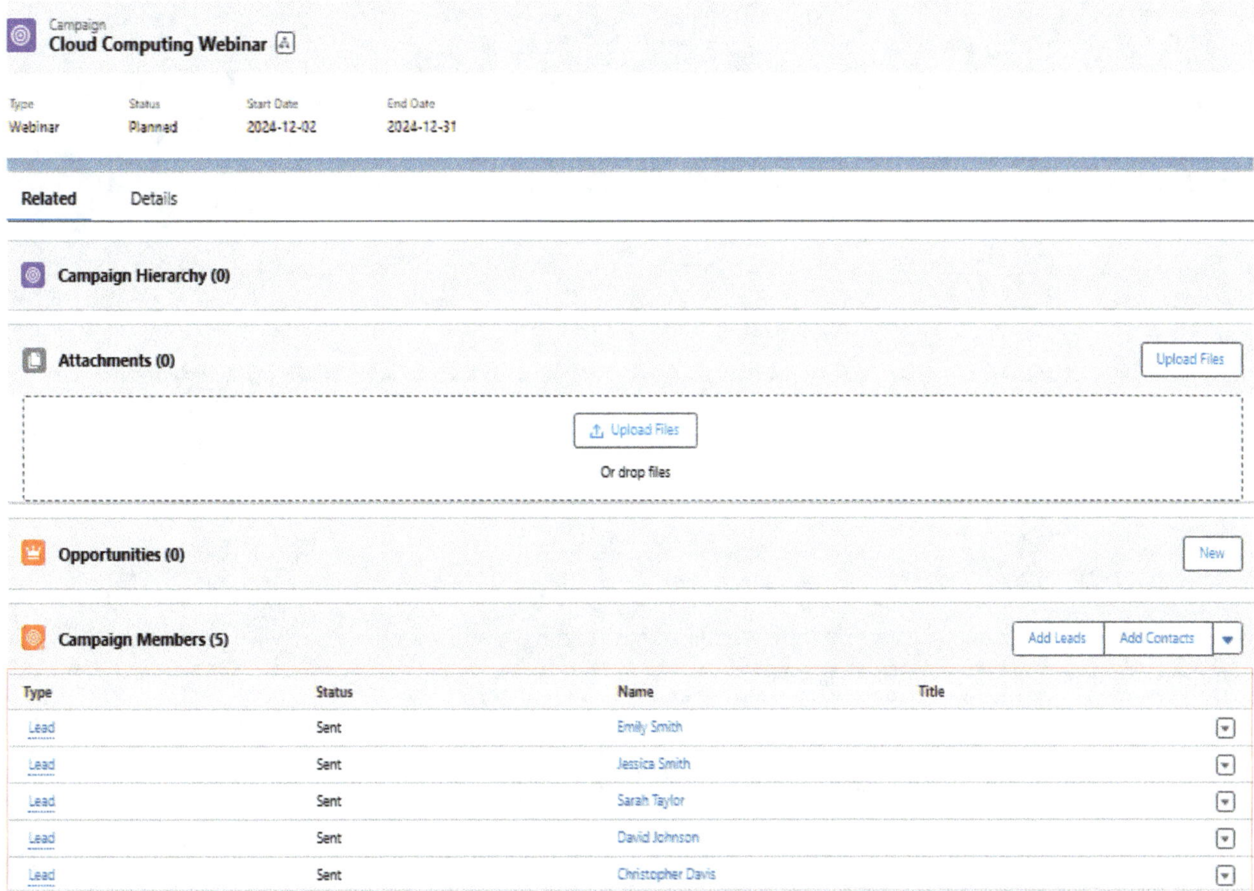

Sales Cloud allows you to send newsletters directly from a campaign to all its members. This feature is particularly useful for distributing campaign-related information, follow-ups, or promotional content to a large group of leads and contacts associated with a specific marketing initiative.

*Click Send List Email on the campaign detail page.*

*Then, write your message, review it, and send it to all campaign members.*

We can also connect an opportunity to a campaign. Connecting an opportunity to a campaign is especially valuable when you want to measure the impact of marketing efforts on revenue. If you're running a targeted campaign, like a webinar for a new product, and several leads who attended the webinar become opportunities, connecting those opportunities to the campaign helps you see the direct revenue impact of the event.

Let's create an example by opening the existing opportunity you want to connect to your campaign.

*Enter the campaign in the Primary Campaign Source field on your Opportunity, and click Save.*

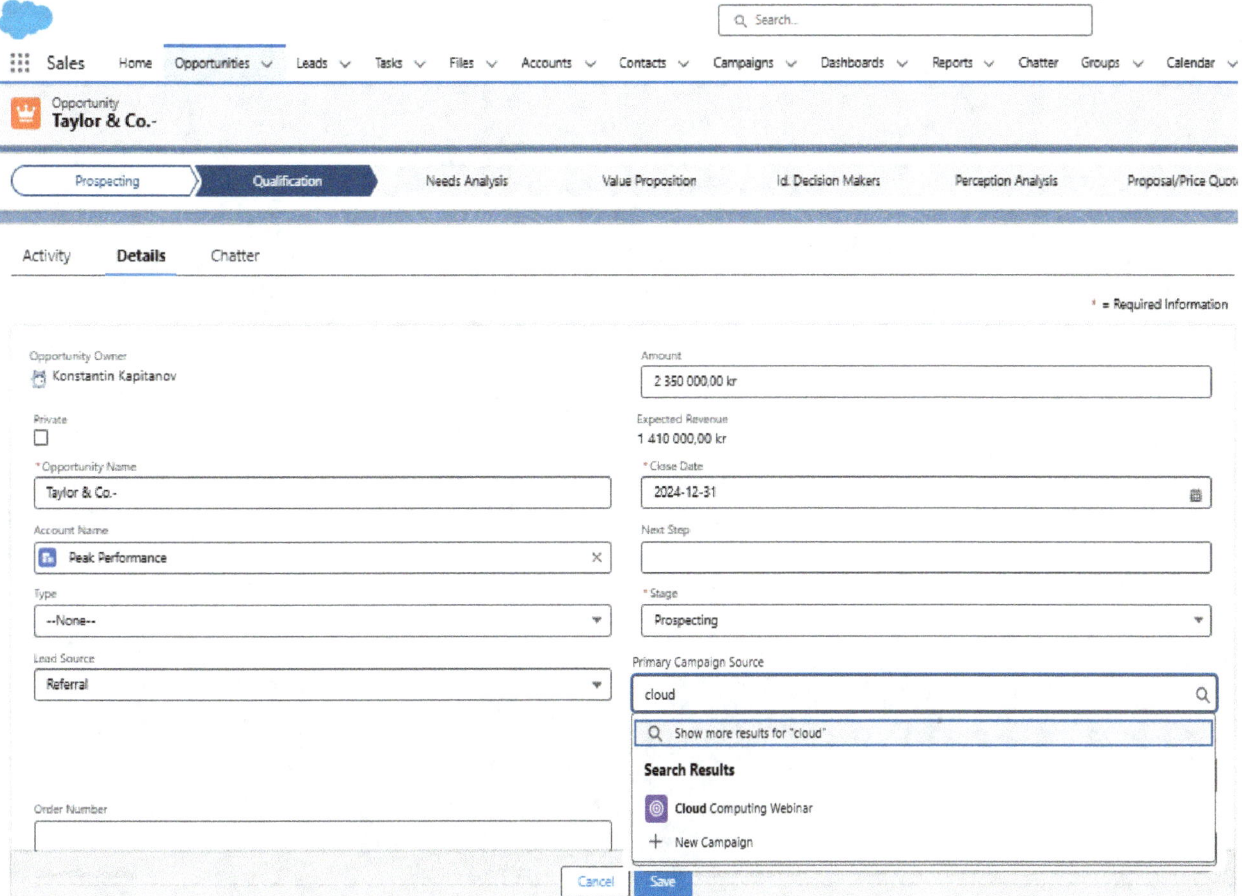

# PART I – Sales Cloud for Sales Managers and Sales Reps

*The connection to the campaign has been created now.*

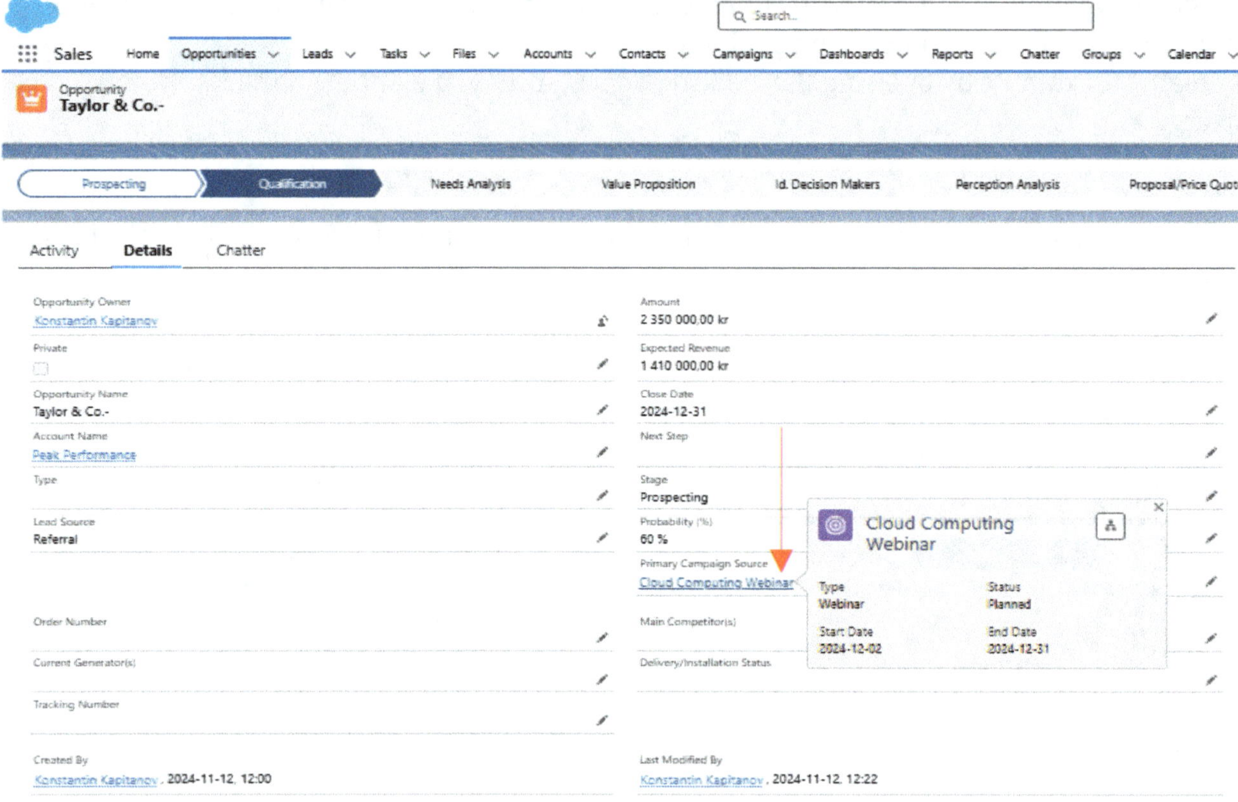

By changing the status of your opportunity to Closed Won and clicking on the campaign source, you can view the opportunity's value as part of the accumulated total in your campaign.

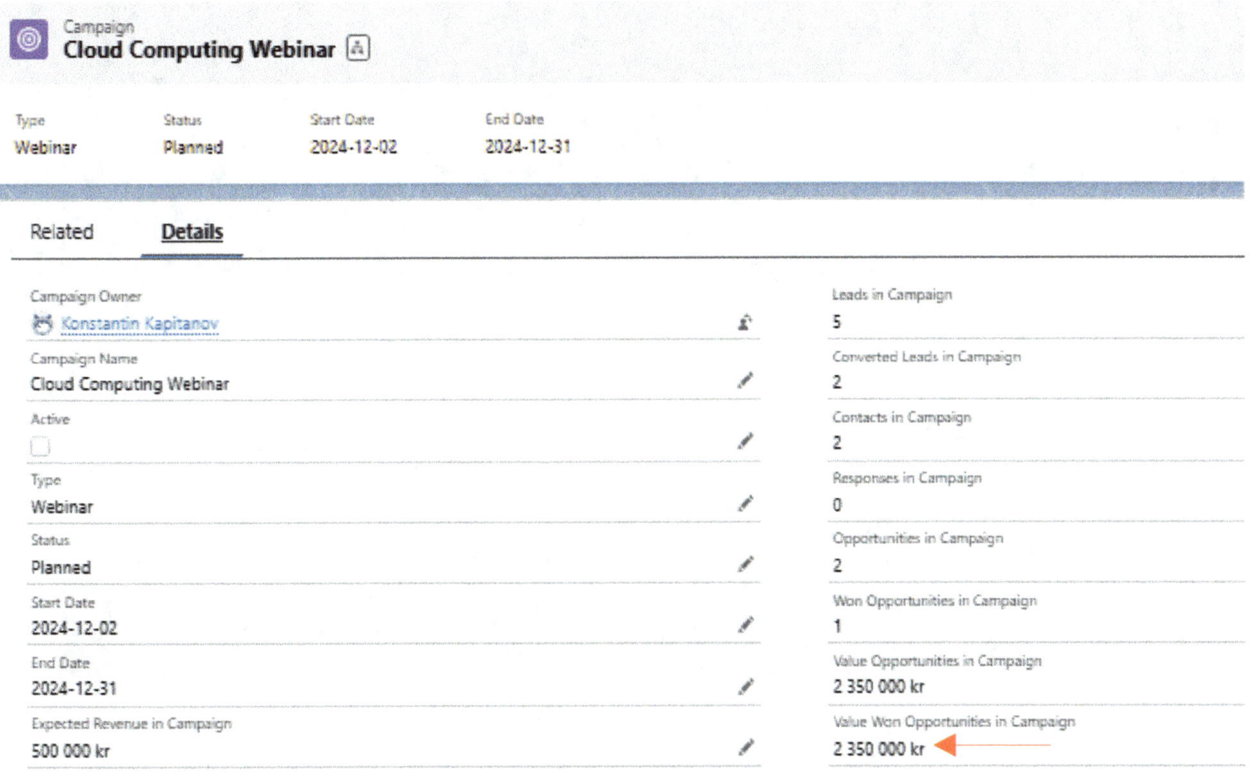

# Chapter 5. Reports

## 5.1 Standard Report Type

Reports in Sales Cloud are tools that help transform raw CRM data into actionable insights. They help us look into our customer and sales information from many different angles. A report can be a simple list of accounts created last week or a complex cross-analysis of opportunities linked to active projects with forecasted revenue per quarter.

Sales Cloud provides different report formats, each serving a different analytical purpose like Tabular, Summary, Matrix, and Joined. Reports can be filtered, grouped, and summarized, and they serve as the data source for dashboards. We'll go over each one, explaining what it is, why it's useful, and how to make it. Along the way, we will use a practical business case from our sample to illustrate each type.

You have access to a rich set of reports, available instantly with no setup required. Sales teams commonly use these reports to track opportunities, accounts, contacts, and activities. Because the reports are prebuilt, you don't have to start from scratch, you simply select a report that matches the question you want answered and then run it.

Let's say your company wants to know which products are associated with open deals. Instead of building a customer report, you can use the standard Opportunities with Products report type. This report lists all opportunities and their associated products when you run it. The report not only shows the product names but also includes quantities, prices, and total amounts.

*Go to → Reports → New Report*

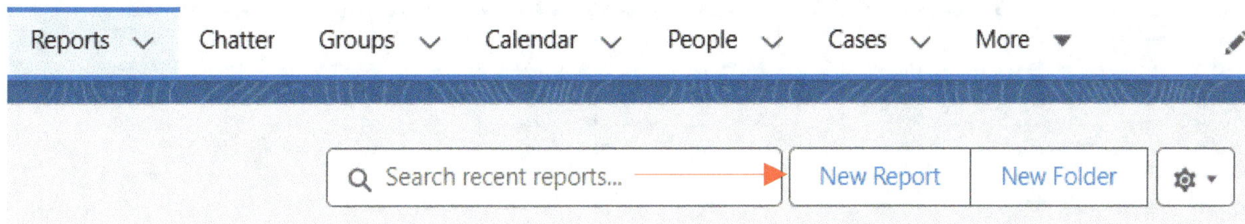

# PART I —  Sales Cloud for Sales Managers and Sales Reps

*Select → Opportunities → Opportunities with Products  → Start Report*

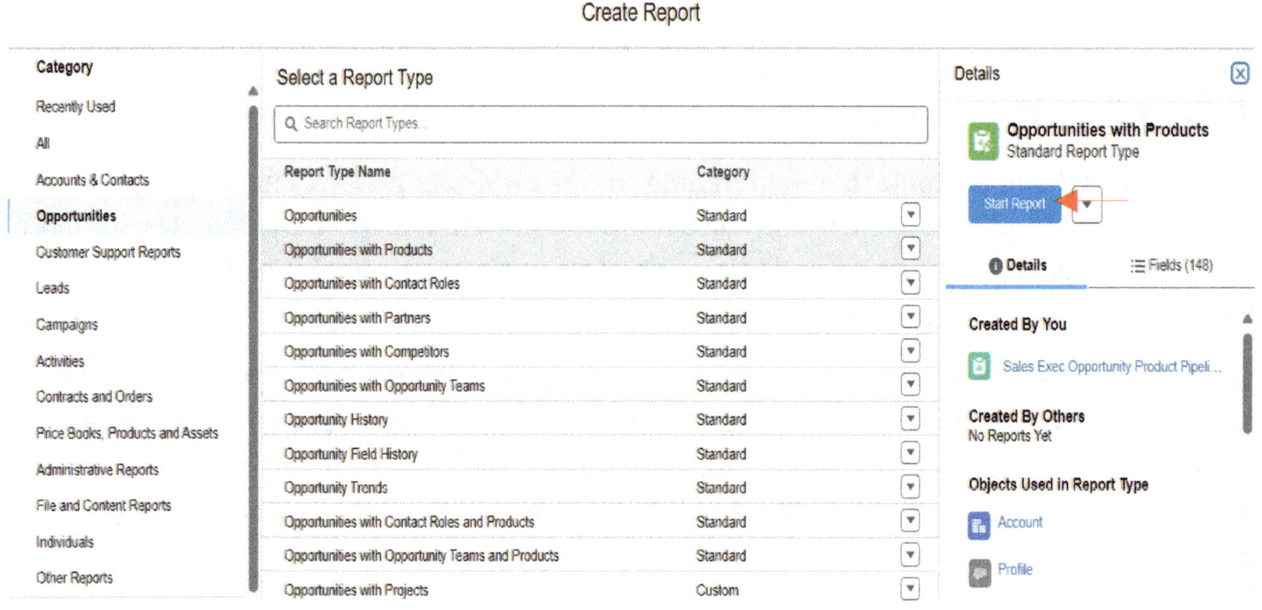



*Click Run.*

*See a list of opportunities that include product line items.*

# 5.2 Custom Report Type

A custom report type lets you design your own reporting framework by choosing the objects and the relationships between them. Once you set up a custom report type, users can build reports that pull data exactly in the way you defined. This is especially useful when working with custom objects or when you need a reporting view that isn't provided by default.

Our case requires analyzing opportunities that are connected to projects. Since Project is a custom object in the Sales Cloud setup (see Chapter 10 for more details), we need to link it to Opportunities in a way that reports can understand. This task is done through a custom report type.

```
Go to Setup → Report Types → Continue
```

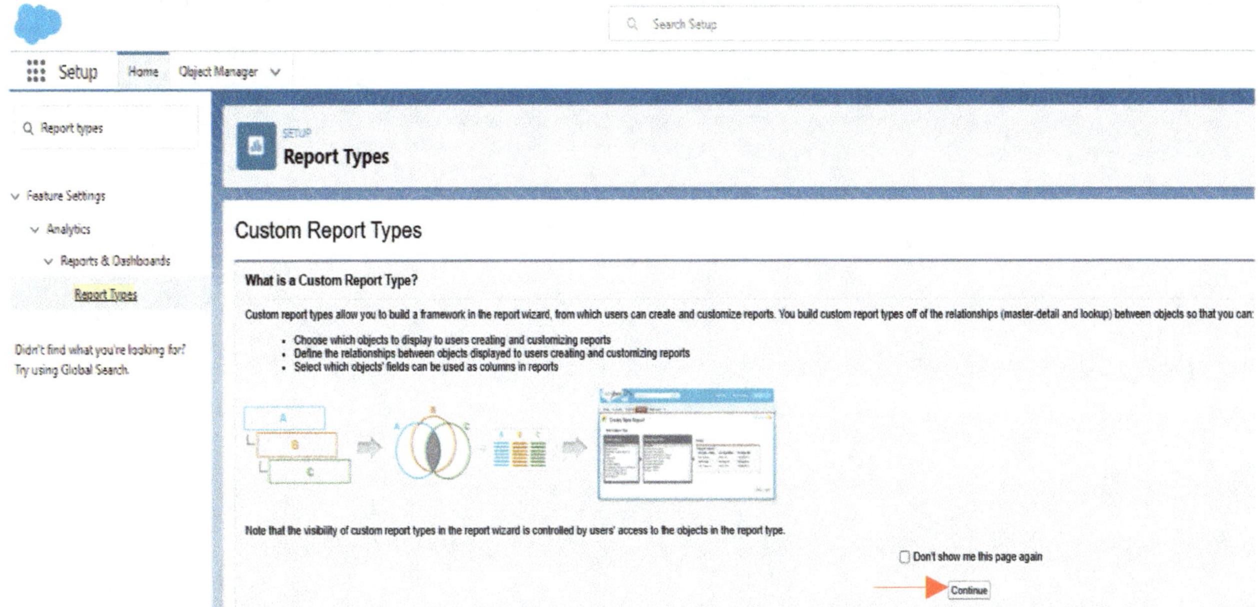

*Click New Custom Report Type.*

## All Custom Report Types

With custom report types, you can enable users to create reports from the predefined objects, object relationships, and fields that you specify.

View: All Custom Report Types   Edit | Create New View

New Custom Report Type

*Put these values in the following fields:*

*Primary Object-select Opportunities.*
*Report Type Label-enter Opportunities with Projects.*
*Store in Category-select Opportunities.*
*Deployment Status-choose Deployed so users can access it immediately.*

*Then click Next.*

## New Custom Report Type

**Step 1. Define the Custom Report Type**

**Report Type Focus**

Specify what type of records (rows) will be the focus of reports generated by this report type.

Example: If reporting on "Contacts with Opportunities with Partners," select "Contacts" as the primary object.

Primary Object: Opportunities

**Identification**

Report Type Label: Opportunities with Projects

Report Type Name: Opportunities_with_Project

*Note: Description will be visible to users who create reports.*

Description: Opportunities with Projects

Store in Category: Opportunities

**Deployment**

A report type with deployed status is available for use in the report wizard. While in development, report types are visible only to authorized administrators and their delegates.

Deployment Status:
- ○ In Development
- ● Deployed

*Click to relate another object.*

New Custom Report Type
## Opportunities with Projects

**Step 2. Define Report Records Set**

This report type will generate reports about Opportunities. You may define which related records from other objects are returned in report results by choosing a relationship to another object.

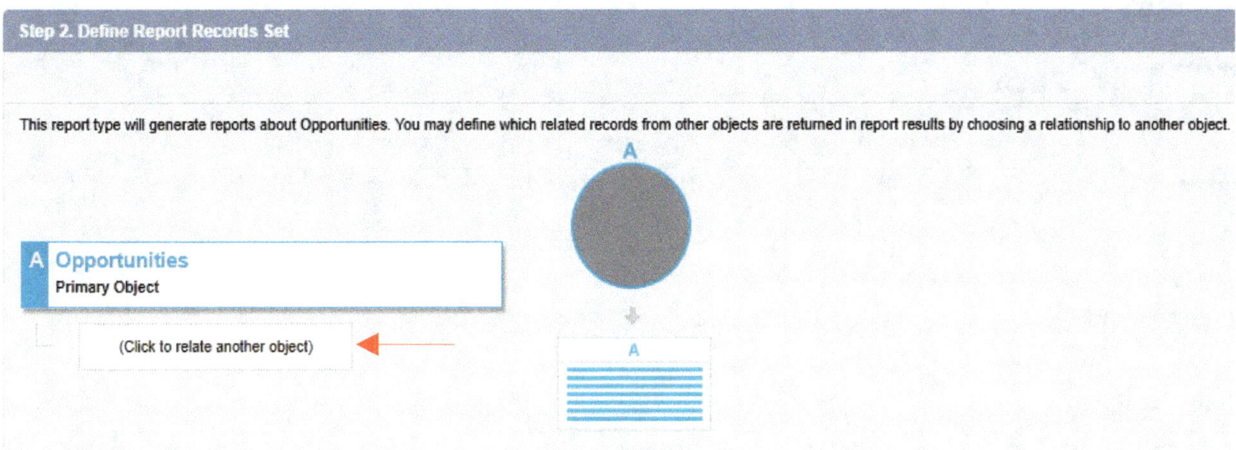

# PART I — Sales Cloud for Sales Managers and Sales Reps

*Add the related object Projects. Define the relationship as Each "A" record must have at least one related "B" record. In our case it means each Opportunity may have one or more related Projects. Then click Save.*

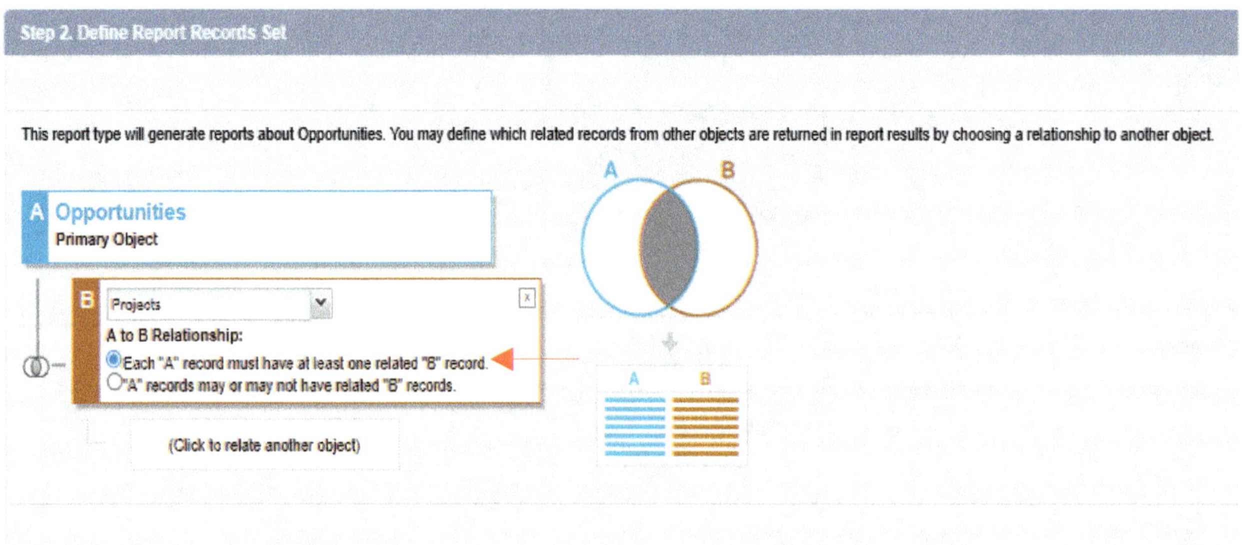

*Our custom report template is created.*

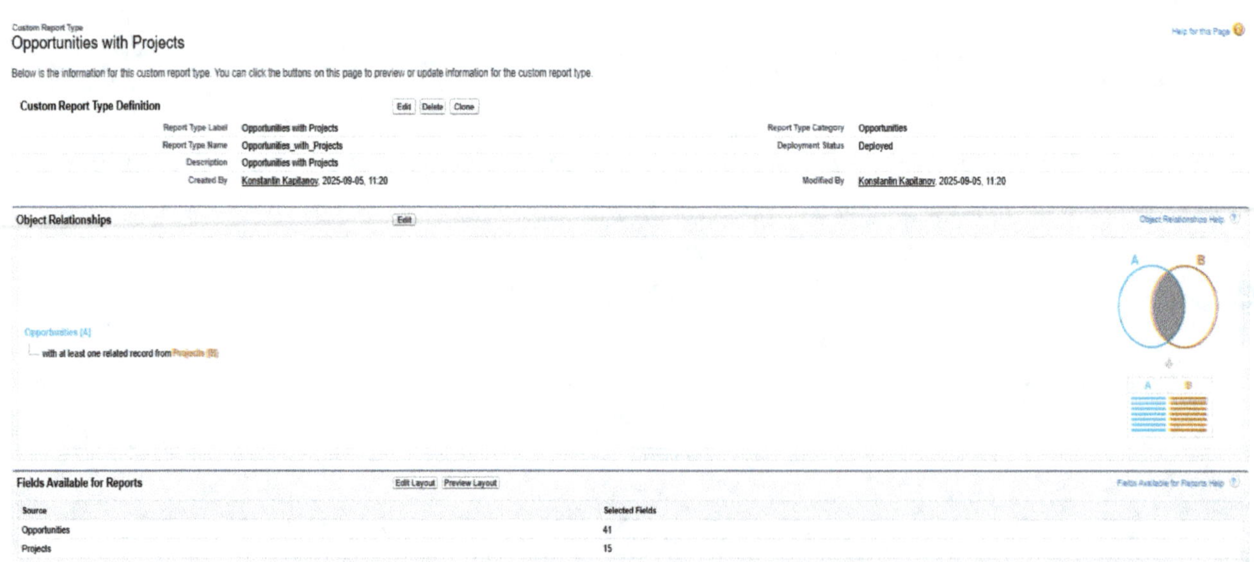

# 5.3 Tabular Reports

The most basic type of report is the tabular report. Think of it like a spreadsheet list. Tabular reports are perfect when you need a straightforward table of records without much grouping or calculation. They are often used for exports or quick overviews.

Suppose the sales manager wants to see a list of all opportunities linked to ongoing projects, showing their stage, expected revenue, and close date. This does not need grouping or subtotals just a clean list.

*Open the Reports tab and click New Report.*

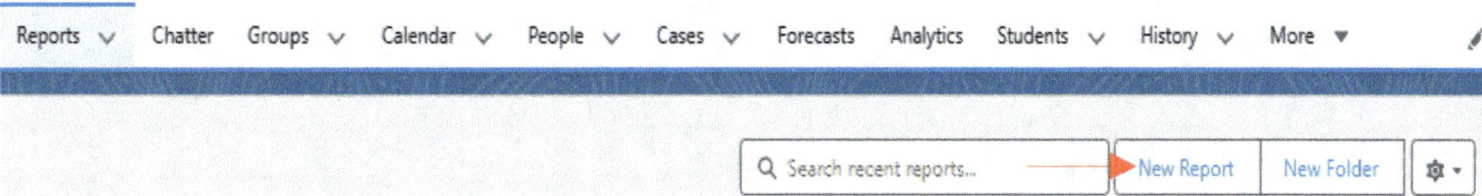

*Choose Category Opportunities and the report type Opportunities with Projects.  Click Start Report.*

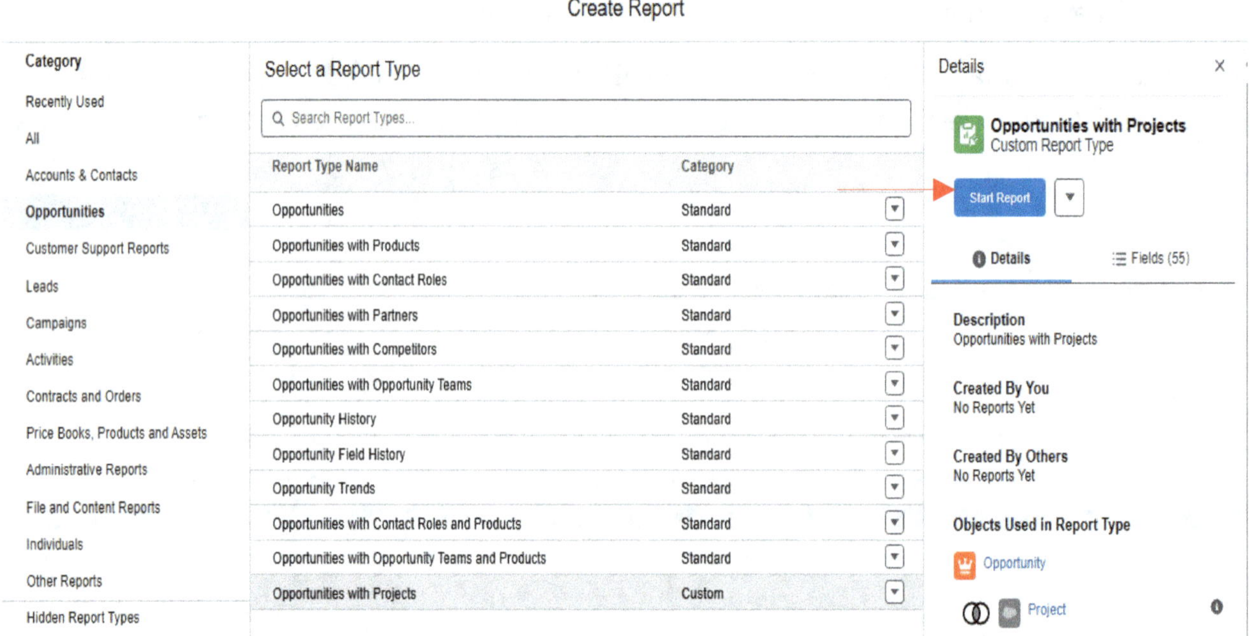

*Select the fields such as: Opportunity Name, Account Name, Project Name, Stage, Amount, and Close Date.*

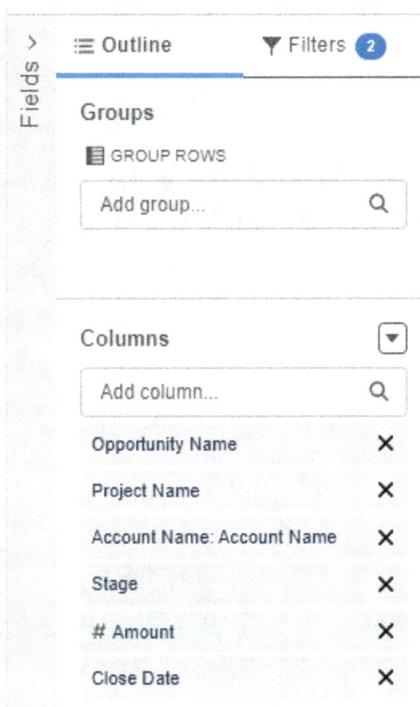

*Apply filters: Close Date = Current FQ, Closed = equals True.*

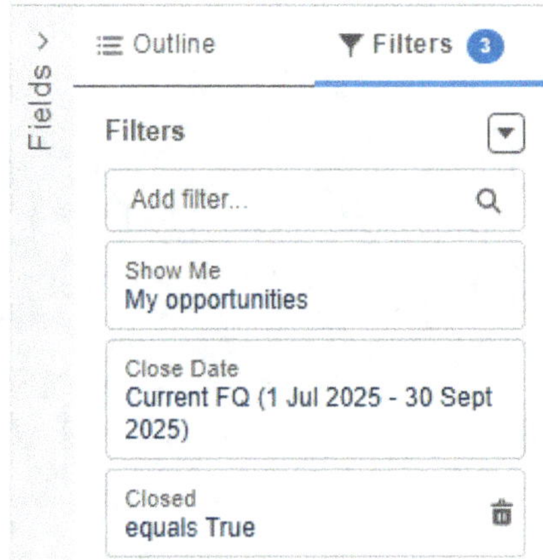

*Click Save & Run.*

*The result is a simple table showing all closed opportunities linked to projects, allowing the sales manager to quickly review the expected revenue in the near future.*

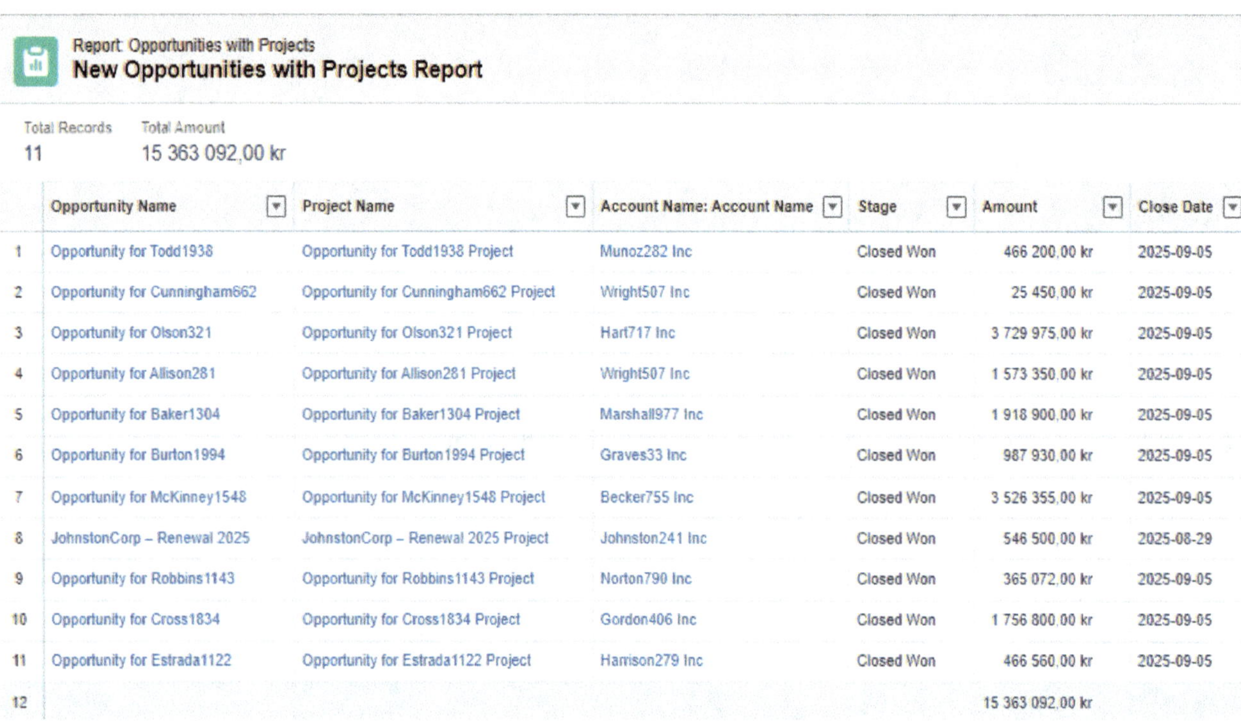

Report: Opportunities with Projects
**New Opportunities with Projects Report**

Total Records
11

Total Amount
15 363 092,00 kr

| | Opportunity Name | Project Name | Account Name: Account Name | Stage | Amount | Close Date |
|---|---|---|---|---|---|---|
| 1 | Opportunity for Todd1938 | Opportunity for Todd1938 Project | Munoz282 Inc | Closed Won | 466 200,00 kr | 2025-09-05 |
| 2 | Opportunity for Cunningham662 | Opportunity for Cunningham662 Project | Wright507 Inc | Closed Won | 25 450,00 kr | 2025-09-05 |
| 3 | Opportunity for Olson321 | Opportunity for Olson321 Project | Hart717 Inc | Closed Won | 3 729 975,00 kr | 2025-09-05 |
| 4 | Opportunity for Allison281 | Opportunity for Allison281 Project | Wright507 Inc | Closed Won | 1 573 350,00 kr | 2025-09-05 |
| 5 | Opportunity for Baker1304 | Opportunity for Baker1304 Project | Marshall977 Inc | Closed Won | 1 918 900,00 kr | 2025-09-05 |
| 6 | Opportunity for Burton1994 | Opportunity for Burton1994 Project | Graves33 Inc | Closed Won | 987 930,00 kr | 2025-09-05 |
| 7 | Opportunity for McKinney1548 | Opportunity for McKinney1548 Project | Becker755 Inc | Closed Won | 3 526 355,00 kr | 2025-09-05 |
| 8 | JohnstonCorp – Renewal 2025 | JohnstonCorp – Renewal 2025 Project | Johnston241 Inc | Closed Won | 546 500,00 kr | 2025-08-29 |
| 9 | Opportunity for Robbins1143 | Opportunity for Robbins1143 Project | Norton790 Inc | Closed Won | 365 072,00 kr | 2025-09-05 |
| 10 | Opportunity for Cross1834 | Opportunity for Cross1834 Project | Gordon406 Inc | Closed Won | 1 756 800,00 kr | 2025-09-05 |
| 11 | Opportunity for Estrada1122 | Opportunity for Estrada1122 Project | Harrison279 Inc | Closed Won | 466 560,00 kr | 2025-09-05 |
| 12 | | | | | 15 363 092,00 kr | |

Reports are most useful when they show the current state of your data and let you act on it quickly. Inline editing is a feature in Salesforce that allows you to update certain fields directly from the report itself, without having to open each individual record. This makes it easier to clean up data, make quick corrections, or adjust values in bulk as you review results.

For example, if you're looking at a report and notice that some opportunities have incorrect stages, you don't need to click into each opportunity record separately. With inline editing, you can simply click into the field within the report, adjust the value, and save.

**Note!** Formula fields can't be edited.

*Click Enable Field Editing Button.*

*Hover over a field that supports inline editing. If the field is editable, its value will be highlighted.*

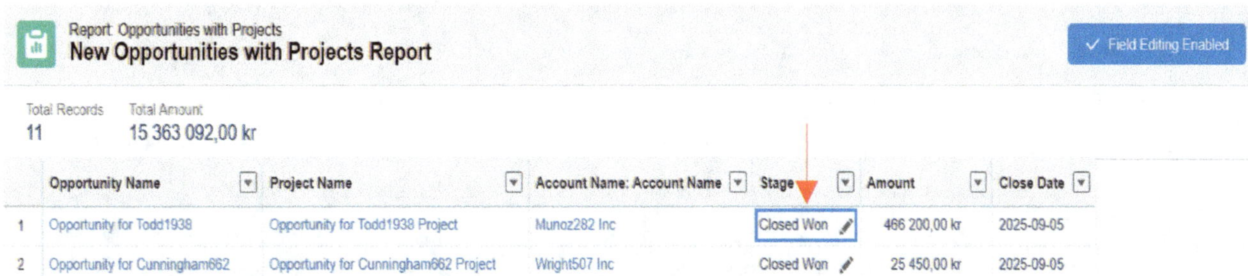

*Edit highlighted field directly.*

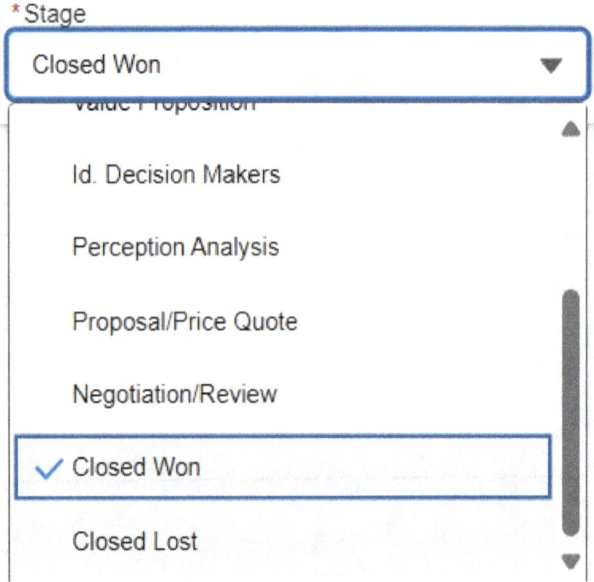

*Click to save your changes in the report.*

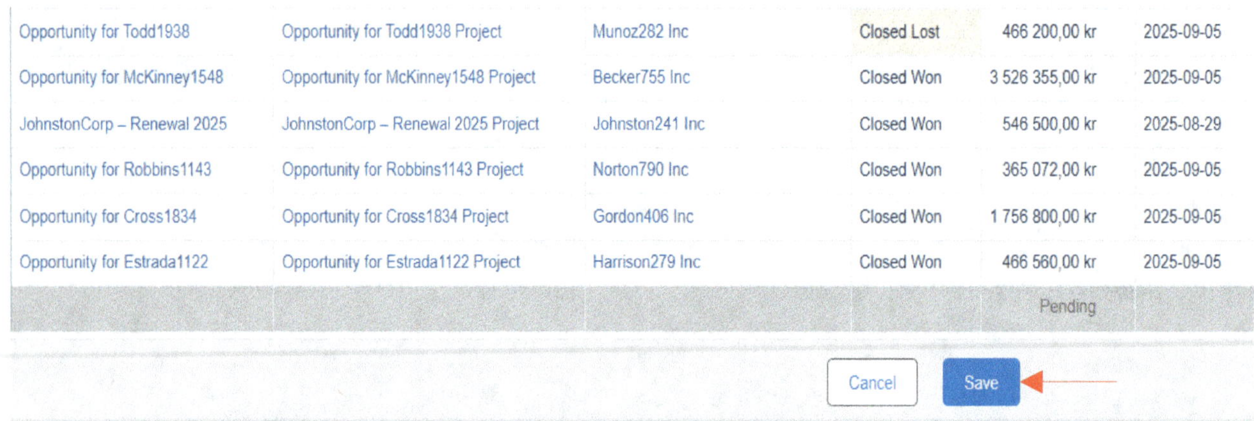

Sometimes it's not enough to view a report inside Salesforce, you may need to share the data with others, run more profound analysis in Excel, or archive a snapshot of results. Exporting a report allows you to take the information out of Salesforce and work with it in a familiar format, like an Excel spreadsheet or a CSV file. This way, sales teams can perform additional calculations and easily circulate results by email or include them in presentations.

*Exporting is straightforward. Once you have a report open, simply click Export option.*

*Select the format you want and click the Export button.*

## Export

**Export View**

### Details Only

Export only the detail rows. Use this to do further calculations or for uploading to other systems.

Format

Excel Format .xls

Encoding

ISO-8859-1 (General US & Western Europea

Cancel    Export

# 5.4 Summary Reports

Summary reports let us move beyond a simple list of records. They allow grouping, sorting, and adding totals, which makes them especially useful for pipeline analysis or revenue by account. Imagine the situation where the CFO wants to understand which accounts bring in the highest opportunity value this quarter. Instead of looking at a long list of opportunities, the report should group them by account and calculate a total per account.

*We will create a new report and select the Opportunities standard report type. Click Start Report.*

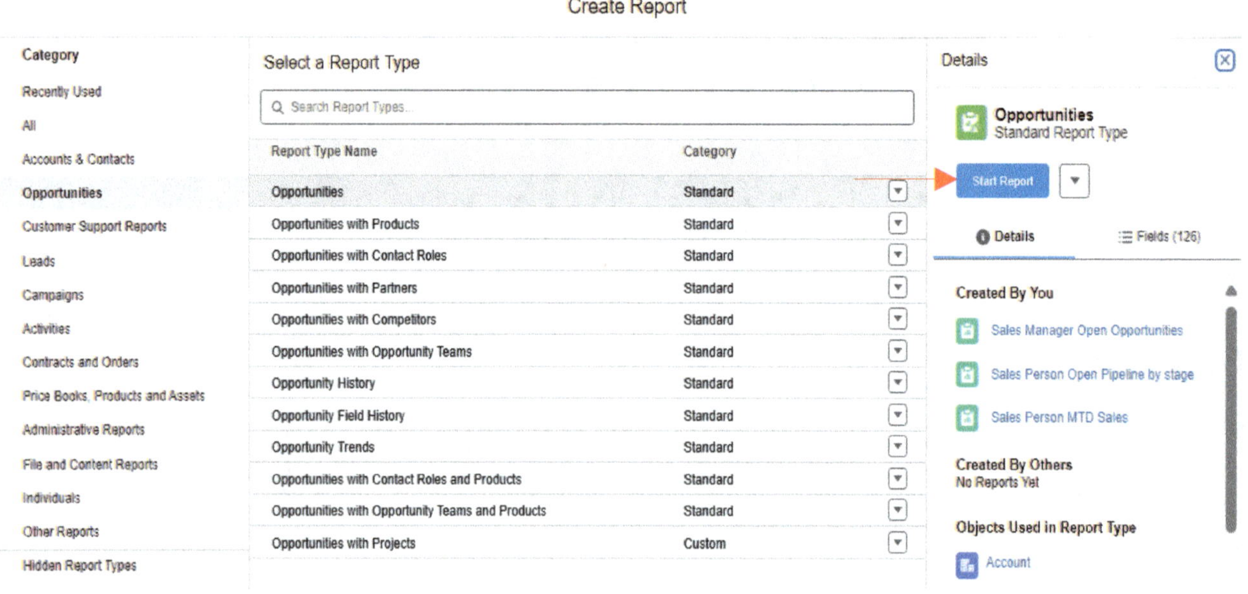

*Add the fields: Account Name, Opportunity Name, Stage, and Amount.*

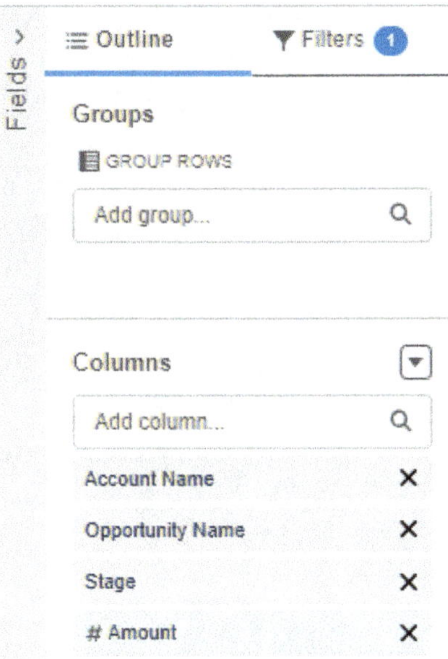

*Group Rows by Account Name.*

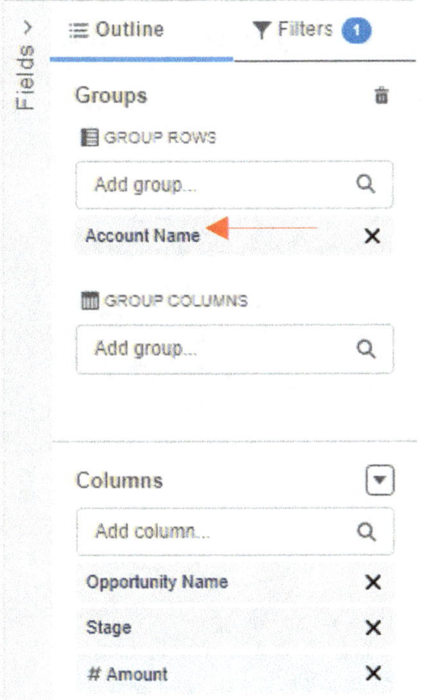

*Add a summary on the Amount field to calculate the total opportunity value per account and Apply.*

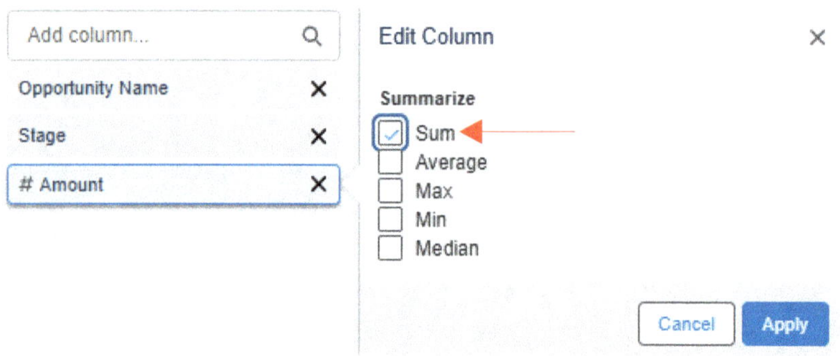

*Click Save & Run.*

Now the report shows each account as a headline, with all its opportunities listed below and a subtotal at the bottom. This makes it clear which accounts are expected to generate the most value in the short term.

| Account Name ↑ | Opportunity Name | Stage | Amount |
|---|---|---|---|
| Subtotal | | | 1 049 880,00 kr |
| Briggs402 Inc (1) | Opportunity for Barker1602 | Needs Analysis | 951 000,00 kr |
| Subtotal | | | 951 000,00 kr |
| Bright Tech (6) | Opportunity for Generators | Prospecting | 45 620,00 kr |
| | Opportunity for Services Renewal | Prospecting | 23 168,00 kr |
| | Opportunity Panel Implementation | Prospecting | 8 971,00 kr |
| | Opportunity Expansion Deal | Prospecting | 63 210,00 kr |
| | Opportunity Equipment Upgrade | Prospecting | 12 536,00 kr |
| | Opportunity System Integration | Prospecting | 900 455,00 kr |
| Subtotal | | | 1 053 960,00 kr |
| Bright Tech South (2) | Annual Subscription | Evaluation | 546 121,00 kr |
| | Mobile Solution Pilot | Prospecting | 542 133,00 kr |
| Subtotal | | | 1 088 254,00 kr |
| Brock75 Inc (1) | Opportunity for Lambert182 | Value Proposition | 1 750 200,00 kr |
| Subtotal | | | 1 750 200,00 kr |
| Brown495 Inc (1) | Opportunity for Gardner1110 | Needs Analysis | 645 700,00 kr |
| Subtotal | | | 645 700,00 kr |
| Bryan926 Inc (1) | Opportunity for Phelps205 | Needs Analysis | 53 325,00 kr |
| Subtotal | | | 53 325,00 kr |

Row Counts ✓  Detail Rows ✓  Subtotals ✓  Grand Total ✓

When working with reports conditional formatting helps by adding simple color cues to your report data, making it easier to spot patterns, successes, or areas of concern. Instead of scanning through long columns of figures, you can immediately see which values stand out like green for strong performance, orange for average, and red for values that may need attention.

This feature works on summary or matrix reports where data is grouped, allowing you to apply thresholds to key metrics such as revenue, deal count, or activity volume. By setting these thresholds, color formatting automatically applies to the summarized values, giving you a quick visual overview of performance across your report.

# PART I —  Sales Cloud for Sales Managers and Sales Reps

*By editing your report click the Conditional Formatting button.*

*Click to add you Conditional Formatting Role.*

*After setting your Conditional Formatting Roles click Done.*

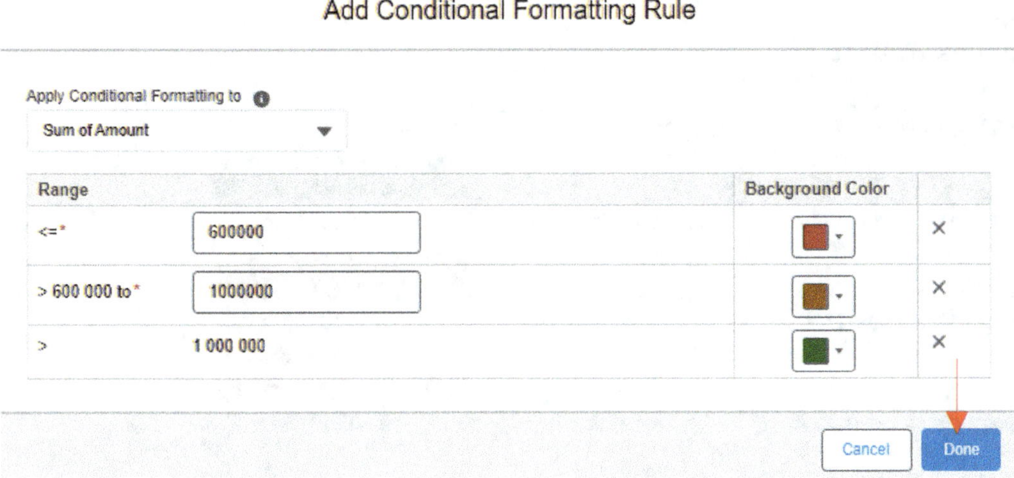


*Click Apply your Conditional Formatting Roles and run your report again.*

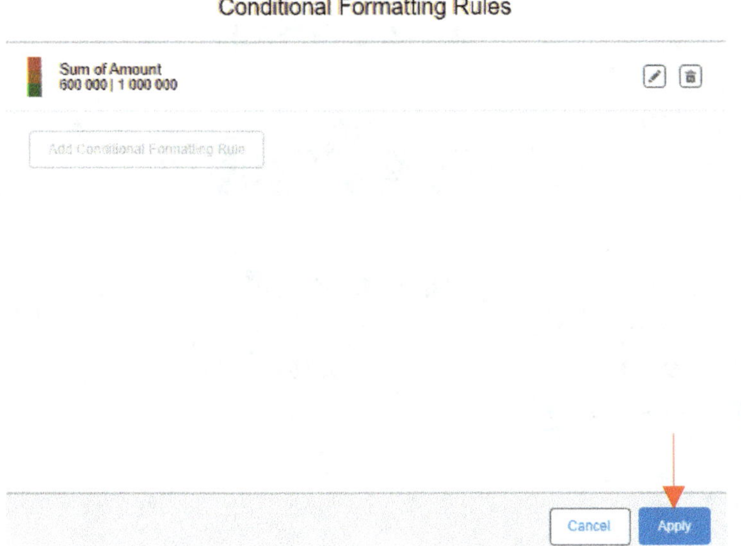

*Now your report highlights values automatically based on your ranges.*

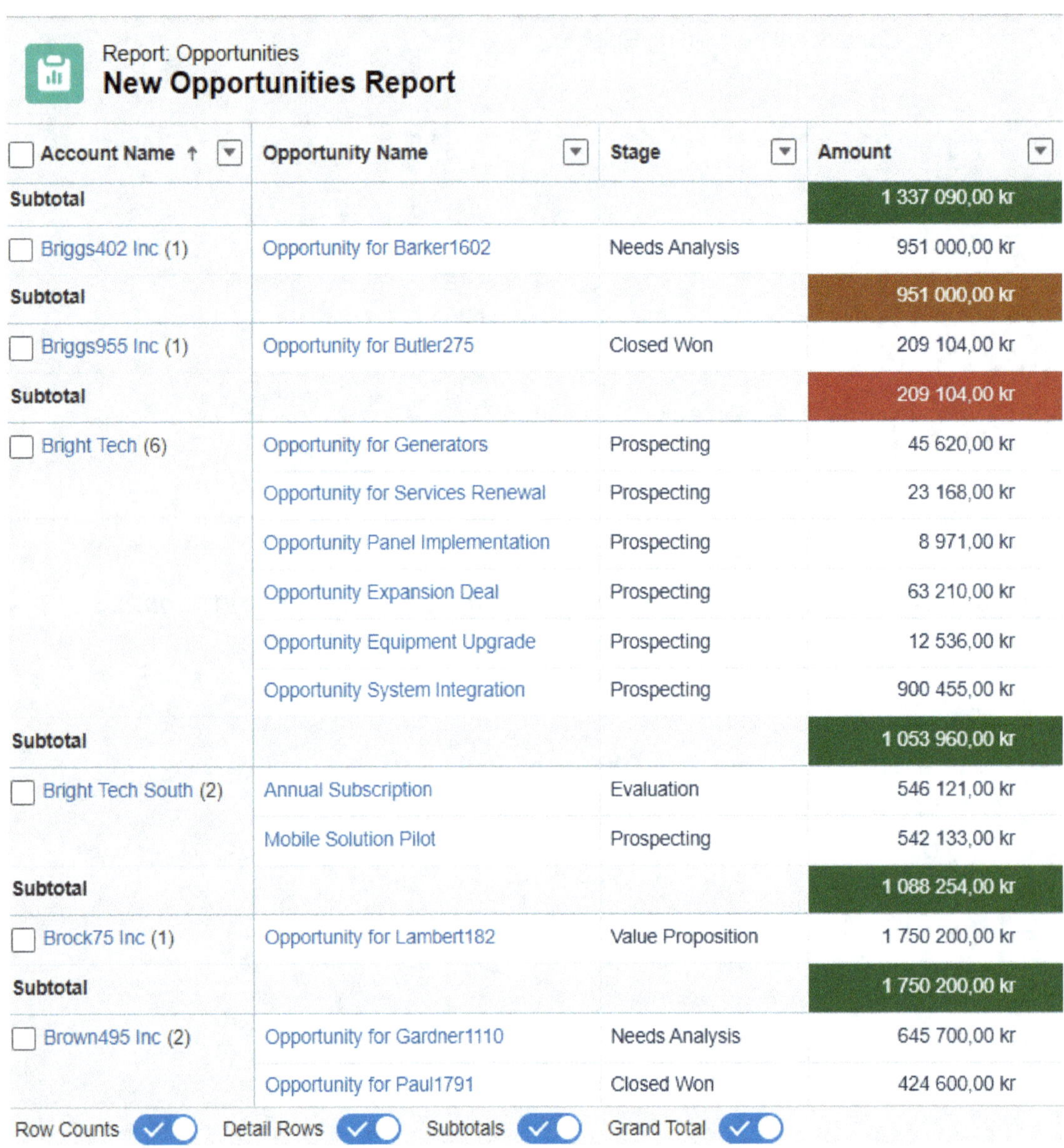

# 5.5 Matrix Reports

Matrix reports give us the possibility to group data both by rows and columns, making comparisons easier. They are especially useful for analyzing how two dimensions interact, like sales stage by region or account by quarter.

The sales director wants to compare how much revenue was expected from opportunities in each stage from last month. This way, it's possible to see not only the time dimension but also where opportunities stand in the pipeline.

*Create a new report and select the Opportunities standard report type. Click Start Report.*

Create Report

| Category | Select a Report Type | | Details |
| --- | --- | --- | --- |
| Recently Used | Q Search Report Types... | | **Opportunities** — Standard Report Type |
| All | | | |
| Accounts & Contacts | **Report Type Name** | **Category** | Start Report |
| Opportunities | Opportunities | Standard | |
| Customer Support Reports | Opportunities with Products | Standard | Details   Fields (126) |
| Leads | Opportunities with Contact Roles | Standard | |
| Campaigns | Opportunities with Partners | Standard | Created By You |
| Activities | Opportunities with Competitors | Standard | Sales Manager Open Opportunities |
| Contracts and Orders | Opportunities with Opportunity Teams | Standard | Sales Person Open Pipeline by stage |
| Price Books, Products and Assets | Opportunity History | Standard | Sales Person MTD Sales |
| Administrative Reports | Opportunity Field History | Standard | |
| File and Content Reports | Opportunity Trends | Standard | Created By Others |
| Individuals | Opportunities with Contact Roles and Products | Standard | No Reports Yet |
| Other Reports | Opportunities with Opportunity Teams and Products | Standard | Objects Used in Report Type |
| Hidden Report Types | Opportunities with Projects | Custom | Account |

*Add the fields: Account Name, Opportunity Name, Stage, Close Date, and Amount.*

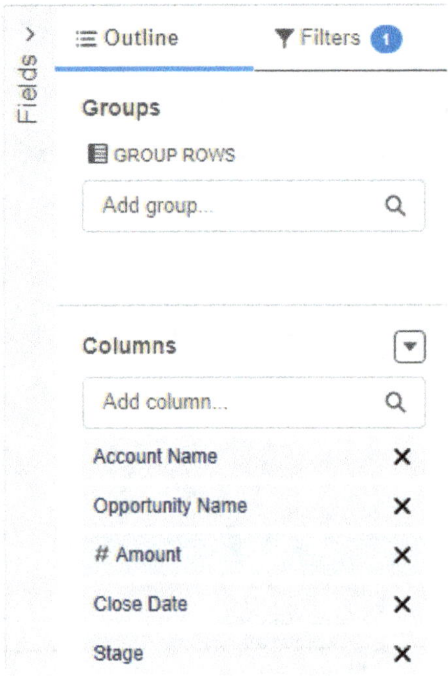

Group rows by Stage and Group columns by Close Date.

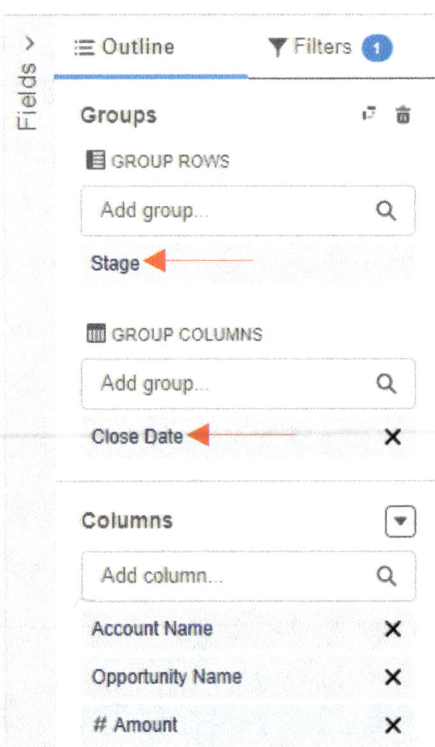

*Click Run.*

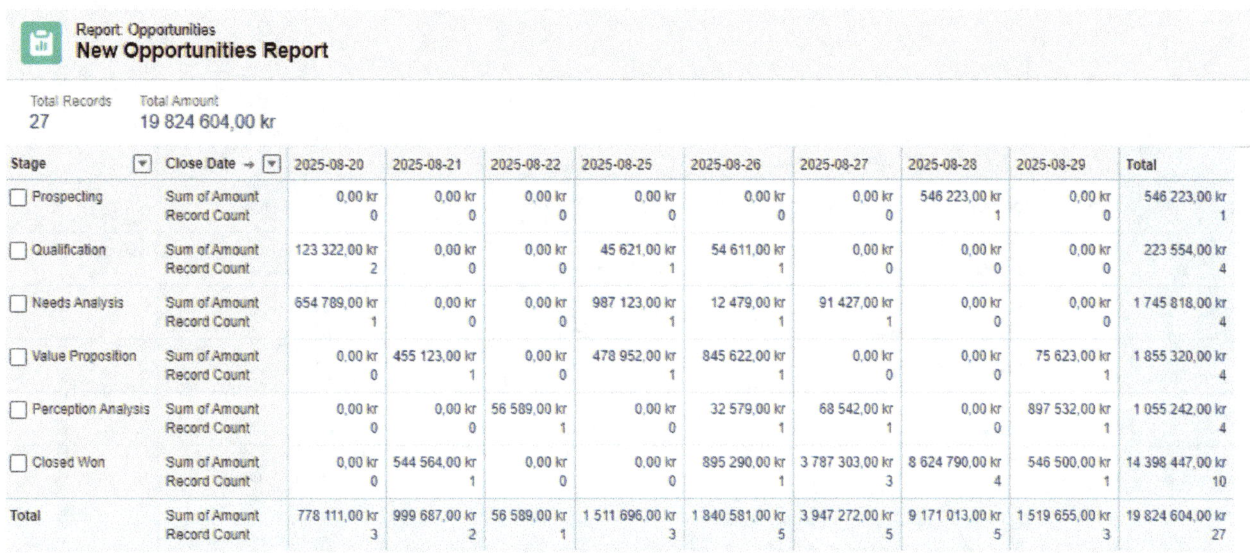

Report: Opportunities
**New Opportunities Report**

Total Records
27

Total Amount
19 824 604,00 kr

| Stage | Close Date → | 2025-08-20 | 2025-08-21 | 2025-08-22 | 2025-08-25 | 2025-08-26 | 2025-08-27 | 2025-08-28 | 2025-08-29 | Total |
|---|---|---|---|---|---|---|---|---|---|---|
| Prospecting | Sum of Amount | 0,00 kr | 0,00 kr | 0,00 kr | 0,00 kr | 0,00 kr | 0,00 kr | 546 223,00 kr | 0,00 kr | 546 223,00 kr |
| | Record Count | 0 | 0 | 0 | 0 | 0 | 0 | 1 | 0 | 1 |
| Qualification | Sum of Amount | 123 322,00 kr | 0,00 kr | 0,00 kr | 45 621,00 kr | 54 611,00 kr | 0,00 kr | 0,00 kr | 0,00 kr | 223 554,00 kr |
| | Record Count | 2 | 0 | 0 | 1 | 1 | 0 | 0 | 0 | 4 |
| Needs Analysis | Sum of Amount | 654 789,00 kr | 0,00 kr | 0,00 kr | 987 123,00 kr | 12 479,00 kr | 91 427,00 kr | 0,00 kr | 0,00 kr | 1 745 818,00 kr |
| | Record Count | 1 | 0 | 0 | 1 | 1 | 1 | 0 | 0 | 4 |
| Value Proposition | Sum of Amount | 0,00 kr | 455 123,00 kr | 0,00 kr | 478 952,00 kr | 845 622,00 kr | 0,00 kr | 0,00 kr | 75 623,00 kr | 1 855 320,00 kr |
| | Record Count | 0 | 1 | 0 | 1 | 1 | 0 | 0 | 1 | 4 |
| Perception Analysis | Sum of Amount | 0,00 kr | 0,00 kr | 56 589,00 kr | 0,00 kr | 32 579,00 kr | 68 542,00 kr | 0,00 kr | 897 532,00 kr | 1 055 242,00 kr |
| | Record Count | 0 | 0 | 1 | 0 | 1 | 1 | 0 | 1 | 4 |
| Closed Won | Sum of Amount | 0,00 kr | 544 564,00 kr | 0,00 kr | 0,00 kr | 895 290,00 kr | 3 787 303,00 kr | 8 624 790,00 kr | 546 500,00 kr | 14 398 447,00 kr |
| | Record Count | 0 | 1 | 0 | 0 | 1 | 3 | 4 | 1 | 10 |
| Total | Sum of Amount | 778 111,00 kr | 999 687,00 kr | 56 589,00 kr | 1 511 696,00 kr | 1 840 581,00 kr | 3 947 272,00 kr | 9 171 013,00 kr | 1 519 655,00 kr | 19 824 604,00 kr |
| | Record Count | 3 | 2 | 1 | 3 | 5 | 5 | 5 | 3 | 27 |

The result is a grid where each row is a sales stage and each column is a day. The intersecting cells display the total revenue for each stage in that day, facilitating the identification of concentrated deals over time.

# 5.6 Joined Reports

Joined reports let us combine different report blocks, each with its fields and filters, into one view. They are useful for comparing related information side by side, especially when we want to analyze different aspects of the same business context.

Sales leadership wants to evaluate the opportunity pipeline and, at the same time, see how customer support cases from the same accounts might influence sales. The idea is to understand whether accounts with high revenue potential also have many open support cases, which could put deals at risk.

# PART I — Sales Cloud for Sales Managers and Sales Reps

*Create a new report, select the Opportunities standard report type and click Start Report.*

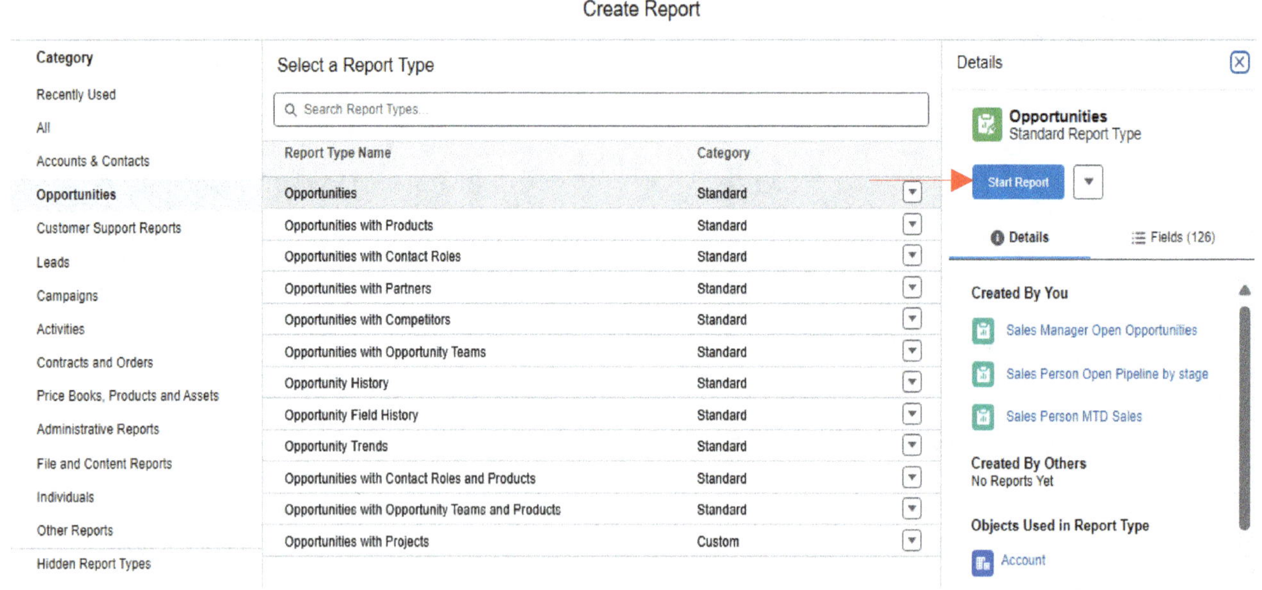

*Add the fields: Account Name, Opportunity Name, Amount, Close Date, and Stage.*

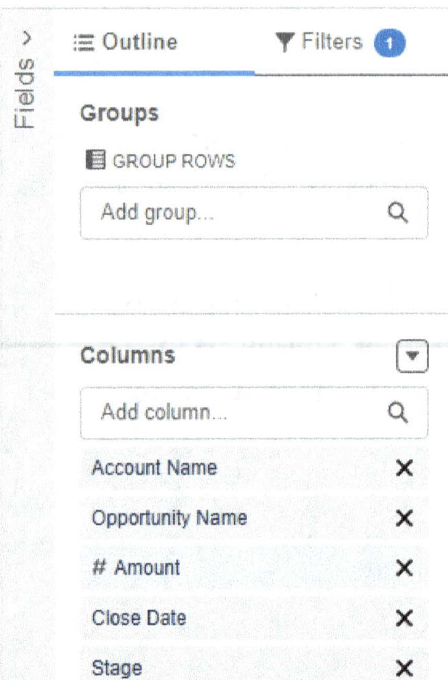

*Click on Report, select Joined Reports and Apply.*

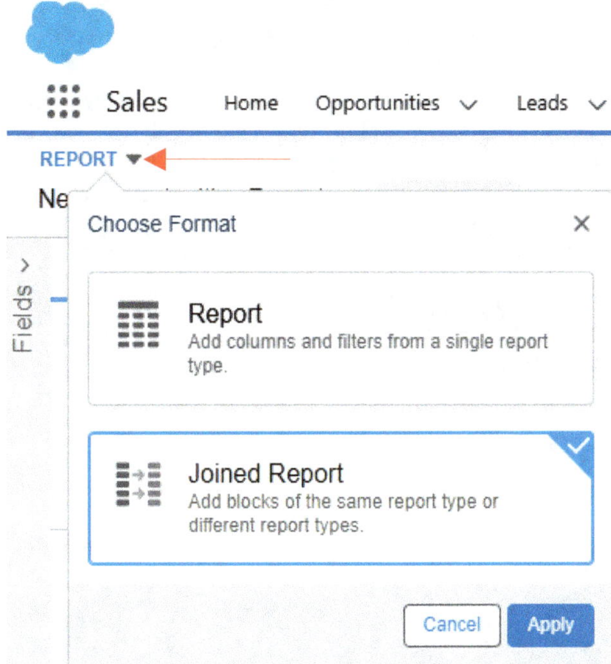


*Select Cases and click Add Block.*

Create Report

| Category | Select a Report Type | | Details |
| --- | --- | --- | --- |
| **Recently Used** | | | **Cases** Standard Report Type |
| All | Recently Used Report Types | | Common fields will come from these objects: Account, User. |
| Accounts & Contacts | | | ☑ Include default columns |
| Opportunities | **Report Type Name** | **Category** | **Add Block** |
| Customer Support Reports | Slices with Bread | Standard | |
| Leads | Tasks and Events | Standard | **Details**    **Fields (132)** |
| Campaigns | Opportunities | Standard | |
| Activities | Opportunities with Products | Standard | **Created By You** |
| Contracts and Orders | Leads | Standard | Trend of Cases Created Report |
| Price Books, Products and Assets | Campaigns with Leads | Standard | Trend of Cases Closed Report |
| Administrative Reports | Leads with converted lead information | Standard | Trend of Case Resolution Time Report |
| File and Content Reports | Campaigns with Opportunities | Standard | |
| Individuals | Campaigns | Standard | **Created By Others** No Reports Yet |
| Other Reports | Cases | Standard | |
| Hidden Report Types | | | |

# PART I — Sales Cloud for Sales Managers and Sales Reps

*The joined report shows two perspectives for each account the opportunities expected to close in the near term and the active support cases. Managers can prioritize risk mitigation by using this combined view, which highlights accounts where unresolved issues may threaten large opportunities.*

Joined Report
**New Opportunities Report**

| | Opportunities — Opportunities block 1 | | | | | Cases — Cases block 1 | | |
|---|---|---|---|---|---|---|---|---|
| | Account Name | Opportunity Name | Stage | Amount | Close Date | Case Number | Subject | Open |
| 34 | Acme Inc | Initial Inquiry for Laptops | Needs Analysis | 546 223,00 kr | 2025-10-03 | 00034181 | Laptop Not Powering On | ☑ |
| 35 | Global Corp | Qualification Call for Business Phones | Perception Analysis | 456 536,00 kr | 2025-10-03 | 00034516 | Battery Drain Issue | ☑ |
| 36 | Tech Solutions | Workshop on Digital Media Solution Requirements | Value Proposition | 546 665,00 kr | 2025-10-03 | 00034517 | Software Compatibility | ☑ |
| 37 | Innovate LLC | Presentation of New Fleet | Prospecting | 564 564,00 kr | 2025-10-03 | 00034518 | Screen Damage | ☑ |
| 38 | Alpha Co | Quote for Smartphones with Service Contract | Prospecting | 548 798,00 kr | 2025-10-03 | 00034519 | Network Connectivity Problem | ☑ |
| 39 | Beta Tech | Negotiating Digital Media License Package | Proposal/Price Q... | 2 133 232,00 kr | 2025-10-03 | 00034520 | Warranty Claim | ☑ |
| 40 | Delta Partners | Contract Sent for Mobile Devices | Negotiation/Review | 123 285,00 kr | 2025-10-03 | 00034521 | Subscription Not Activated | ☑ |
| 41 | Epsilon Ltd | Digital Media Package | Negotiation/Review | 954 213,00 kr | 2025-10-03 | 00033894 | Streaming Quality Issue | ☑ |
| 42 | Zeta Group | Purchase of 250 Tablets | Proposal/Price Q... | 95 423,00 kr | 2025-10-03 | 00033895 | Login Problems | ☑ |
| 43 | Omega Inc | Evaluation of Laptop Leasing Model | Id. Decision Mak... | 54 213,00 kr | 2025-10-03 | 00033896 | Payment Failure | ☑ |

# 5.7 Report Charts

Reports in Sales Cloud give you raw data in a table format, with rows and columns showing leads, opportunities, or accounts. But tables can be overwhelming. That's where report charts come in. A report chart is a visual representation of report data, making it easier to see patterns, trends, and insights at a glance. Instead of reading through hundreds of rows, you immediately see what matters. In the following example, we'll take a single report and show how a Stacked Bar and a Donut chart answer different questions.

*Go to → Reports → New Report→ Select Opportunities → Start Report*

Create Report

| Category | Select a Report Type | | Details |
|---|---|---|---|
| Recently Used | | | **Opportunities** Standard Report Type |
| All | Q Search Report Types... | | |
| Accounts & Contacts | | | **Start Report** |
| Opportunities | Report Type Name | Category | |
| Customer Support Reports | Opportunities | Standard | **1** Details / **Fields (126)** |
| Leads | Opportunities with Products | Standard | |
| Campaigns | Opportunities with Contact Roles | Standard | **Created By You** |
| Activities | Opportunities with Partners | Standard | Sales Manager Open Opportunities |
| Contracts and Orders | Opportunities with Competitors | Standard | Sales Person Open Pipeline by stage |
| Price Books, Products and Assets | Opportunities with Opportunity Teams | Standard | Sales Person MTD Sales |
| Administrative Reports | Opportunity History | Standard | |
| File and Content Reports | Opportunity Field History | Standard | **Created By Others** No Reports Yet |
| Individuals | Opportunity Trends | Standard | |
| Other Reports | Opportunities with Contact Roles and Products | Standard | **Objects Used in Report Type** |
| Hidden Report Types | Opportunities with Opportunity Teams and Products | Standard | Account |
| | Opportunities with Projects | Custom | |

# PART I — Sales Cloud for Sales Managers and Sales Reps

*Group rows by Stage and Group columns by Close Month.*

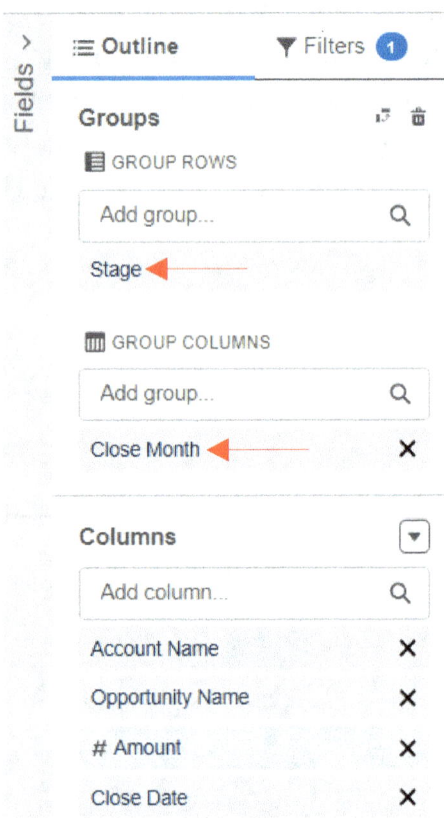

*Add a summary on the Amount field to calculate the total opportunity value per account and Apply.*

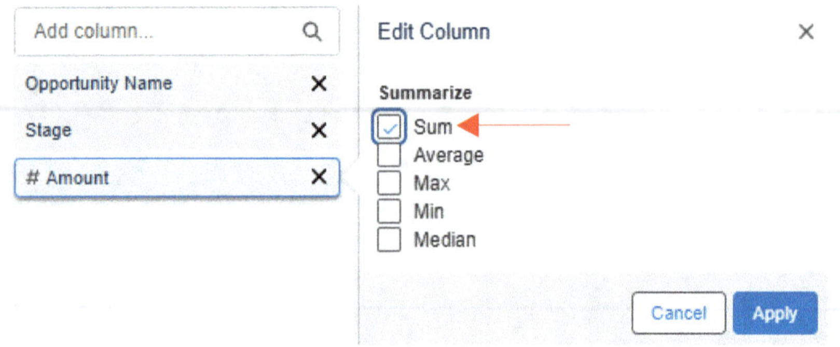

*Click Save & Run.*

*Click the Toggle Chart button at the top.*

*Click the Chart Properties button and select Stacked Bar with Y-Axis- Close Month and X-Axis-Record Count settings.*

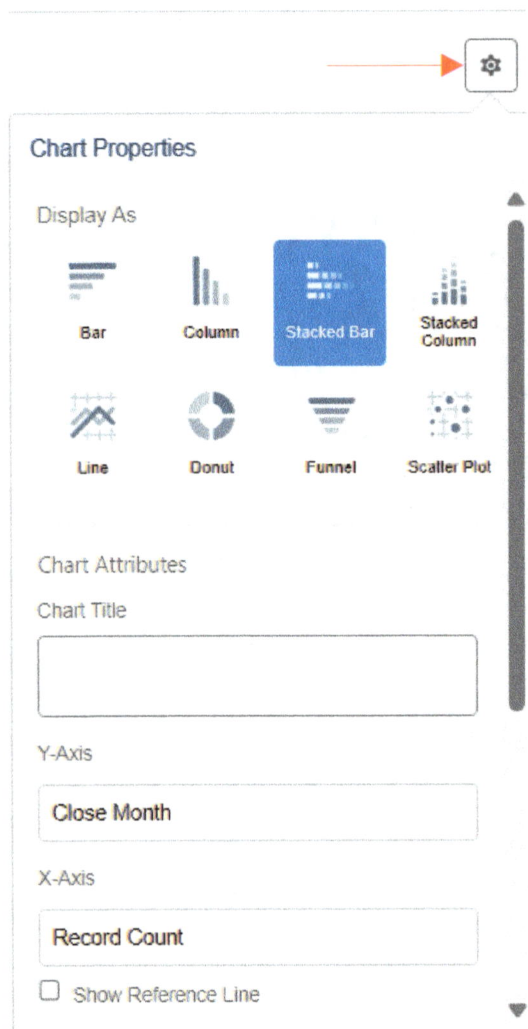

*Each column represents a month and the colors within each column represent stages. You can quickly see whether the pipeline is growing or shrinking month by month.*

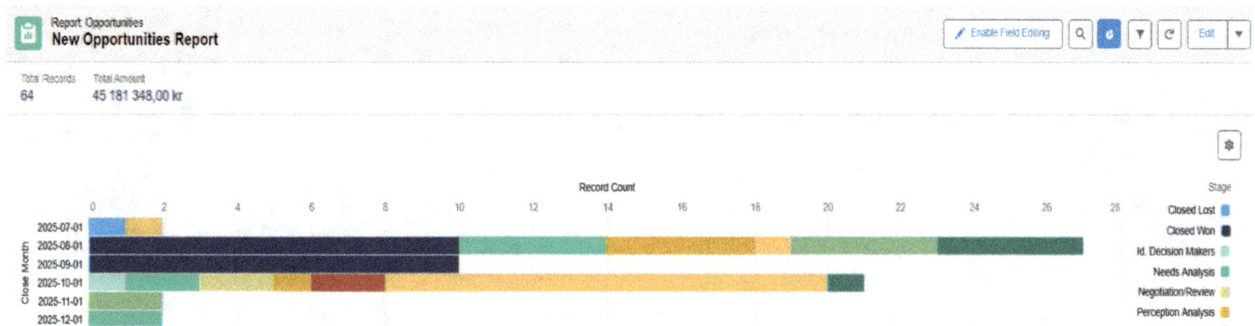

*Click the Chart Properties button and select Donut with Value-Sum of Amount and Sliced By-Stage.*

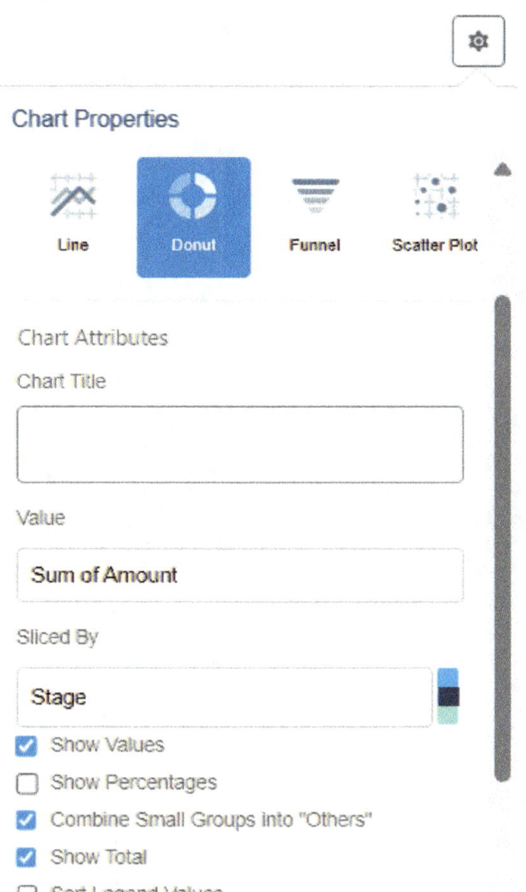

*The Donut chart ignores the monthly breakdown and instead focuses on the distribution of revenue by stage. This chart shifts the perspective from number of deals to value of deals.*

Sales Cloud gives you a toolbox of chart types, and the most effective one always depends on the question you want to answer. By experimenting with different formats, you can turn the same report data into entirely new perspectives.

# Chapter 6. Dashboards

## 6.1 Standard Dashboards

While reports give you the detailed rows and columns of information, dashboards take that data and present it as easy-to-read charts. Think of a dashboard as a control panel it gathers the most important numbers and trends in one place so that sales teams, managers, or executives can quickly see how the business is performing.

A dashboard is made up of individual components, and each component is based on a report. For example, you could have a Bar chart showing how many opportunities are in each stage of the sales pipeline or a Donut chart that breaks down revenue by product line. By combining several components, a dashboard gives a complete picture of sales performance, customer activity, or any other key business process.

Dashboards in Sales Cloud are not static, they update automatically as the underlying data are changed. This means you're always looking at the most current state of your business. Dashboards can also be customized by choosing which reports are included, how the data is grouped, or by setting filters to focus on specific regions, teams, or time periods.

For teams, dashboards are also a way to align everyone around the same goals. A sales manager might use them to track team quotas, while a salesperson may use their personal dashboard to focus only on their pipeline. Executives often rely on dashboards for high-level summaries across multiple departments.

In short, dashboards transform raw data into meaningful insights, helping everyone from individual sales reps to company leadership make smarter, faster decisions.

A common use case for dashboards is helping sales teams track their pipeline. In this example, we will build a Sales Pipeline Dashboard that presents sales reps, managers, and executives a clear view of opportunities at different stages.

# PART I — Sales Cloud for Sales Managers and Sales Reps

*Go to Dashboards → New Folder.*

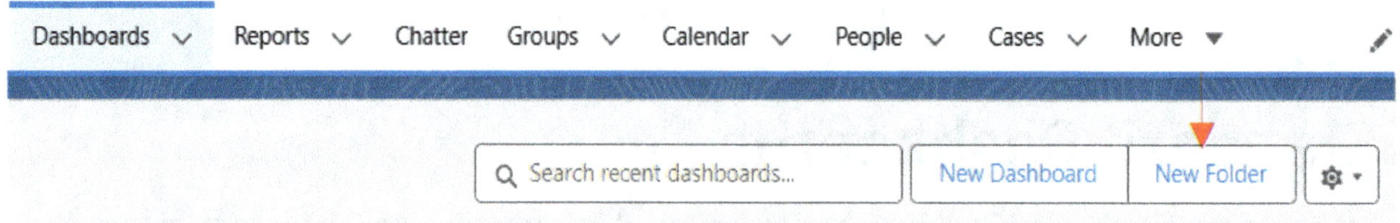

*Set up the Folder Label and click Save.*

## Create folder

* Folder Label

Sales Pipeline

* Folder Unique Name

SalesPipeline

Cancel    Save

*In the newly created folder click New Dashboard.*

*Set up the Name and click Select Folder.*

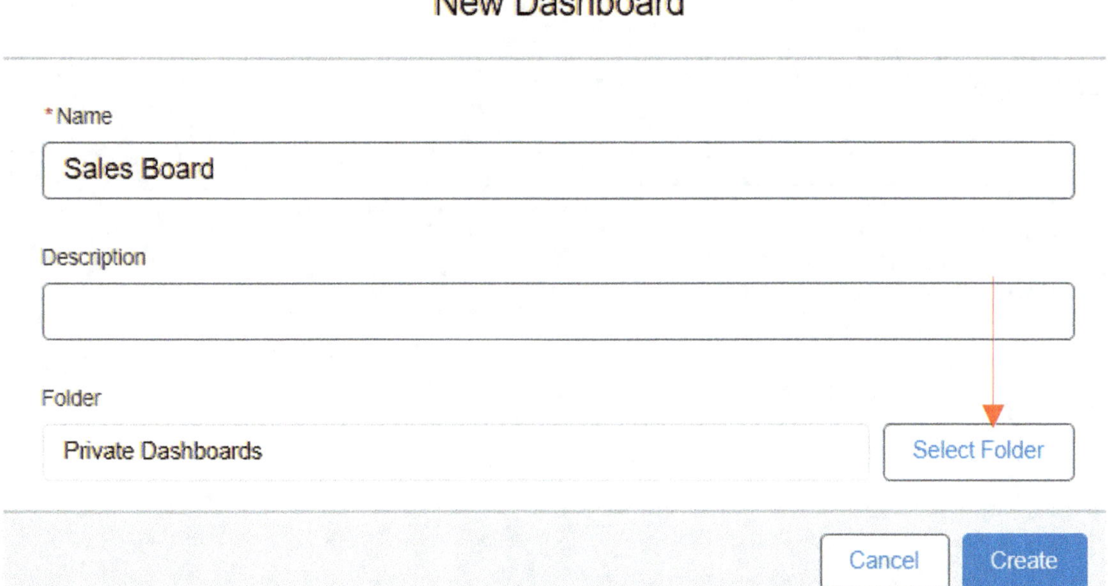

*Select the newly created folder and click Select Folder button.*

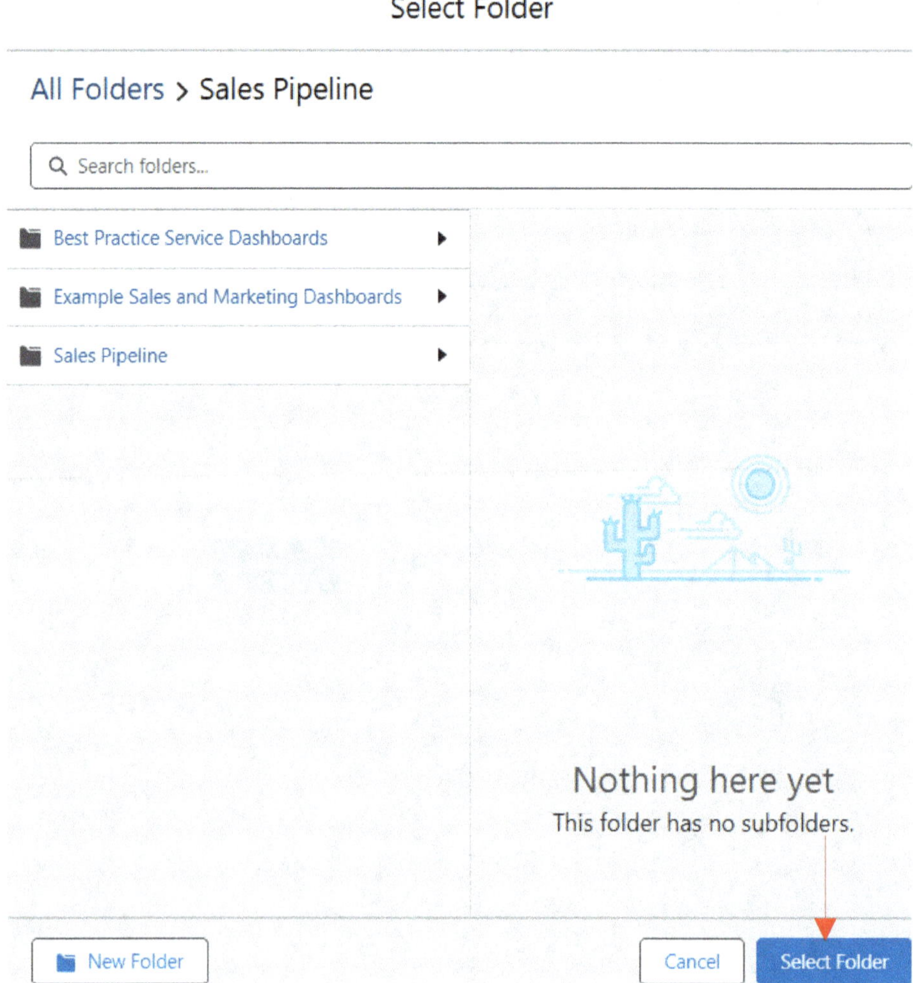

*Then the right folder is selected, click Create.*

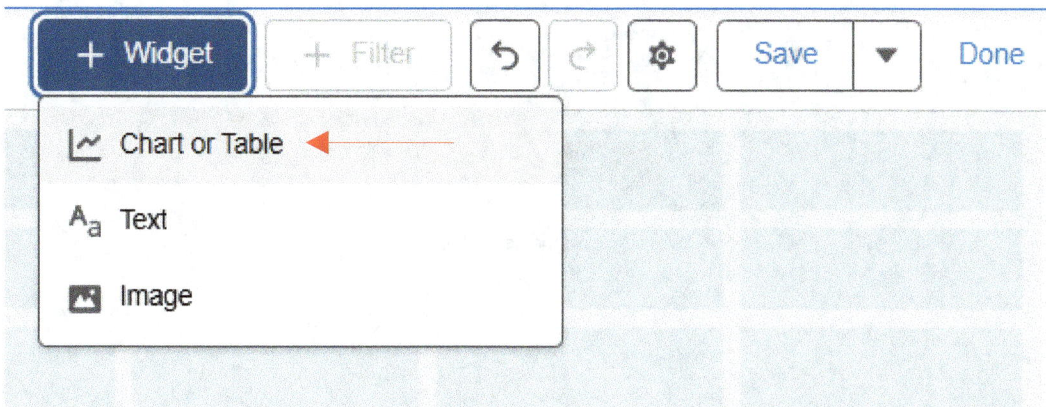

*Click "+ Widget" and select "Chart" or "Table" to add any reports to your newly created dashboard.*

# PART I — Sales Cloud for Sales Managers and Sales Reps

*Select the report you want to add and click the Select button.*

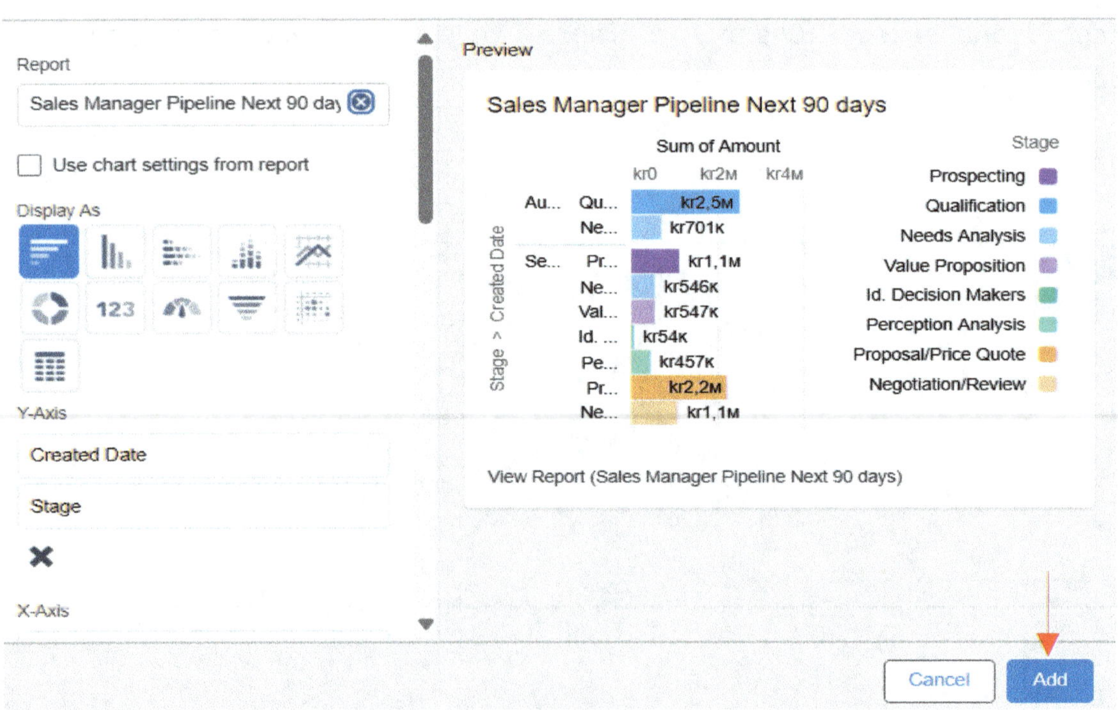


*Choose a chart type you want to display and click Add button.*

*Then select another reports in the same way you want to add and click the Save button.*

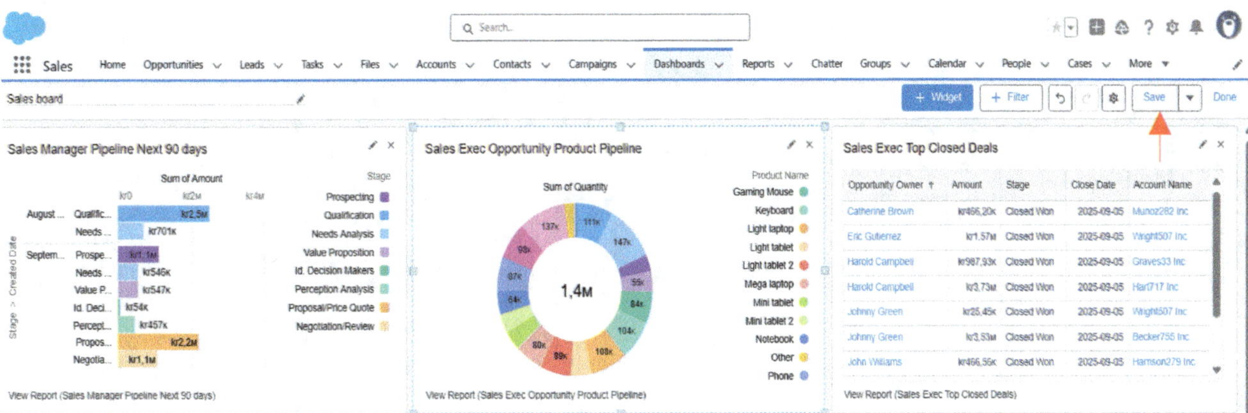

# 6.2 Dynamic dashboards

Dynamic dashboards in Salesforce are dashboards that show data tailored to the user who is viewing them, instead of showing the same fixed data for everyone. This can add flexibility if the viewer can switch perspectives for example, they could view the dashboard as themselves, their manager, or another user depending on permissions. It´s great for sales managers who want to see what the dashboard looks like for different team members.

*Click on Edit Dashboard Properties button.*

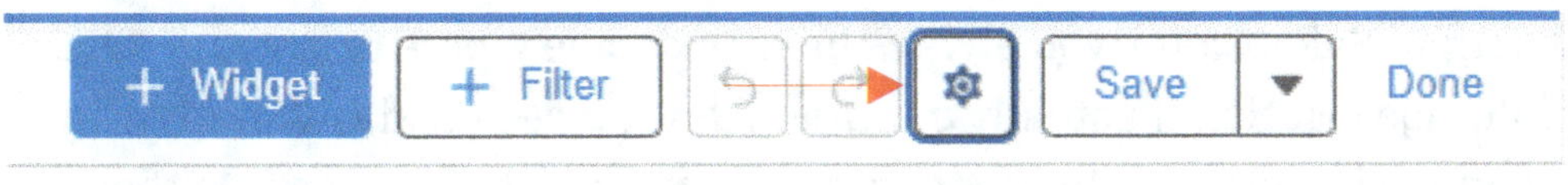

*You can select two dynamic options here and save your choices.*

***The dashboard viewer*** *always runs as whoever is logged in. Each user automatically sees only their own data.*

*Let dashboard viewers choose whom they view the dashboard as,* here the user can switch the view to themselves, their team colleagues, or another available user depending on access.

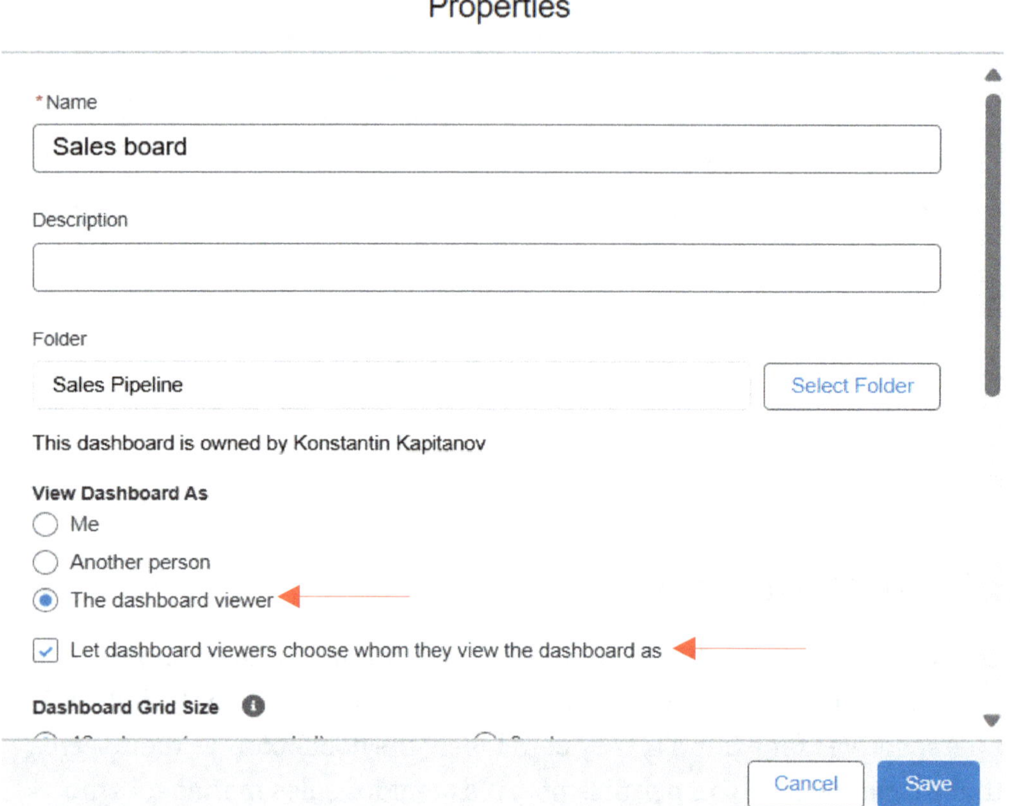

# 6.3 Sharing dashboards

When you create a dashboard in Sales Cloud, you always have to decide where to save it.  The folder is more than just a storage location it actually controls who can see the dashboard, who can edit it, and who can manage its settings.  In other words, if someone lacks access to the folder, they cannot see the dashboard, even if they know it exists. There are two main types of folders.

- Personal Folders: Only you can see dashboards saved here.

- Shared Folders: Dashboards here can be shared with specific users, roles, or public groups.

The power of a shared folder lies in the way you can control access. You can decide exactly who or which groups of people should have permission to see what's inside. For example, you might give the entire sales team access to view a folder, but only allow managers to make edits. Sales Cloud even lets you share a folder with roles and their subordinates, so a sales director can automatically see the same dashboards as their managers and reps.

Dynamic dashboards enhance flexibility by displaying distinct results based on the user's login status. But even here, the folder is still the gatekeeper. A user must first have access to the folder before they can open the dashboard. Only then will the dynamic dashboard adjust the data to reflect that person's access level.

*Select our created Folder Sales Pipeline and click Share.*

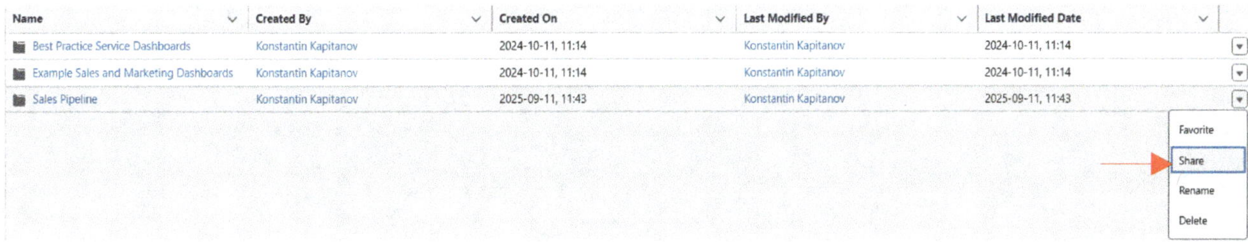

*You can select users access level to the dashboard and then click the Done button.*

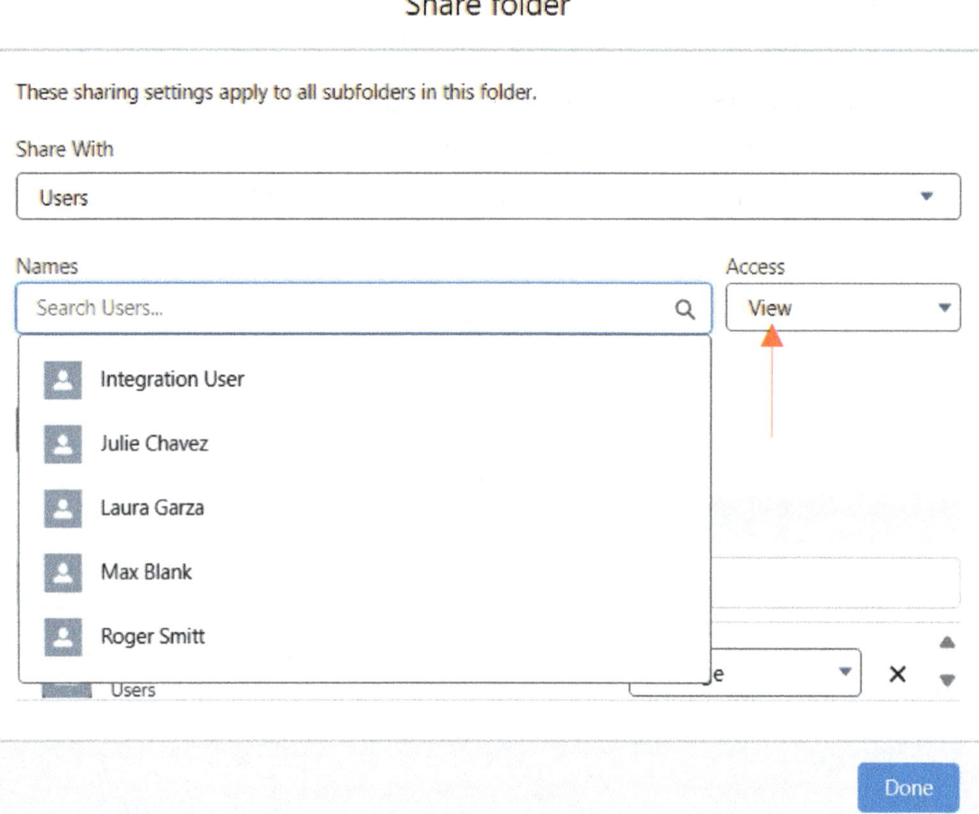


# 6.4 Embedding Dashboards & Reports

In App Builder, dashboards are intended to present multiple reports and visualizations brought together into a single, interactive panel. You can embed a dashboard directly into a Lightning app page or the Home page using the Dashboard component, which lets users interact with real-time data and apply filters. You can also embed a single report chart onto some page types using a different component, such as a Report Chart widget. This feature gives a quick view of one set of metrics but is not as versatile or comprehensive as a dashboard since it doesn't support multiple data sources or dashboard-level interactivity.

*Go to the Home Page.*

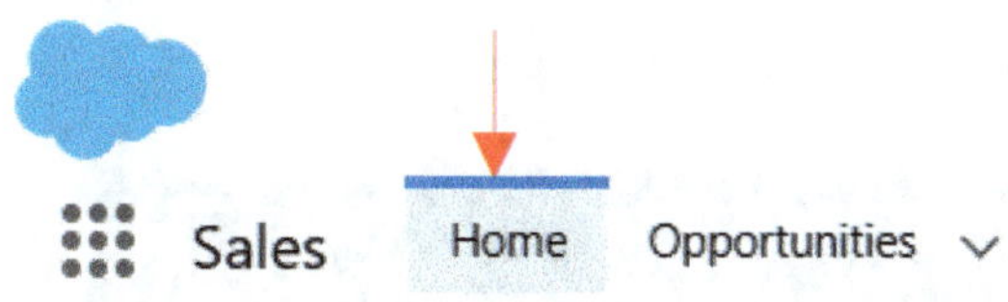

*Go to Setup→ Edit Page*

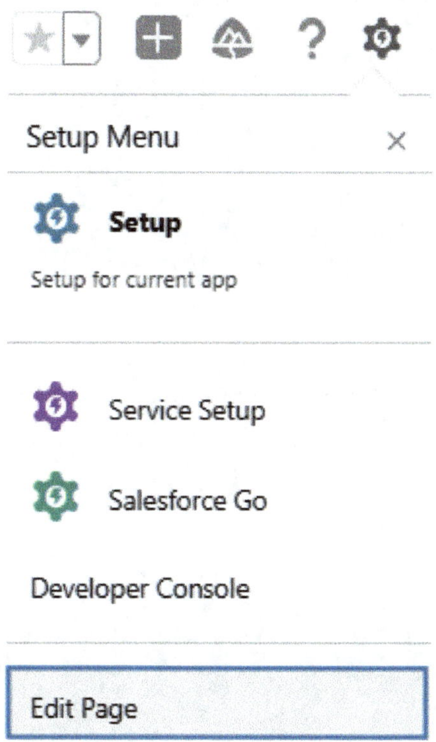

*Drag the Dashboard component from the sidebar into the section of the page layout where it should be displayed.*

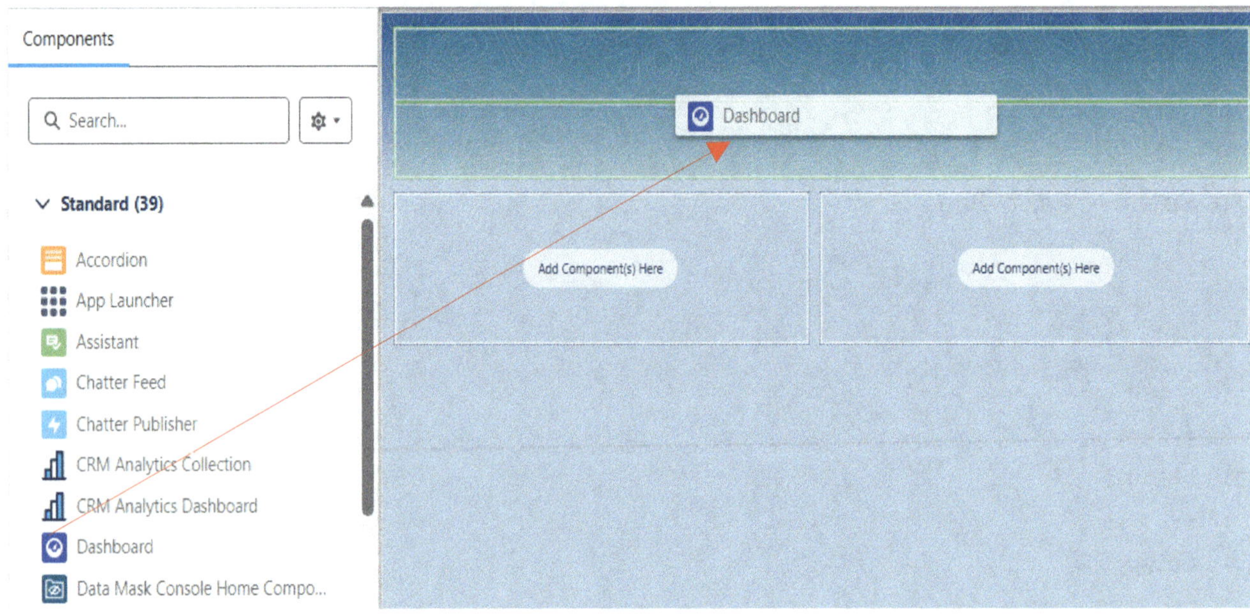

*Drag the Report chart component from the sidebar into the next section of the page layout where it should be displayed.*

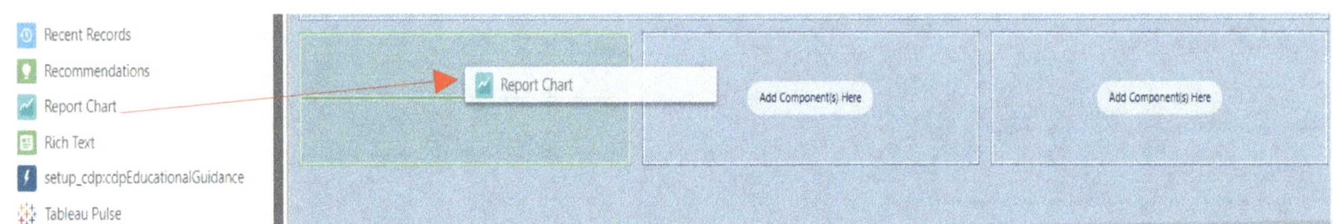

*Click Save.*

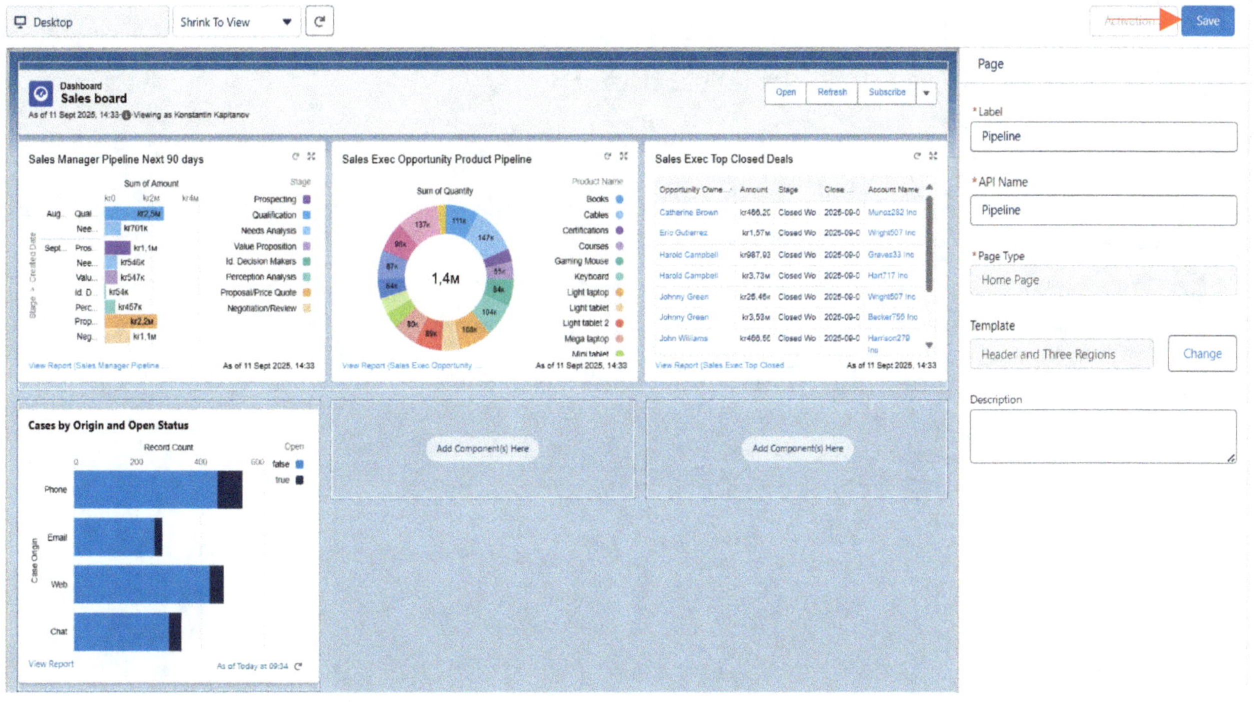

*Use the Activation settings to define whether the page should be assigned to specific apps or user profiles. For the demonstration purpose, we select Assign as Org Default.*

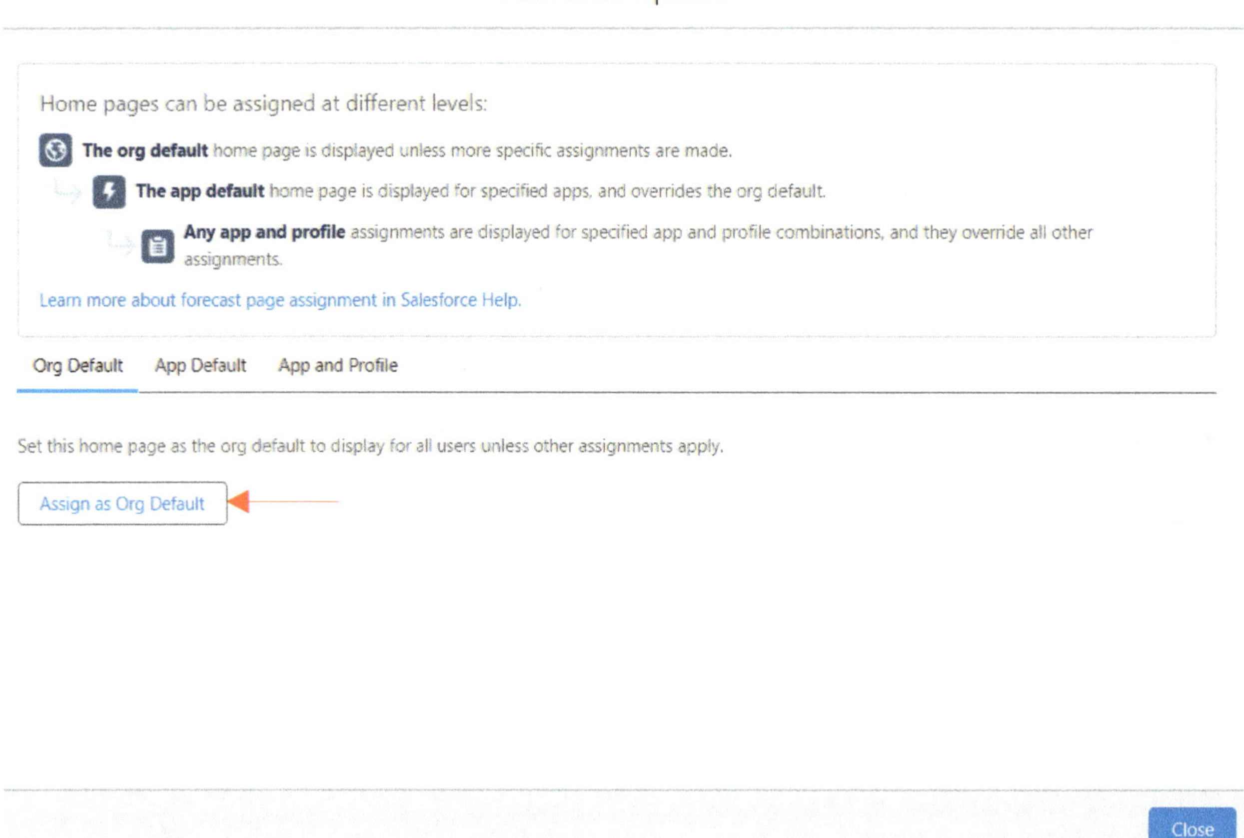

*Click Save.*

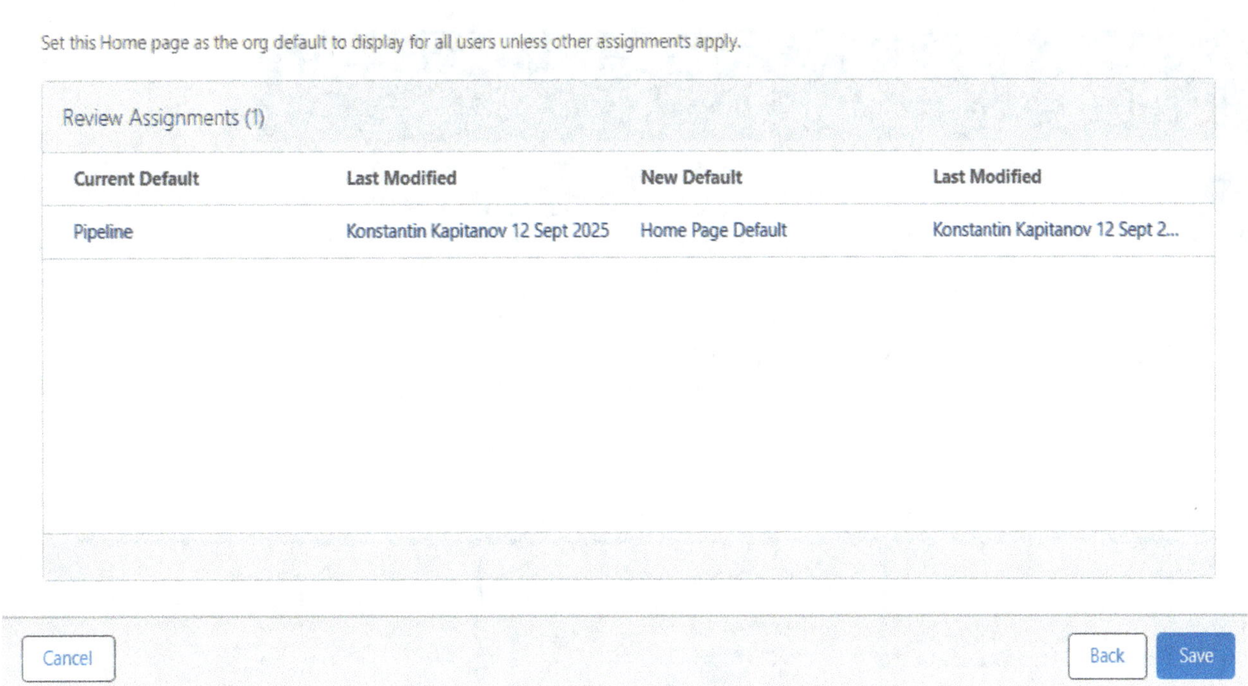

Set as Org Default: Home Page Default

Set this Home page as the org default to display for all users unless other assignments apply.

| Current Default | Last Modified | New Default | Last Modified |
|---|---|---|---|
| Pipeline | Konstantin Kapitanov 12 Sept 2025 | Home Page Default | Konstantin Kapitanov 12 Sept 2... |

*After clicking Save an Activation should be successful.*

*Click the Back button on the top left.*

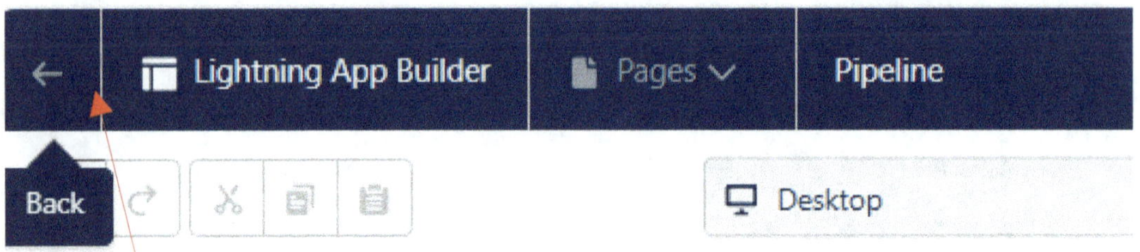

*The Home page shows embedded components.*

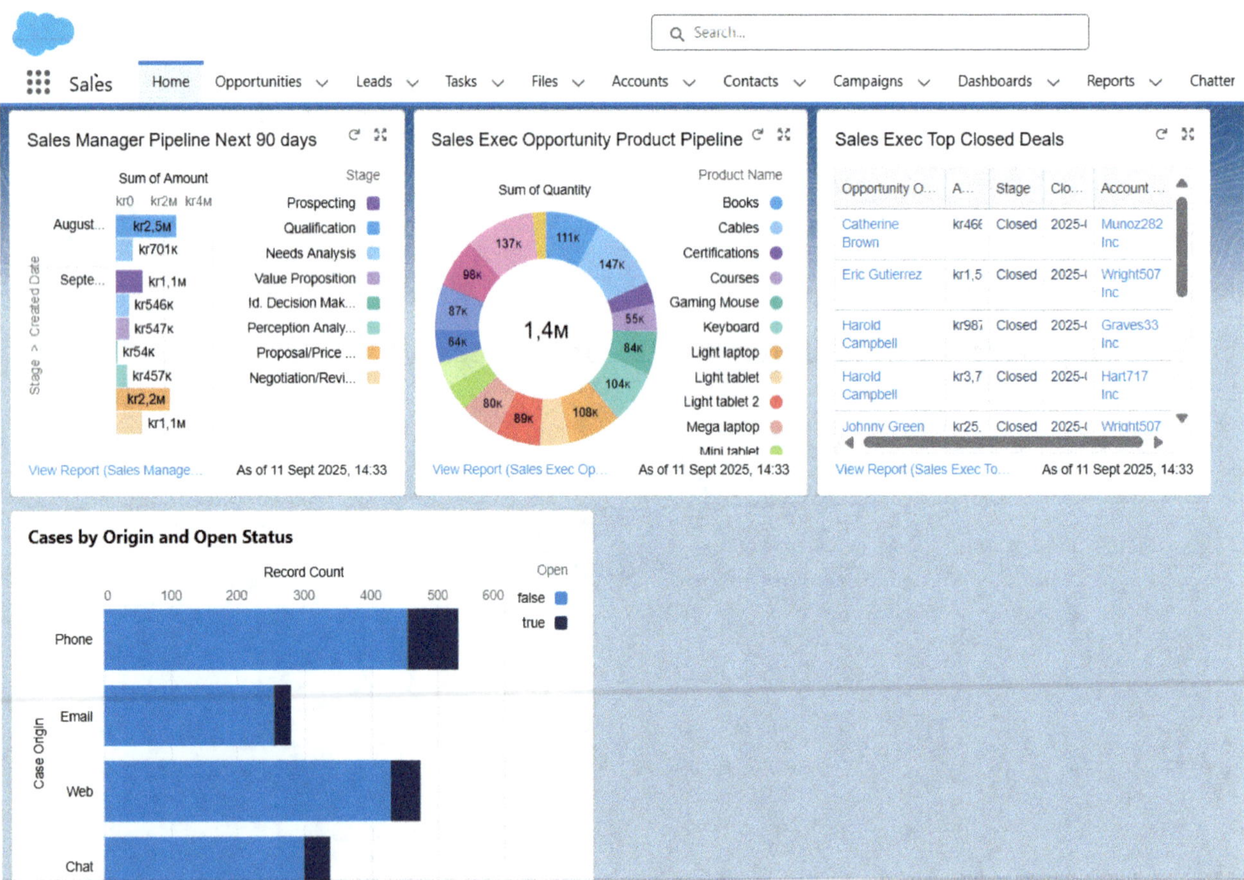

# 6.5 Favorite Dashboards and Reports

Sales Cloud allows users to quickly access the dashboards and reports they rely on most by marking them as a Favorites list. This feature reduces navigation time and ensures critical insights are always just one click away. Favoriting is a user-level action, meaning each user can create their own personalized list of dashboards and reports without affecting others.

*Navigate to the desired dashboard and report. Click the star icon in the header toolbar to add the items to the Favorites list.*

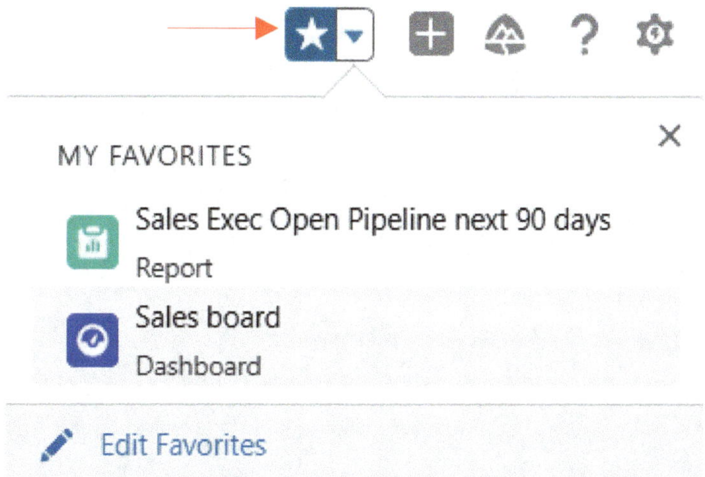



# 6.6 Subscribe Option

The subscription feature allows users to receive automated notifications for dashboards and reports. Subscriptions facilitate the delivery of critical business insights on a scheduled basis, eliminating the need for users to manually open the dashboard or report each time.

*Open the report you want to monitor and click the Subscribe button located at the top of the page.*

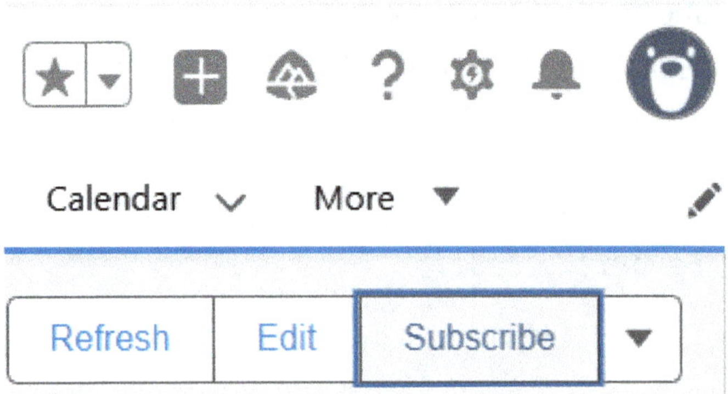

*Configure the subscription details and click Save.*

## Edit Subscription

Schedule dashboard refreshes and subscribe to receive results.

### Settings

Frequency

Daily | Weekly | Monthly

Days

Sun | Mon | Tue | Wed | Thu | Fri | Sat

Time

11:00

### Recipients

⚠ Recipients see the same report data as the person running the report.

☑ Receive new results by email when dashboard is refreshed. ⓘ

Send email to
Me

Edit Recipients

Cancel    Save

# Chapter 7. Salesforce Mobile App

## 7.1 Introduction

The Salesforce mobile app delivers a robust, intuitive experience that enables sales representatives to manage accounts, leads, tasks, and more, all from the convenience of a smartphone or tablet. Professionals on the move can easily access essential customer data and sales tools, regardless of their location. This app is packed with valuable features for a sales rep. At its core, it provides instant access to customer accounts, contacts, and opportunities, which lets salespeople look up critical details before client meetings or calls. Users can also use smart search capabilities to locate information in seconds, which enhances productivity.

Collaboration is another significant element. With features like integrated feeds and notifications, sales reps can discuss their pipelines, share updates, or request support from colleagues. The app also enables seamless file sharing and Chatter integration, keeping communication centralized and efficient. Offline mode ensures users can still access and edit records even without a reliable internet connection changes are synced once the device is back online.

# PART I — Sales Cloud for Sales Managers and Sales Reps

Getting started involves a few steps that ensure both ease of use and organizational security. The app itself is available to download for free on both iOS and Android devices via the App Store or Google Play. Once access is enabled by the administrator, users receive their credentials to log in to the app. Users can jump between different menus using the App Launcher to see a different navigation bar.  We'll choose Sales for demonstration purposes.

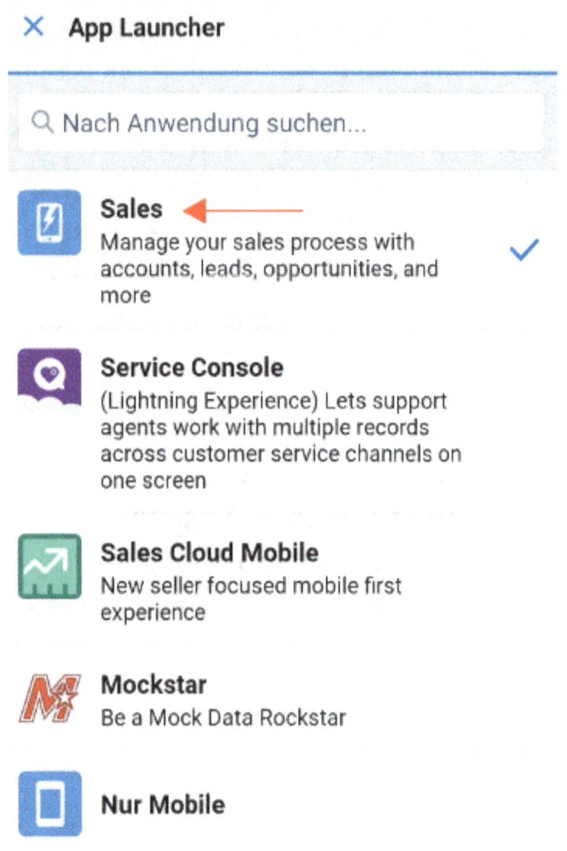

# 7.2 Daily Tasks with Mobile App

*With a fresh cup of coffee, your day starts by opening the Salesforce Mobile App to review tasks and upcoming meetings. On the home screen, you check your Tasks.*

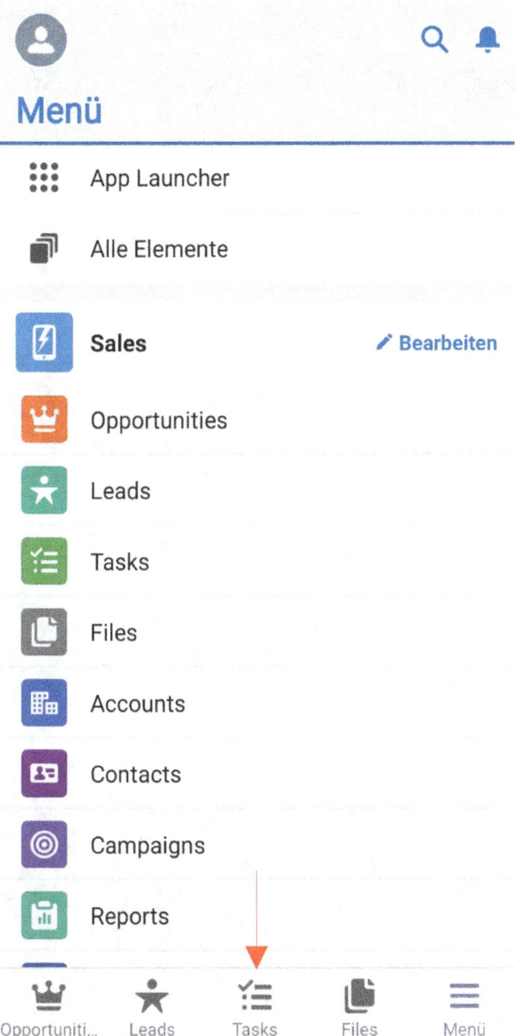

*By clicking Tasks you see that you have a meeting with Abba GmbH at 10:00 AM and is linked to the respective Account in Sales Cloud.*

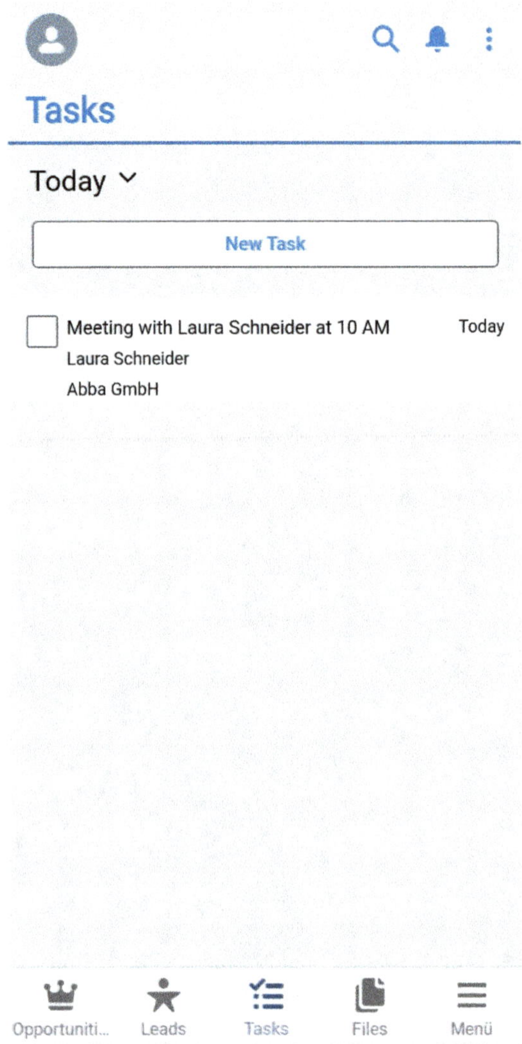

*At 10:00 AM, you arrive at Abba GmbH's headquarters in Munich. You meet with Laura S, Head of Procurement. During the conversation, she mentions interest in upgrading their current service package to include premium support and integration with their ERP system. By clicking New, you create a new Opportunity called ERP Integration & Premium Support linked to Abba GmbH.*

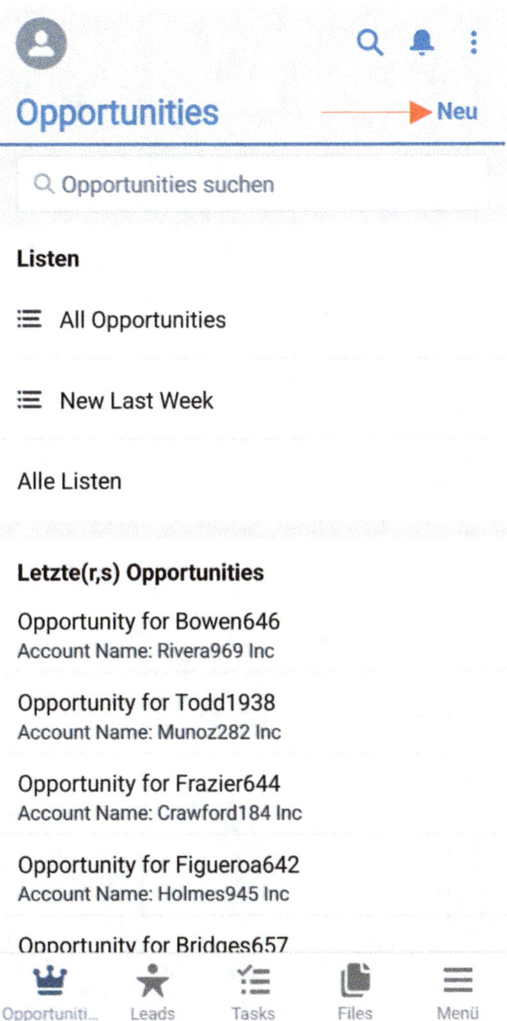

*You set the Close Date, a value and mark the Stage as Prospecting. Then click Save.*

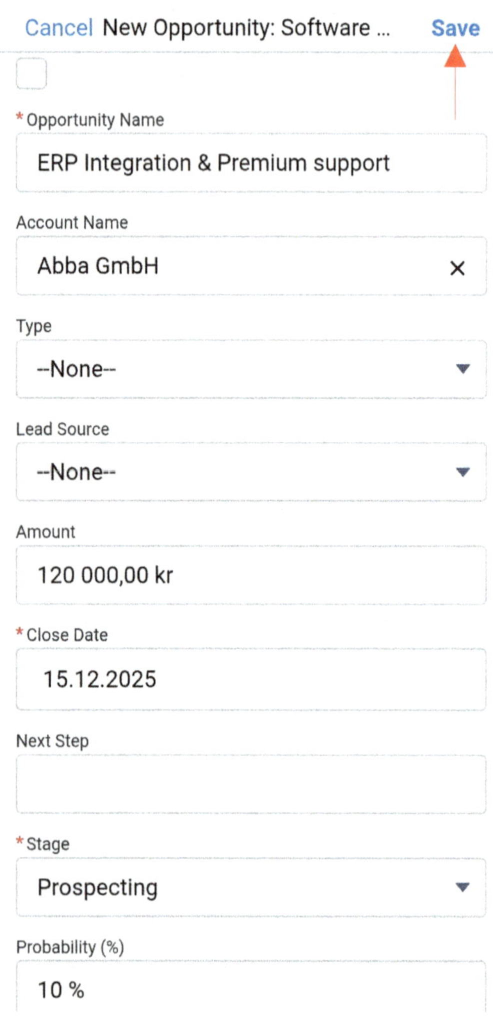

*A new opportunity is created.*

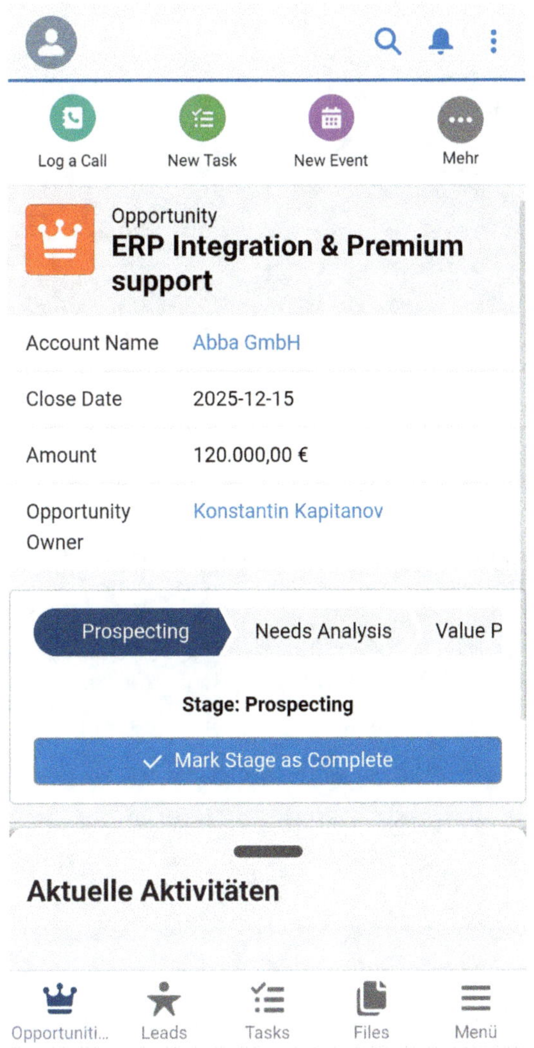

# PART I — Sales Cloud for Sales Managers and Sales Reps

*Add quickly Meeting Notes such as „Client is highly interested in ERP integration, send detailed proposal asap" and click Save.*

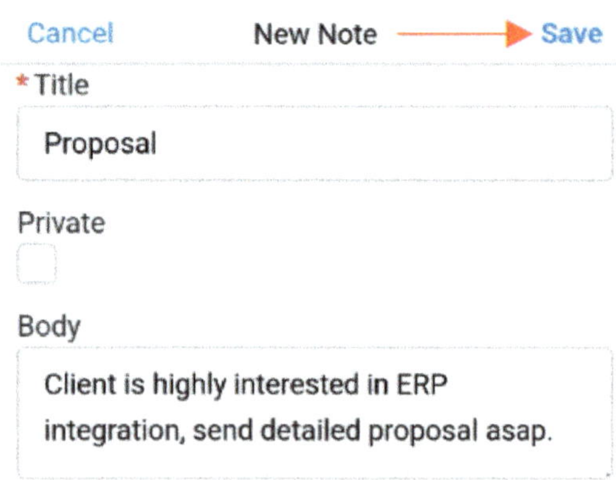


*To stay on track, you create a Task: Prepare a proposal. Then set up a Due Date, assign it to yourself and click Save.*

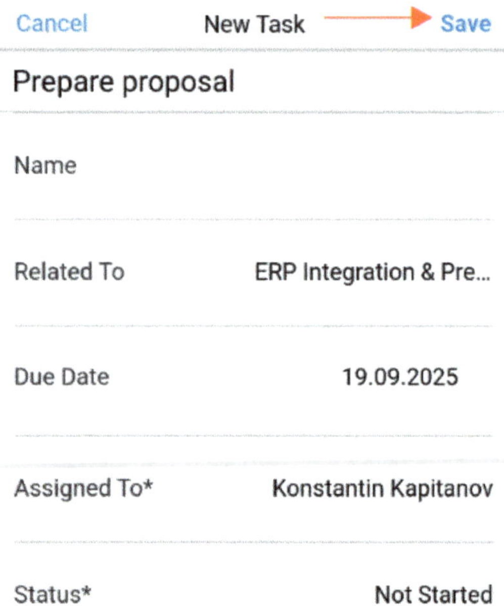

*Now, the opportunity with related Activities is created in Salesforce, and you won't forget the follow-up.*

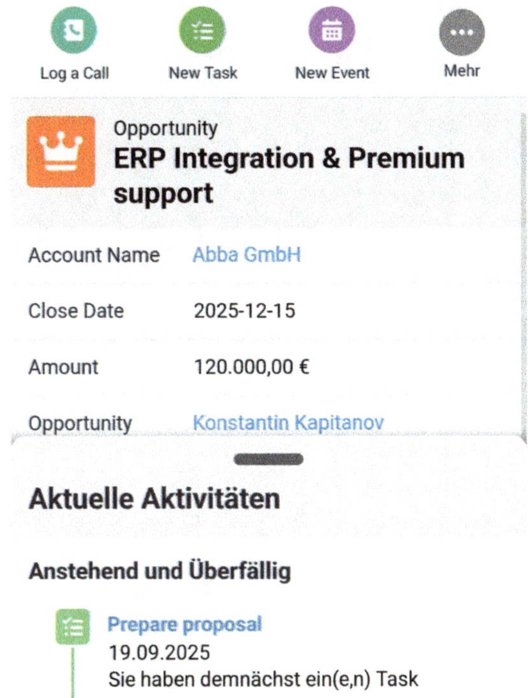

# PART II — SALES CLOUD FOR PRODUCT OWNERS, IT MANAGERS, AND ADMINS

## Configuration, Security, and Implementation Guidance

# Chapter 8. Settings and Customization

## 8.1 Company Settings

A foundational part of Sales Cloud setup is configuring your Company Information and Fiscal Year settings correctly. These settings affect how your system behaves, how data is displayed, and how your reports and forecasts align with your organization's business structure.

**The Company Information page** contains critical details about your instance and system limits. This page includes your company name, address, primary contact, default locale, and time zone, ensuring that your business's regional and operational preferences are reflected across your org. It also displays your Organization ID, a unique identifier used when interacting with Salesforce Support or managing integrations, and your instance, indicating the server your organization's data is hosted on. Additionally, the Company Information page provides essential visibility into your license usage. It also displays your data storage and file storage usage, which helps administrators monitor and manage storage limits proactively. Keeping this information accurate and up to date ensures your Salesforce Org aligns with your company's official details and enables efficient support and operational consistency.

*To view your Company Information click the Gear Icon in the upper right -> Setup.*

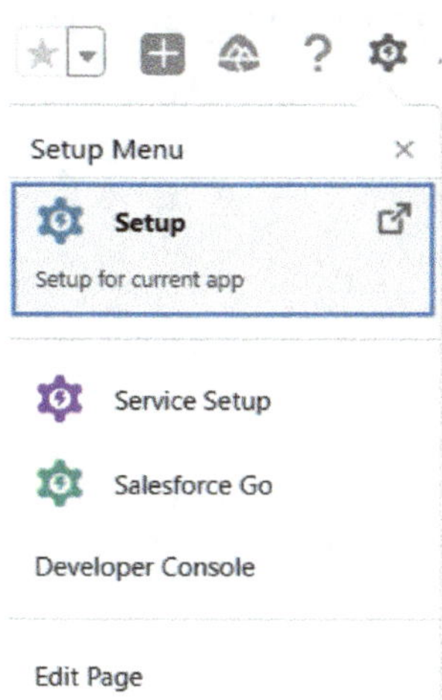

*In the Quick Find box, type "Company" and select in under Company Information.*

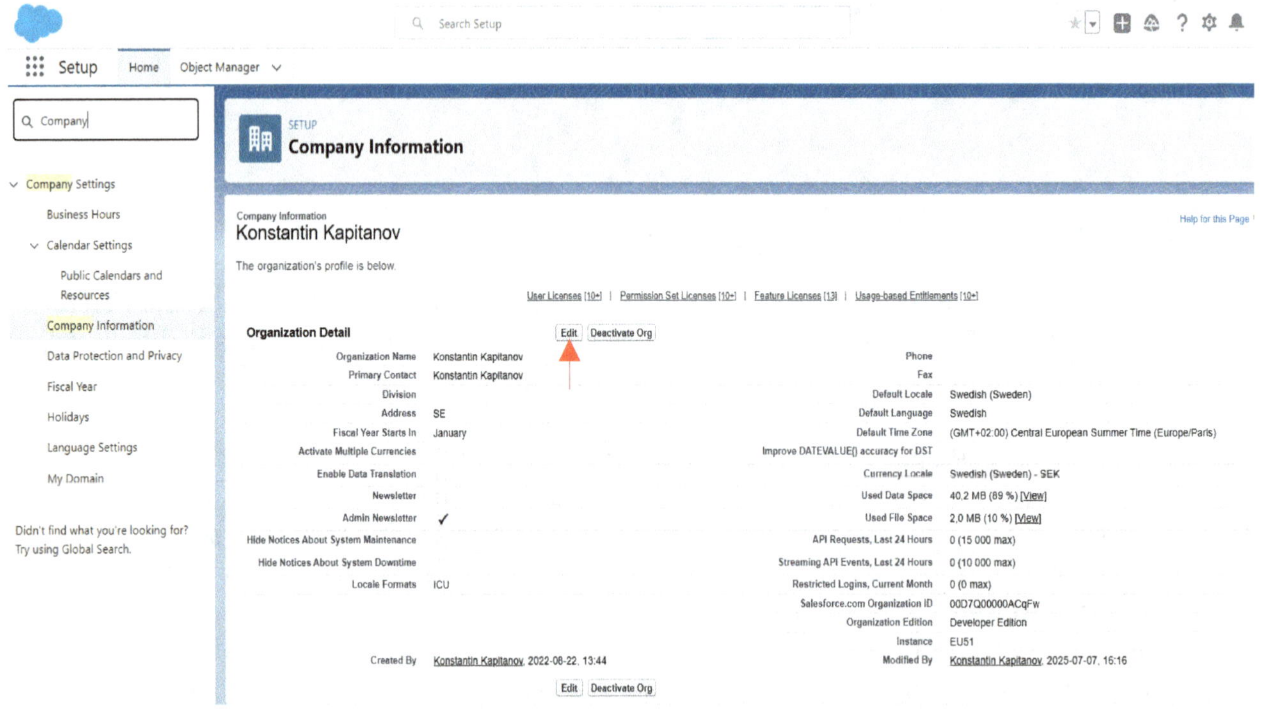

If you need to update your company's address or contact information, click Edit, make the necessary changes, and click Save. Further, Sales Cloud allows you to configure your fiscal year so that reporting and forecasting align with your company's financial reporting periods. By default, it uses the Standard Fiscal Year, which follows the 12-month calendar structure. However, you can define the month in which your fiscal year starts. For example, if your fiscal year begins in April, you can configure accordingly, ensuring reports and forecasts align with your business's financial periods. The Standard Fiscal Year is straightforward to configure and is compatible with all features.

*In the Quick Find box, type "fiscal" and select under Fiscal Year.*

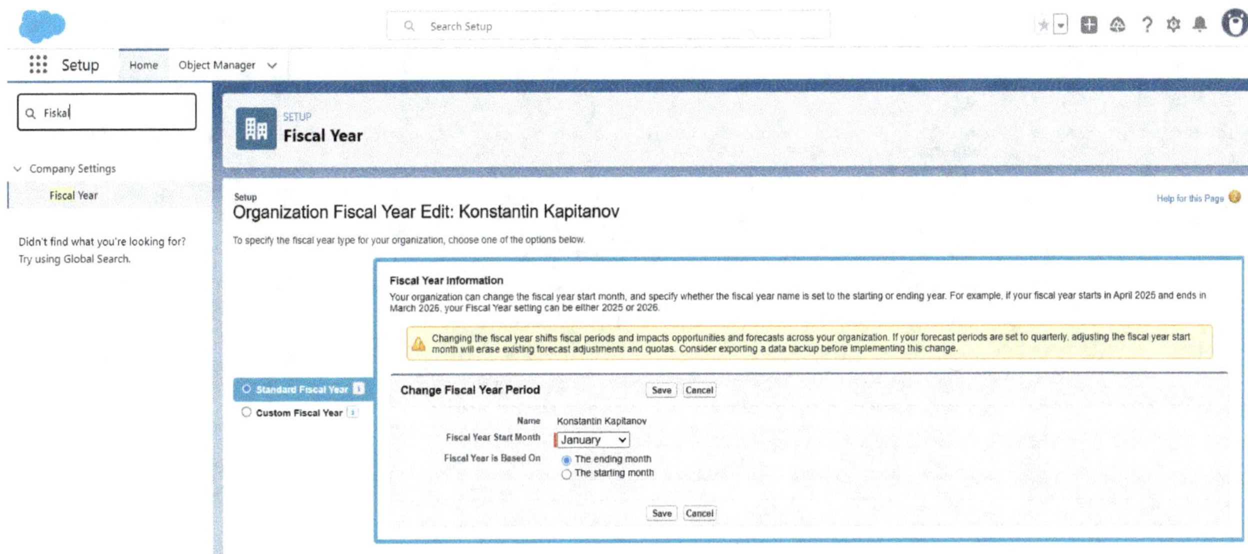

If your organization uses a non-standard fiscal calendar, Sales Cloud offers the Custom Fiscal Year feature. This allows for advanced fiscal structures but requires careful planning, as Custom Fiscal Year cannot be disabled once enabled. Additionally, some features may not fully support Custom Fiscal Year. Enabling is generally suitable for organizations with complex financial calendars and specific reporting requirements.

*If you require a Custom Fiscal Year, check the Enable Custom Fiscal Year checkbox as below.*

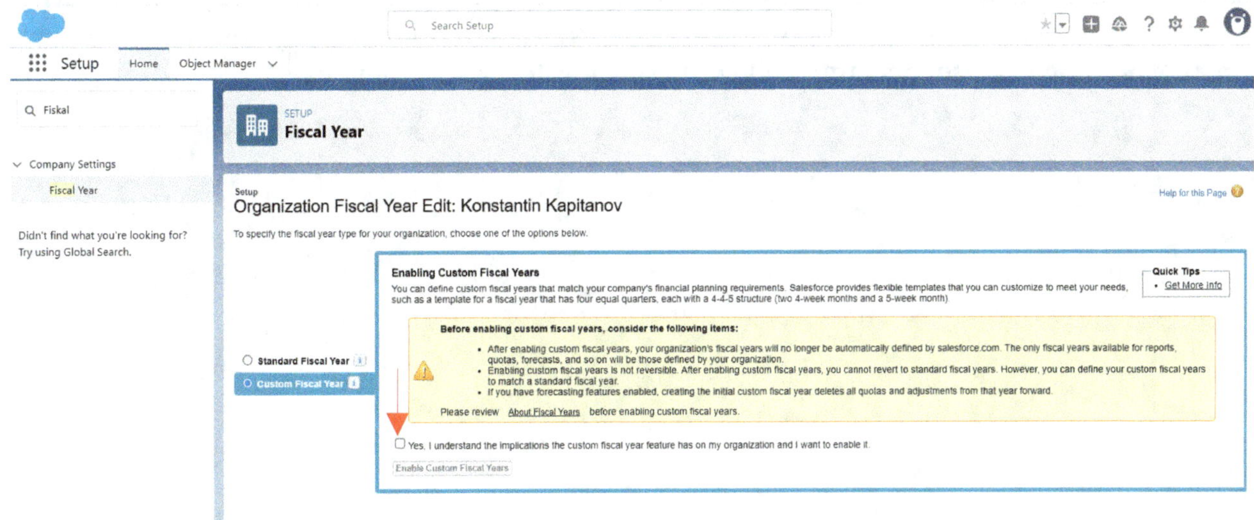

*Define your custom periods according to your company's financial structure.*

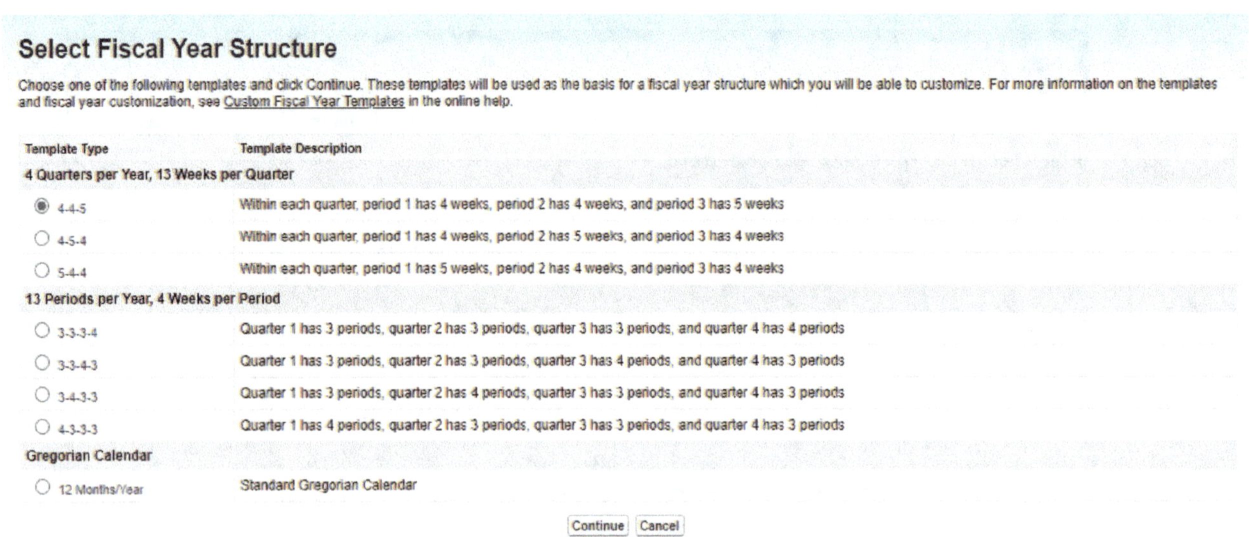


# 8.2 User Management

User management in Salesforce is a fundamental administrative responsibility that ensures that the right people have access to your Sales Cloud environment. This includes creating users, assigning the appropriate licenses and profiles, managing user activation status, and resetting passwords when required. Effective user management supports data integrity, system security, and user accountability within your Salesforce org. When a new employee joins your sales team, they will need a user account. Follow these steps to create a new user.

*Navigate to Setup.*

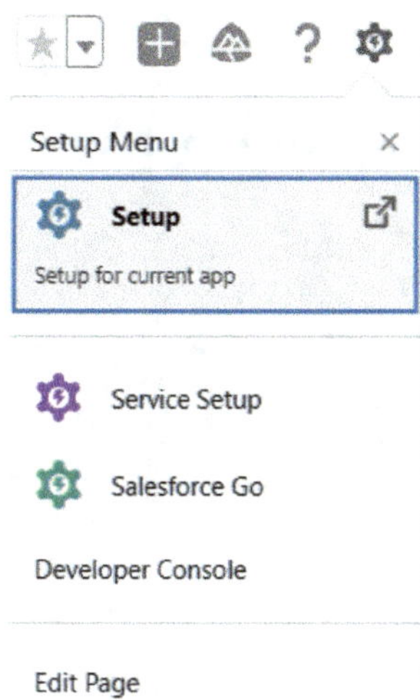

*In the Quick Find box, type "user", select Users and then click New User.*

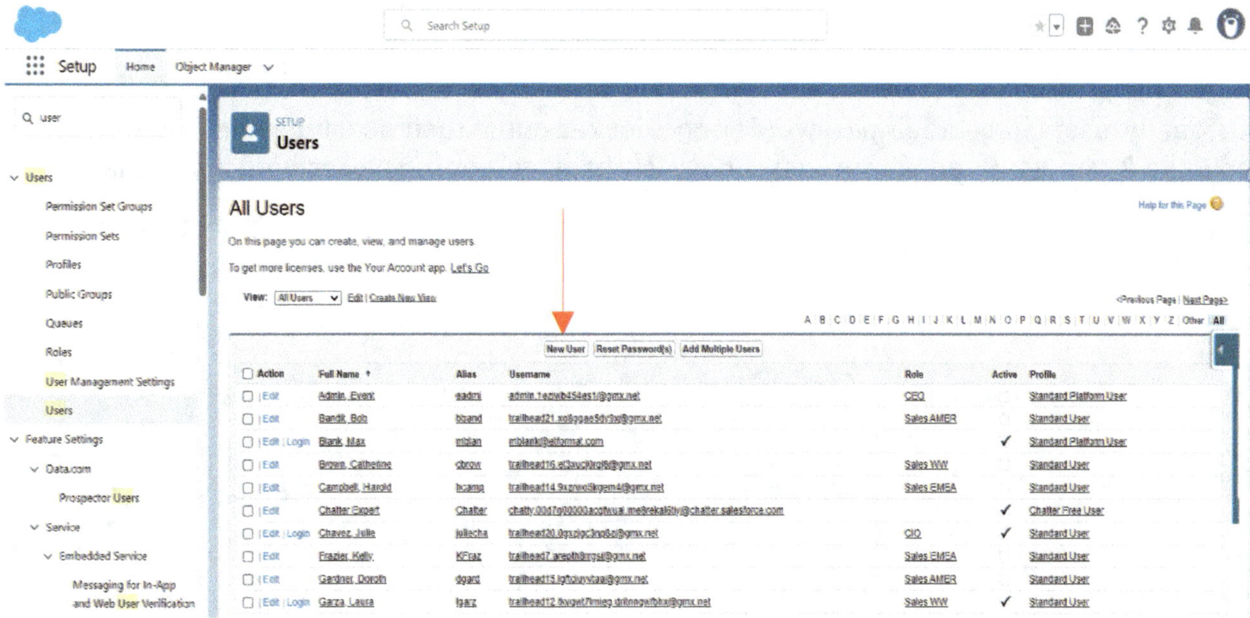

# PART II – Sales Cloud for Product Owners, IT Managers, and  Admins

*On the New User page, complete the required fields and click Save.*

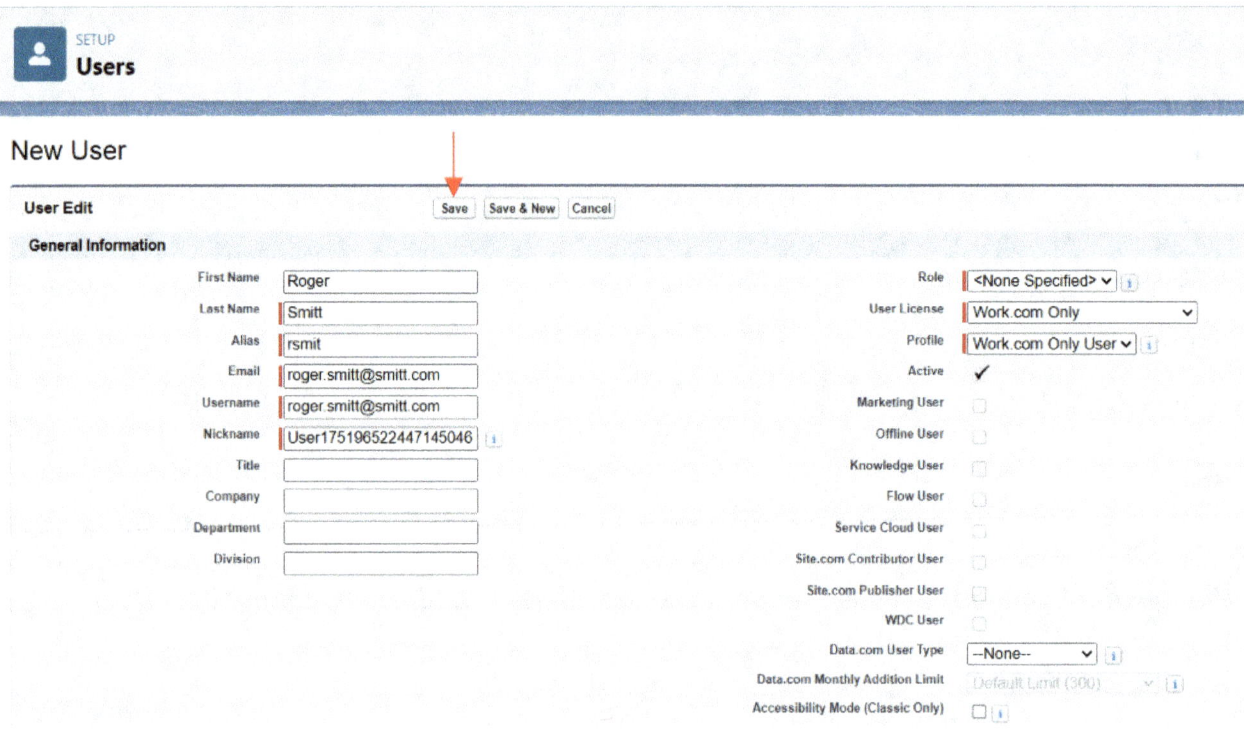

Occasionally, users forget their passwords or get locked out of their accounts after multiple failed login attempts. As an admin, you can assist them by sending a password reset email.

*Click the Reset Password button.*

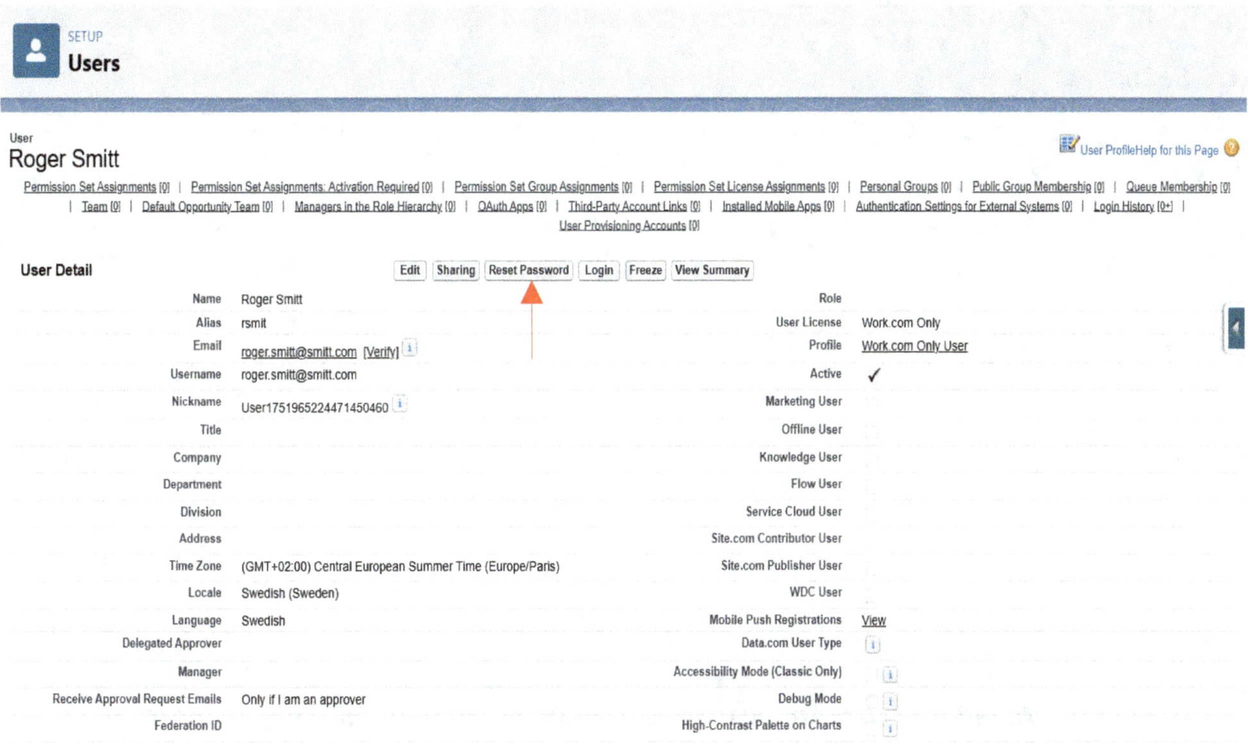

The user will receive an activation email with instructions to set or reset a password and log in to the cloud.

# 8.3 Business Processes

Record Types in Sales Cloud allow you to configure different business processes, picklist values, and page layouts for different groups of users working with the same object.
Business Processes define picklist stages for specific standard objects for example Sales Processes as Opportunity Stage picklist, Lead Processes as Lead Status picklist or Support Processes as Case Status picklist.

In many sales organizations, different teams handle different products or regions with varying sales stages, required data, and workflows. Record Types and Business Processes allow you to support these differences systematically while maintaining clean data within a single object structure.

# PART II — Sales Cloud for Product Owners, IT Managers, and  Admins

To illustrate this practice, we'll create two simple Sales Processes based on a company that sells both Hardware and Software Subscriptions. Because we want to track Opportunities with different sales stages per product line.

*Go to Setup.*

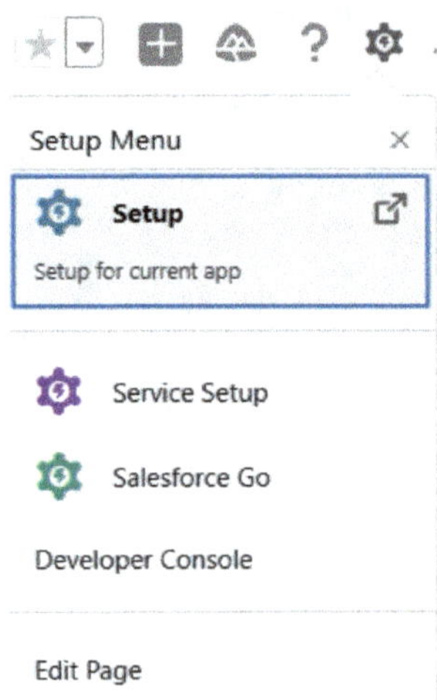

*Then in Object Manager type in Quick Find box "Opp" and select Opportunity object.*

*In the Opportunity object click Fields & Relationships on the left menu. Then type "Stage" in Quick Find box and select.*

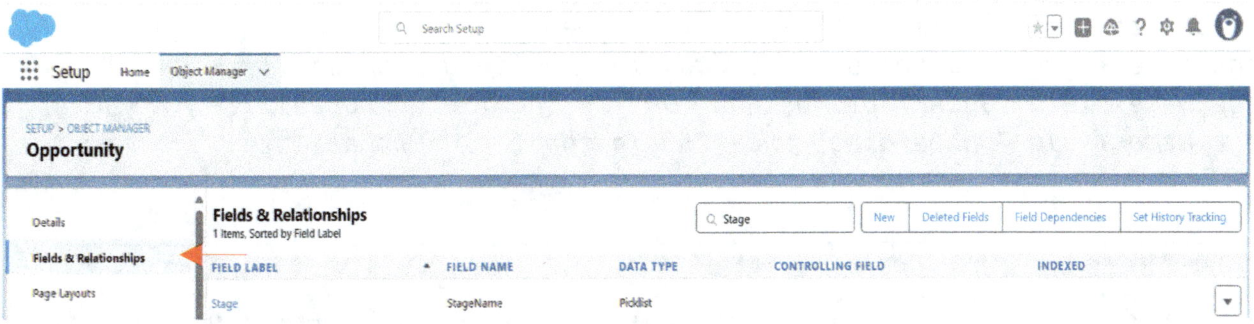

Scroll down to the Opportunity Stages Picklist Values and click New.

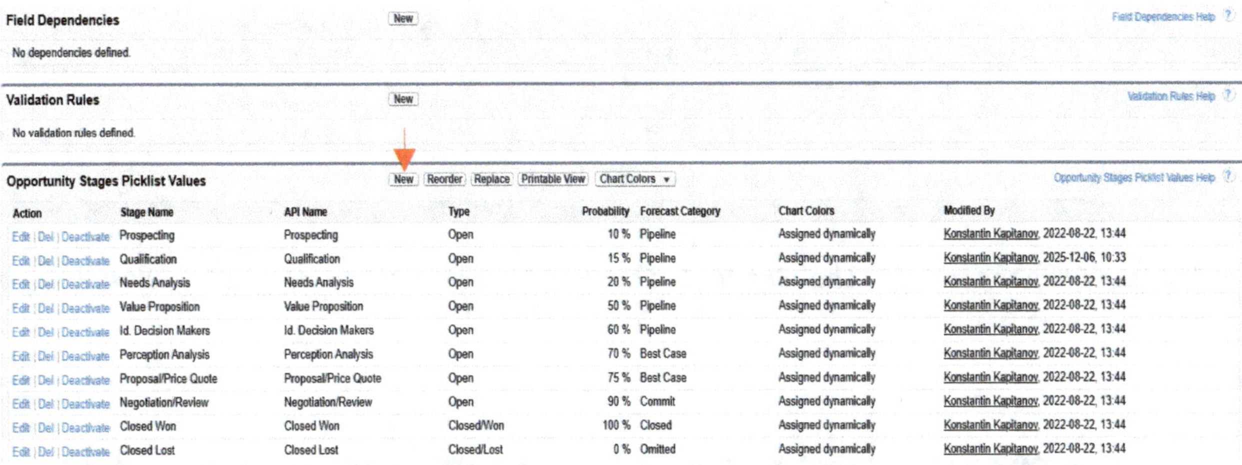

Set the Stage Name field to "Trial" and enter "80" in the Probability field, then save the changes.

## Opportunity Stages

Modify or Add the stage to fit your sales process. Note that the Type and Forecast Category values affect each other. The Forecast Category automatically determines how opportunities are tracked in a forecast, but these values can be revised

⚠ Changing the Type or Forecast Category updates all opportunities that have this stage value. If you change the Type or Forecast Category, this global update can require several hours, depending on the amount of data you have. We send you an email v
The process doesn't interrupt your users' work, but it sometimes updates the Last Modified By date and time in affected records.

Save   Save & New   Cancel

Stage Name: Trial
Type: Open
Description:

Probability: 80
Forecast Category: Pipeline
Chart Color: Assigned dynamically

*Then create the following values in the same way:*
*Stage Name field "Evaluation" and "85" in the field Probability.*
*Stage Name field "Subscription" and "90" in the field Probability.*
*Stage Name field "Onboarding" and "95" in the field Probability.*

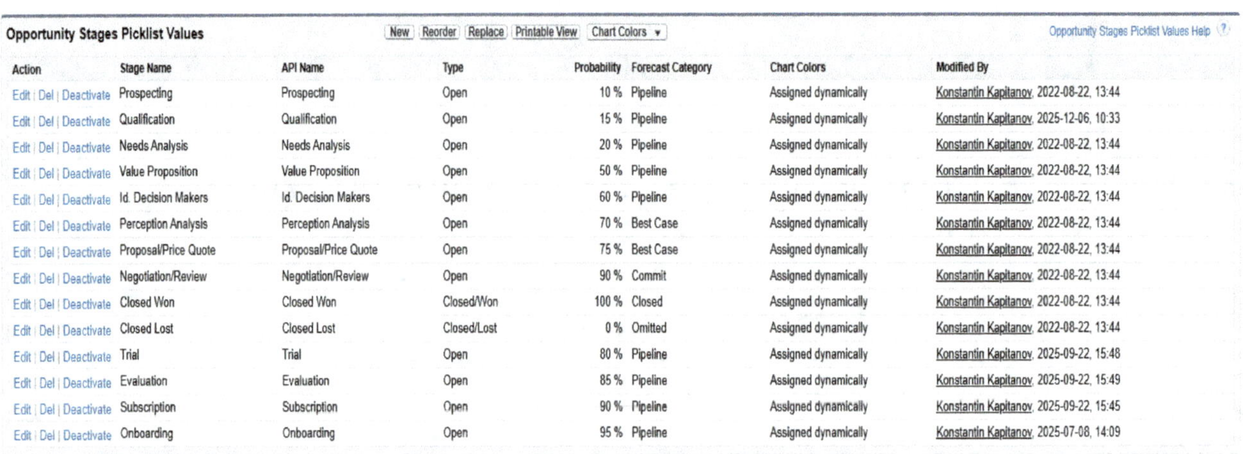

| Opportunity Stages Picklist Values | | | | | | | |
|---|---|---|---|---|---|---|---|
| Action | Stage Name | API Name | Type | Probability | Forecast Category | Chart Colors | Modified By |
| Edit \| Del \| Deactivate | Prospecting | Prospecting | Open | 10 % | Pipeline | Assigned dynamically | Konstantin Kapitanov, 2022-08-22, 13:44 |
| Edit \| Del \| Deactivate | Qualification | Qualification | Open | 15 % | Pipeline | Assigned dynamically | Konstantin Kapitanov, 2025-12-06, 10:33 |
| Edit \| Del \| Deactivate | Needs Analysis | Needs Analysis | Open | 20 % | Pipeline | Assigned dynamically | Konstantin Kapitanov, 2022-08-22, 13:44 |
| Edit \| Del \| Deactivate | Value Proposition | Value Proposition | Open | 50 % | Pipeline | Assigned dynamically | Konstantin Kapitanov, 2022-08-22, 13:44 |
| Edit \| Del \| Deactivate | Id. Decision Makers | Id. Decision Makers | Open | 60 % | Pipeline | Assigned dynamically | Konstantin Kapitanov, 2022-08-22, 13:44 |
| Edit \| Del \| Deactivate | Perception Analysis | Perception Analysis | Open | 70 % | Best Case | Assigned dynamically | Konstantin Kapitanov, 2022-08-22, 13:44 |
| Edit \| Del \| Deactivate | Proposal/Price Quote | Proposal/Price Quote | Open | 75 % | Best Case | Assigned dynamically | Konstantin Kapitanov, 2022-08-22, 13:44 |
| Edit \| Del \| Deactivate | Negotiation/Review | Negotiation/Review | Open | 90 % | Commit | Assigned dynamically | Konstantin Kapitanov, 2022-08-22, 13:44 |
| Edit \| Del \| Deactivate | Closed Won | Closed Won | Closed/Won | 100 % | Closed | Assigned dynamically | Konstantin Kapitanov, 2022-08-22, 13:44 |
| Edit \| Del \| Deactivate | Closed Lost | Closed Lost | Closed/Lost | 0 % | Omitted | Assigned dynamically | Konstantin Kapitanov, 2022-08-22, 13:44 |
| Edit \| Del \| Deactivate | Trial | Trial | Open | 80 % | Pipeline | Assigned dynamically | Konstantin Kapitanov, 2025-09-22, 15:48 |
| Edit \| Del \| Deactivate | Evaluation | Evaluation | Open | 85 % | Pipeline | Assigned dynamically | Konstantin Kapitanov, 2025-09-22, 15:49 |
| Edit \| Del \| Deactivate | Subscription | Subscription | Open | 90 % | Pipeline | Assigned dynamically | Konstantin Kapitanov, 2025-09-22, 15:45 |
| Edit \| Del \| Deactivate | Onboarding | Onboarding | Open | 95 % | Pipeline | Assigned dynamically | Konstantin Kapitanov, 2025-07-08, 14:09 |

*Type "Sales Processes" in the Setup Quick Find, select it and click New.*

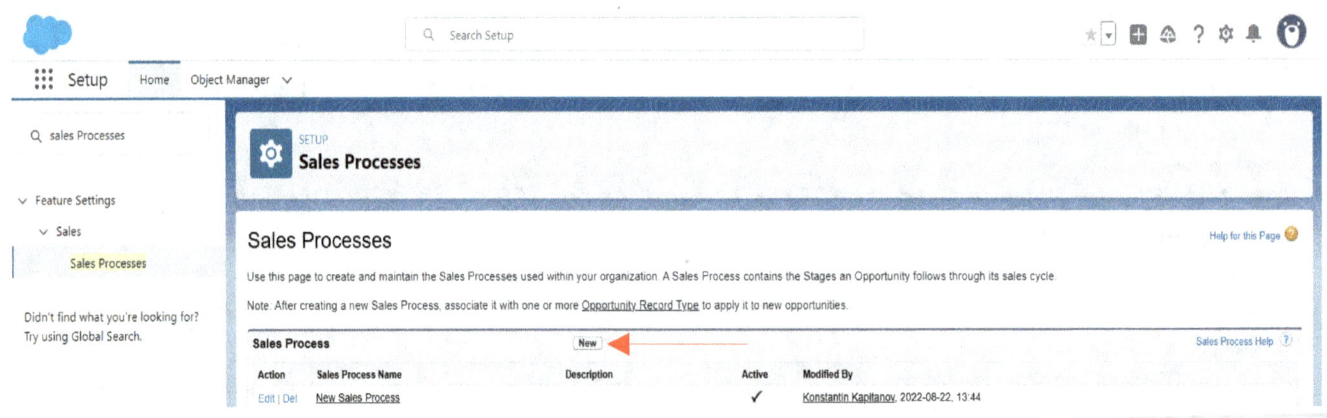

*Enter the Sales Process Name as the Hardware Sales Process, then click Save.*

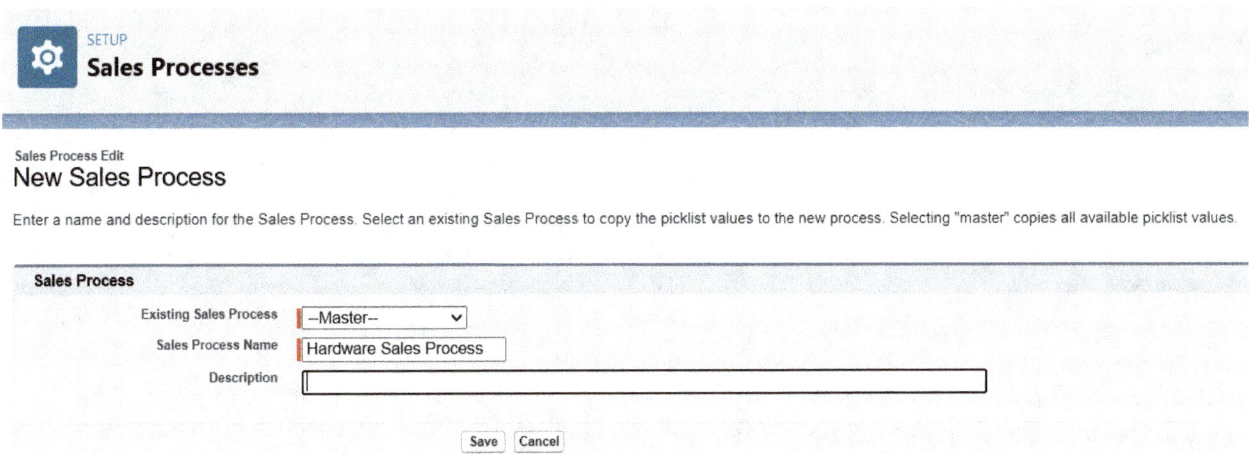

*Select the values for your new Hardware Sales Process and Save.*

*A new Hardware Sales Process is created now.*

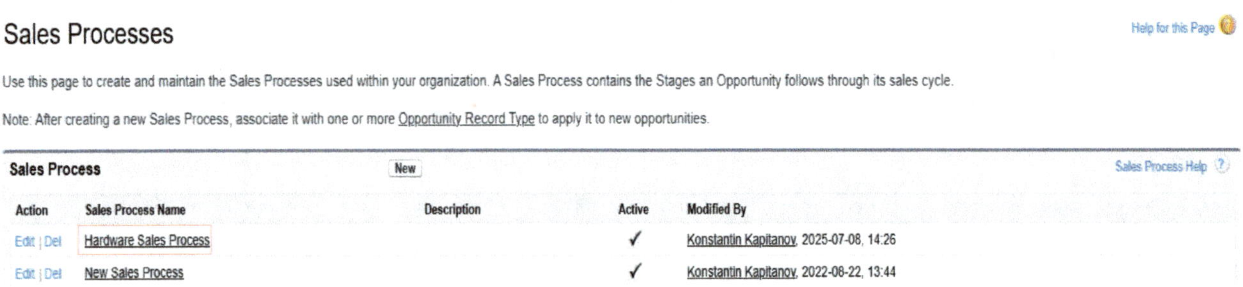

*Now, add a second Sales Process by entering Software Sales Process as the Sales Process Name, then click Save.*

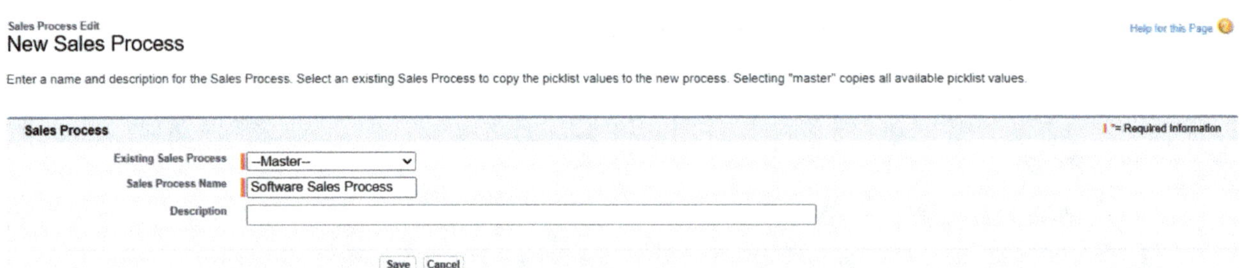

*Select the values for your new Software Sales Process and Save.*

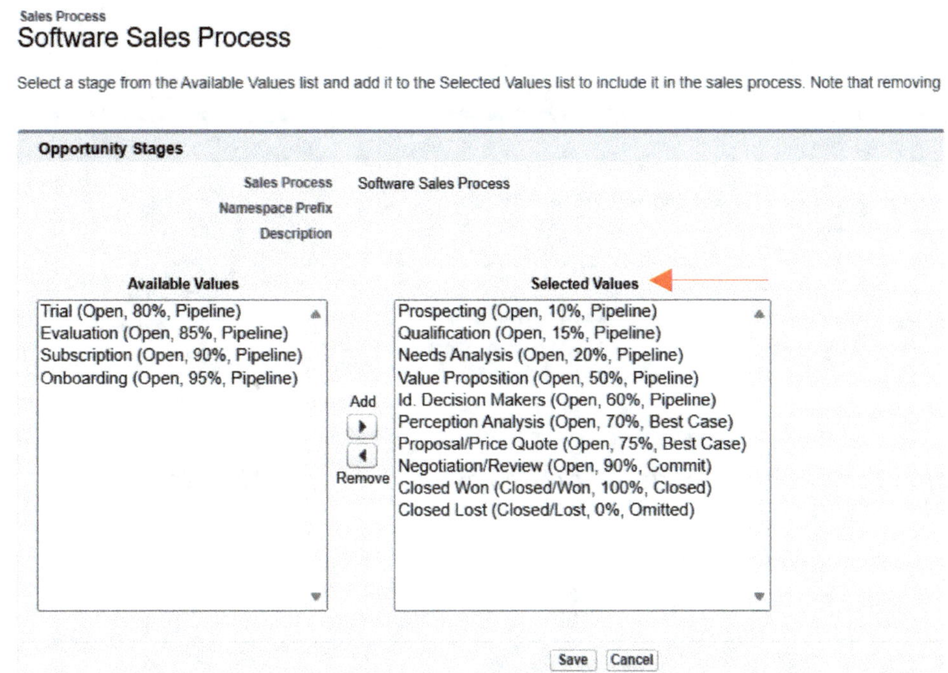



*After you have created Sales Processes to define specific values for the opportunity stage picklist in your business workflows, you need to tie these Sales Processes to record types and assign appropriate page layouts.*

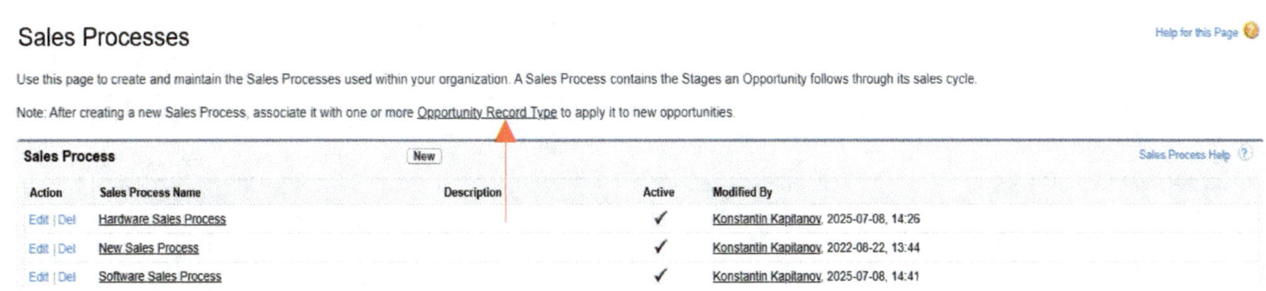

# PART II – Sales Cloud for Product Owners, IT Managers, and Admins

*To create a new Record Type click New.*

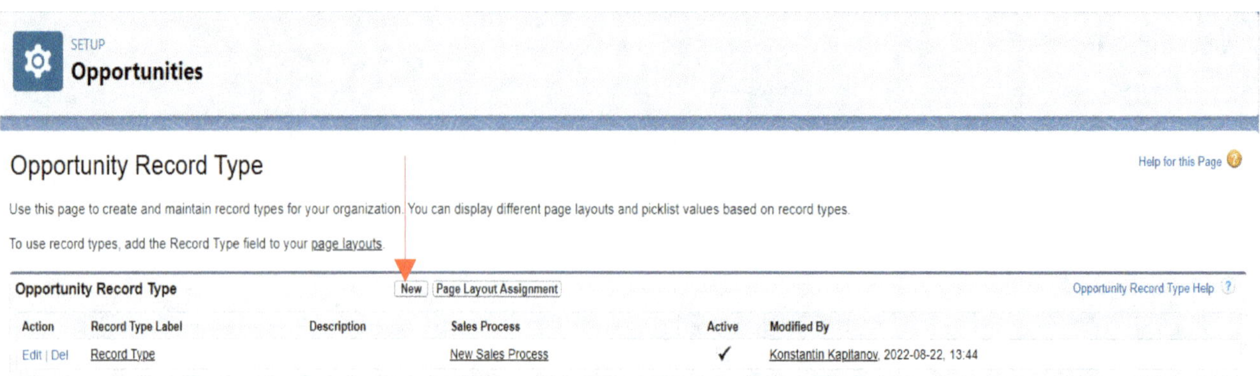

*Fill out the fields, choose available user profiles and click the Next button.*

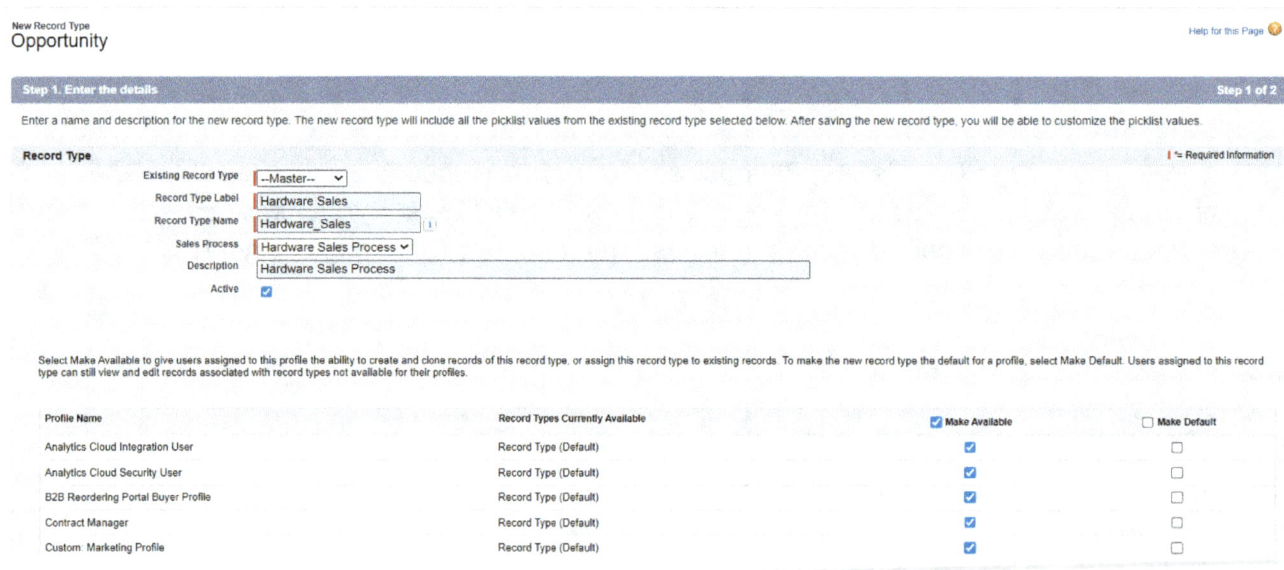

*Select the page layout and Save.*

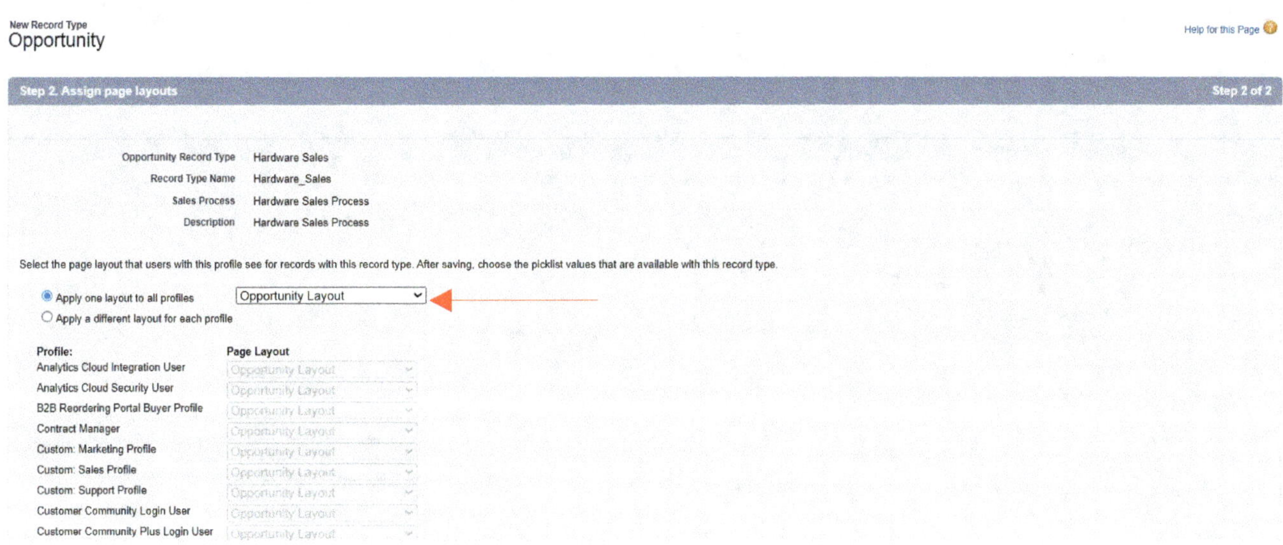

*The new Record Type for Hardware Sales has now been created.*

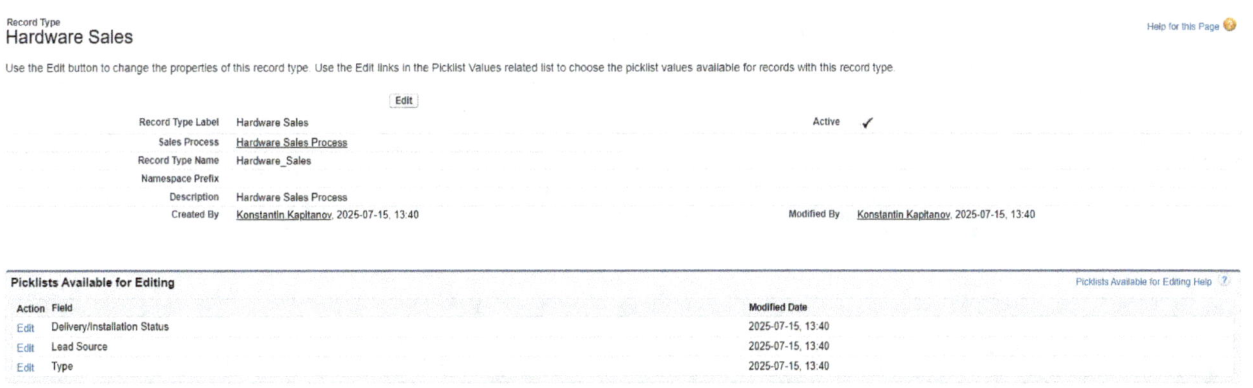

# PART II — Sales Cloud for Product Owners, IT Managers, and  Admins

*We are doing the same to create a Software Sales Record Type by filling out the fields, choosing available user profiles and clicking the Next button.*

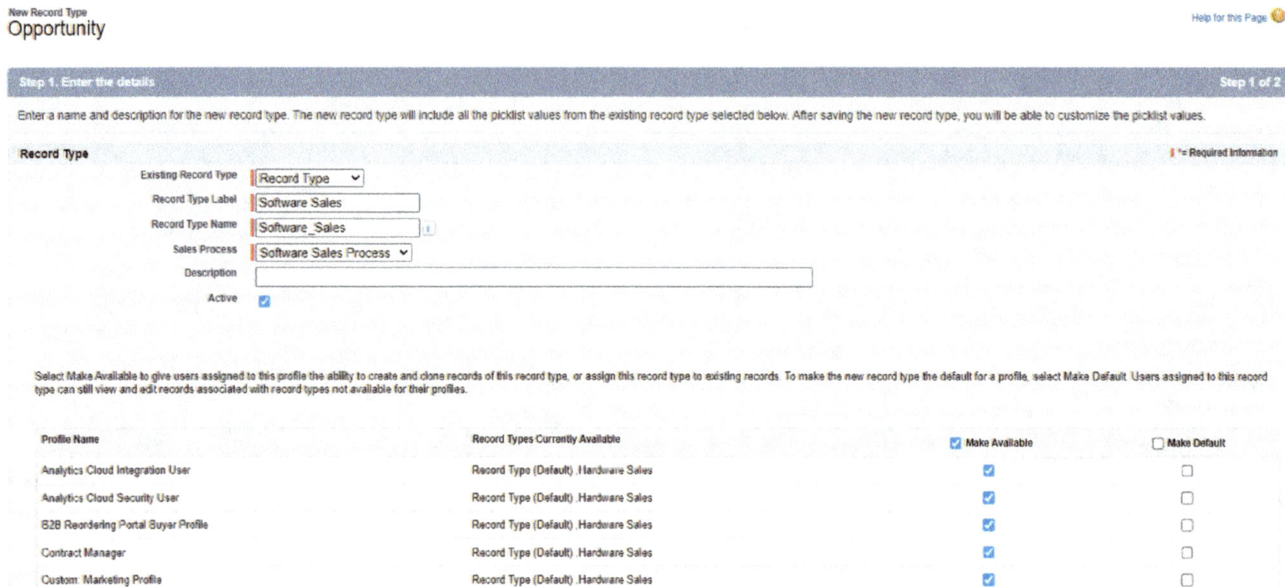

*Also select the page layout and save it.*

*The new Record Type for Software Sales has now been created.*

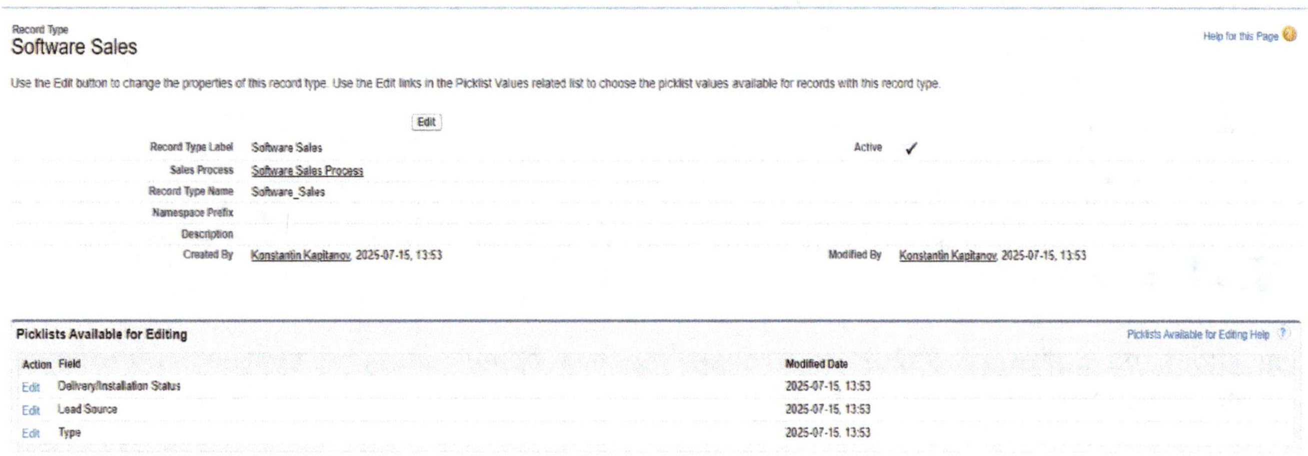

*Now we will create a new Opportunity and see the two new record types appear.*

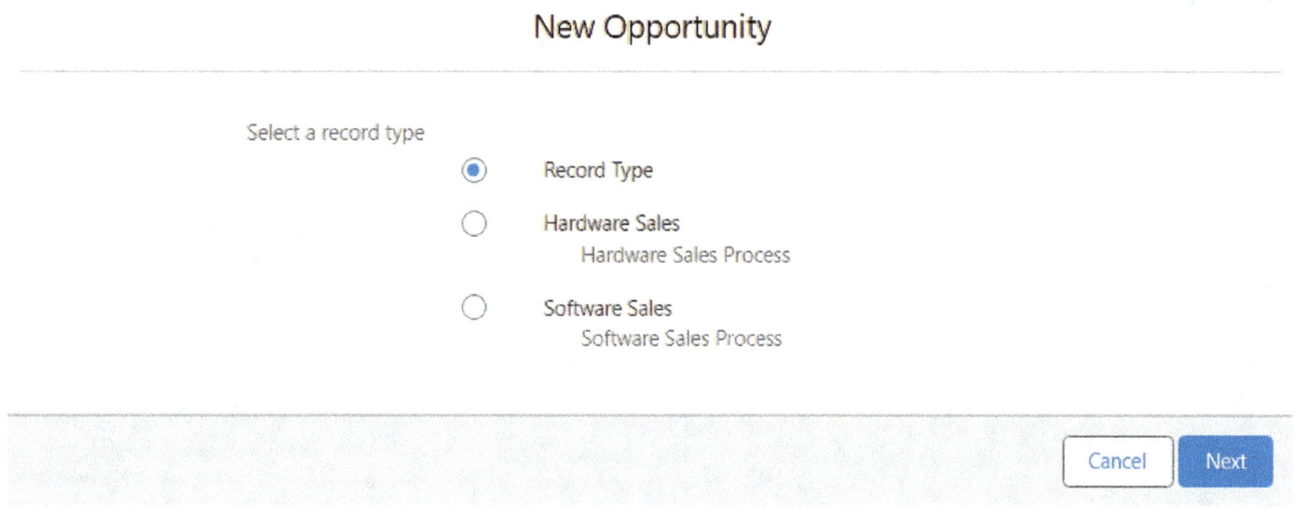

# PART II – Sales Cloud for Product Owners, IT Managers, and  Admins

*By choosing Hardware Sales we create the new opportunity with the Hardware Sales Process dedicated stages.*

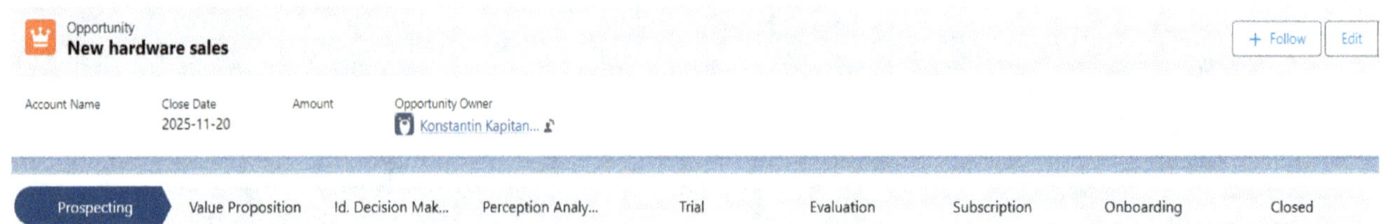

*By choosing Software Sales we create the new opportunity with the Software Sales Process dedicated stages.*

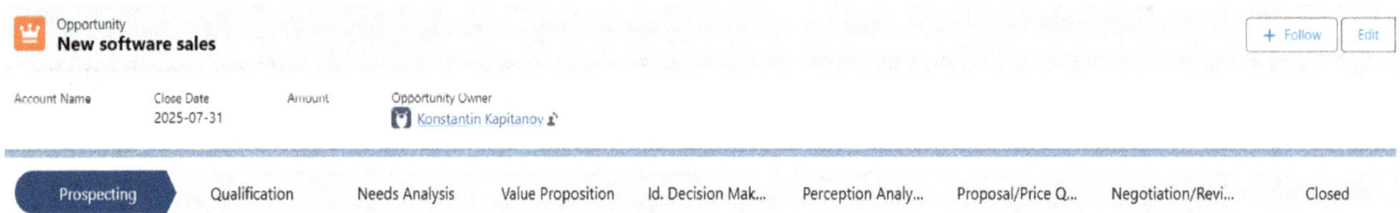

# Chapter 9. Understanding Data Access and Security

## 9.1 Profiles and Permission Sets

In Salesforce, user access management is a cornerstone of both security and operational efficiency. The platform uses a layered approach, where profiles establish baseline permissions and permission sets provide additional flexibility. Together, they ensure users have the correct level of access required for their roles while protecting sensitive data and business processes from unauthorized activity.

A profile defines the foundational level of access for a user. It represents the default configuration of what a user can view or do within the system. Object access determines which standard and custom objects a user can interact with, such as creating, reading, editing, and deleting records. Field-level security, as the next layer, regulates visibility and edit permissions for individual fields within objects.

It represents the general responsibilities of a user role in the organization. It acts as a baseline, ensuring that users receive only the access necessary to perform their job functions.

While profiles establish the basics of permissions, permission sets act as incremental extensions. A permission set grants additional capabilities beyond those defined in the assigned profile, without requiring any changes to the profile itself. This makes permission sets especially useful for temporary, project-based, or feature-specific access adjustments.

Such flexibility could be used in ways including, but not limited to:

- Granting temporary access to certain objects or fields.
- Enabling newly deployed functionality for a subset of users.
- Extending permissions for users involved in cross-functional initiatives.

Now that we understand what profiles and permission sets are, let's create two custom profiles to see them in action. This exercise will give you hands-on experience setting up user permissions for a sales team.

*As a first step, we will create a Custom Sales Rep Profile with the following configuration:*
*Leads: Read/Create*
*Opportunities: Read/Create/Edit*
*Accounts: Read only*

*Then we'll build a Custom Sales Manager Profile with broader capabilities:*
*Leads: Read/Create/Edit*
*Opportunities: Read/Create/Edit/Delete*
*Accounts: Read/Create/Edit*

*Go to Setup → Profiles → New Profile*

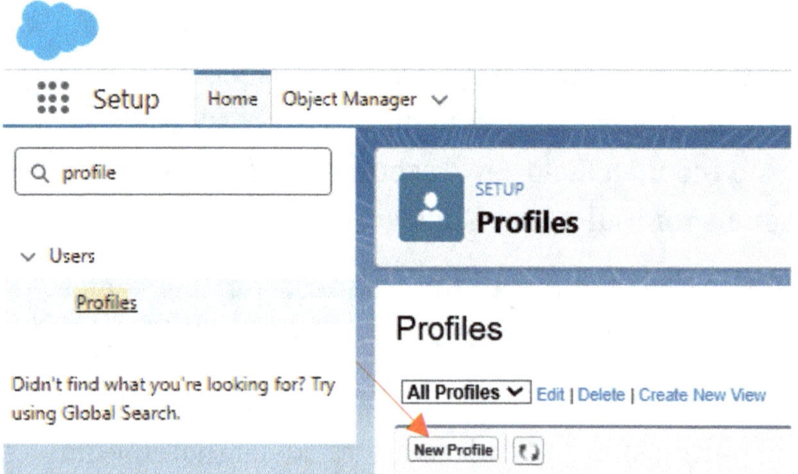

*Select Standard User Profile to clone, set up Profile Name in the field and Save.*

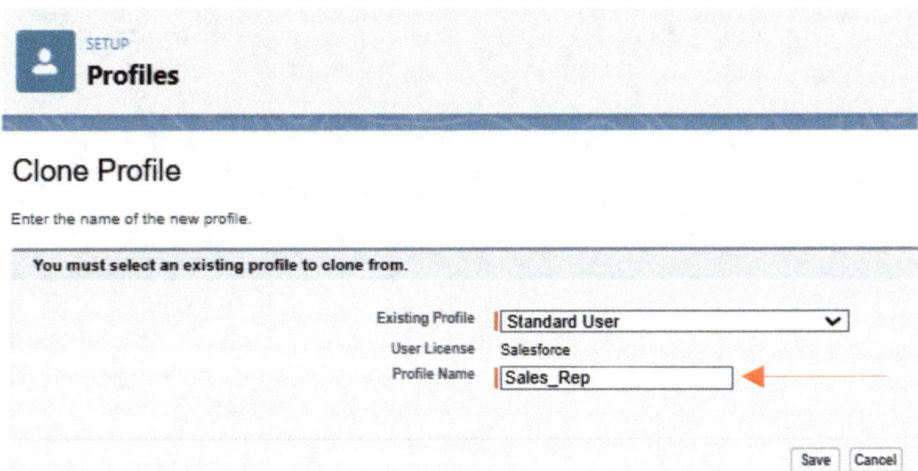

*Then click Edit.*

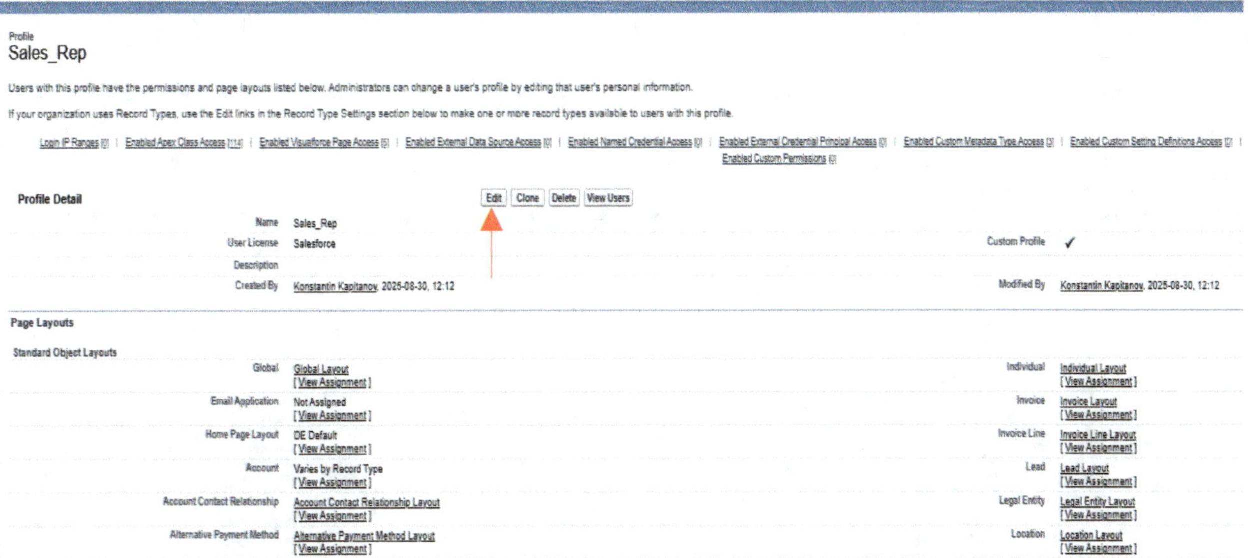

*Set up the Object Permissions and Save.*

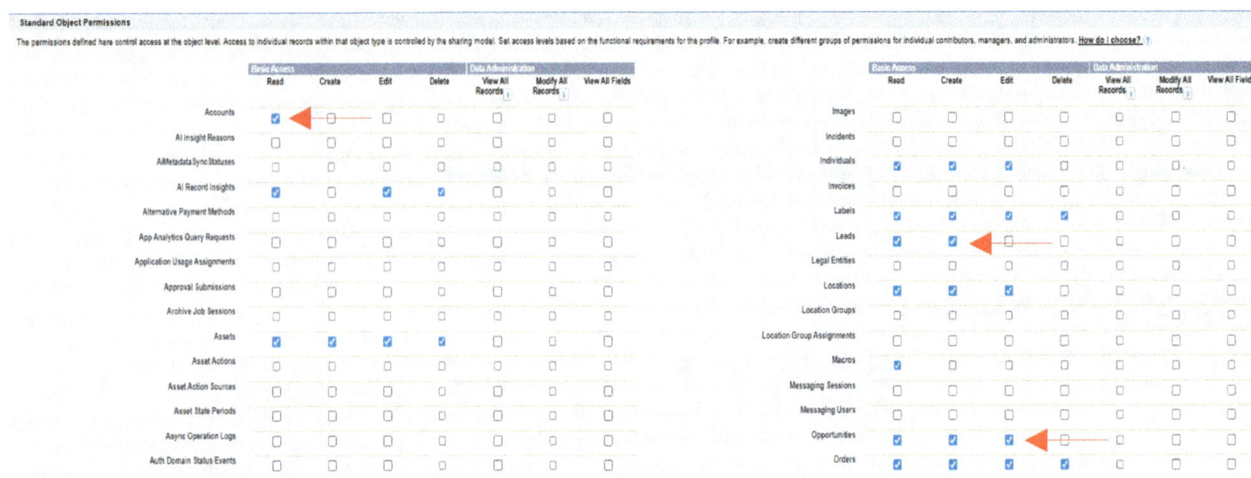

*Clone the newly created Sales Rep Profile to create a Sales Manager Profile as well.*

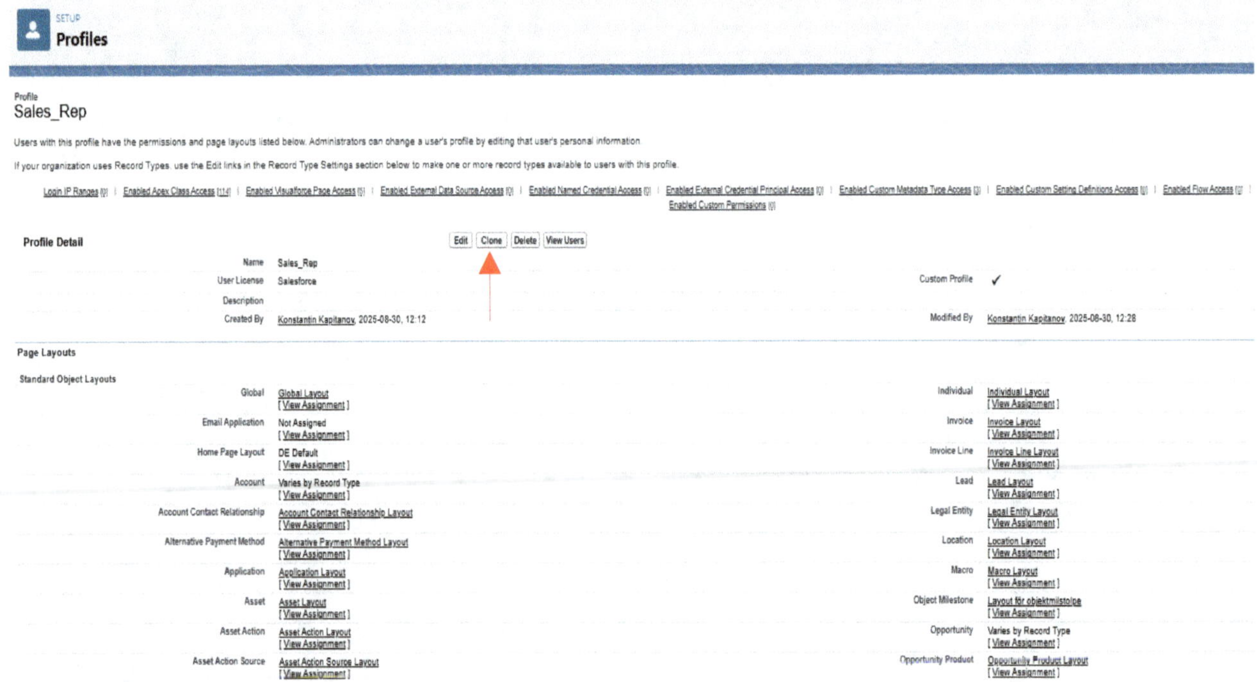

*Set up Profile Name in the field and Save.*

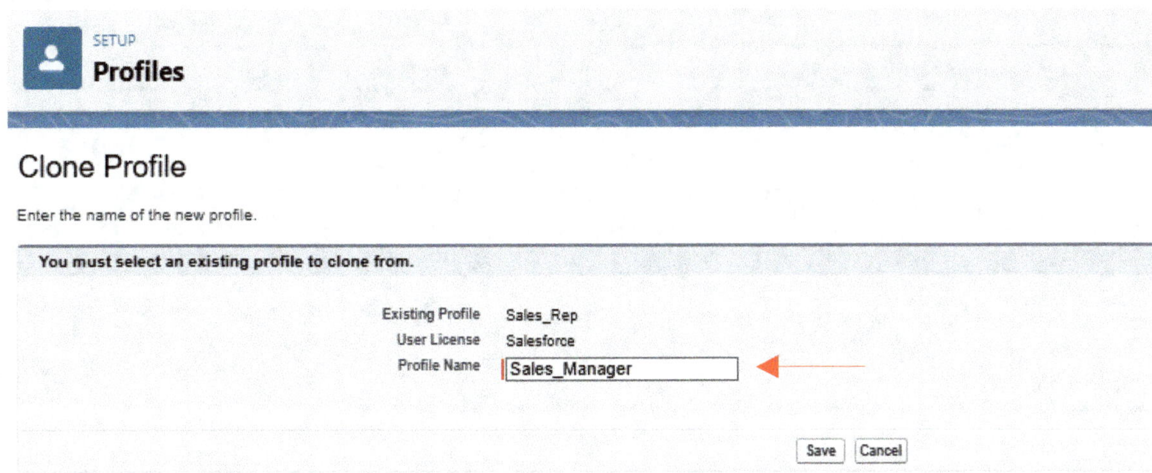

*Click Edit.*

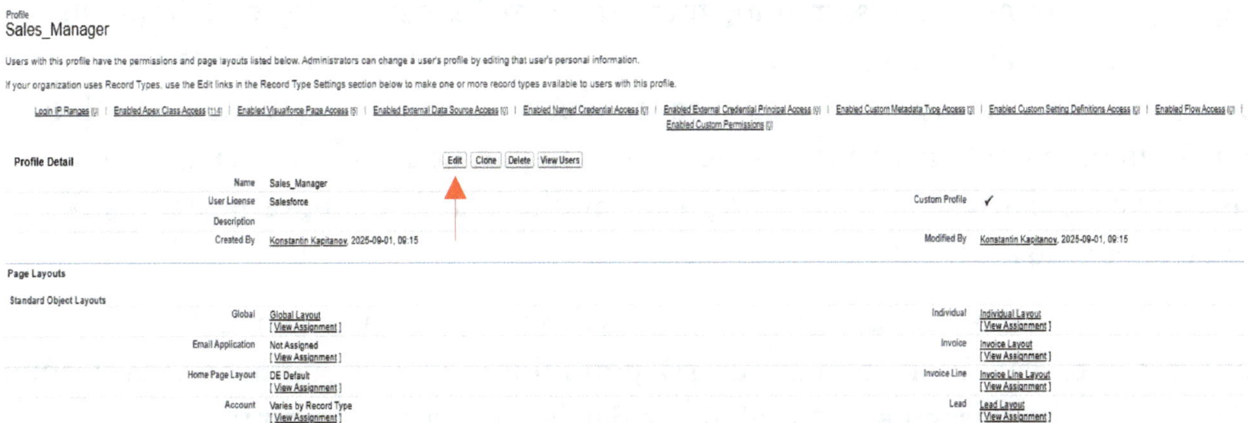

*Set up the Object Permissions and Save.*

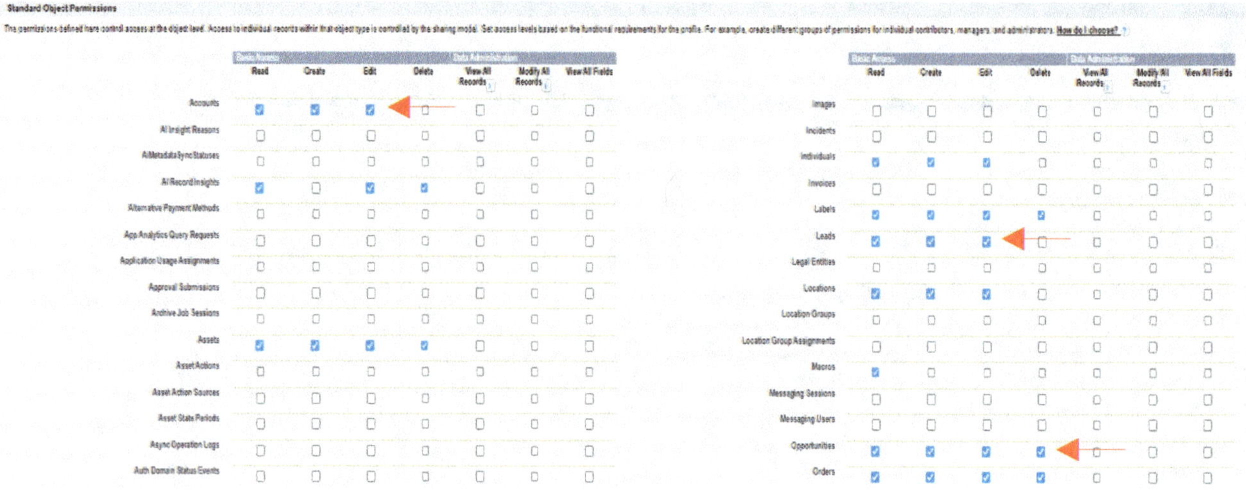

**Standard Object Permissions**

The permissions defined here control access at the object level. Access to individual records within that object type is controlled by the sharing model. Set access levels based on the functional requirements for the profile. For example, create different groups of permissions for individual contributors, managers, and administrators. How do I choose?

| | Basic Access | | | | Data Administration | | |
| --- | --- | --- | --- | --- | --- | --- | --- |
| | Read | Create | Edit | Delete | View All Records | Modify All Records | View All Fields |
| Accounts | ✓ | ✓ | ✓ | | | | |
| AI Insight Reasons | | | | | | | |
| AI Metadata Sync Statuses | | | | | | | |
| AI Record Insights | ✓ | | ✓ | ✓ | | | |
| Alternative Payment Methods | | | | | | | |
| App Analytics Query Requests | | | | | | | |
| Application Usage Assignments | | | | | | | |
| Approval Submissions | | | | | | | |
| Archive Job Sessions | | | | | | | |
| Assets | ✓ | ✓ | ✓ | ✓ | | | |
| Asset Actions | | | | | | | |
| Asset Action Sources | | | | | | | |
| Asset State Periods | | | | | | | |
| Async Operation Logs | | | | | | | |
| Auth Domain Status Events | | | | | | | |

| | Basic Access | | | | Data Administration | | |
| --- | --- | --- | --- | --- | --- | --- | --- |
| | Read | Create | Edit | Delete | View All Records | Modify All Records | View All Fields |
| Images | | | | | | | |
| Incidents | | | | | | | |
| Individuals | ✓ | ✓ | ✓ | | | | |
| Invoices | | | | | | | |
| Labels | ✓ | ✓ | ✓ | ✓ | | | |
| Leads | ✓ | ✓ | ✓ | | | | |
| Legal Entities | | | | | | | |
| Locations | ✓ | ✓ | ✓ | | | | |
| Location Groups | | | | | | | |
| Location Group Assignments | | | | | | | |
| Macros | ✓ | | | | | | |
| Messaging Sessions | | | | | | | |
| Messaging Users | | | | | | | |
| Opportunities | ✓ | ✓ | ✓ | ✓ | | | |
| Orders | ✓ | ✓ | ✓ | ✓ | | | |

While profiles define the baseline access for a user, Salesforce provides another flexible tool called a Permission Set. It's a collection of settings and permissions that can be assigned to one or more users, granting them additional access on top of their profile. But it does not replace or modify the profile. Instead, they act as an add-on layer of security and allow extra permissions to be granded to specific users without creating and maintaining multiple custom profiles. For example, if only one Sales Rep needs temporary access to a feature, assigning a Permission Set is far more efficient than cloning or editing the profile.

Let's look at a practical example that illustrates this usage. A Sales Rep profile is configured to prevent users from deleting Opportunities. However, during a data cleanup activity, a specific person needs the ability to delete duplicate Opportunities for one week. Instead of editing the Sales Rep profile we can create a Permission Set that grants only this additional Delete permission for Opportunities.

*Go to Setup → Permission Sets → New*

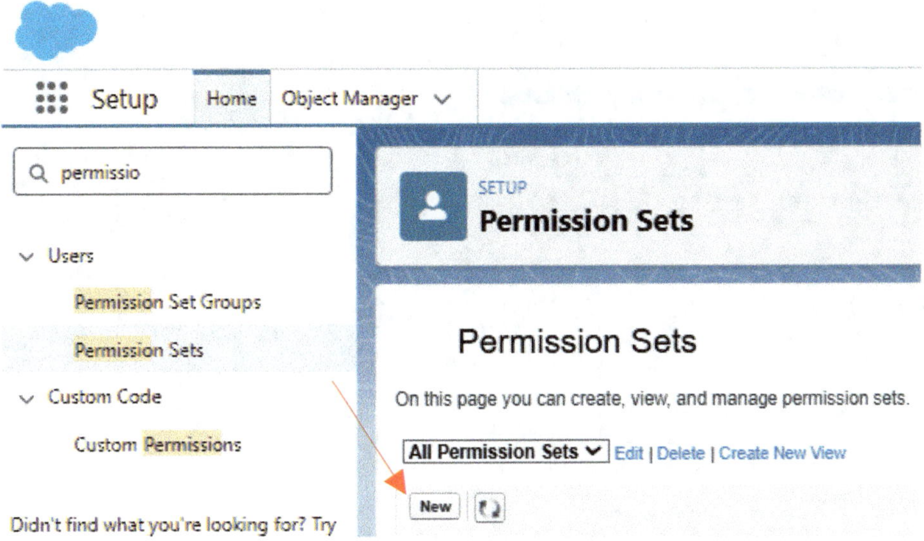

*Set up value "Opportunity Delete Access" in the Label field and Save.*

Permission Set
## Create

Save | Cancel

**Enter permission set information**

| | |
|---|---|
| Label | Opportunity Delete Access |
| API Name | Opportunity_Delete_Access |
| Description | |
| Session Activation Required | ☐ |

**Select the type of users who will use this permission set**

Who will use this permission set?

-Choose '--None--' if you plan to assign this permission set to multiple users with different user and permission set licenses.
-Choose a specific user license if you want users with only one license type to use this permission set.
-Choose a specific permission set license if you want this permission set license auto-assigned with the permission set.

Not sure what a permission set license is? Learn more here.

| License | --None-- |
|---|---|

Save | Cancel

*Open an Object Settings.*

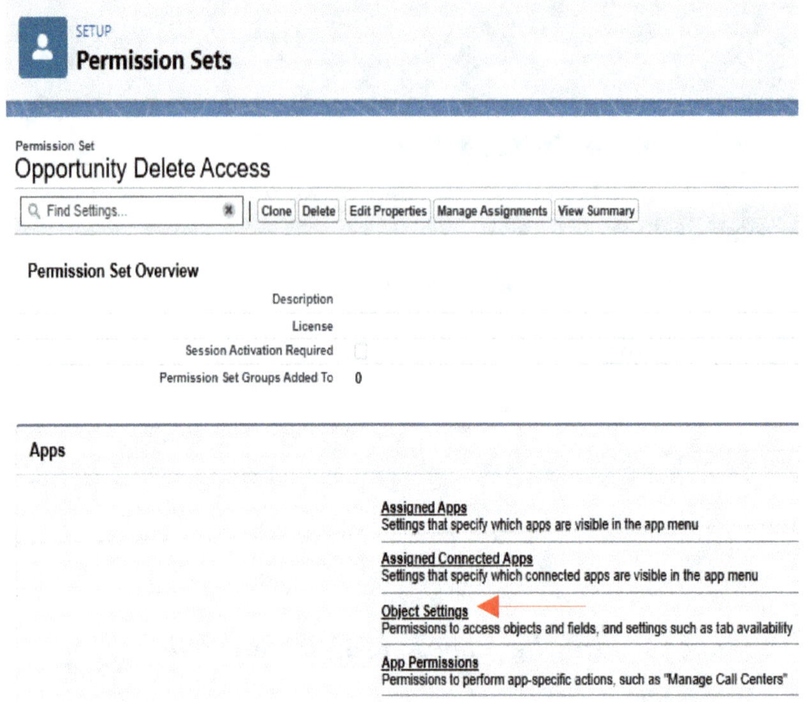

*Select Opportunities and click Edit.*

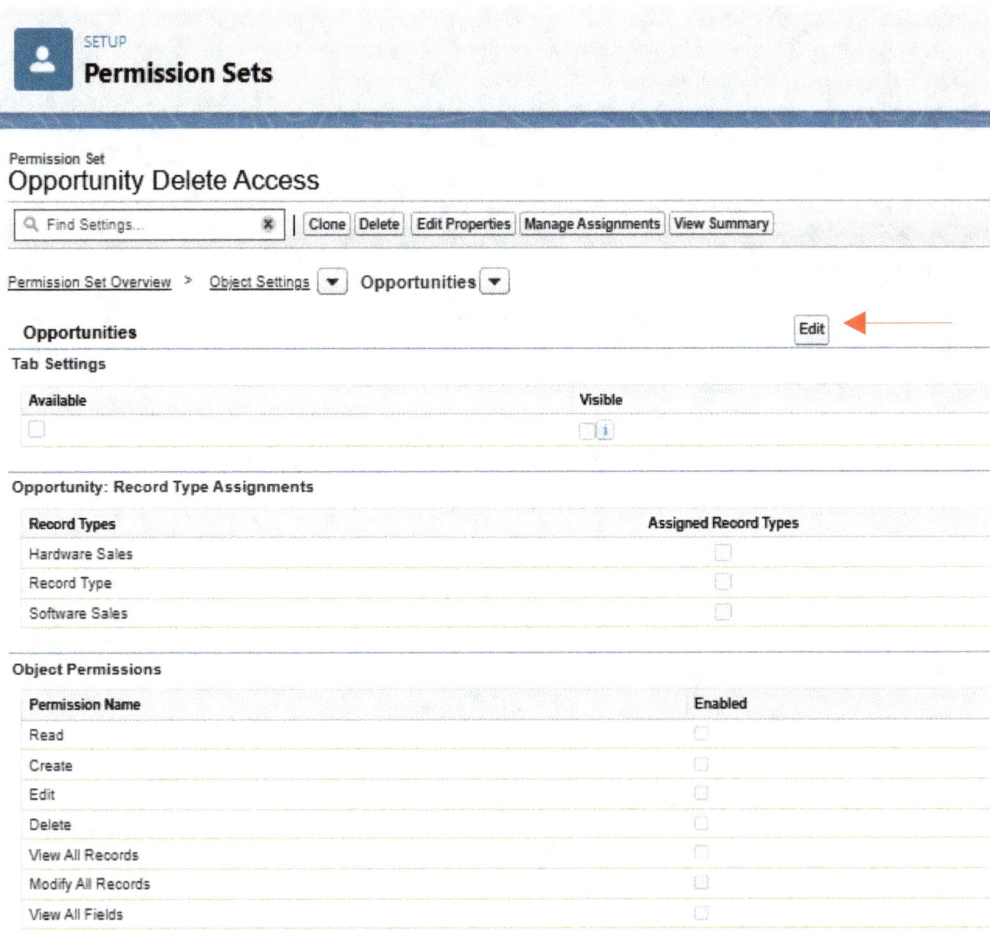

*Enable Delete Object Permission and Save.*

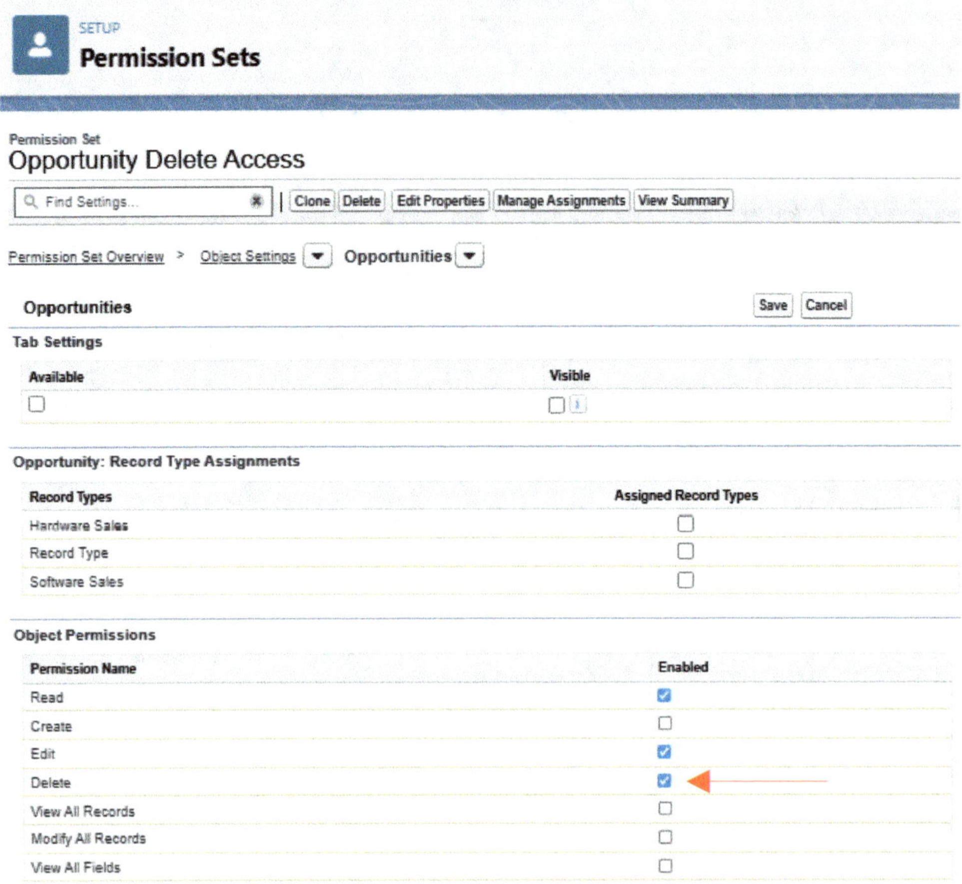

*Click Manage Assignments.*

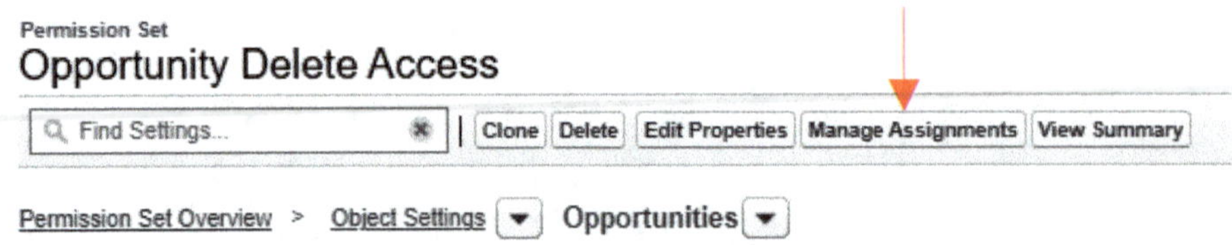

*Click Add Assignment*

*Select Users you want to add and click Next.*

Select Users to Assign

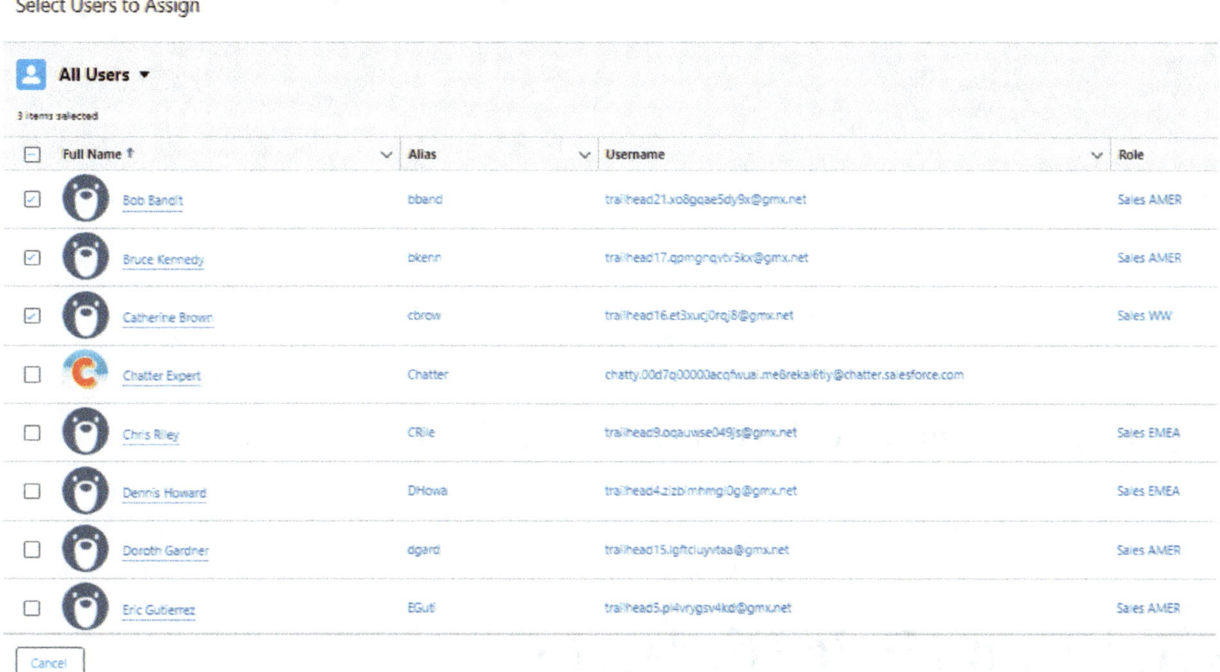

*Specify an expiration date and click Assign.*

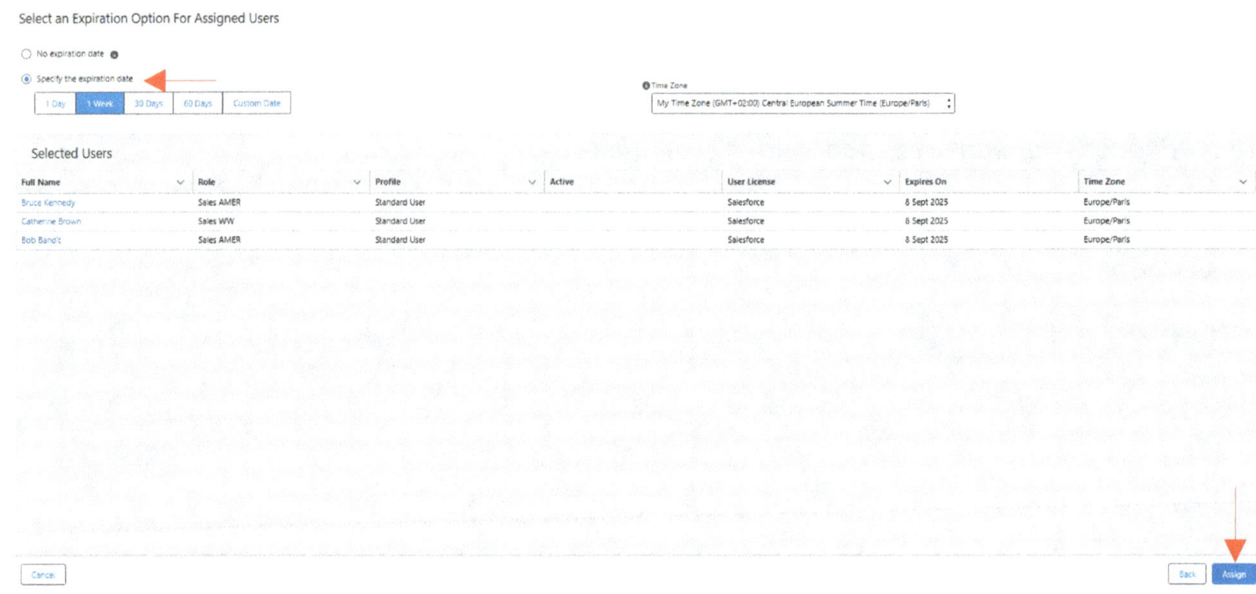

Some sales reps now can delete opportunities for a limited time.

# 9.2 Roles and Role Hierarchy

Roles can define levels of authority and data access, independent of an organizational chart. This allows for flexible access control based on business needs rather than reporting structure. This system ensures controlled data visibility and helps in sales management, especially for pipeline and territory management. Roles differ from profiles and determine record-level access, while profiles control permissions for objects and fields.

**Key capabilities are:**

- Access control: Restricts record visibility based on user responsibilities.

- Reporting: Enables managers to view consolidated sales data for all direct and subordinate reports.

- Adaptable structures: Roles do not have to precisely match organizational job titles but should reflect required access levels.

Let's go ahead and create two roles.

*Go to Setup → Roles → Set up Roles*

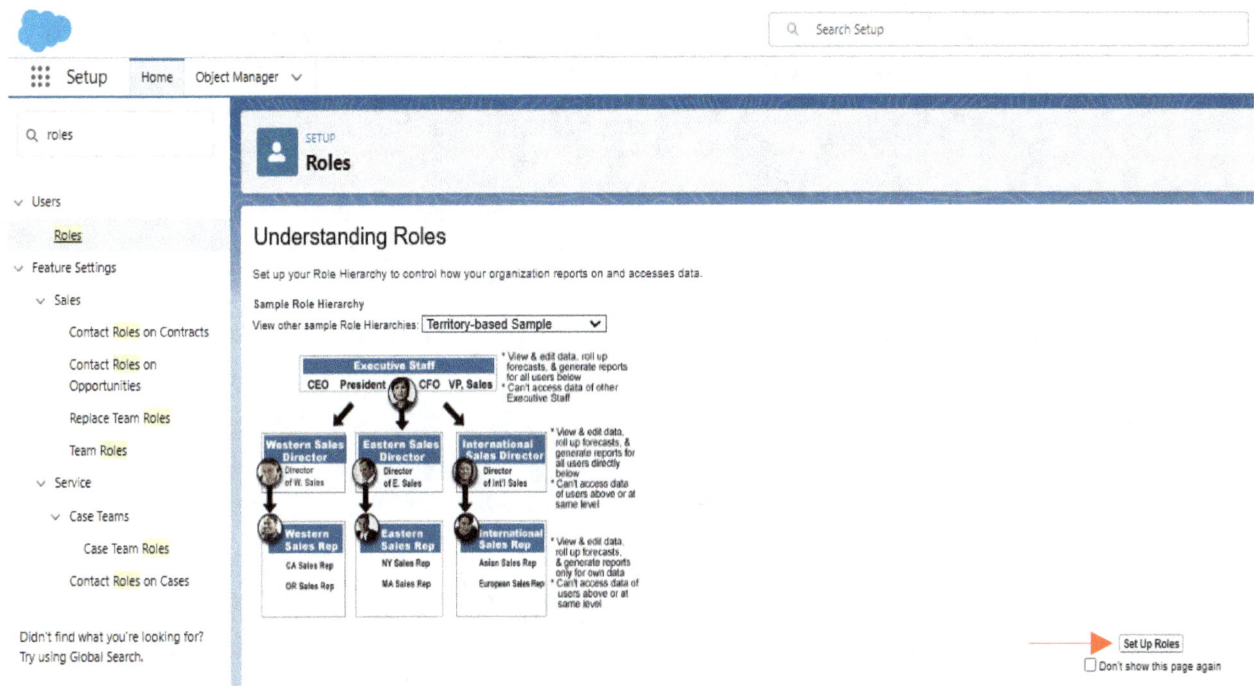

*In the hierarchy view, click Add Role.*

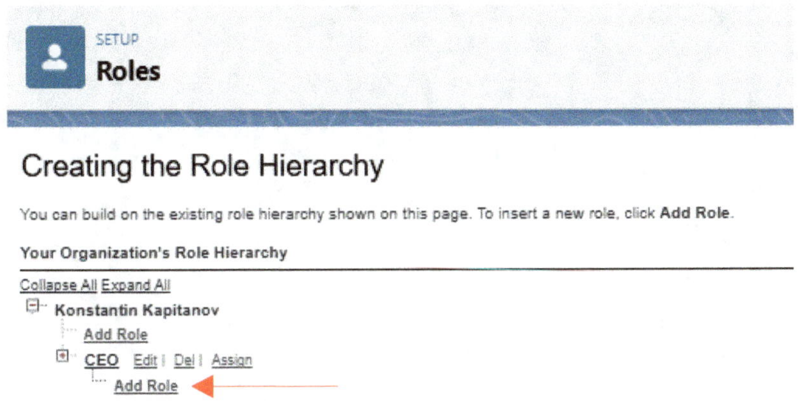

## Creating the Role Hierarchy

You can build on the existing role hierarchy shown on this page. To insert a new role, click **Add Role**.

**Your Organization's Role Hierarchy**

Collapse All Expand All

- **Konstantin Kapitanov**
  - Add Role
  - **CEO**   Edit | Del | Assign
    - Add Role

*Put the Field Label "VP of Sales", select this role reports to GEO and click Save & New.*

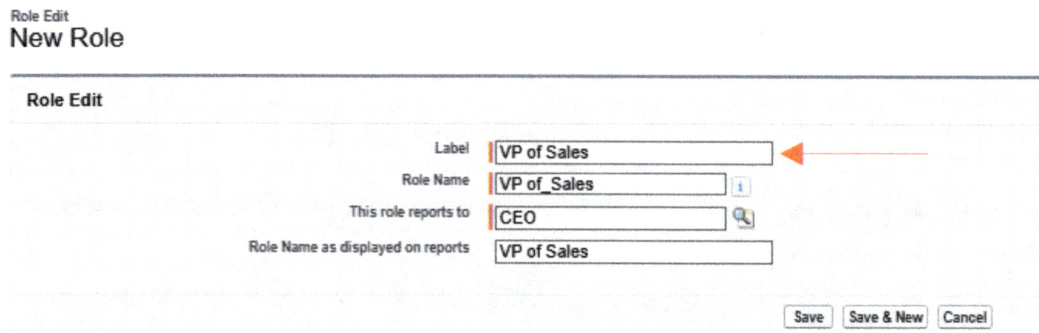

*Put the Field Label "Sales Representative", select this role reports to VP of Sales and click Save.*

*We've now created a new Role Hierarchy with two additional roles and can assign users to it.*

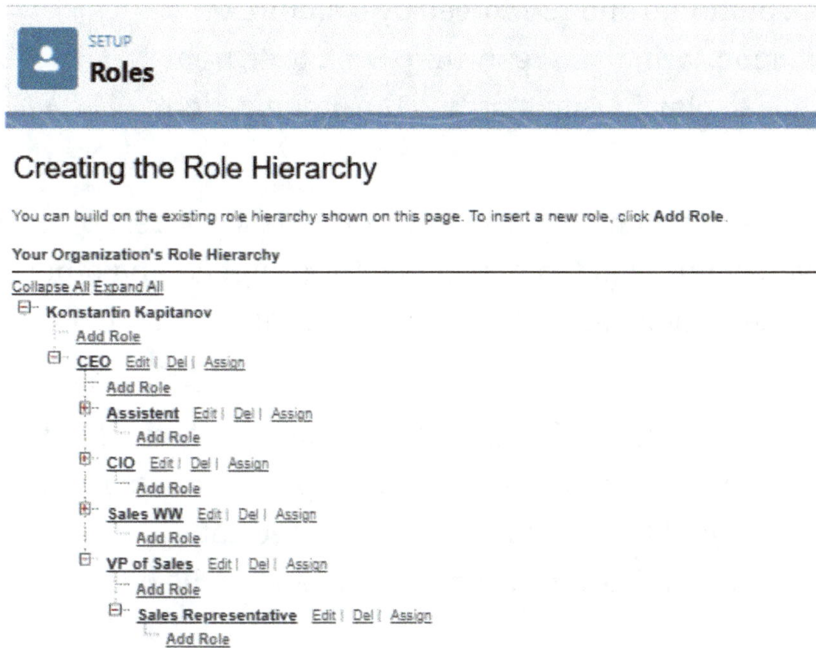

## 9.3 Data Management in Sales Cloud

At its core, Salesforce data management is about organizing, protecting, and optimizing all the data that enters and flows through the platform, supporting every business function from sales to customer service and beyond. Organizations must set out a clear strategy at the beginning of the data management journey. This often starts with understanding what data should be captured and defining how that information will be used across different departments. Regardless of whether a business deals with a few hundred records or millions, success hinges on establishing well-planned rules around data input, validation, storage, user access, and compliance, aligning every aspect of data management. Data quality efforts may involve routine audits for duplicates, missing fields, or outdated data, as well as ongoing validation to maintain consistency. This ensures teams trust and can base decisions on solid ground.

Another critical pillar is compliance. Every organization must align with legal requirements like GDPR, CCPA, or industry-specific regulations which means having clear policies for data retention, documentation, and timely deletion when necessary. This regulatory awareness must be built into and reinforced by a culture of accountability established through monitoring and reporting. Each user, from administrator to executive, has a role to play in safeguarding the organization's information assets.

Integration is also crucial for effective data management. Most organizations rely on more than just Salesforce, often using additional tools for marketing, finance, and other business functions. By leveraging integrations and APIs, businesses can ensure that data flows reliably across all systems.

As companies grow and the volume of data expands, Sales Cloud offers the flexibility to adapt through scalable cloud infrastructure that evolves with changing business needs. During periods of rapid expansion or digital transformation, a proactive data management strategy helps maintain control, minimize risks, and ensure the business retains high-value data.

# 9.4 Data Import Wizard

The Data Import Wizard is a native tool designed to help users import and update data in a straightforward way. It is ideal for handling small to medium data volumes and supports import operations on several standard and custom objects. The tool offers a guided interface that simplifies mapping data fields from CSV files into Salesforce objects.

However, be aware of certain limitations when using the Data Import Wizard which include a limit of up to 50,000 records in a single import, a limit of files to 100 MB in size, and the ability to handle up to 90 fields per record. Some standard objects, such as Opportunities and Cases, are not supported, and the tool does not support deleting records or automated-scheduled imports. These considerations may influence whether the Data Import Wizard is suitable for a particular data management task or if more advanced tools like Data Loader or Workbench are required.

*To import the data, prepare a CSV file formatted as shown below or similarly.*

| | A | B | C | D | E |
|---|---|---|---|---|---|
| 1 | First Name | Last Name | Email | Phone | Account Name |
| 2 | John | Doe | john.doe@example.com | 123-456-7890 | Acme Inc |
| 3 | Jane | Smith | jane.smith@example.com | 234-567-8901 | Global Corp |
| 4 | Alice | Johnson | alice.johnson@example.com | 345-678-9012 | Tech Solutions |
| 5 | Bob | Brown | bob.brown@example.com | 456-789-0123 | Innovate LLC |
| 6 | Carol | Williams | carol.williams@example.com | 567-890-1234 | Alpha Co |
| 7 | Mike | Davis | mike.davis@example.com | 678-901-2345 | Beta Tech |
| 8 | Nancy | Wilson | nancy.wilson@example.com | 789-012-3456 | Delta Partners |
| 9 | Chris | Lee | chris.lee@example.com | 890-123-4567 | Epsilon Ltd |
| 10 | Patricia | Moore | patricia.moore@example.com | 901-234-5678 | Zeta Group |
| 11 | Steven | Taylor | steven.taylor@example.com | 012-345-6789 | Omega Inc |

*Go to Setup → Data Import Wizard → Launch Wizard*

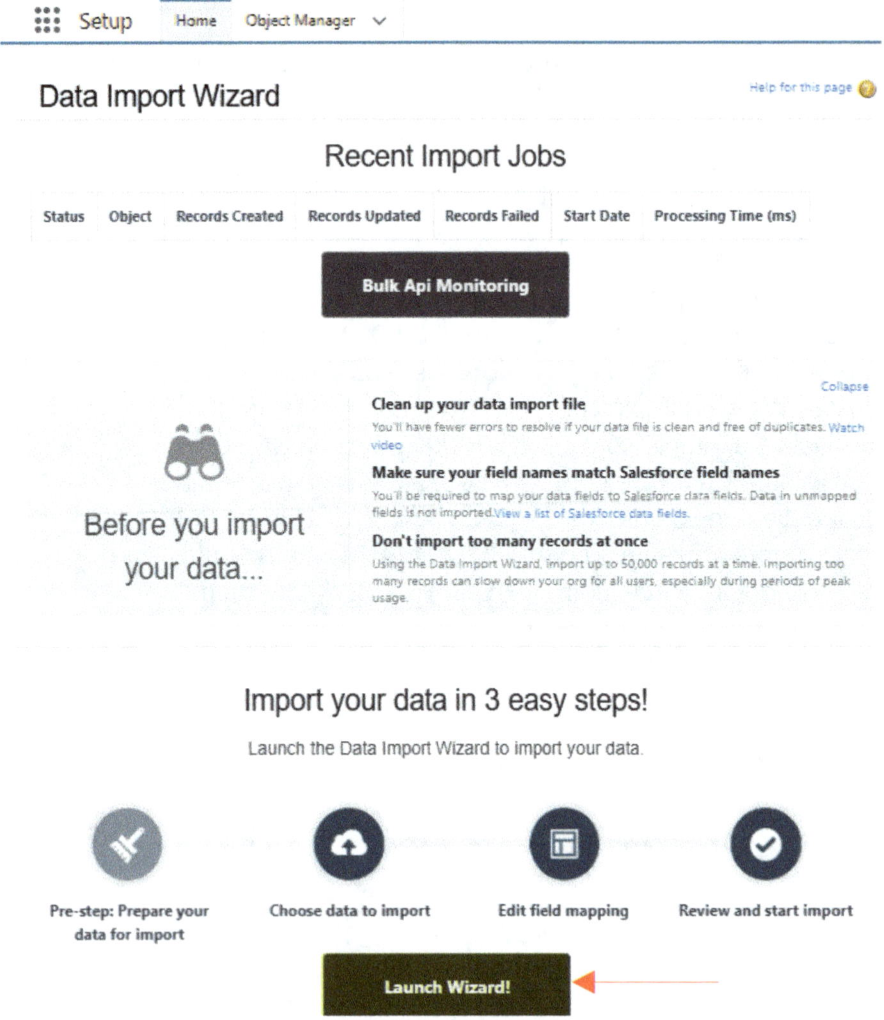

*Select your Object, matching fields, drag your CSV file to upload and click Next.*

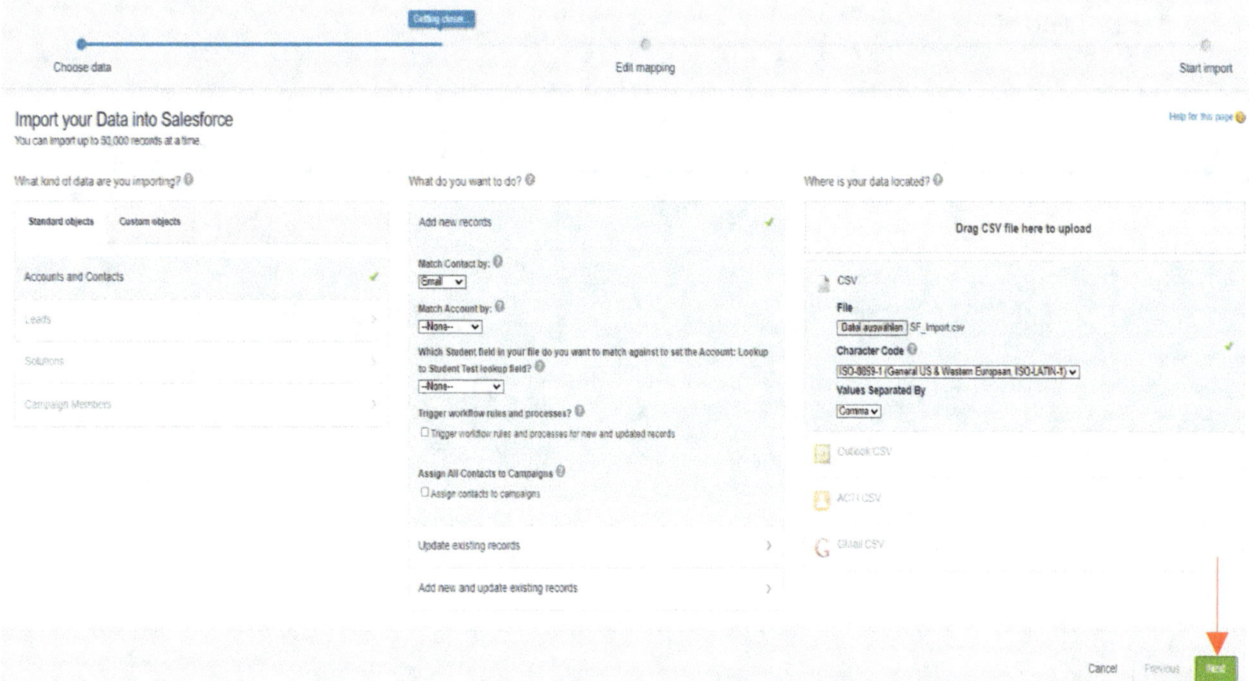

Check your field mapping and click Next.

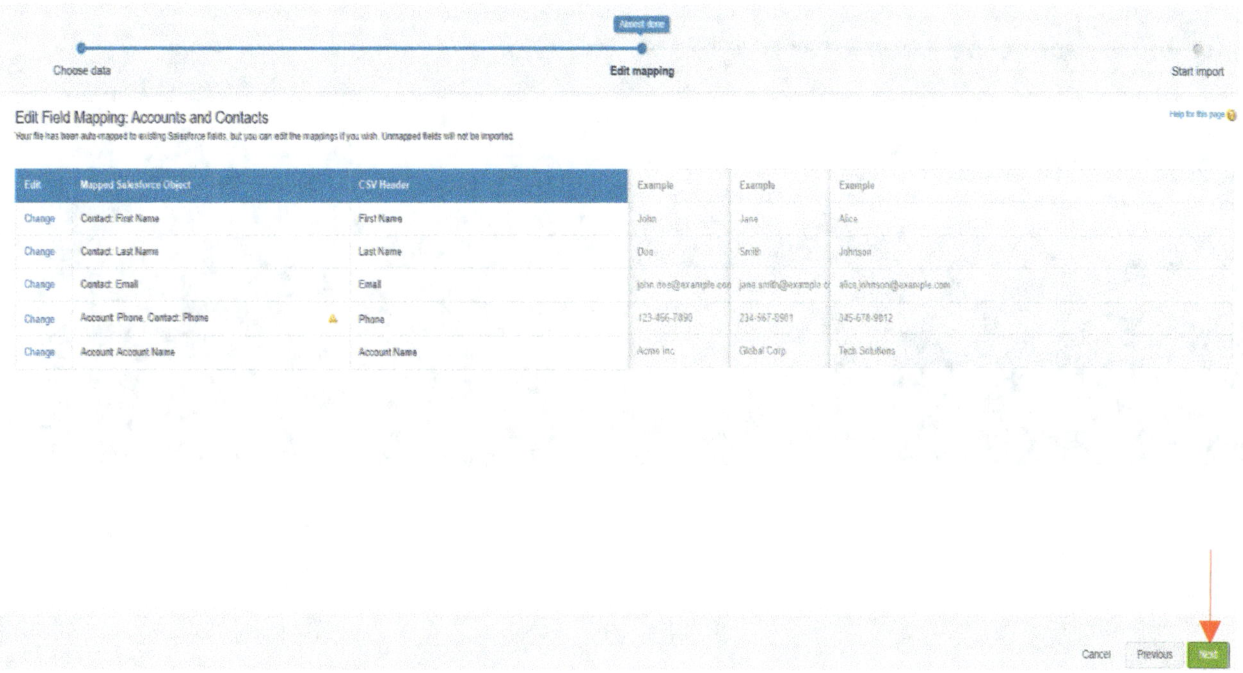

*Click Start Import.*

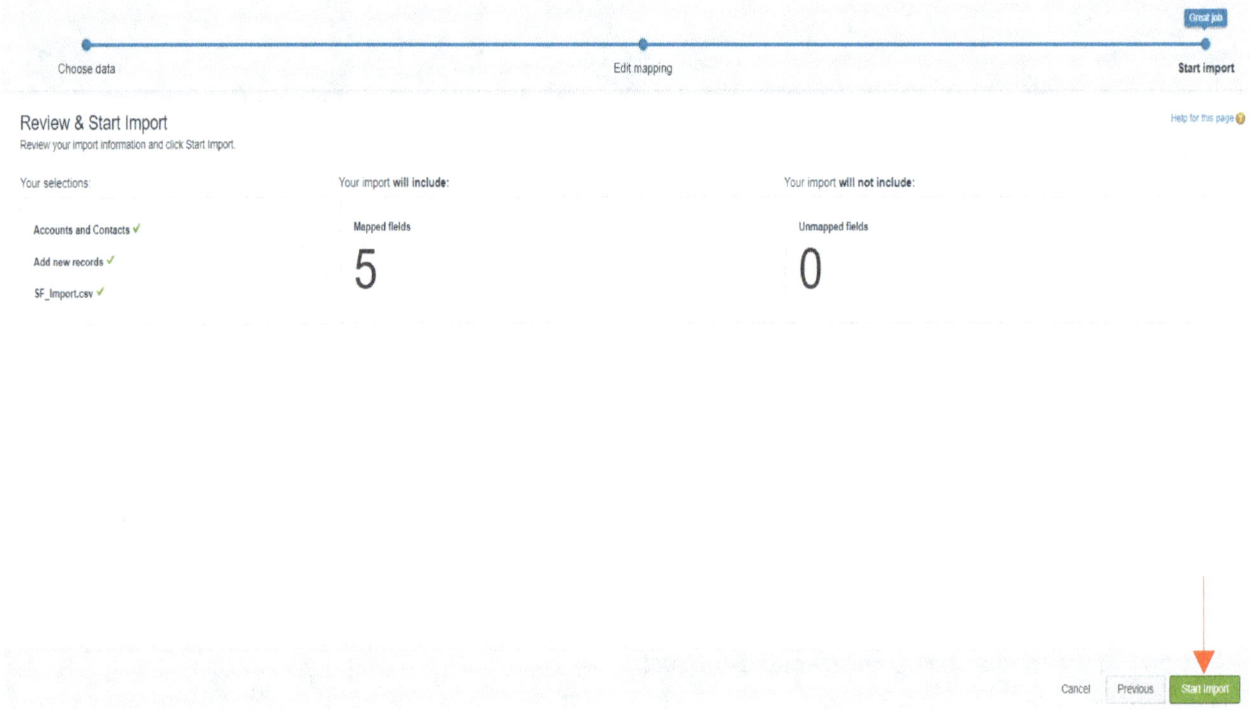

*After your import as been started click to view a status.*

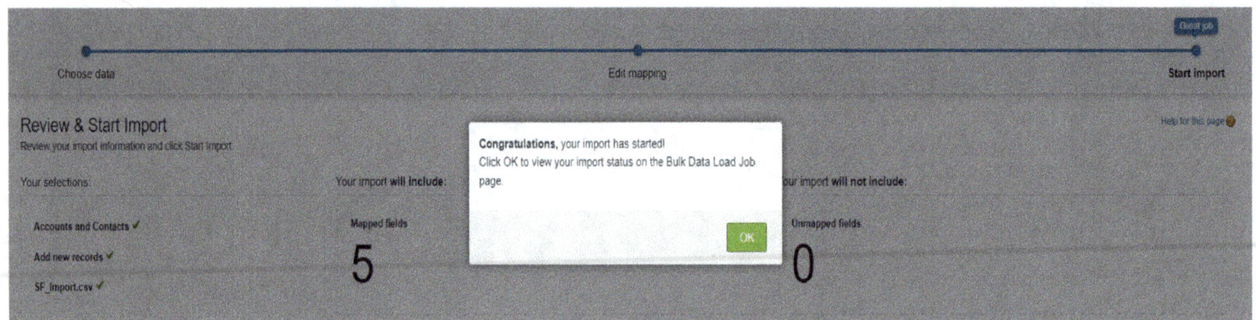

*If the import status of the records number is completed, your records are successfully imported.*

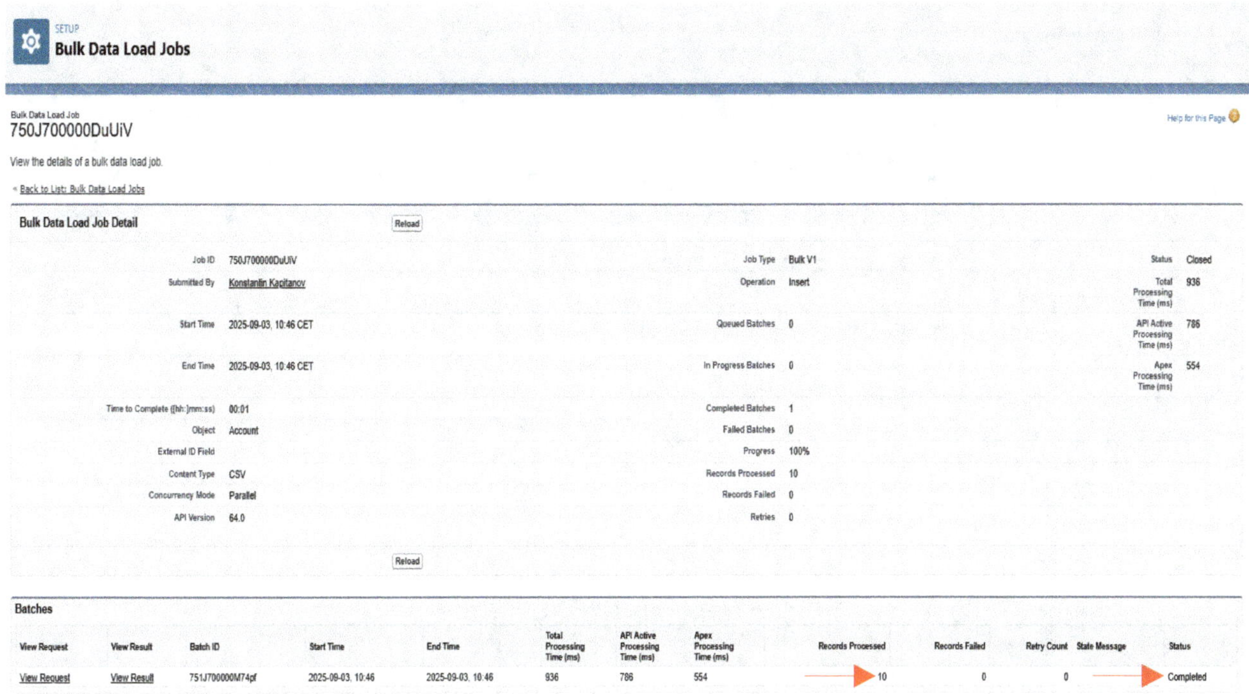

# 9.5 Data Export Tool

Salesforce provides several ways to export data from the platform, and one commonly used option is the Data Export Tool. This tool allows users to export records and related files into CSV format for backup, analysis, or transfer purposes. It supports manual exports on demand or scheduled exports that run automatically on a weekly or monthly basis, depending on the Salesforce edition. This tool is useful for creating a comprehensive snapshot of your data, but it has some limitations, such as export frequency restrictions and file size considerations.

*Go to Setup → Data Export → Schedule Export*

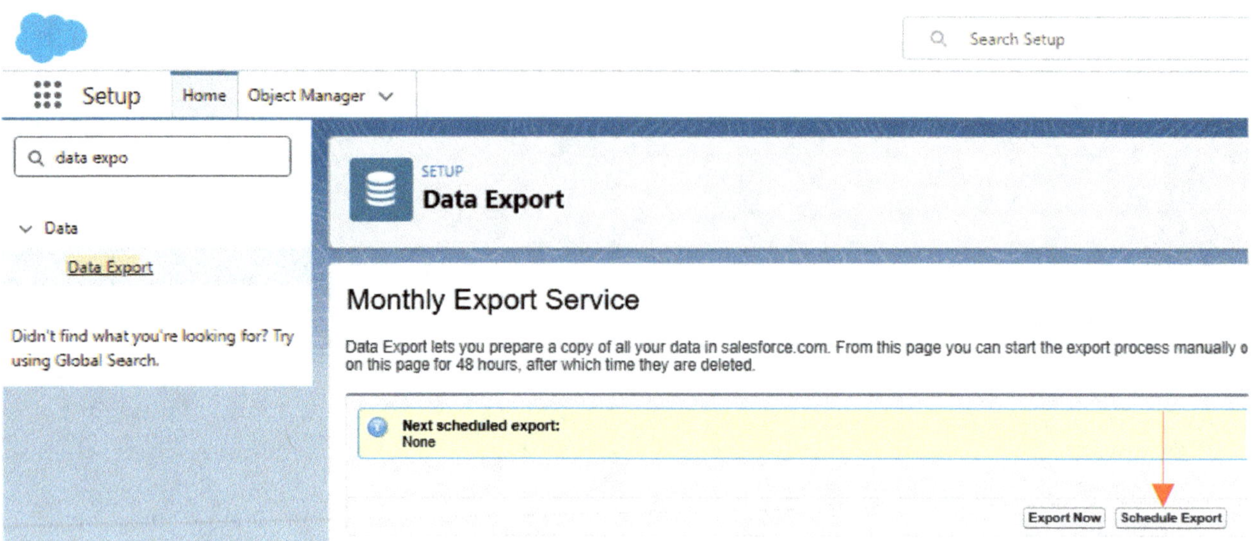

*Select Frequency, Objects to include and click Save.*

Schedule Data Export

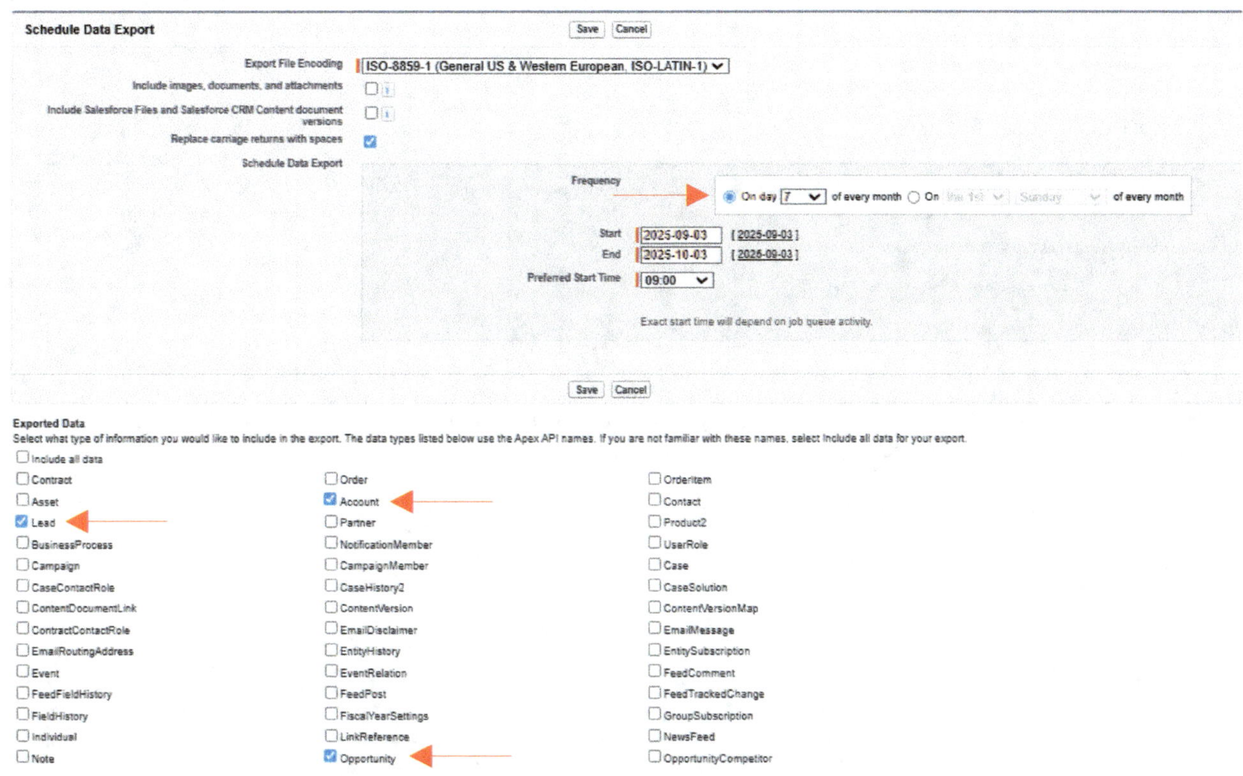

The next scheduled export is created. Alternatively, you can export the data manually whenever you need to. To do this, click Export Now.

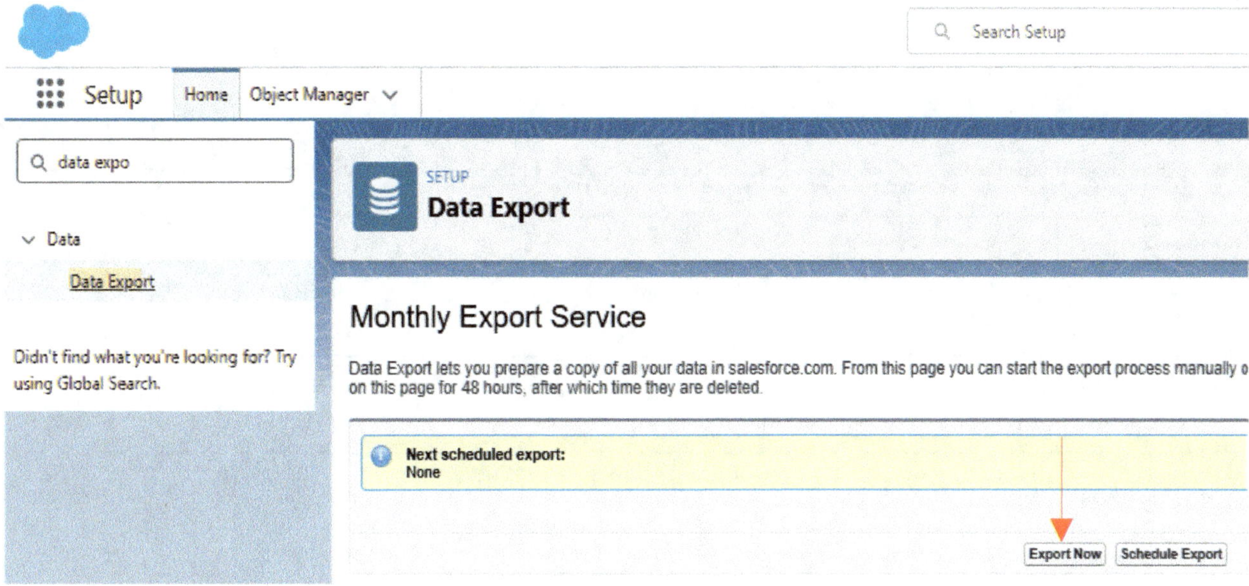

*Select the objects you need and click Start Export.*

## Monthly Export Service

| | |
|---|---|
| Export File Encoding | ISO-8859-1 (General US & Western European, ISO-LATIN-1) ⌄ |
| Include images, documents, and attachments | ☐ ⓘ |
| Include Salesforce Files and Salesforce CRM Content document versions | ☐ ⓘ |
| Replace carriage returns with spaces | ☑ |

Start Export    Cancel

**Exported Data**

Select what type of information you would like to include in the export. The data types listed below use the Apex API names. If you are not familiar with these names, select Include all data for your export.

☐ Include all data

| | | |
|---|---|---|
| ☐ Contract | ☐ Order | ☐ OrderItem |
| ☐ Asset | ☑ Account | ☐ Contact |
| ☑ Lead | ☐ Partner | ☐ Product2 |
| ☐ BusinessProcess | ☐ NotificationMember | ☐ UserRole |
| ☐ Campaign | ☐ CampaignMember | ☐ Case |
| ☐ CaseContactRole | ☐ CaseHistory2 | ☐ CaseSolution |
| ☐ ContentDocumentLink | ☐ ContentVersion | ☐ ContentVersionMap |
| ☐ ContractContactRole | ☐ EmailDisclaimer | ☐ EmailMessage |
| ☐ EmailRoutingAddress | ☐ EntityHistory | ☐ EntitySubscription |
| ☐ Event | ☐ EventRelation | ☐ FeedComment |
| ☐ FeedFieldHistory | ☐ FeedPost | ☐ FeedTrackedChange |
| ☐ FieldHistory | ☐ FiscalYearSettings | ☐ GroupSubscription |
| ☐ Individual | ☐ LinkReference | ☐ NewsFeed |
| ☐ Note | ☑ Opportunity | ☐ OpportunityCompetitor |

*You'll get an email with a link to download your file. Please click the link to download your file.*

## Monthly Export Service

Help for this Page ❓

Data Export lets you prepare a copy of all your data in salesforce.com. From this page you can start the export process manually or schedule it to run automatically. When an export is ready for download you will receive an email containing a link that allows you to download the file(s). The export files are also available on this page for 48 hours, after which time they are deleted.

> ⓘ **Next scheduled export:**
> 2025-09-07, 09:00

Export Now    Schedule Export

| | |
|---|---|
| Scheduled By | Konstantin Kapitanov |
| Schedule Date | 2025-09-03 |
| Export File Encoding | ISO-8859-1 (General US & Western European, ISO-LATIN-1) |

| Action | File Name | File Size |
|---|---|---|
| download | WE_00D7Q00000ACqFwUAL_1.ZIP | 159.7K |

# 9.6 Territory management

Territory Management is a feature that enables to organize and manage their sales territories effectively. It helps in dividing accounts, leads, and opportunities into specific geographic or strategic segments called territories. This segmentation allows businesses to allocate sales resources, assign ownership, and balance workloads in a structured and transparent way. It supports complex sales organizations by enabling hierarchical territory structures, rule-based account assignments, and integrated forecasting and reporting. Sales teams can focus on defined market segments, improving both coverage and performance.

Territories directly influence data visibility and access. When accounts and related records are assigned to a territory, members of that territory gain access to these records based on sharing settings. This means that data security is closely tied to territory assignment, sales reps see only the accounts and opportunities associated with their territories. Sales Cloud uses territory-based sharing rules to grant or restrict access, complementing role hierarchies and other sharing models. This ensures that data exposure matches organizational structure and sales responsibilities, enabling secure, role-appropriate data access.

*Go to Setup → Search for Territory Settings → Enable Sales Territory*

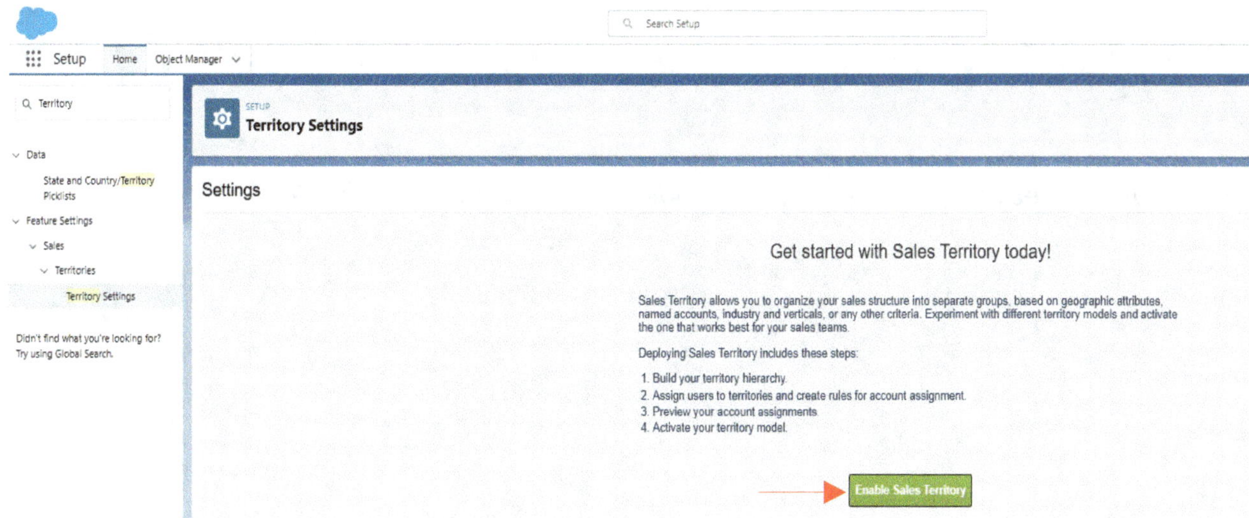

*Select your preferable settings and Save.*

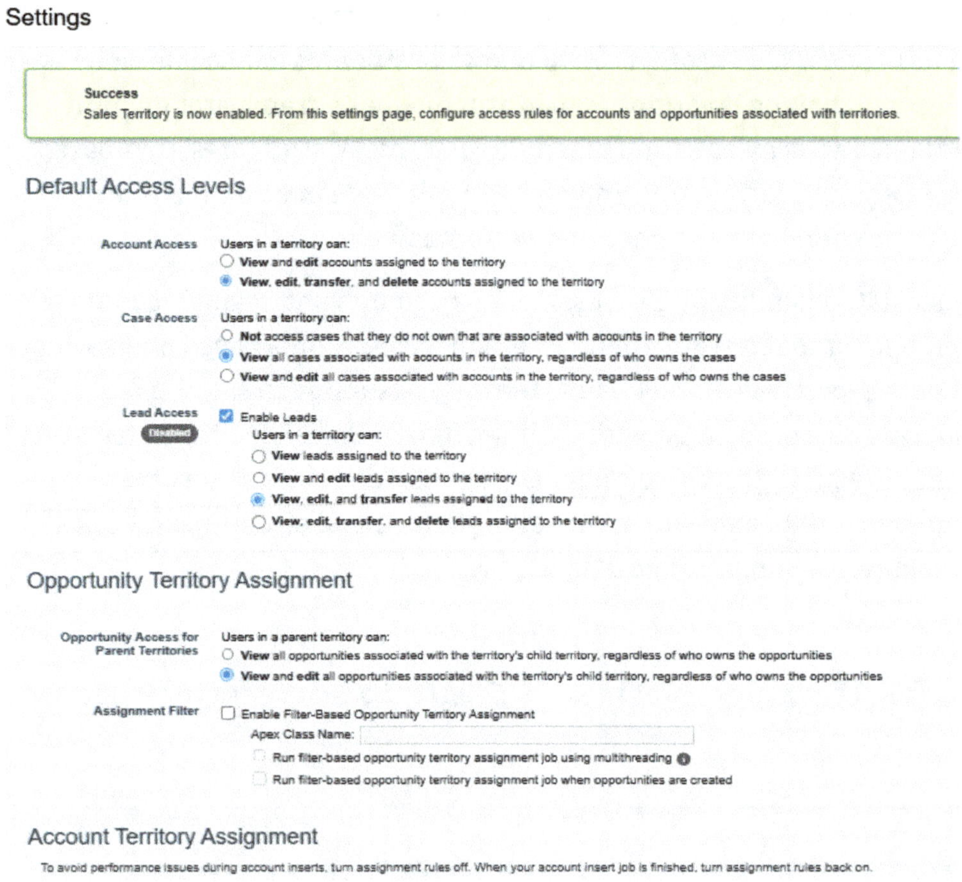

Settings

**Success**
Sales Territory is now enabled. From this settings page, configure access rules for accounts and opportunities associated with territories.

## Default Access Levels

**Account Access**
Users in a territory can:
- ○ **View** and **edit** accounts assigned to the territory
- ◉ **View**, **edit**, **transfer**, and **delete** accounts assigned to the territory

**Case Access**
Users in a territory can:
- ○ **Not** access cases that they do not own that are associated with accounts in the territory
- ◉ **View** all cases associated with accounts in the territory, regardless of who owns the cases
- ○ **View** and **edit** all cases associated with accounts in the territory, regardless of who owns the cases

**Lead Access**
**Disabled**
☑ Enable Leads
Users in a territory can:
- ○ **View** leads assigned to the territory
- ○ **View** and **edit** leads assigned to the territory
- ◉ **View**, **edit**, and **transfer** leads assigned to the territory
- ○ **View**, **edit**, **transfer**, and **delete** leads assigned to the territory

## Opportunity Territory Assignment

**Opportunity Access for Parent Territories**
Users in a parent territory can:
- ○ **View** all opportunities associated with the territory's child territory, regardless of who owns the opportunities
- ◉ **View** and **edit** all opportunities associated with the territory's child territory, regardless of who owns the opportunities

**Assignment Filter**
☐ Enable Filter-Based Opportunity Territory Assignment
Apex Class Name:
- ☐ Run filter-based opportunity territory assignment job using multithreading ⓘ
- ☐ Run filter-based opportunity territory assignment job when opportunities are created

## Account Territory Assignment

To avoid performance issues during account inserts, turn assignment rules off. When your account insert job is finished, turn assignment rules back on.

*Go to Setup → Search for Territory Models → New Territory Model*

*Put the Label "North Region" in the New Territory Model and click Save.*

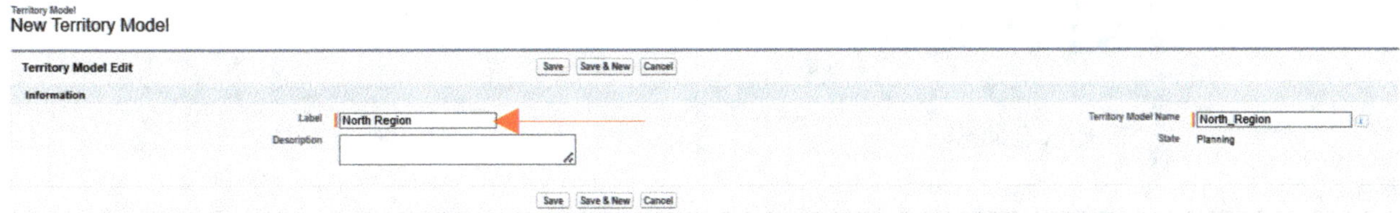

*Go to Setup → Search for Territory Setting → New Territory Type*

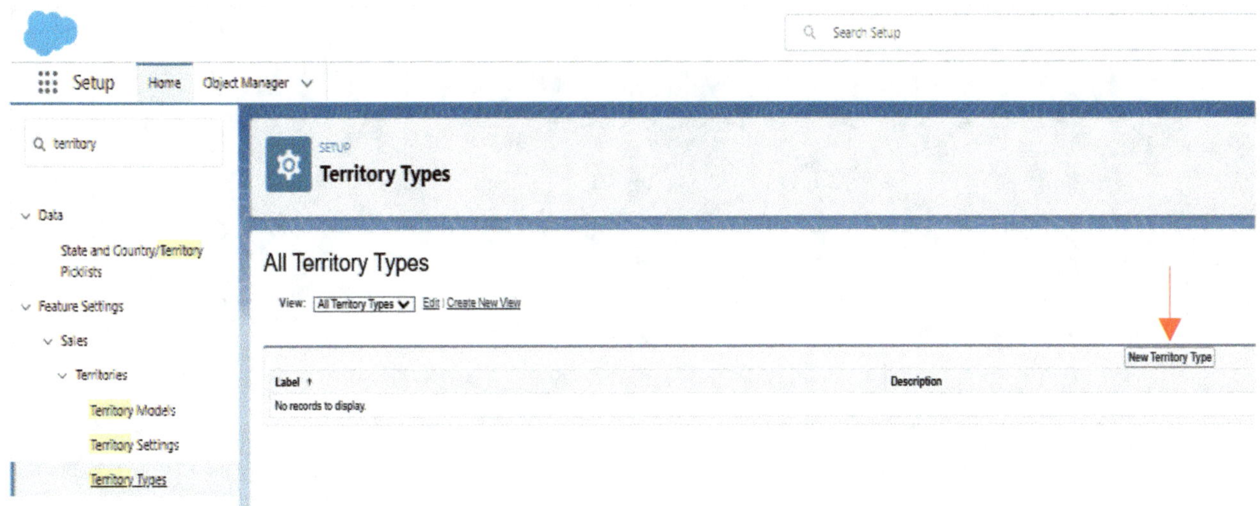

# PART II – Sales Cloud for Product Owners, IT Managers, and  Admins

*Put the label "Region", Priority 1 and click Save.*

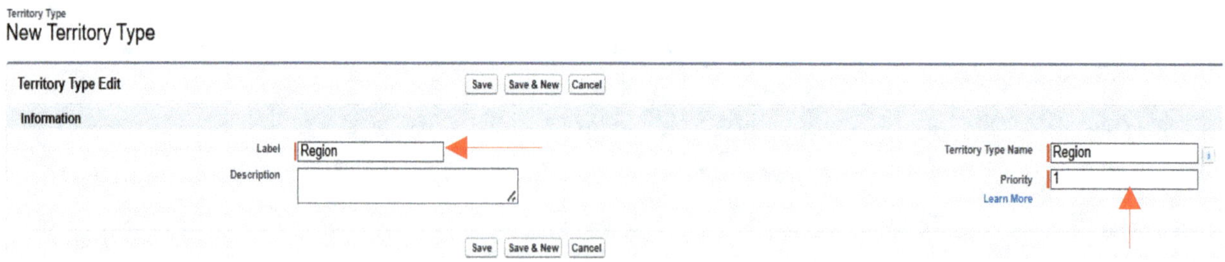

*Please return to the Territory Model and select the North Region.*

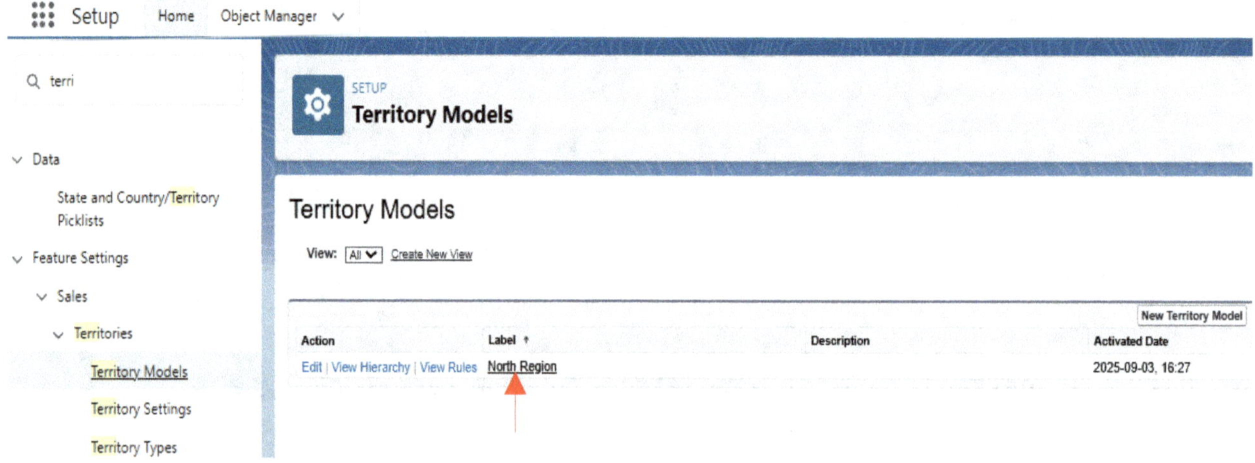

*Then click View Hierarchy.*

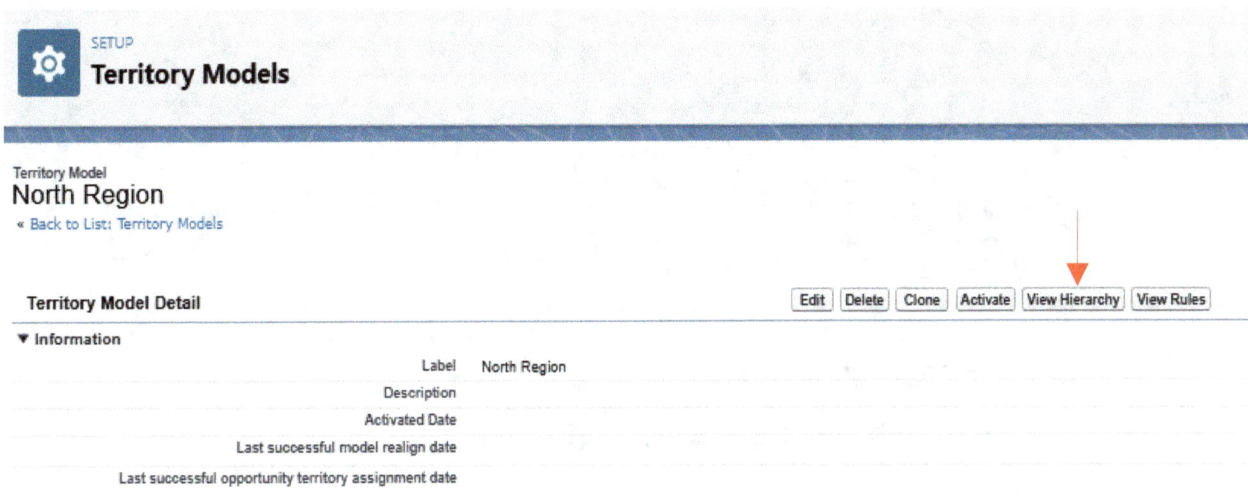

*Click Create Territory.*

## North Region Territory Hierarchy (Planning)

*Put Territory Label "Northwest", Select Region as a Territory Type and click Save & New.*

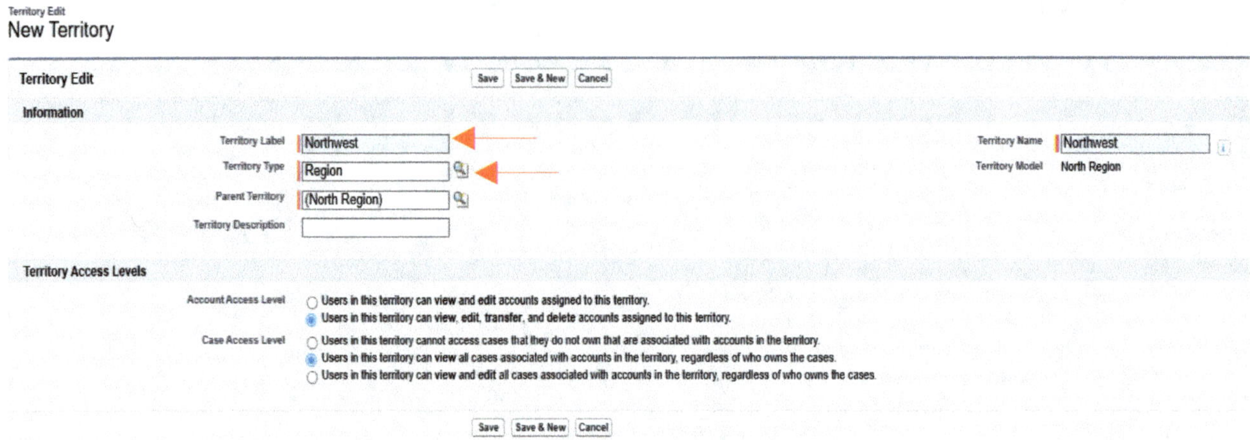

*Put Territory Label "Northeast", Select Region as a Territory Type and click Save.*

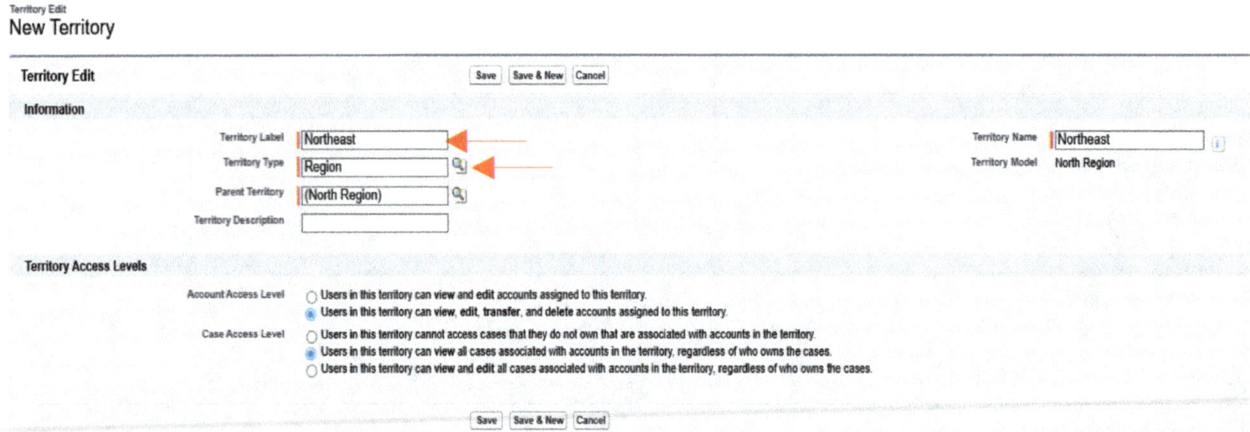

*Click Northwest Territory.*

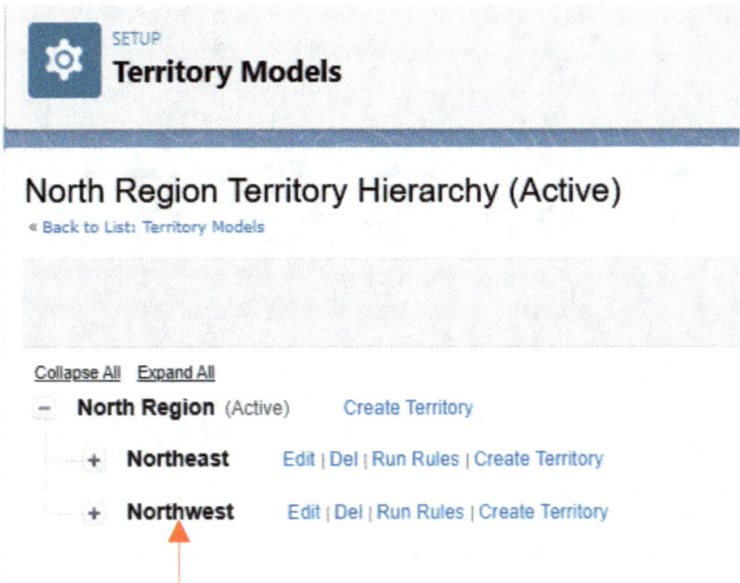

*Click Add Accounts in Northwest Territory.*

Territory
## Northwest
Hierarchy: <u>North Region</u> » Northwest



### Territory Detail

[ Edit ]  [ Delete ]  [ Clone ]  [ View Accounts ]

| | |
|---|---|
| Territory Label | Northwest |
| Territory Type | <u>Region</u> |
| Parent Territory | (North Region) |
| Territory Description | |

▼ **System Information**

| | |
|---|---|
| Last Modified By | <u>Konstantin Kapitanov</u>, 2025-09-03, 15:47 |

▼ **Territory Access Levels**

| | |
|---|---|
| Account Access Level | Users in this territory can view, edit, transfer, and delete accounts assigned to this territory. |
| Case Access Level | Users in this territory can view all cases associated with accounts in the territory, regardless of who owns the cases. |

### Assigned Users

[ Manage Users ]

No records to display

### Object Access

| Action | Object | Access Level |
|---|---|---|
| Edit | Lead | Transfer |

### Manually Assigned Accounts

[ Add Accounts ]  ←

No records to display

### Inherited Assignment Rules

No records to display

*Select Accounts for Northwest Territory and click Assign.*

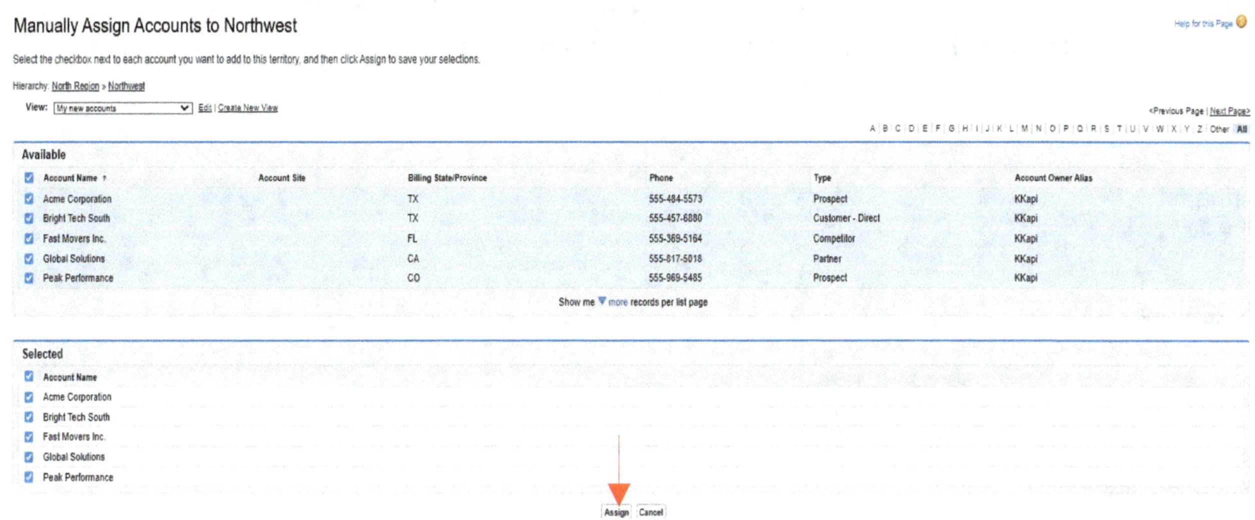

*Accounts now assigned to Northwest Territory.*

Territory
# Northwest
Hierarchy: North Region » Northwest

Assigned Users [0]  |  Object Access [1]  |  Manually Assigned Accounts [5]  |  Inherited Assignment Rules [0]  |

**Territory Detail**      [ Edit ] [ Delete ] [ Clone ] [ View Accounts ]

| | |
|---|---|
| Territory Label | Northwest |
| Territory Type | Region |
| Parent Territory | (North Region) |
| Territory Description | |

**▼ System Information**

| | |
|---|---|
| Last Modified By | Konstantin Kapitanov, 2025-09-03, 15:47 |

**▼ Territory Access Levels**

| | |
|---|---|
| Account Access Level | Users in this territory can view, edit, transfer, and delete accounts assigned to this territory. |
| Case Access Level | Users in this territory can view all cases associated with accounts in the territory, regardless of who owns the cases. |

**Assigned Users**      [ Manage Users ]

No records to display

**Object Access**

| Action | Object | Access Level |
|---|---|---|
| Edit | Lead | Transfer |

**Manually Assigned Accounts**      [ Add Accounts ]

| Action | Account Name |
|---|---|
| Remove | Fast Movers Inc. |
| Remove | Acme Corporation |
| Remove | Peak Performance |
| Remove | Global Solutions |
| Remove | Bright Tech South |

*Select the Northeast Territory as you did in the previous step for the Northwest Territory. Then, click Add Accounts within the Northeast Territory, choose the appropriate accounts, and click Assign to complete the process. Thereafter, click Manage Users in the Northeast Territory.*

Territory
### Northeast
Hierarchy: North Region » Northeast

Assigned Users [0]  |  Object Access [1]  |  Manually Assigned Accounts [5]  |  Inherited Assignment Rules [0]

**Territory Detail**     Edit | Delete | Clone | View Accounts

| | |
|---|---|
| Territory Label | **Northeast** |
| Territory Type | Region |
| Parent Territory | (North Region) |
| Territory Description | |

**▼ System Information**

Last Modified By    Konstantin Kapitanov, 2025-09-03, 15:48

**▼ Territory Access Levels**

Account Access Level    Users in this territory can view, **edit**, **transfer**, and **delete** accounts assigned to this territory.

Case Access Level    Users in this territory can view all cases associated with accounts in the territory, regardless of who owns the cases.

**Assigned Users**     Manage Users ←

No records to display

*Select users for Northeast Territory and click Save.*

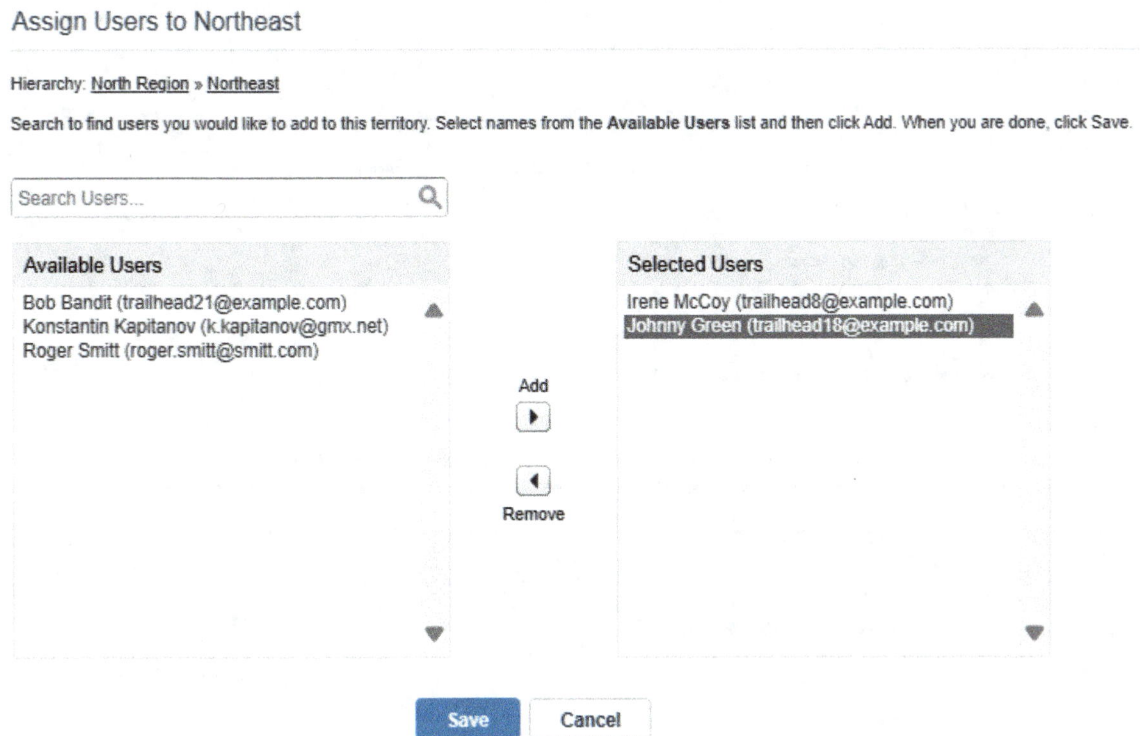

*The users are assigned for Northeast Territory.*

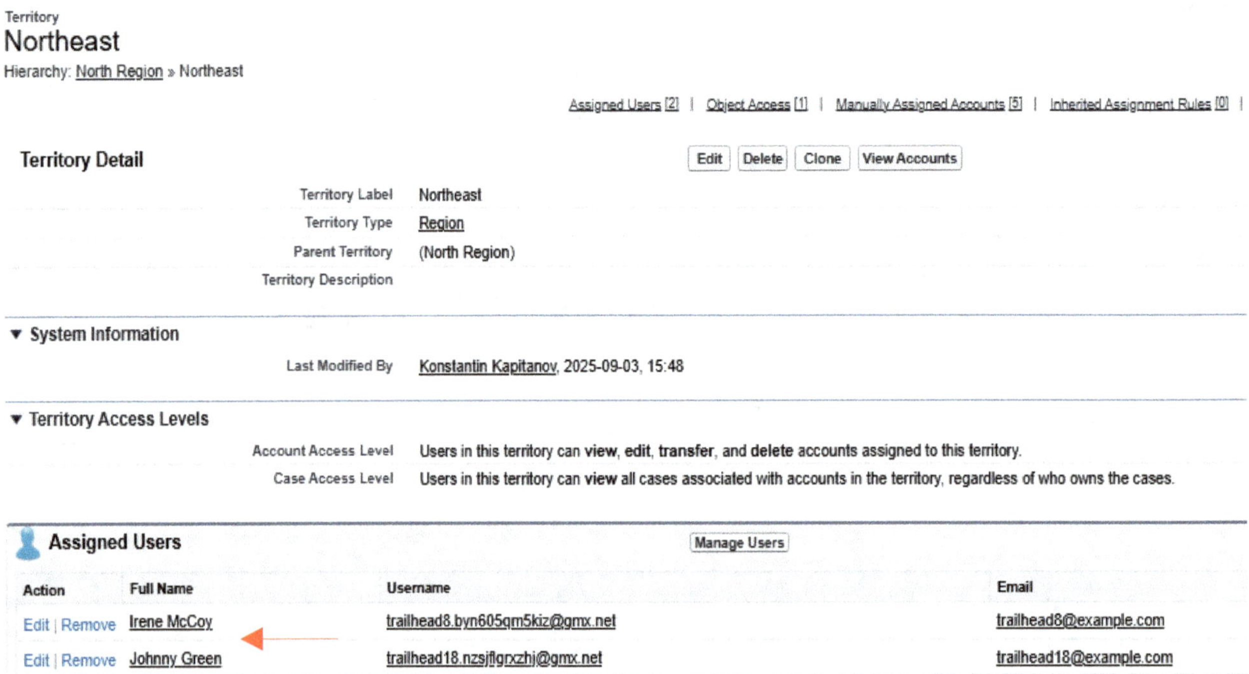

**Territory**

## Northeast

Hierarchy: North Region » Northeast

Assigned Users [2]  |  Object Access [1]  |  Manually Assigned Accounts [5]  |  Inherited Assignment Rules [0]  |

**Territory Detail**    [ Edit ] [ Delete ] [ Clone ] [ View Accounts ]

| | |
|---|---|
| Territory Label | Northeast |
| Territory Type | Region |
| Parent Territory | (North Region) |
| Territory Description | |

**▼ System Information**

| | |
|---|---|
| Last Modified By | Konstantin Kapitanov, 2025-09-03, 15:48 |

**▼ Territory Access Levels**

| | |
|---|---|
| Account Access Level | Users in this territory can view, edit, transfer, and delete accounts assigned to this territory. |
| Case Access Level | Users in this territory can view all cases associated with accounts in the territory, regardless of who owns the cases. |

**Assigned Users**    [ Manage Users ]

| Action | Full Name | Username | Email |
|---|---|---|---|
| Edit | Remove | Irene McCoy | trailhead8.byn605qm5kiz@gmx.net | trailhead8@example.com |
| Edit | Remove | Johnny Green | trailhead18.nzsjflgrxzhj@gmx.net | trailhead18@example.com |

*Please follow the same steps to manage users in the Northwest Territory by selecting them and clicking Assign, just as you did for the Northeast Territory. Thereafter, go back to the North Region and click the Activate button.*

# Chapter 10. Practice Lab with Example Data

## 10.1 Creating the Project Object

Often, closing a deal is not the end, it marks the beginning of a delivery phase that includes implementation, onboarding, and setup. For organizations using Sales Cloud, it is essential to track these projects directly in the CRM, providing visibility to sales teams and delivery leads.

In the next steps, we will focus on configuring Sales Cloud to support implementation project tracking for new customers. This setup introduces a custom object, automation, and summary features. The goal is to make implementation status, revenue, cost, and automation visible directly in the Opportunity workflow, improving both accountability and customer satisfaction.

You will create a new custom object called Project in the first step to extend the standard Salesforce data model and track implementation work. This object will serve as the container for project-related information and will be linked to Opportunities.

*Go to Setup → Object Manager → Create → Custom Object.*

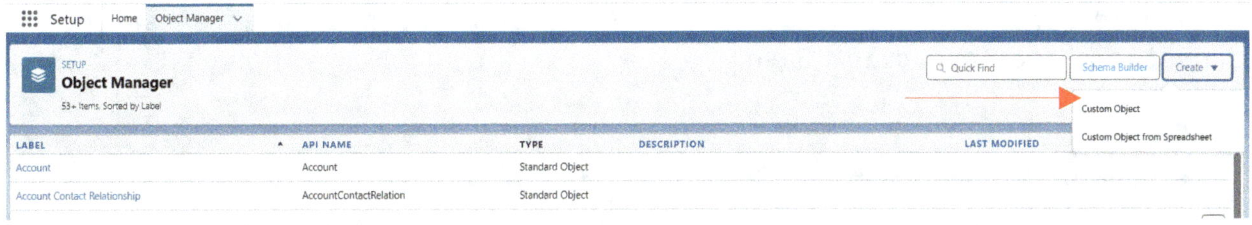

*Enable the options Allow Reports, Allow Activities, and Track Field History to make the object reportable and auditable.*

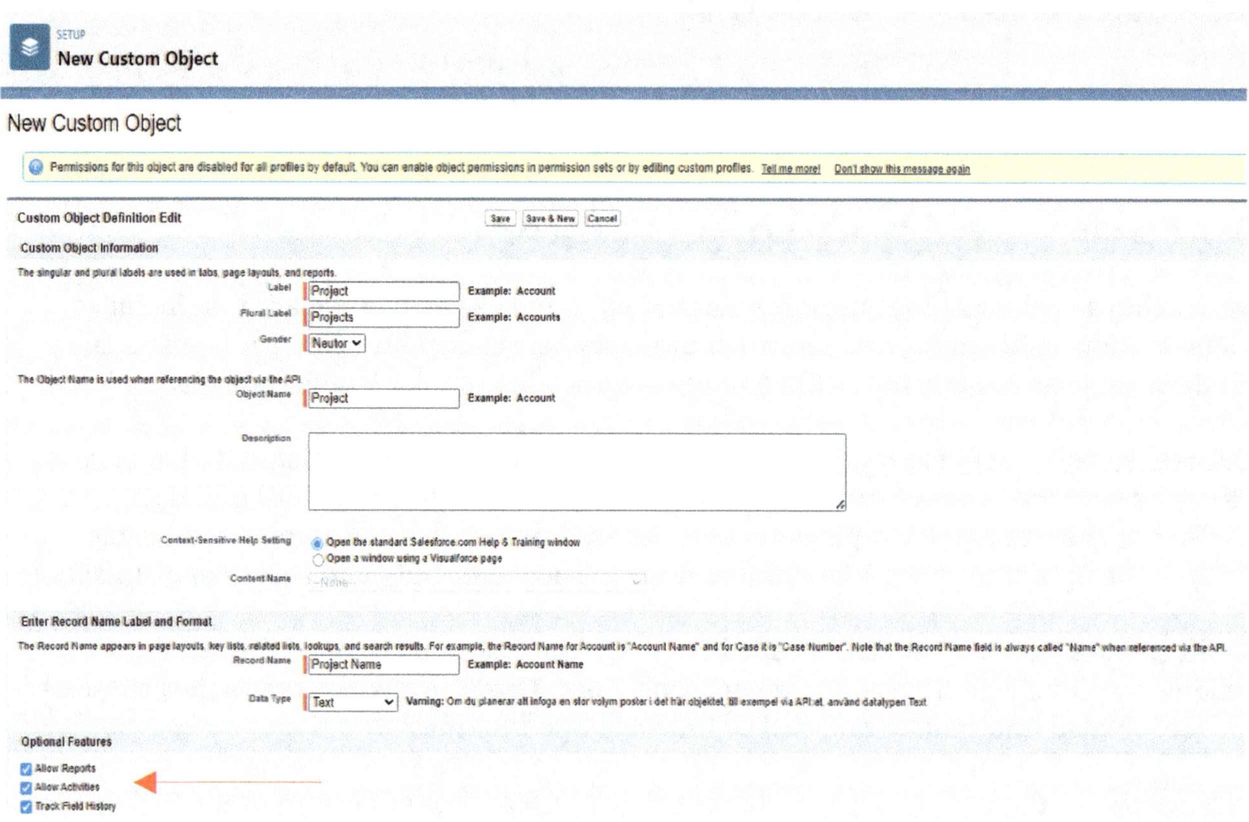

*After enable also the option Launch the New Custom Tab Wizard after saving this custom object and click Save.*

*Use this wizard to assign a tab icon and color, and then add the object to the Sales App Navigation Bar so that it is visible for end users and click Next.*

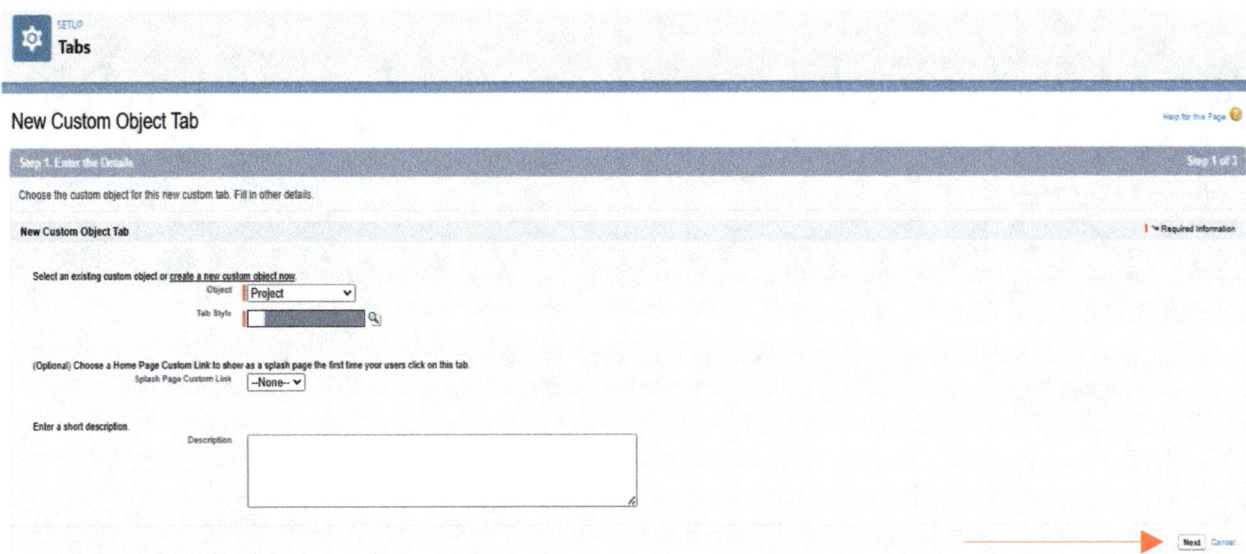

*Choose the user profiles for which the new custom tab will be available. For simplicity, select Visible for all profiles as the default, click Next, and Save. You may also review or adjust tab visibility later based on each profile's details and edit pages.*

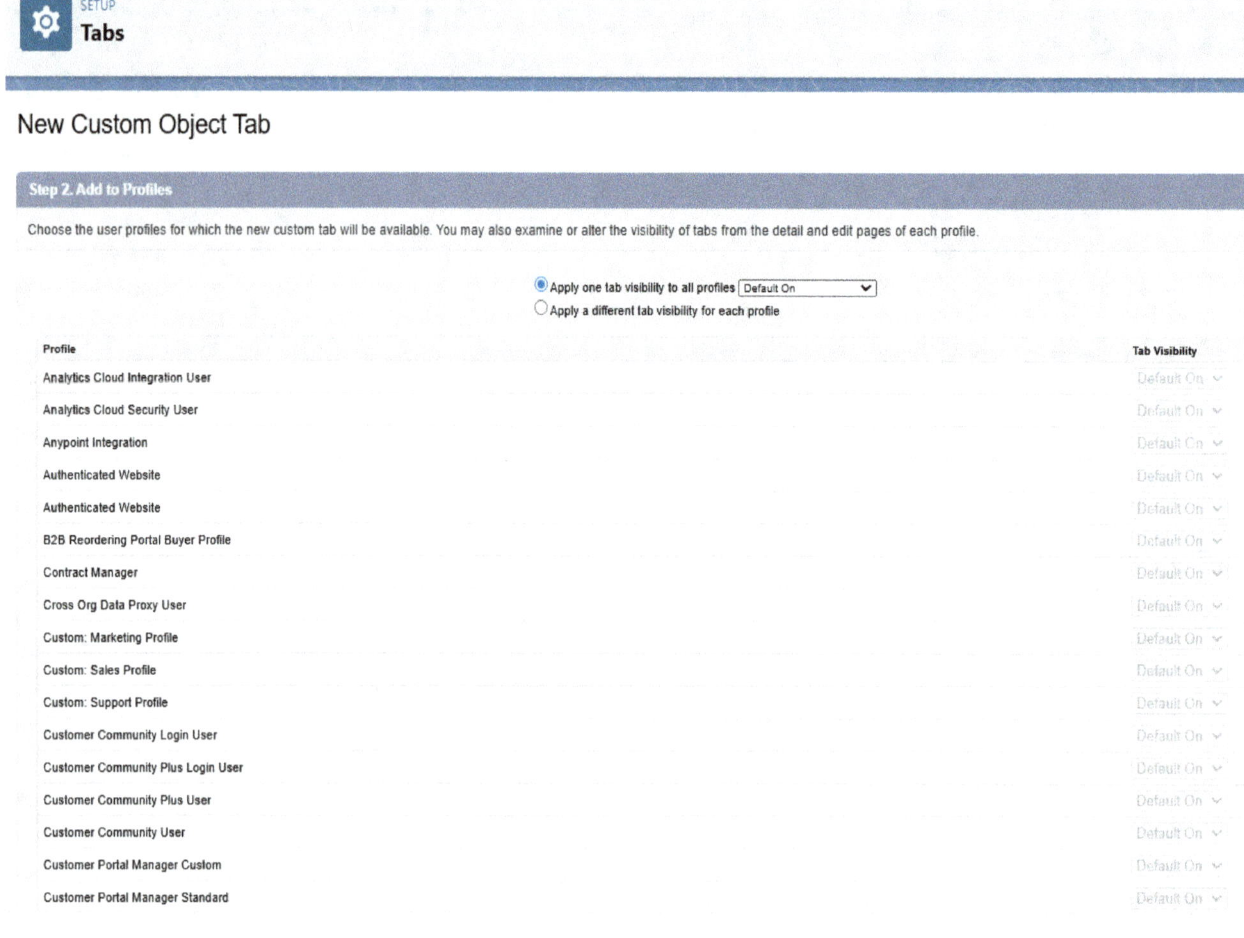



| Profile | Tab Visibility |
|---|---|
| Analytics Cloud Integration User | Default On |
| Analytics Cloud Security User | Default On |
| Anypoint Integration | Default On |
| Authenticated Website | Default On |
| Authenticated Website | Default On |
| B2B Reordering Portal Buyer Profile | Default On |
| Contract Manager | Default On |
| Cross Org Data Proxy User | Default On |
| Custom: Marketing Profile | Default On |
| Custom: Sales Profile | Default On |
| Custom: Support Profile | Default On |
| Customer Community Login User | Default On |
| Customer Community Plus Login User | Default On |
| Customer Community Plus User | Default On |
| Customer Community User | Default On |
| Customer Portal Manager Custom | Default On |
| Customer Portal Manager Standard | Default On |

*After completing the wizard, add the object to the Sales App Navigation Bar so that it is visible for end users.*

*Go to Setup → App Manager → Select App Name Sales → Developer Name LightningSales →  Click Edit*

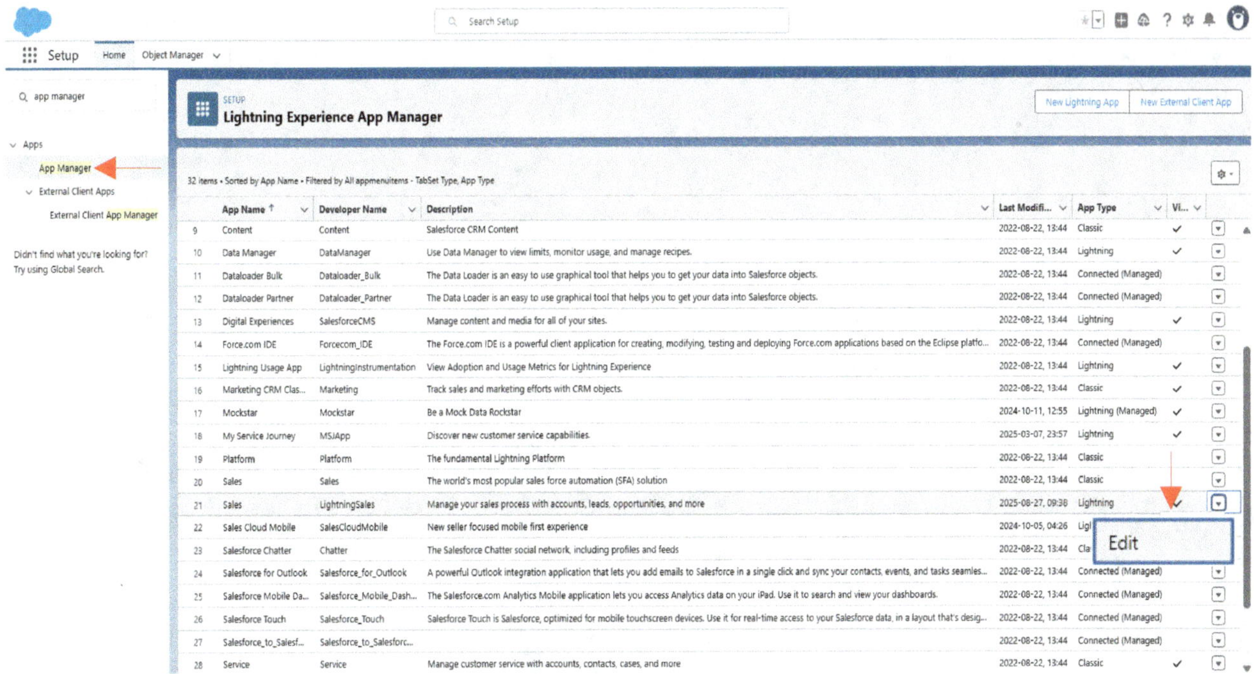

*Go to Navigation Items and search for Project in Available Items.*

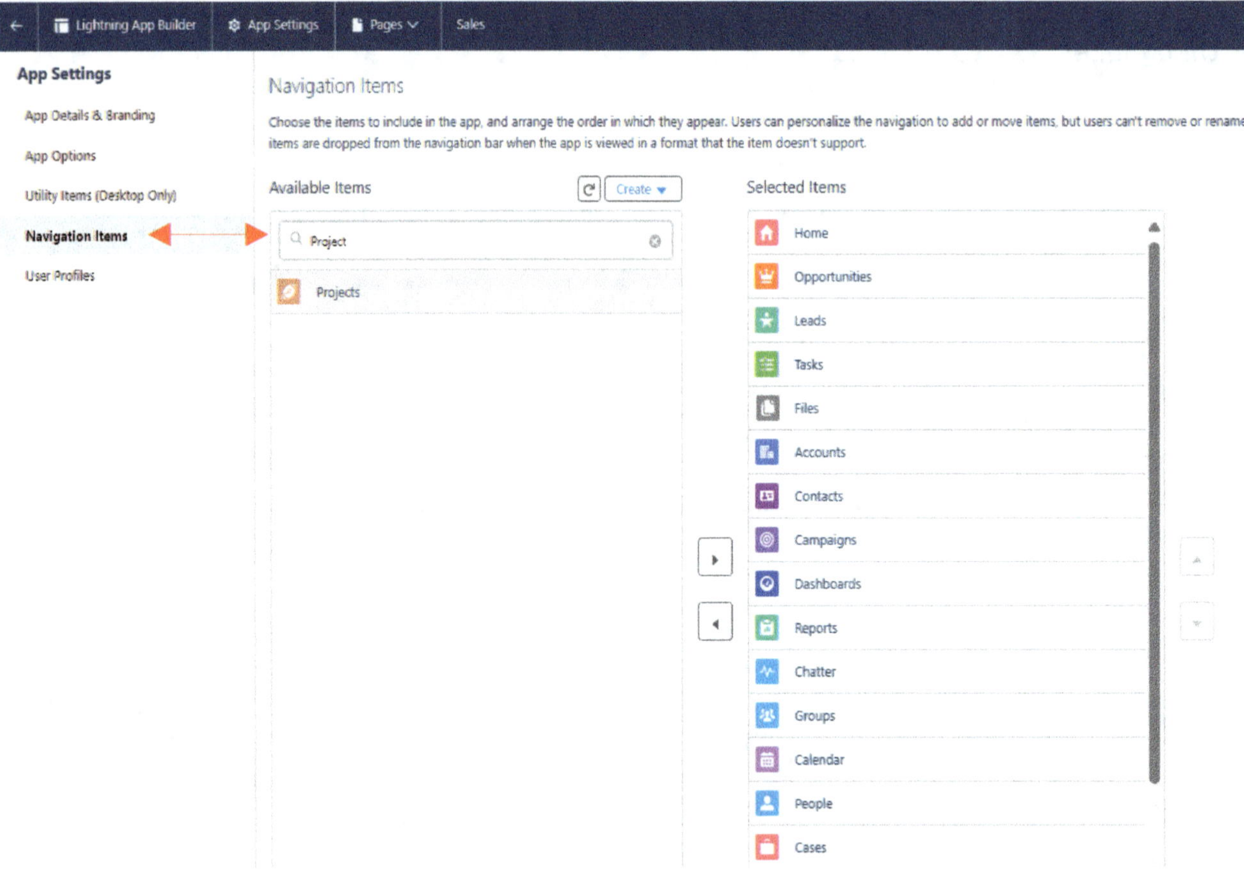

*Add the Project to Selected Items and Save.*

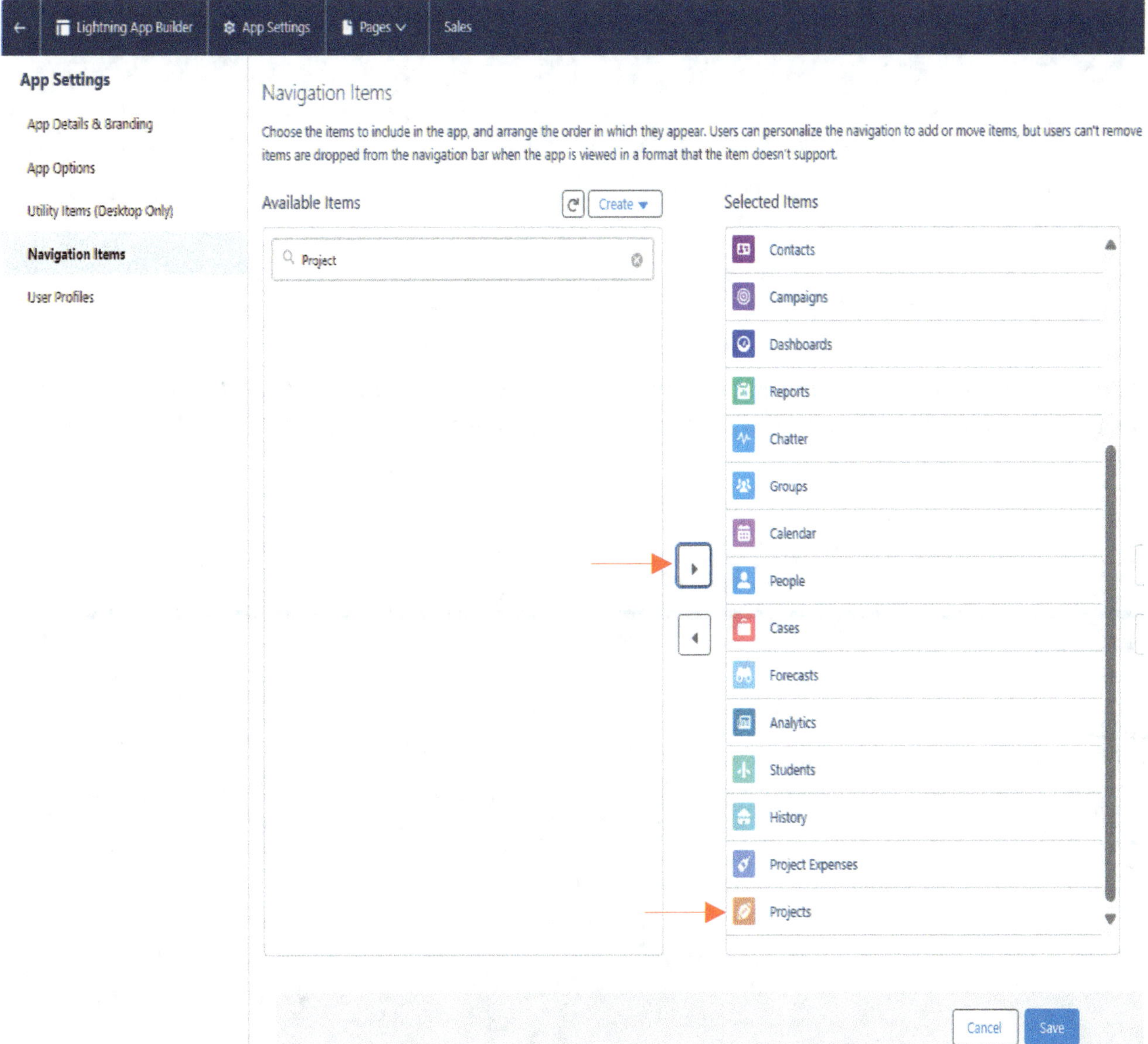

# PART II — Sales Cloud for Product Owners, IT Managers, and  Admins

*Open a new created custom object Project in Setup→Object Manager.*

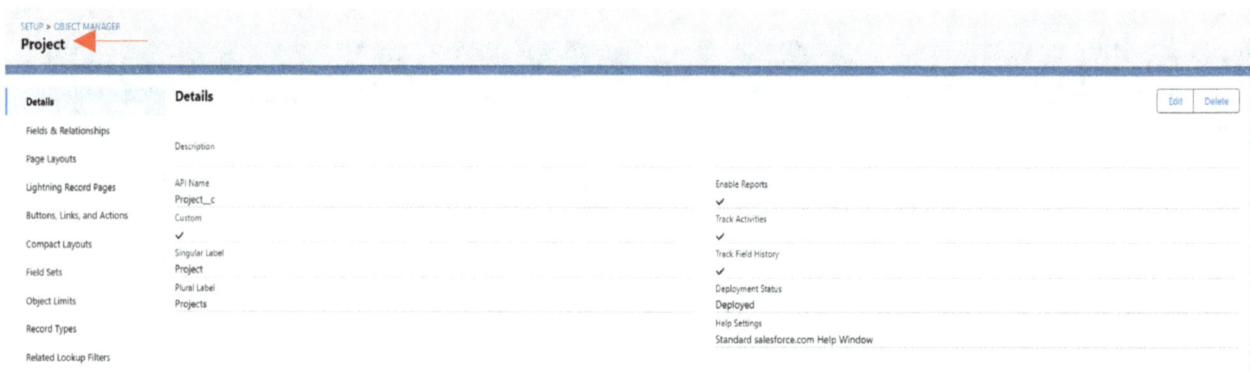

*In this newly created custom object we will define custom fields to capture essential project information. Go to Fields & Relationships and click the New button.*

***Opportunity as a Lookup to Opportunity field:*** *Select Lookup Relationship, choose Opportunity as the related object. This ensures each Project record links back to the originating Opportunity.*

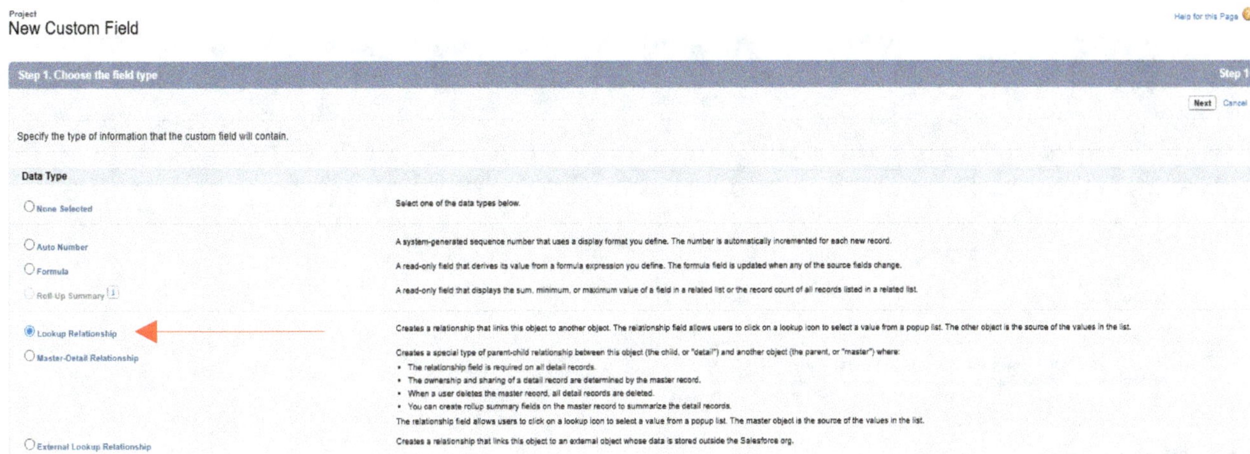

*Choose Related To Opportunity in the selection list and click Next.*

*Label the field as "Opportunity", and select the check box Always require a value in this field to save a record. Click Next.*

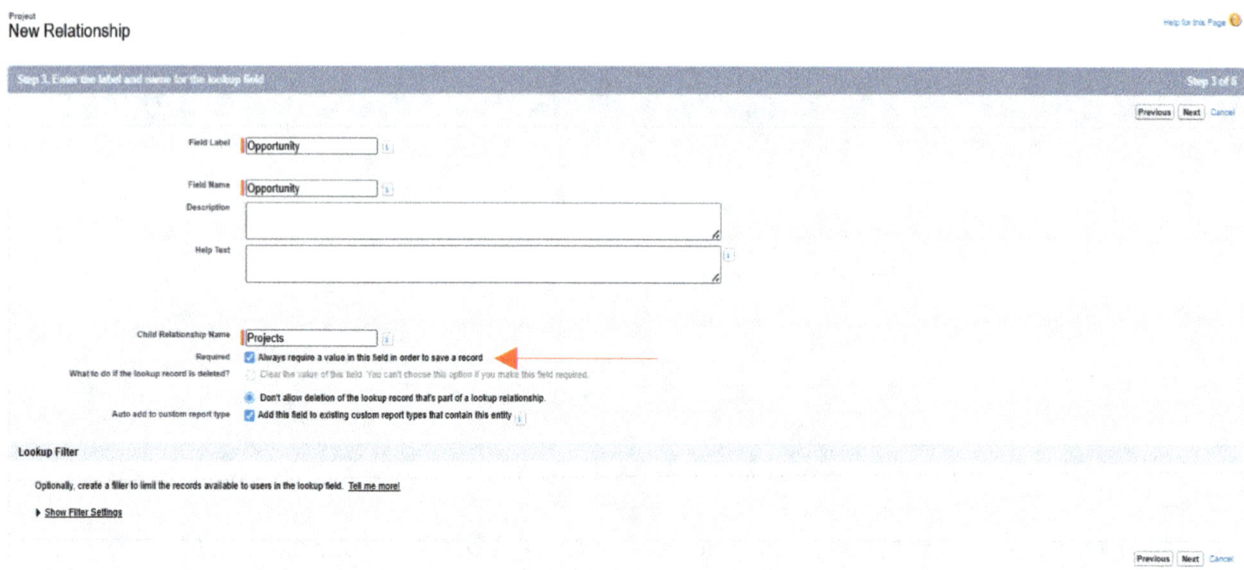

*Once Visible is selected, click Next.*

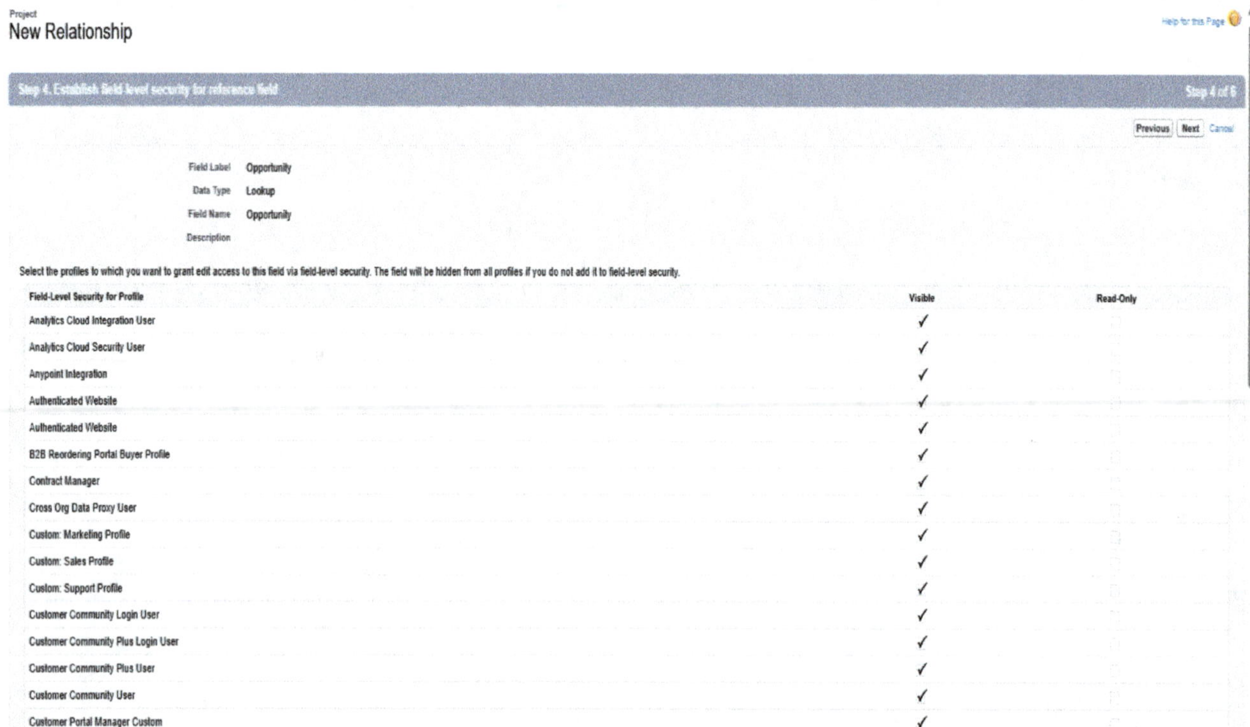

*Check if this field is assigned to Project Layout and click Next.*

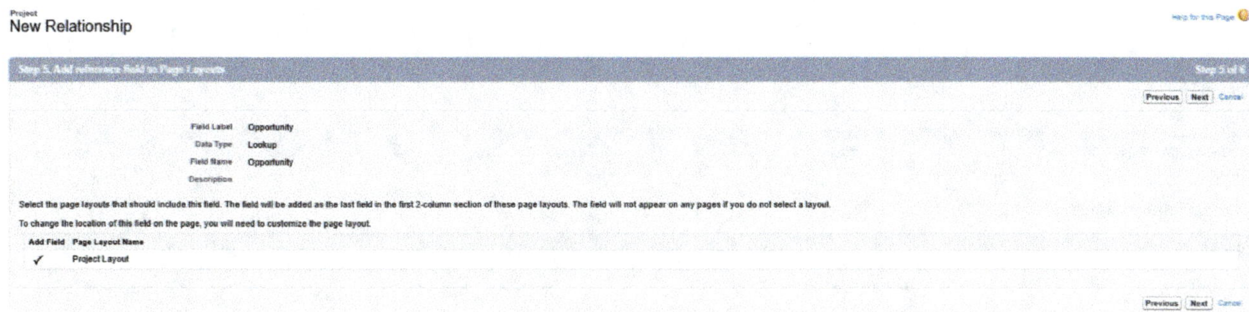

*Select all available Layouts and click Save.*

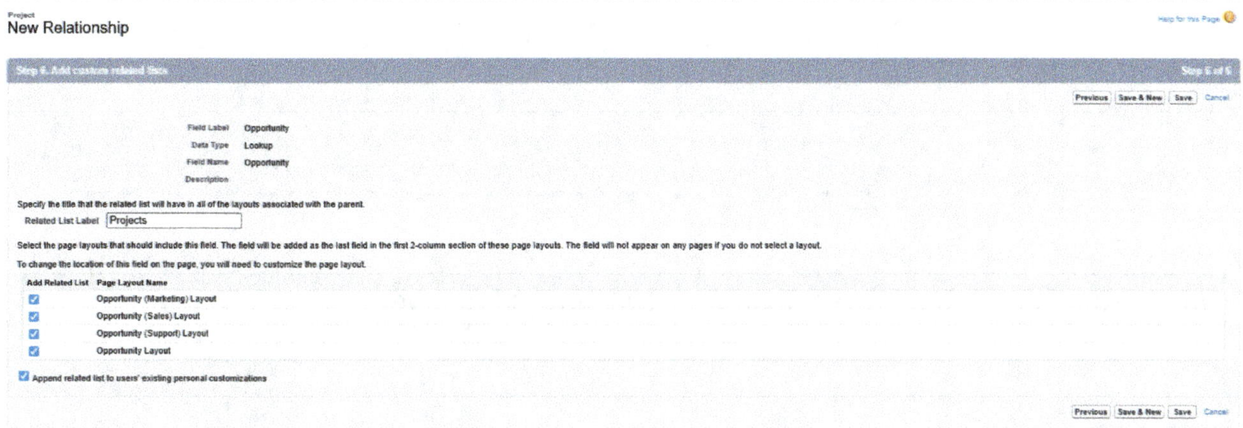

*A new lookup Opportunity custom field is created now.*

## Fields & Relationships

5 Items, Sorted by Field Label

| FIELD LABEL | FIELD NAME | DATA TYPE |
|---|---|---|
| Created By | CreatedById | Lookup(User) |
| Last Modified By | LastModifiedById | Lookup(User) |
| Opportunity | Opportunity__c | Lookup(Opportunity) |
| Owner | OwnerId | Lookup(User,Group) |
| Project Name | Name | Text(80) |

# PART II — Sales Cloud for Product Owners, IT Managers, and  Admins

***Expected Start Date as a Date field:*** *Add a new custom Date field to capture when the project is planned to begin. Select Date and click Next.*

*Put the Field Label "Expected Start Date" and click Next.*

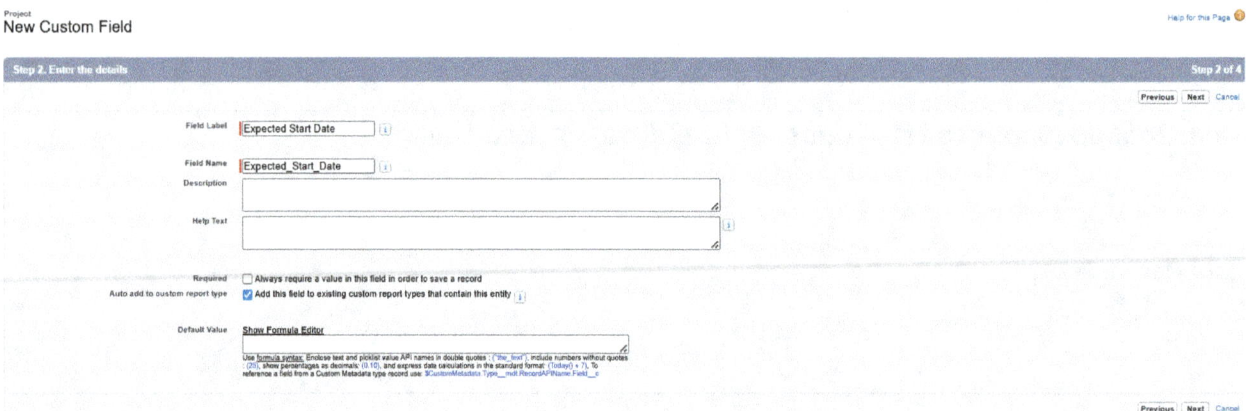

*Select Visible for all profiles and click Next.*

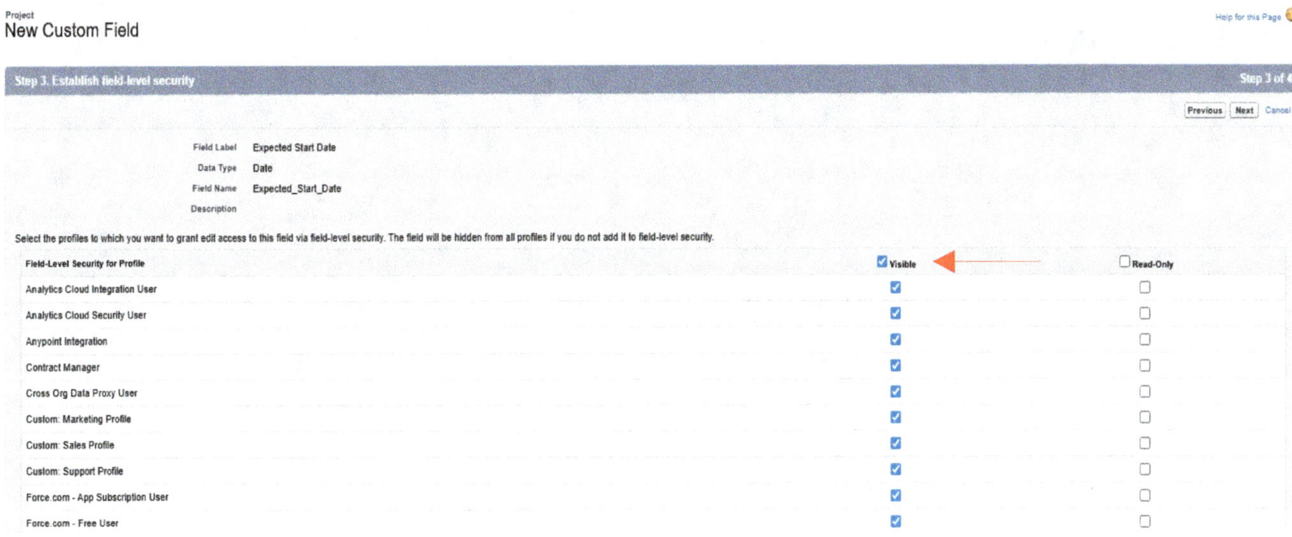

*Click Save.*

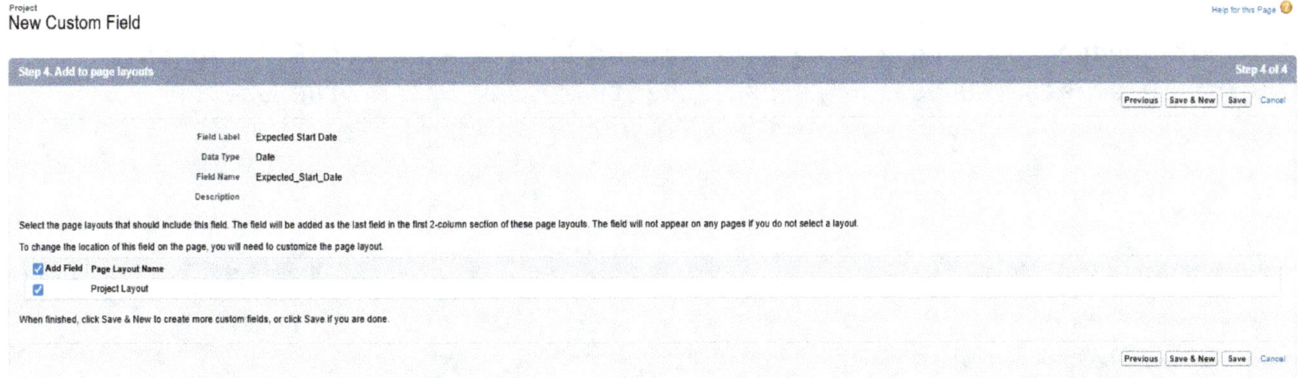

# PART II — Sales Cloud for Product Owners, IT Managers, and Admins

*A new data custom field Expected Start Date is created now.*

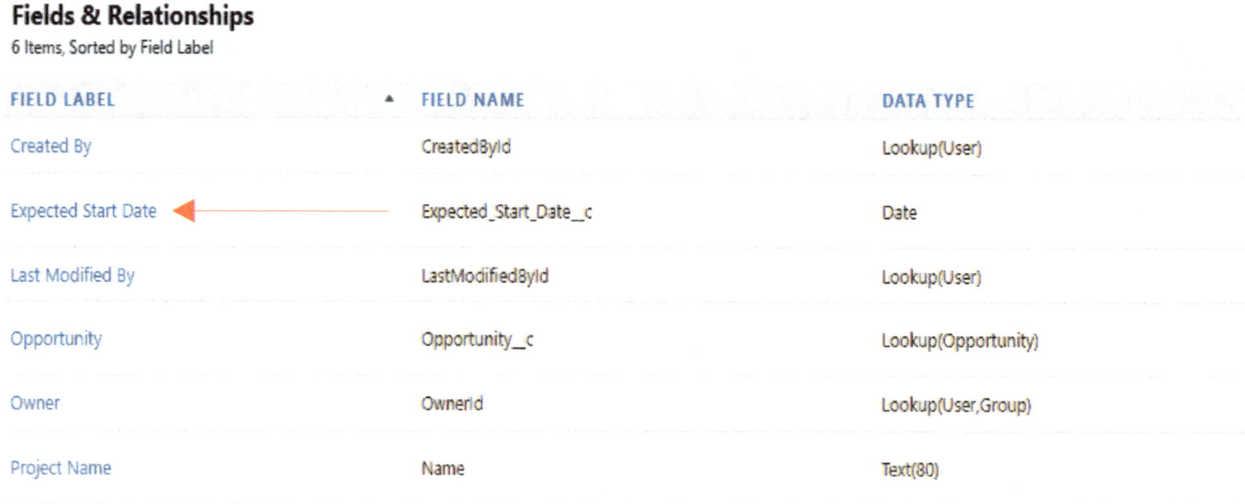

**Expected End Date as a Date field:** Add a Date field to capture the planned completion date by following the same steps used to create the previous custom field Expected Start Date.

**Project Manager as a Lookup to User field:** Create a Lookup Relationship field. This lets you assign responsibility to any Salesforce user.

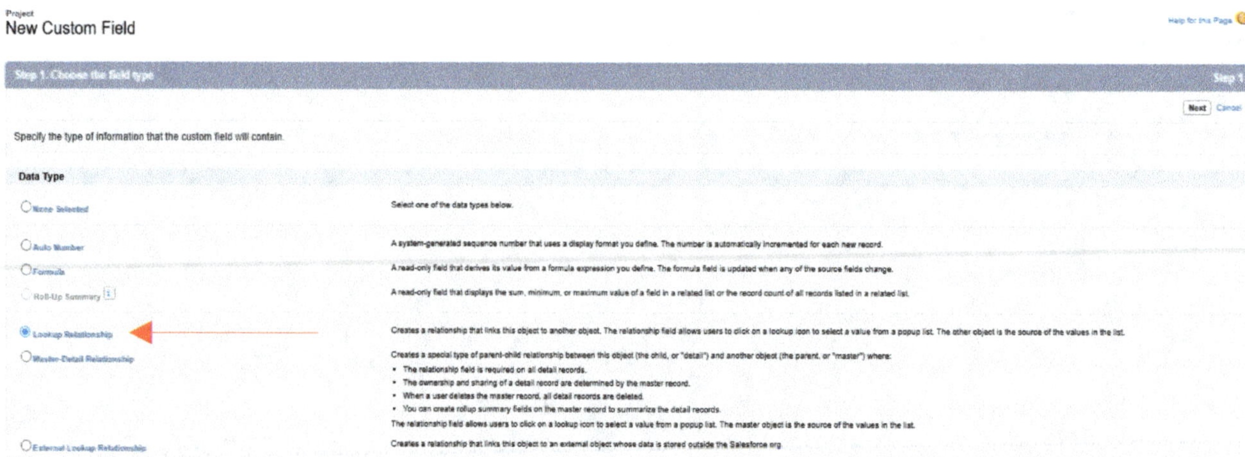

*Choose Related To User in selection list. Click Next.*

*Put the Field Label "Project Manager" and click Next.*

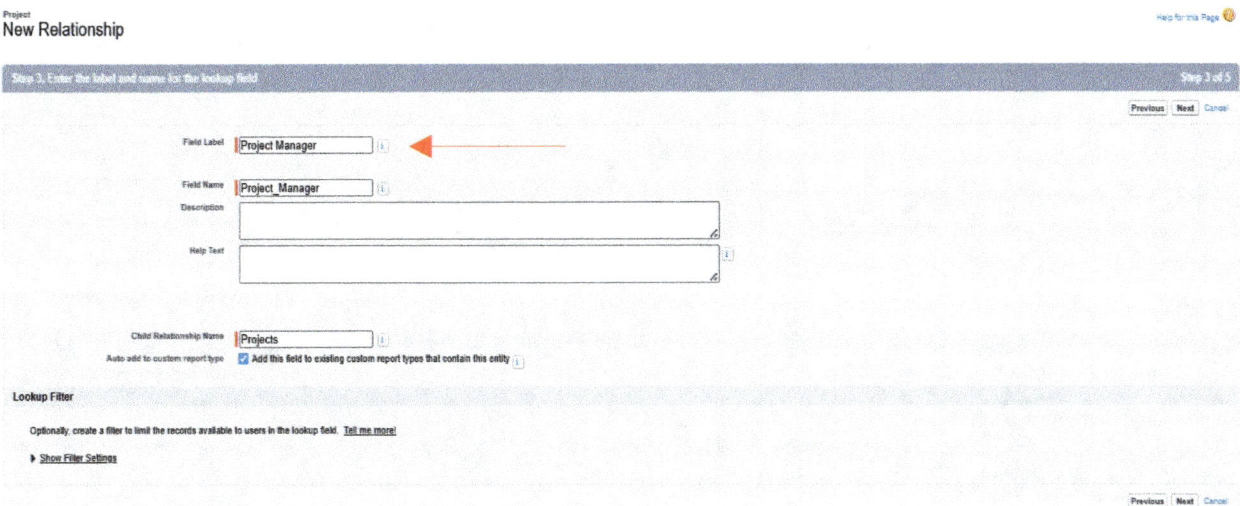

*Select Visible for all profiles and click Next.*

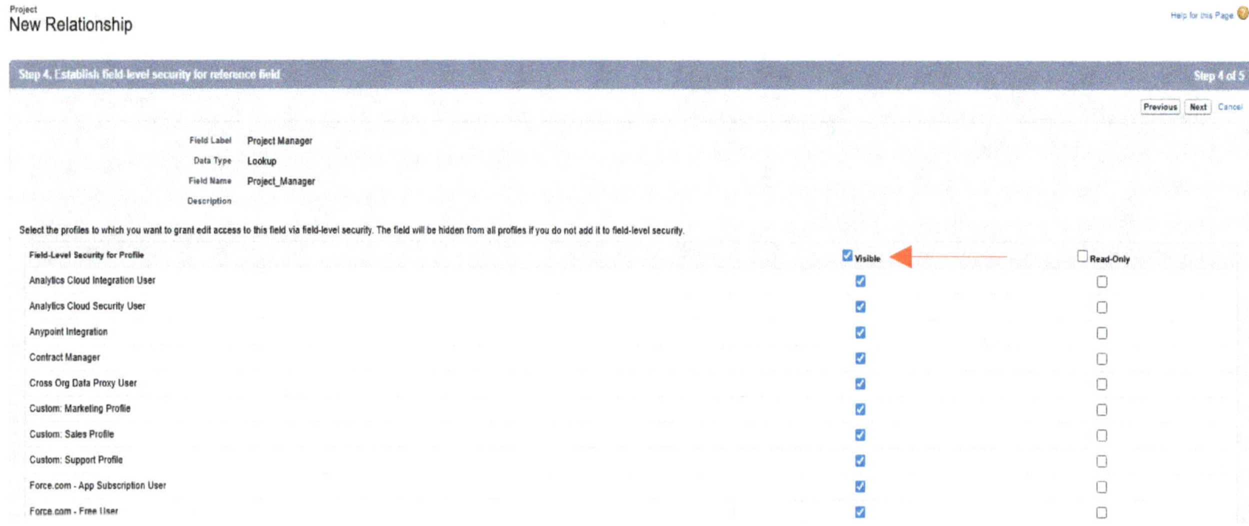

*Click Save.*

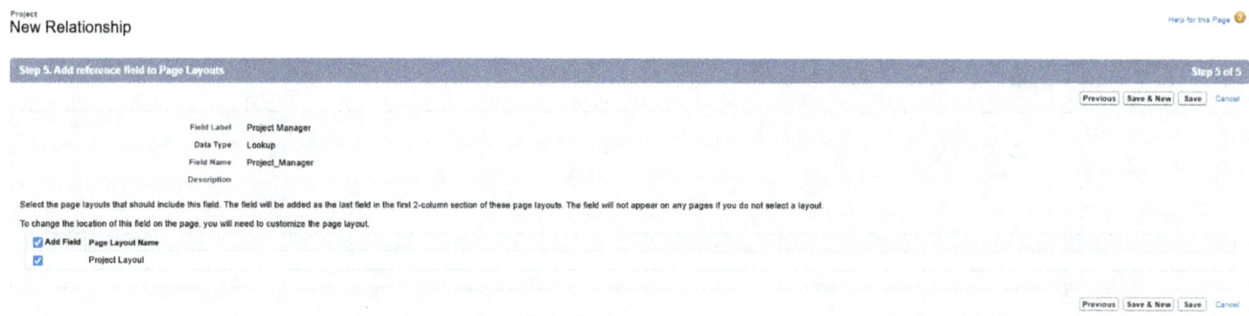

*A new lookup custom field Project Manager is created now.*

## Fields & Relationships

7 Items, Sorted by Field Label

| FIELD LABEL | FIELD NAME | DATA TYPE |
| --- | --- | --- |
| Created By | CreatedById | Lookup(User) |
| Expected Start Date | Expected_Start_Date__c | Date |
| Last Modified By | LastModifiedById | Lookup(User) |
| Opportunity | Opportunity__c | Lookup(Opportunity) |
| Owner | OwnerId | Lookup(User,Group) |
| Project Manager | Project_Manager__c | Lookup(User) |
| Project Name | Name | Text(80) |

***Status as a Picklist field:*** *Add a Picklist field by selecting Picklist. This field helps track project progress. Click Next.*

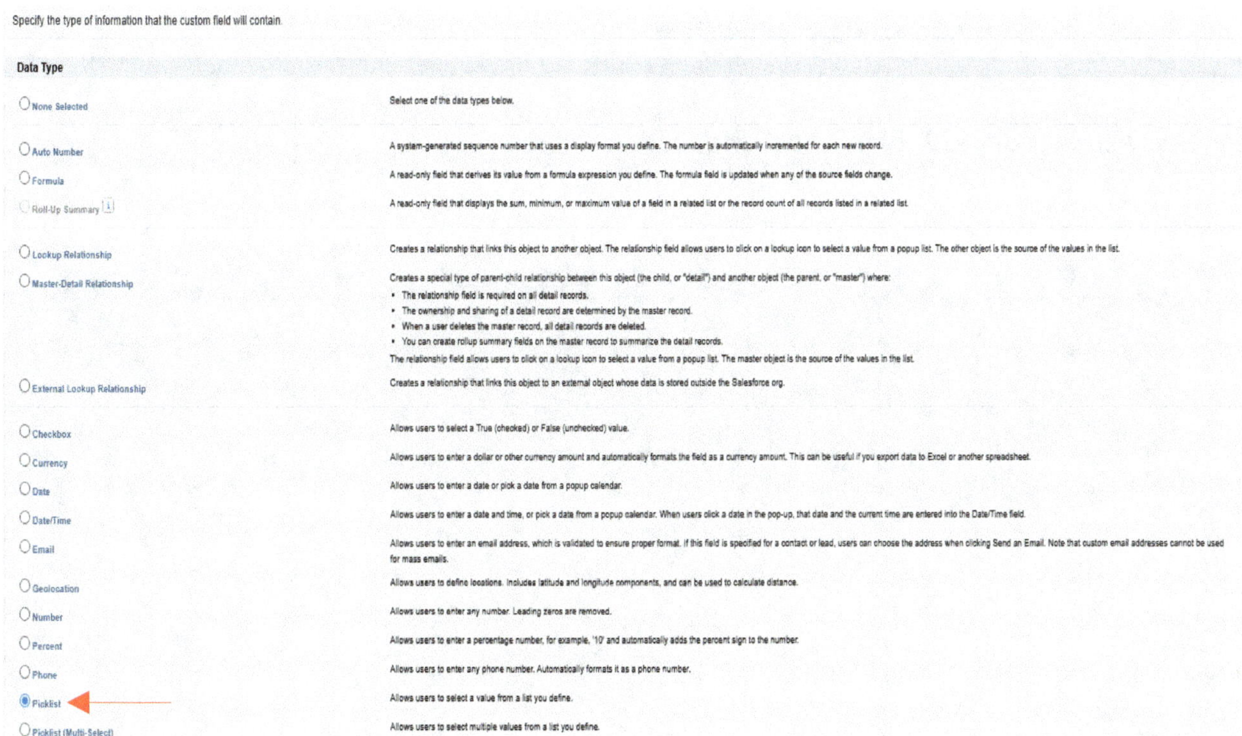

*Put the Field Label "Status" and enter values such as Planned, In Progress, and Completed separated by a new line. Click Next.*

*Select Visible for all profiles and click Next.*

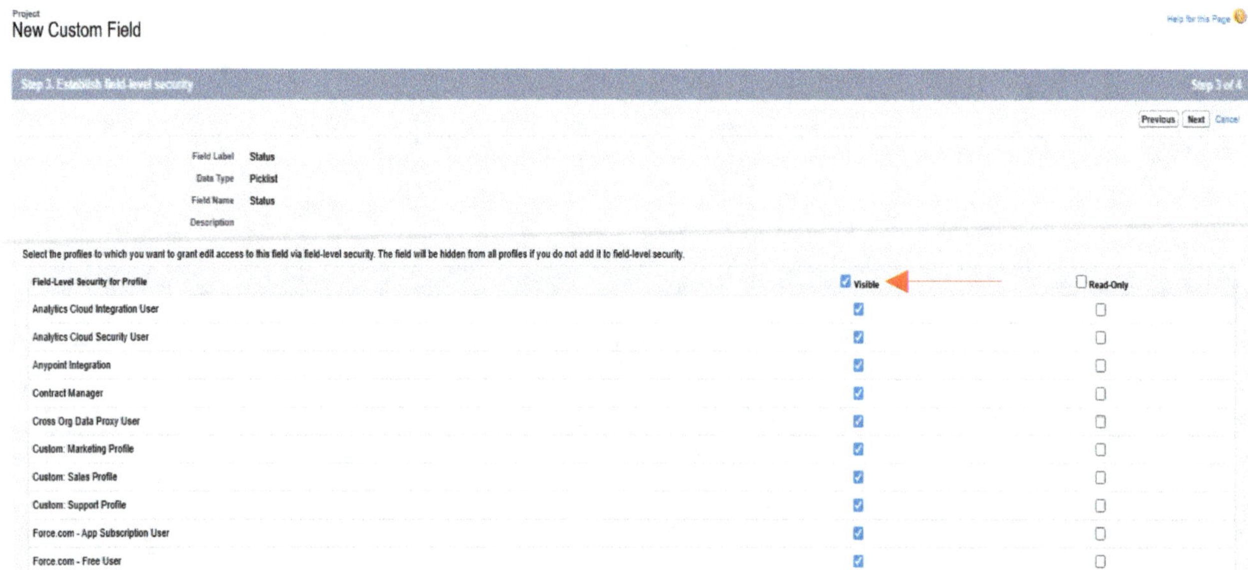

*Click Save.*

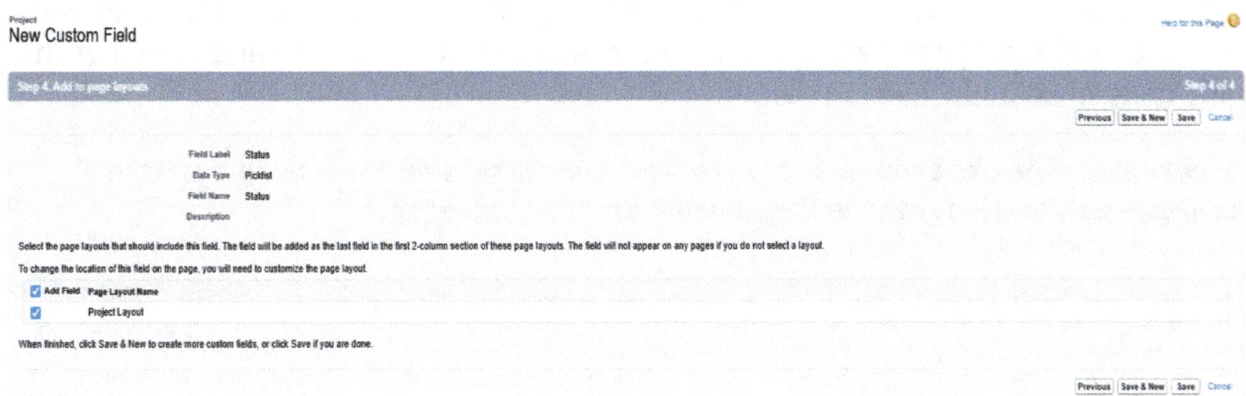

*A new custom Picklist field Status is created now.*

## Fields & Relationships

9 Items, Sorted by Field Label

| FIELD LABEL ▲ | FIELD NAME | DATA TYPE |
|---|---|---|
| Created By | CreatedById | Lookup(User) |
| Expected End Date | Expected_End_Date__c | Date |
| Expected Start Date | Expected_Start_Date__c | Date |
| Last Modified By | LastModifiedById | Lookup(User) |
| Opportunity | Opportunity__c | Lookup(Opportunity) |
| Owner | OwnerId | Lookup(User,Group) |
| Project Manager | Project_Manager__c | Lookup(User) |
| Project Name | Name | Text(80) |
| Status | Status__c | Picklist |

# 10.2 Creating the Project Expense Object

To support financial tracking, create an additional related custom object named Project Expense. This object stores detailed cost and revenue estimate entries associated with already created custom object Project.

*To create this new custom object, follow the same steps we used for the custom object Project at the beginning of this chapter.*

**Note!** When you create a custom object, Salesforce does not automatically create a Tab and App Settings in Lightning App Builder for it. Without a Tab, it cannot appear in the menu. To make your new custom object visible, follow the same steps that you used for the custom object Project.

Once your new custom object, Project Expense, is created, we'll add new custom fields to it as well.

***Project as a Master-Detail Relationship to a Project field:*** *To Links each expense record back to its parent project. Select a new Master-Detail Relationship custom field and click Next.*

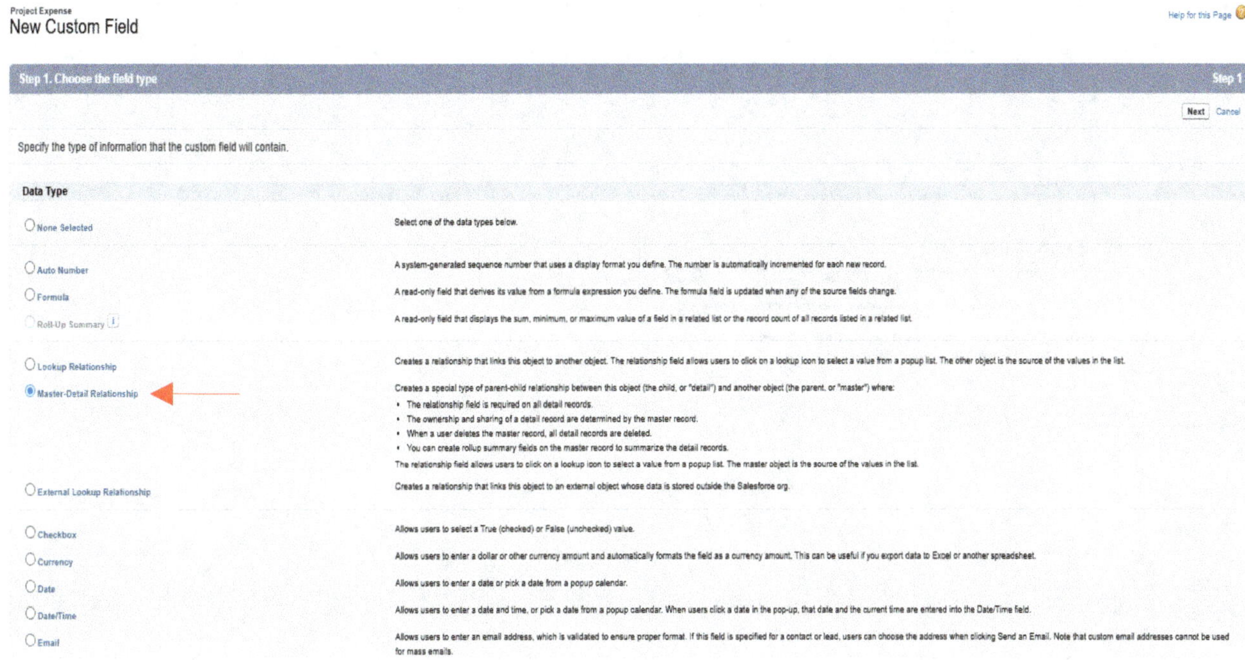

*Choose Related to Project in selection list. Click Next.*

*Put the Field Label "Project" and click Next.*

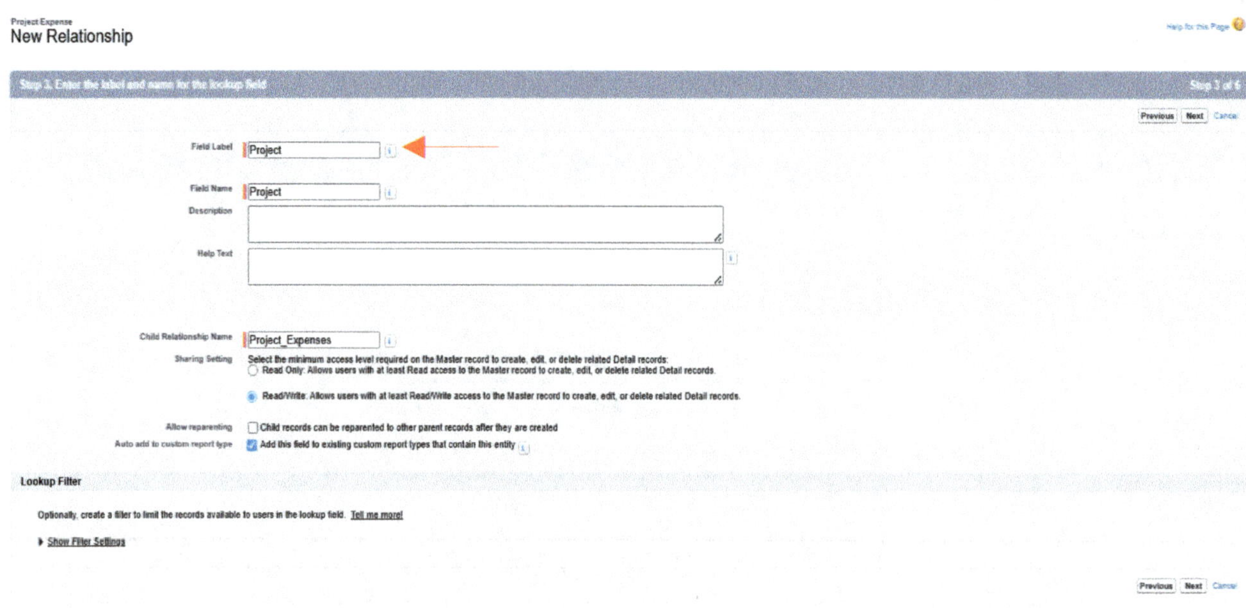

*Then Visible is selected click Next.*

*Check if this field is assigned to Project Layout and click Next.*

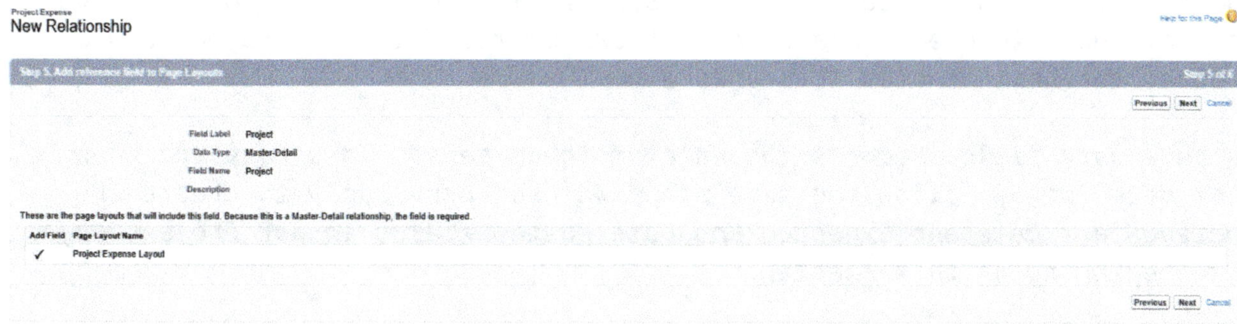

*Click Save.*

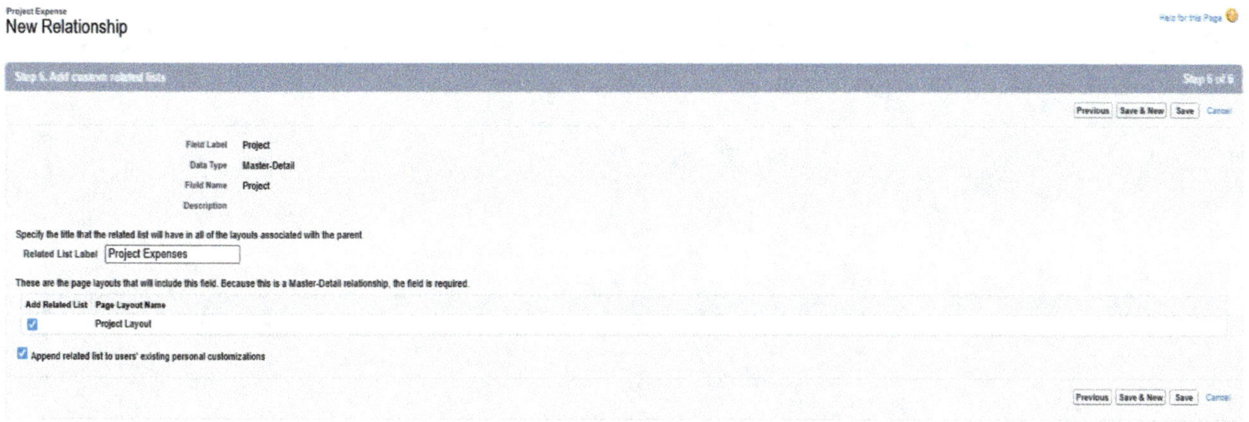

*A new Master-Detail Relationship Project field has been created on the Project Expense object.*

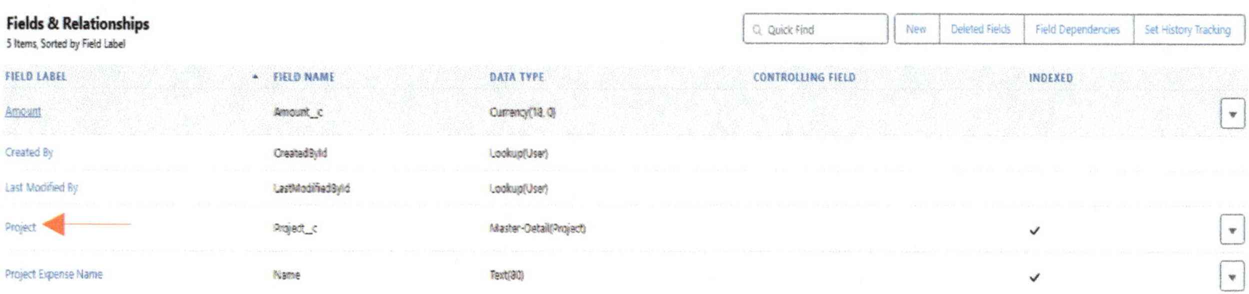

***Type as a Picklist field:*** *Create a Picklist with the values Internal, External, and Billing Estimate. These categories will be used in roll-up summaries later. To create this new custom field, follow the same steps we used previously to create Status as a Picklist field in our Project custom object at the beginning of this chapter.*

***Date as a Date field:*** *Records the date of the expense. To create this new custom date field, follow the same steps we used previously to create the Expected Start Date and Expected End Date custom fields in our Project object at the beginning of this chapter.*

***Amount as a Currency field:*** *Captures the monetary value of the record. Select a new currency field and click Next.*

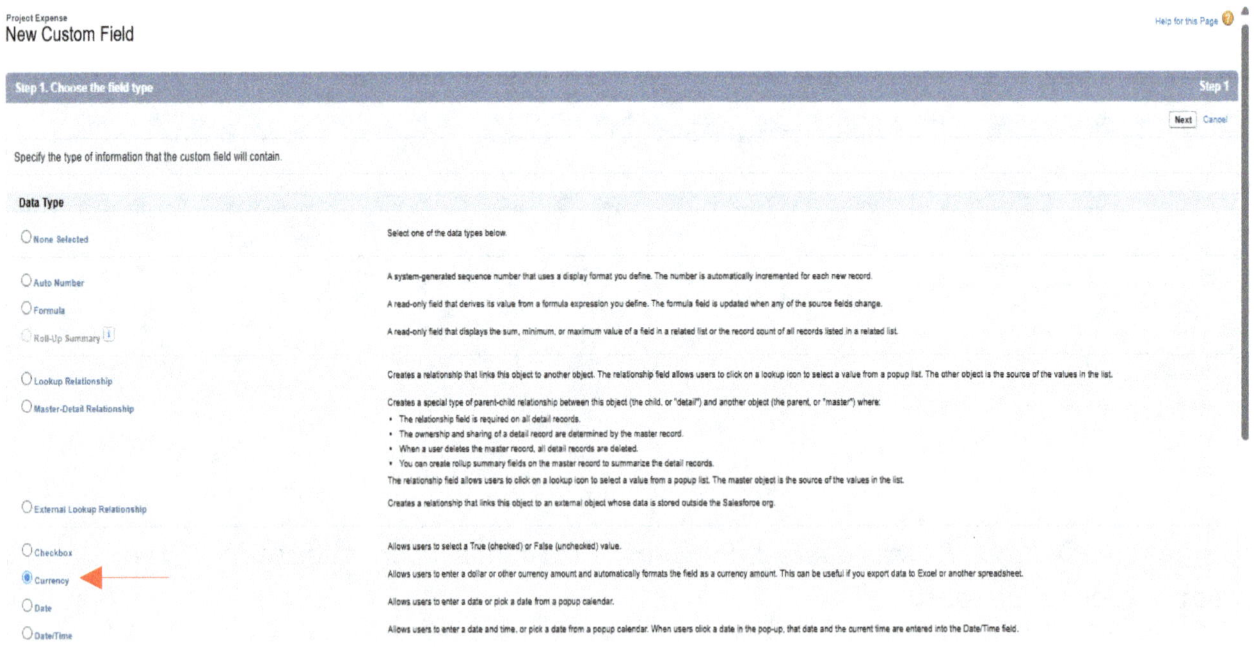

*Put the Field Label "Amount" and click Next.*

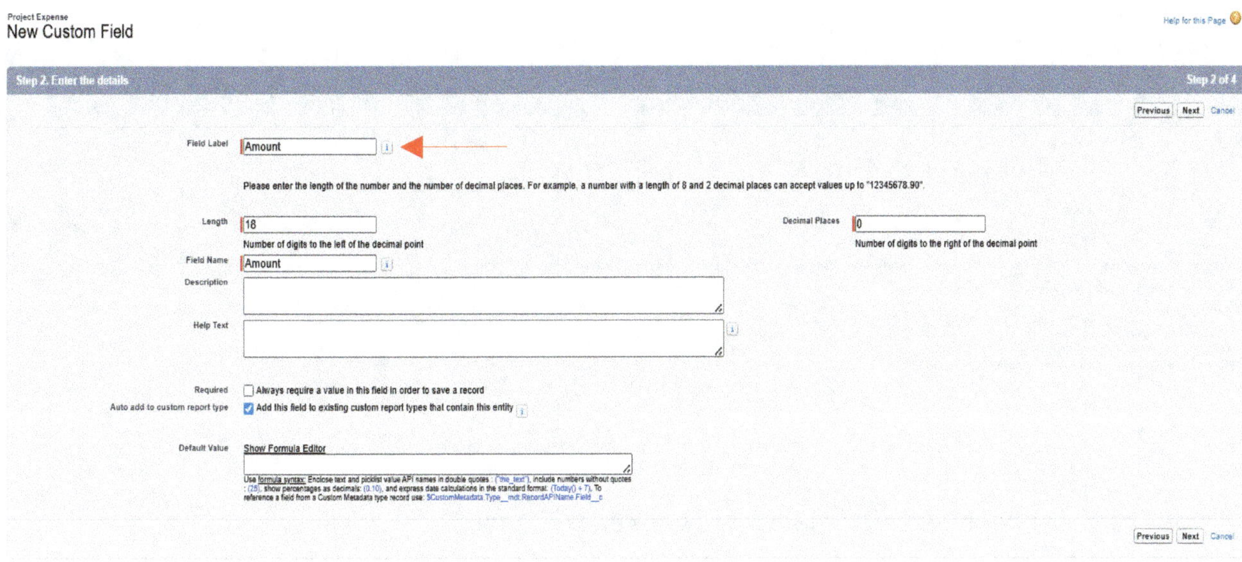

*Select Visible for all profiles and click Next.*

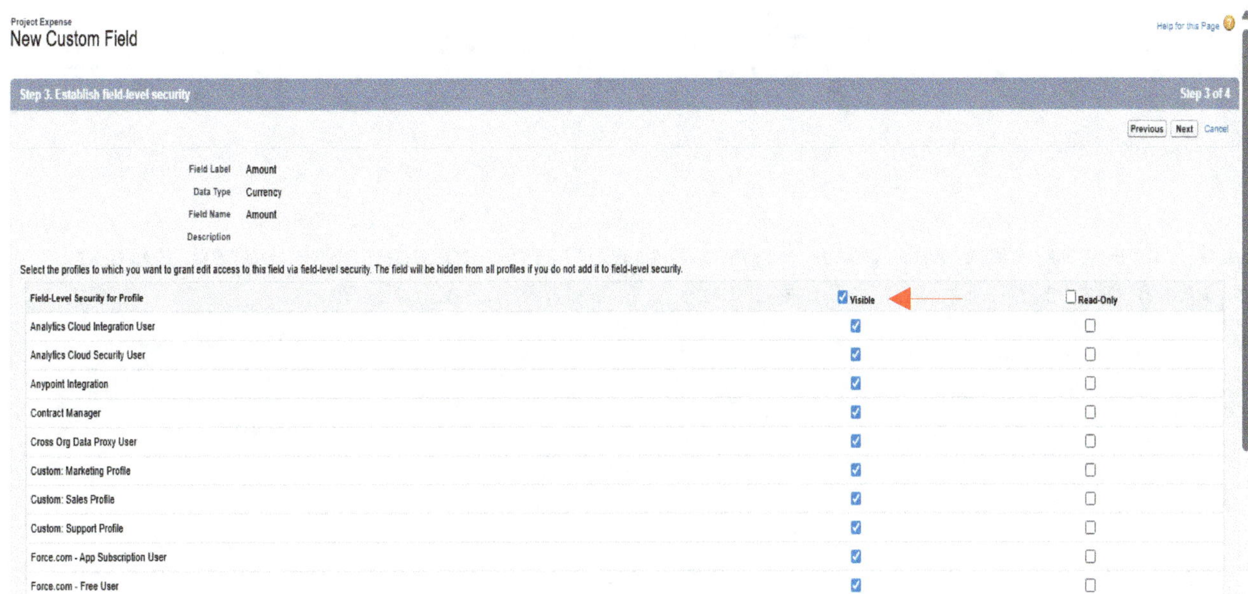

*Click Save.*

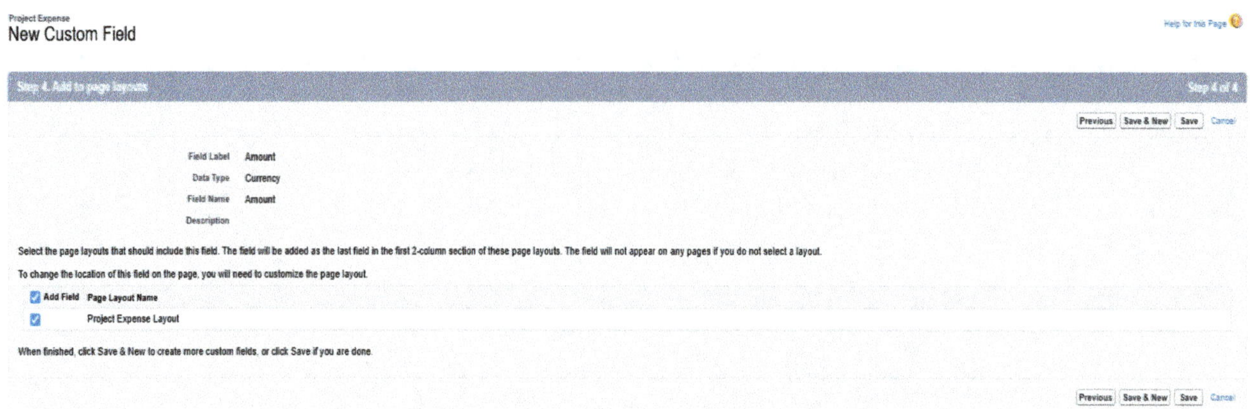

*A new custom currency field Amount is created now.*

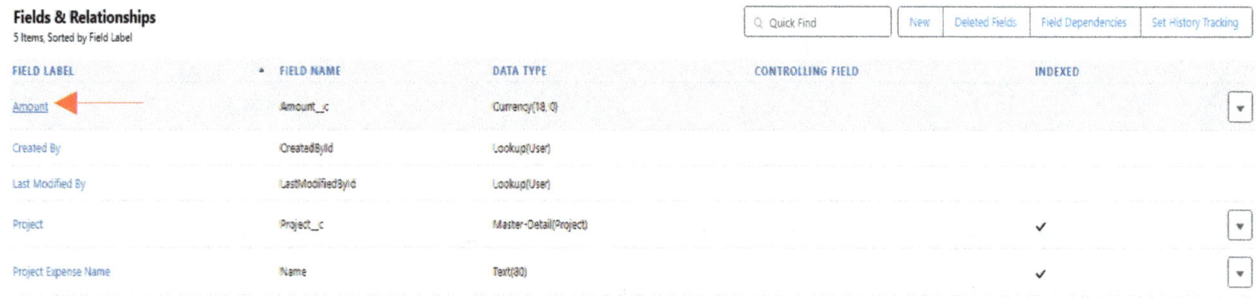

**Amount_Internal_External as a Formula field:** to aggregate selected values
from Amount field. Select a new formula field and click Next.

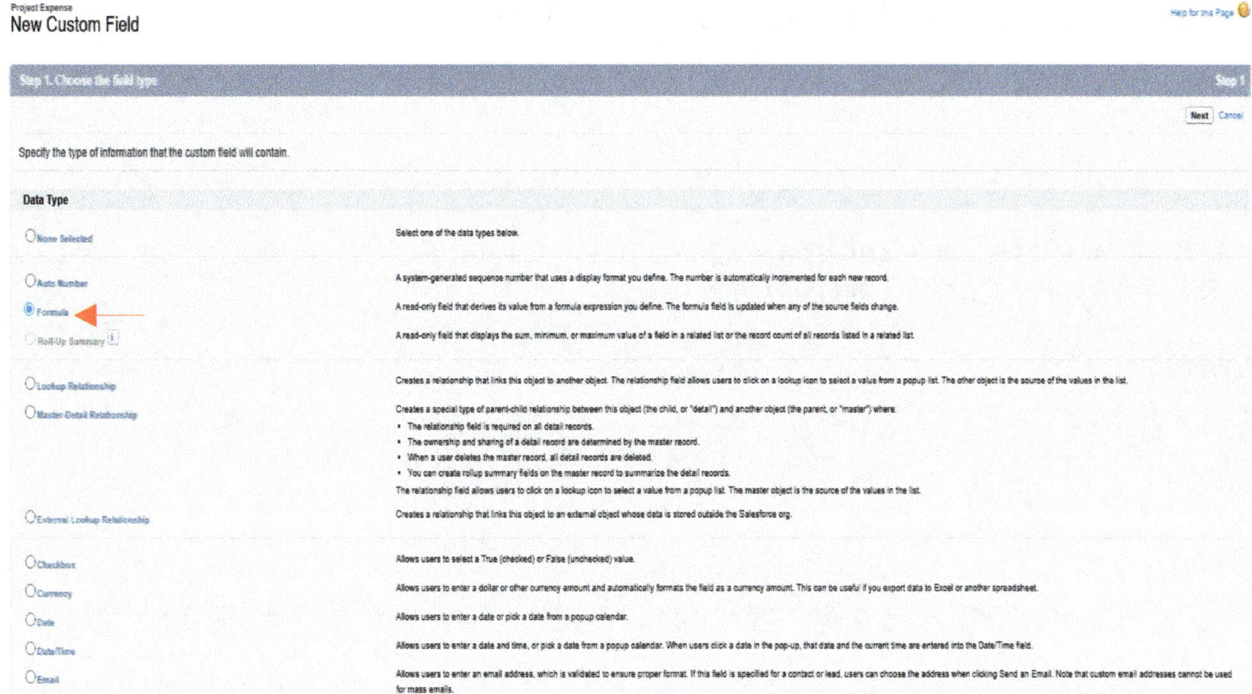

Put the Field Label "Amount_Internal_External", choose Currency as Formula Return Type and click Next.

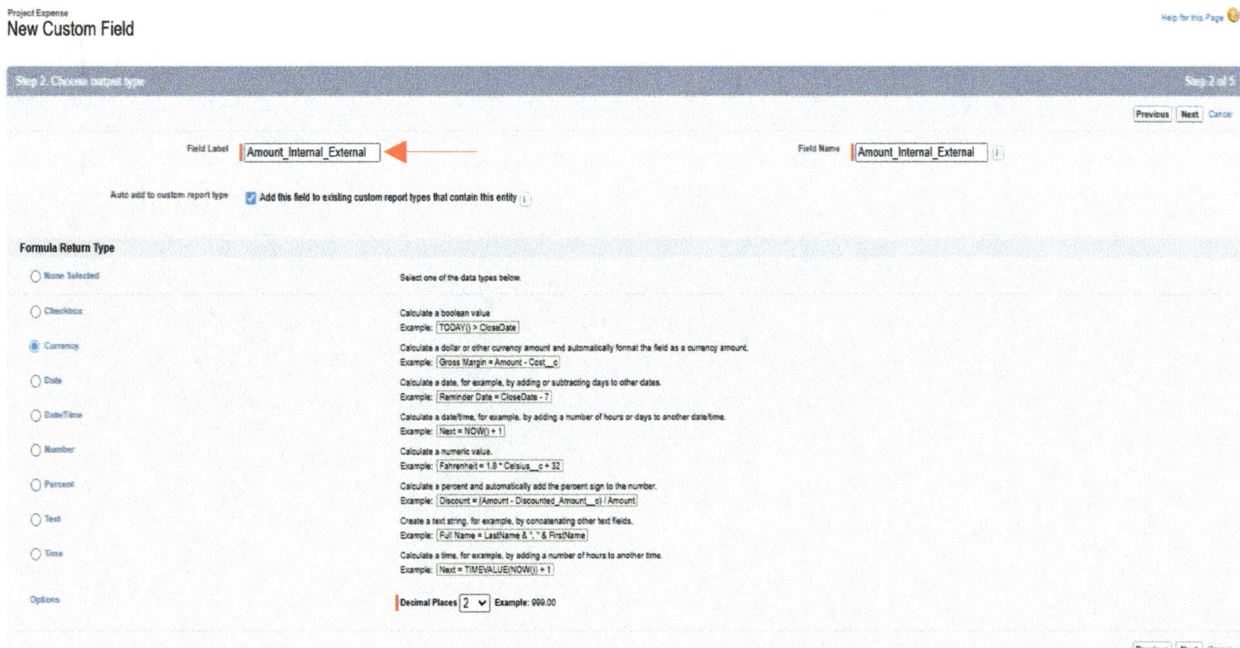

*Add the formula to calculate the value and click Next.*

```
IF(
  OR(
    ISPICKVAL(Type__c, "Internal"),
    ISPICKVAL(Type__c, "External")
  ),
  Amount,
  0
)
```

Project Expense
**New Custom Field**

Help for this Page

**Step 3. Enter formula**  Step 3 of 5

Previous  Next  Cancel

Quick Tips

Enter your formula and click Check Syntax to check for errors. Click the Advanced Formula subtab to use additional fields, operators, and functions.

- Getting Started
- Operators & Functions

Example:  Gross Margin = Amount - Cost__c  More Examples...

Simple Formula  Advanced Formula

Select Field Type    Insert Field
Project Expense ▾   -- Insert Merge Field --   ▾      Insert Operator ▾

Amount_Internal_External (Currency) =

```
IF(
  OR(
    ISPICKVAL(Type__c, "Internal"),
    ISPICKVAL(Type__c, "External")
  ),
  Amount__c,
  0
)
```

*Select Visible for all profiles and click Next.*

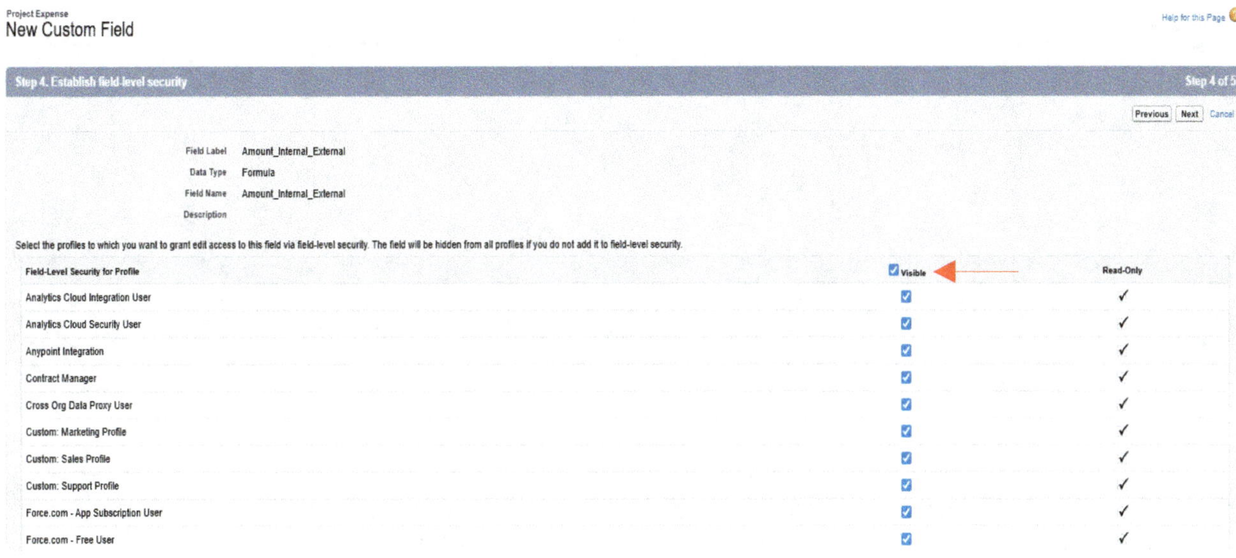

*Click Save.*

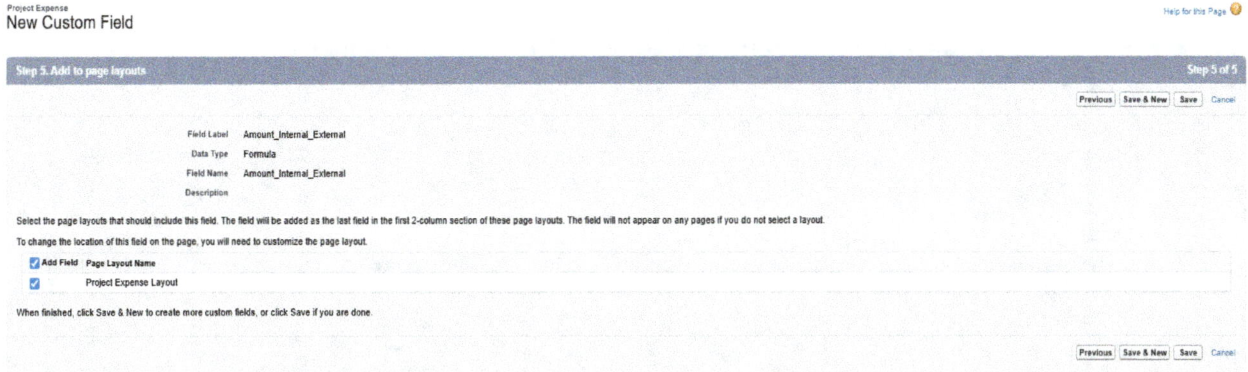

*A new custom formula field Amount_Internal_External is created now.*

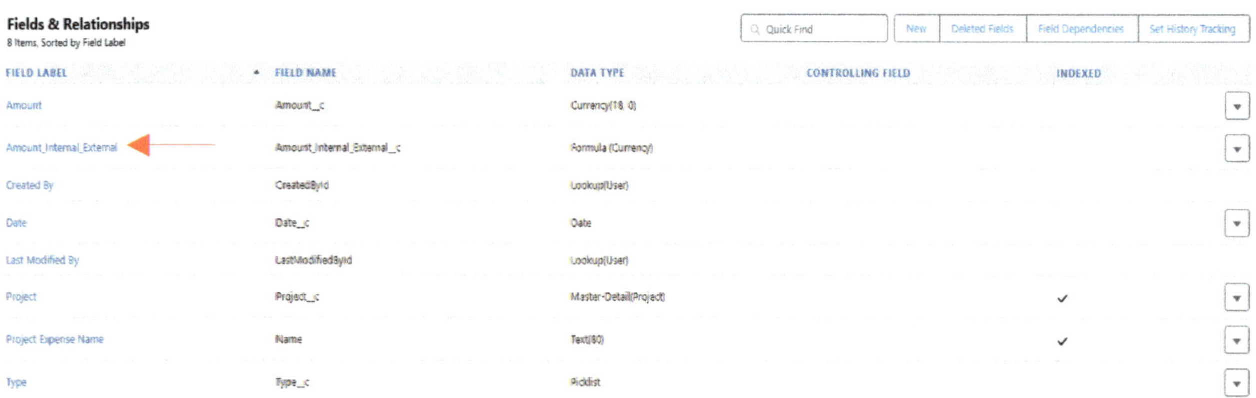

*Once our Project Expense custom fields are in place, return to the already created Project custom object and add the next fields to it.*

*Go to Setup → Object Manager → Project→ Fields & Relationships*

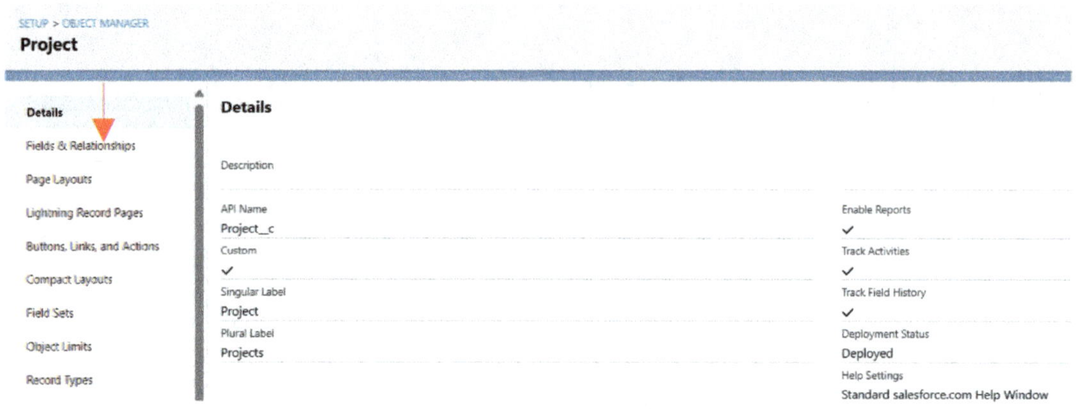

**Total Estimated Revenue as a Currency Roll-up Summary field:** *Create a roll-up summary field that sums the Amount field of related Project Expense records where Type = Billing.*

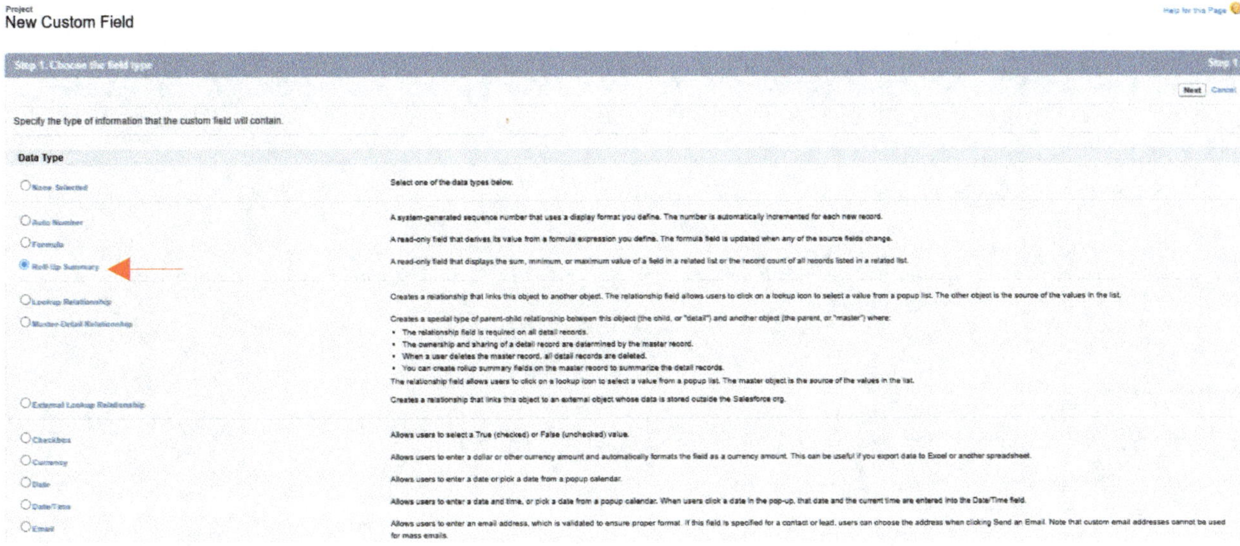

Put the Field Label "Total Estimated Revenue" and click Next.

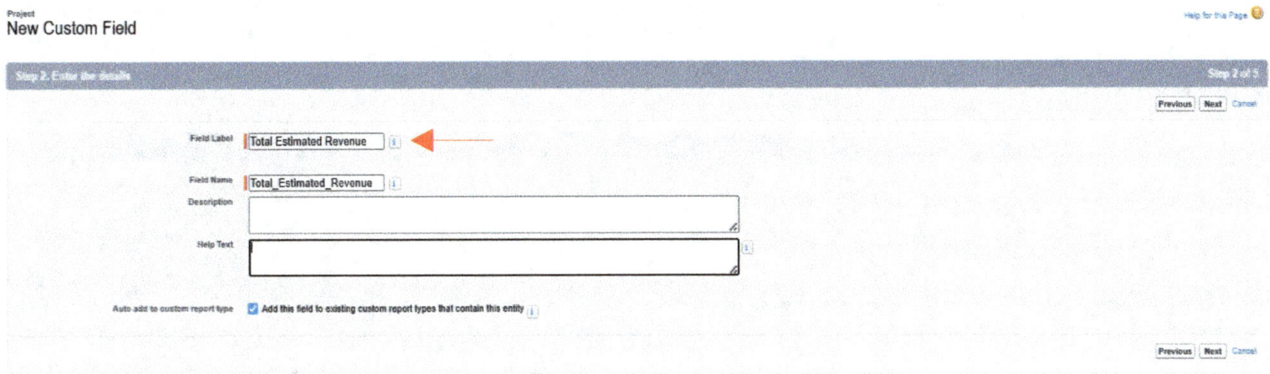

Choose SUM Roll-Up Type and select Filter Criteria:

Field-Type
Operator-equals
Value-Billing

Click Next.

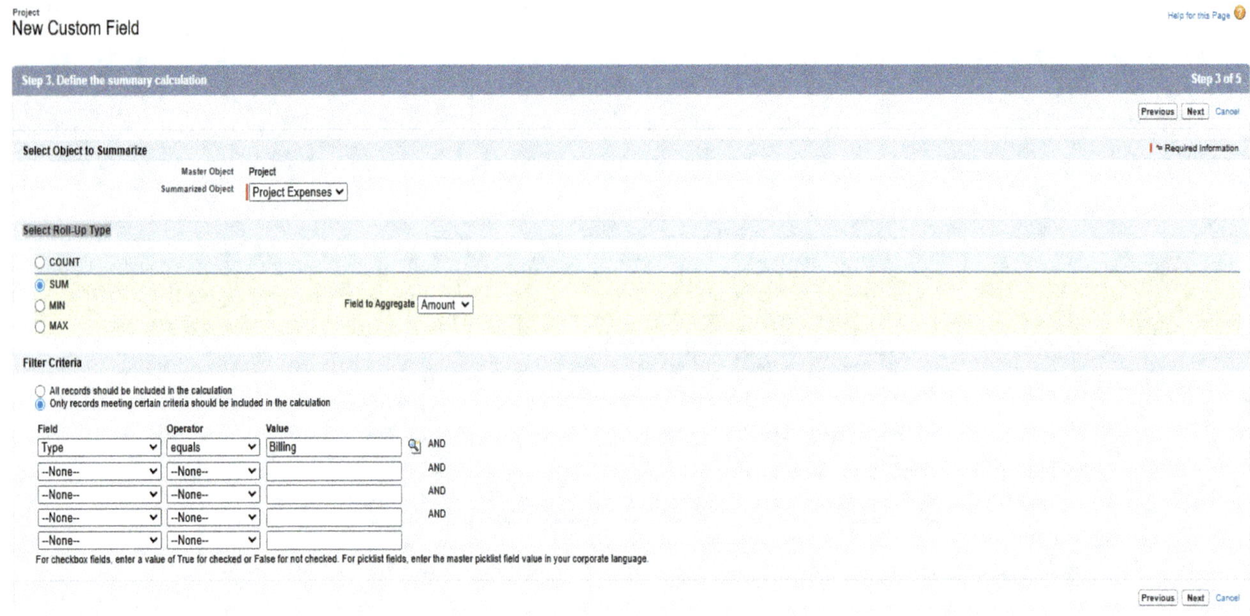

*Select Visible for all profiles and click Next.*

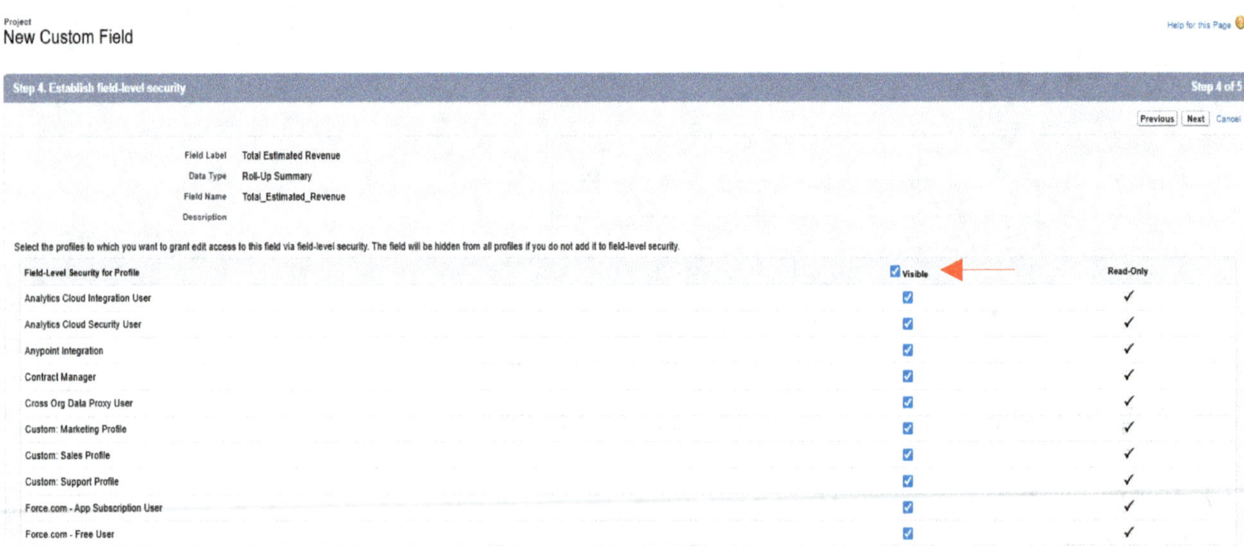

*Click Save.*

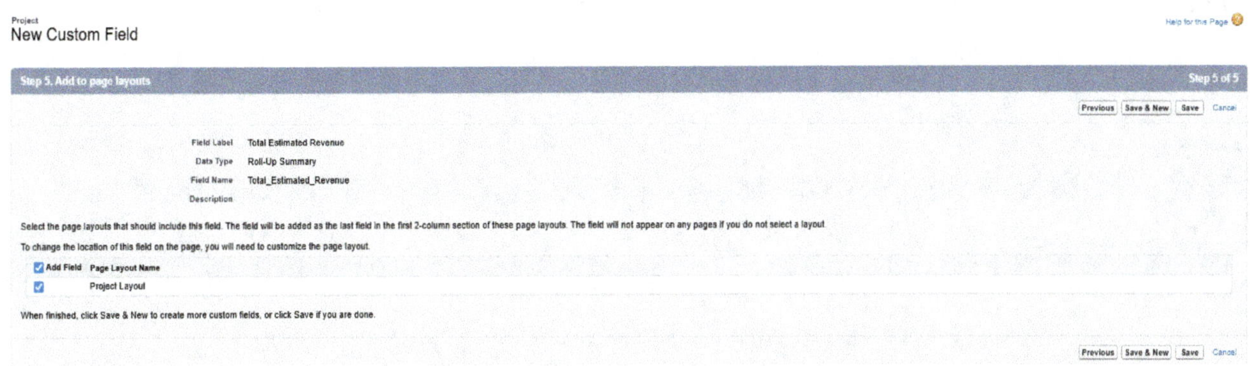

*A new custom Roll-up summary field Total Estimated Revenue is created now.*

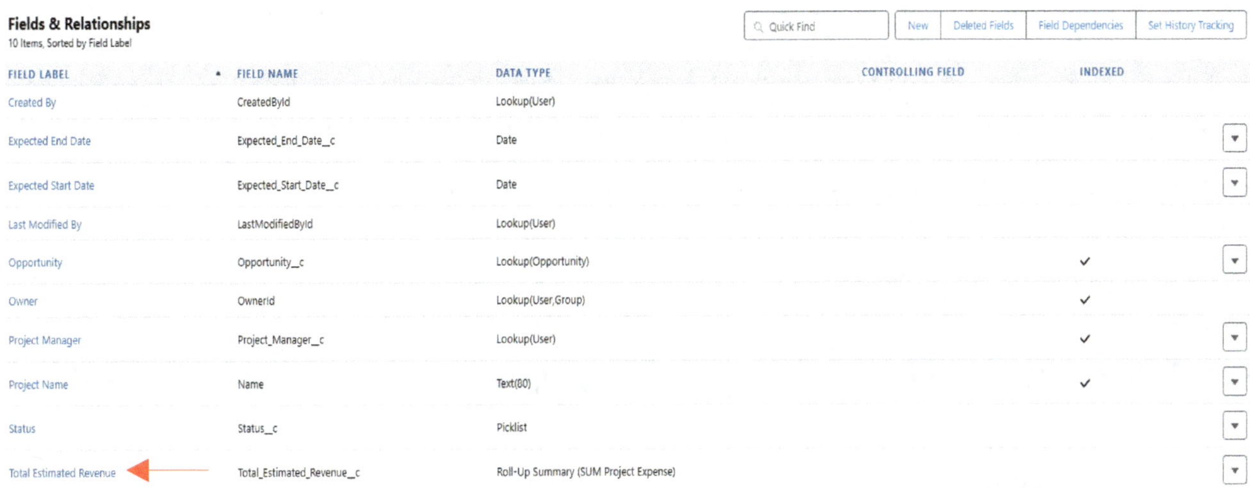

***Total Expenses as a currency Roll-up Summary field:*** *Create a roll-up summary field that sums of related Project Expense records where Type = Internal or External.*

*Put the Field Label "Total Expenses" and click Next.*

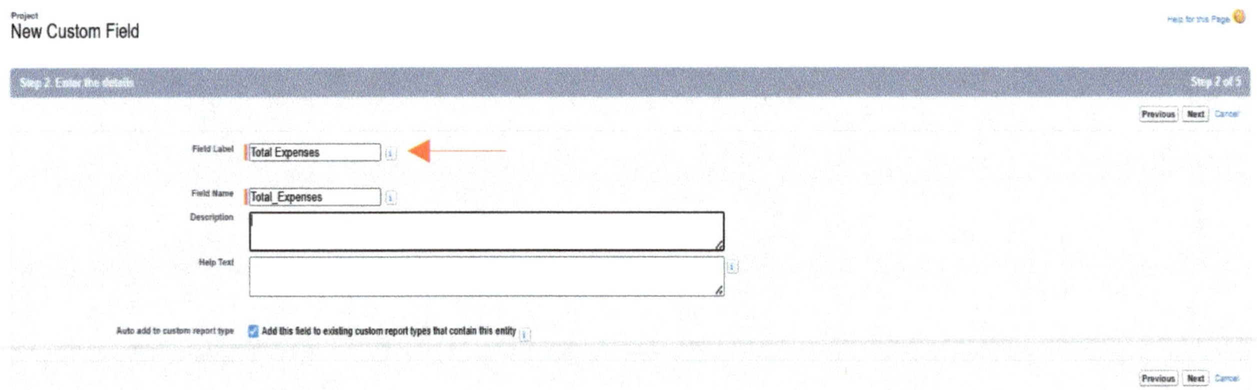

*Choose SUM Roll-Up Type and Amount_Internal_External field to aggregate.*
*Click Next.*

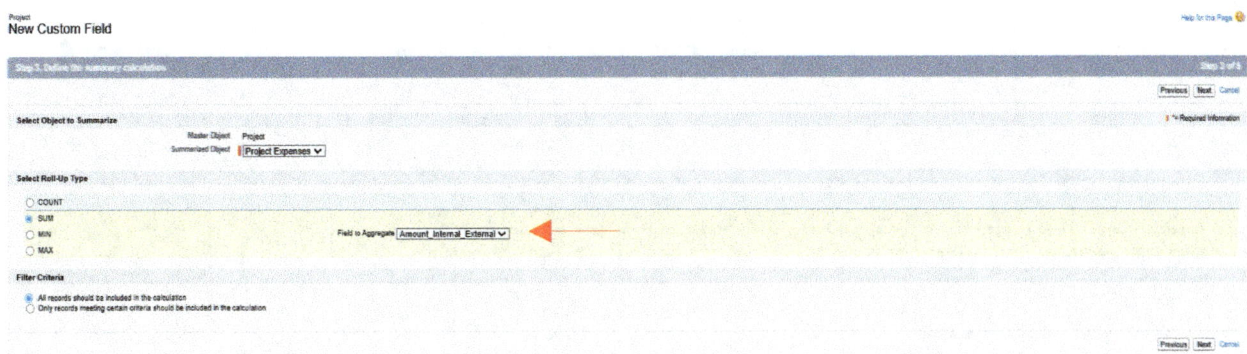

*Select Visible for all profiles and click Next.*

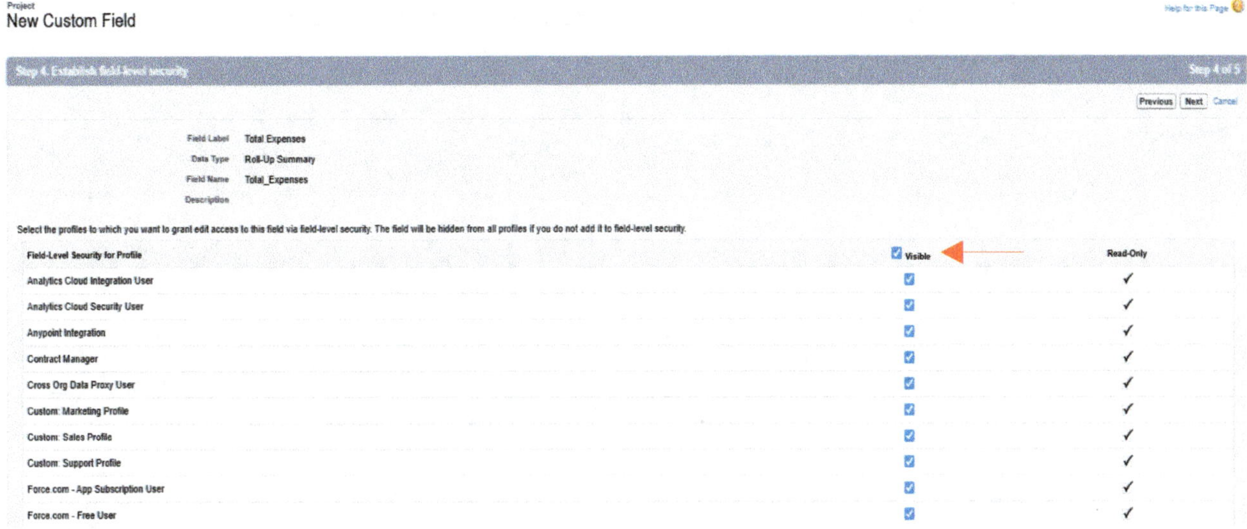

*Click Save.*

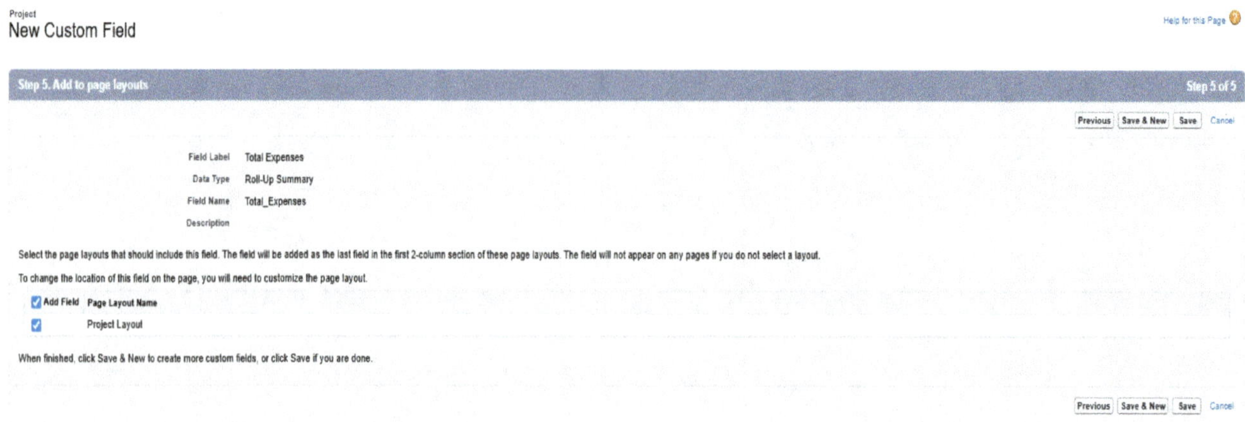

*A new custom Roll-up summary field Total Expenses is created now.*

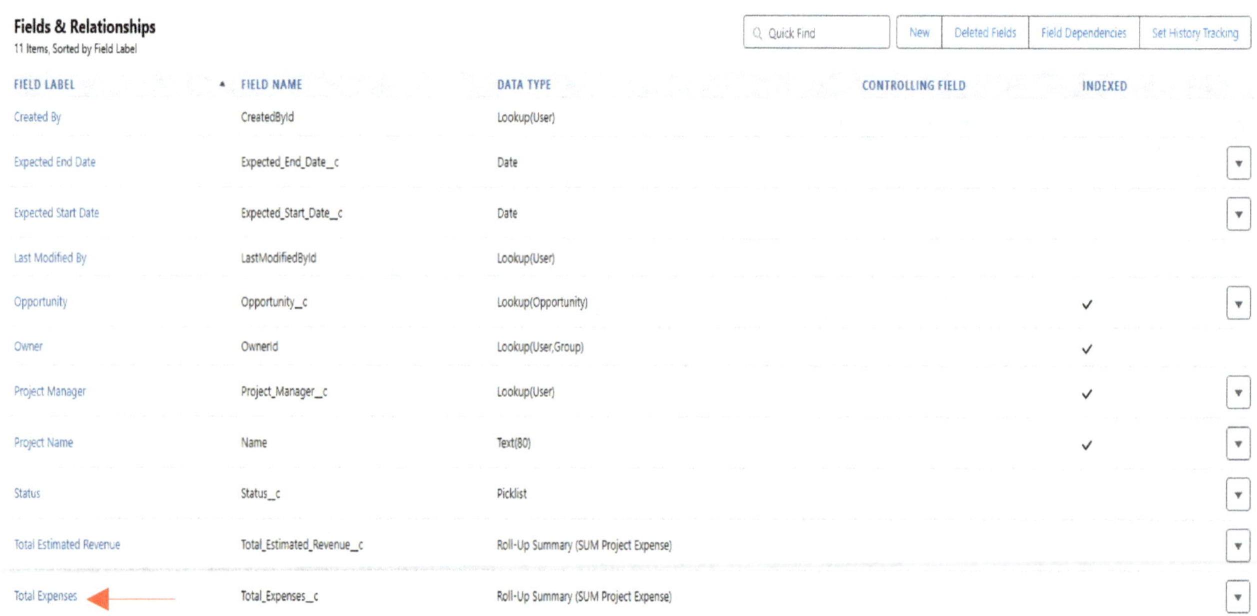

**Projected Profit as Currency Formula field:** *Create Formula field with the formula Total_Estimated_Revenue_c - Total_Expenses_c. This automatically calculates the difference between revenue and expenses.*

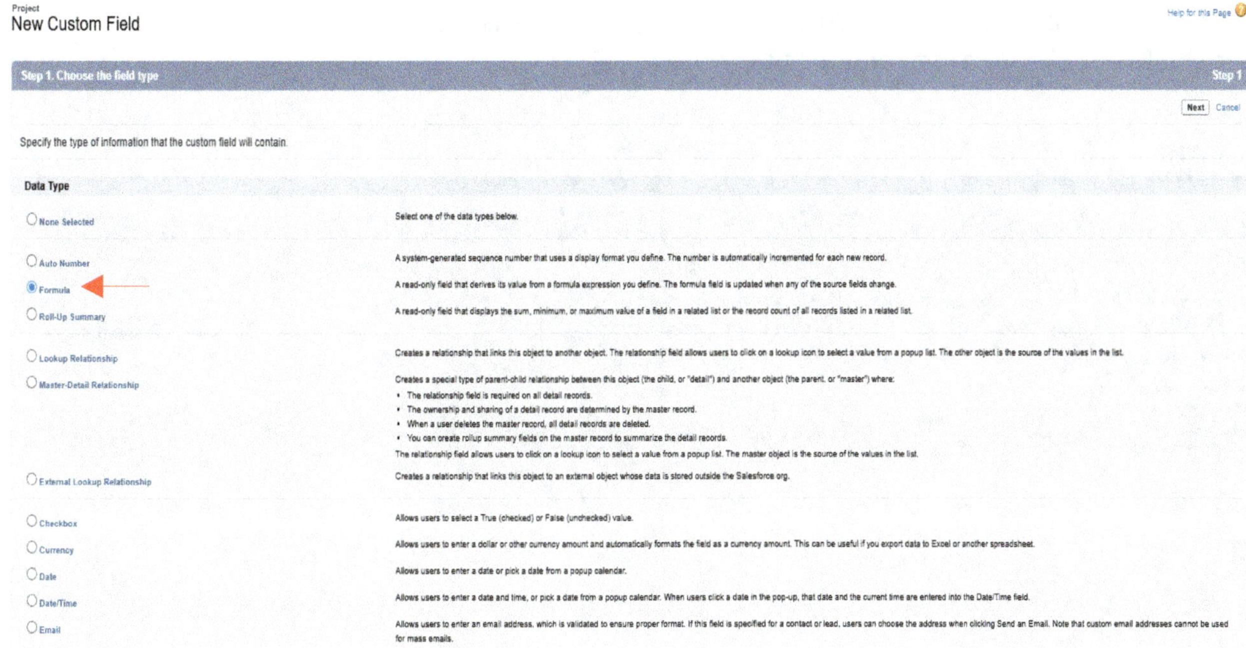

Put the Field Label "Projected Profit", choose Currency as Formula Return Type and click Next.

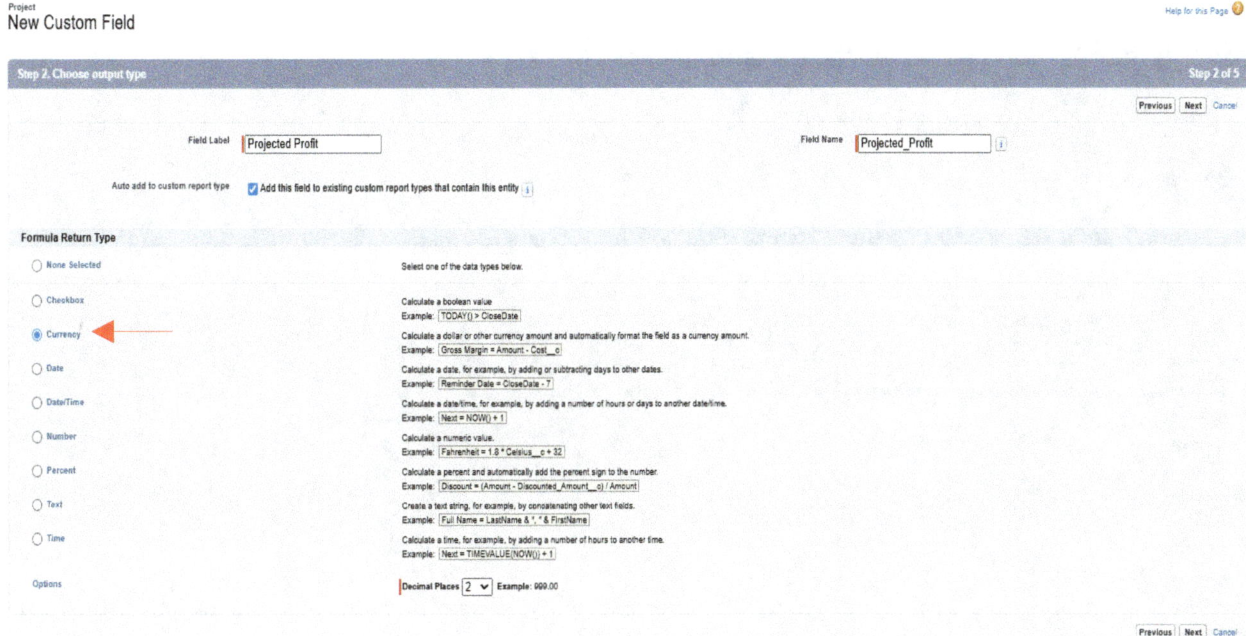

# PART II — Sales Cloud for Product Owners, IT Managers, and  Admins

*Add the formula Total_Estimated_Revenue_c - Total_Expenses_c*
*to calculate the profit and click Next.*

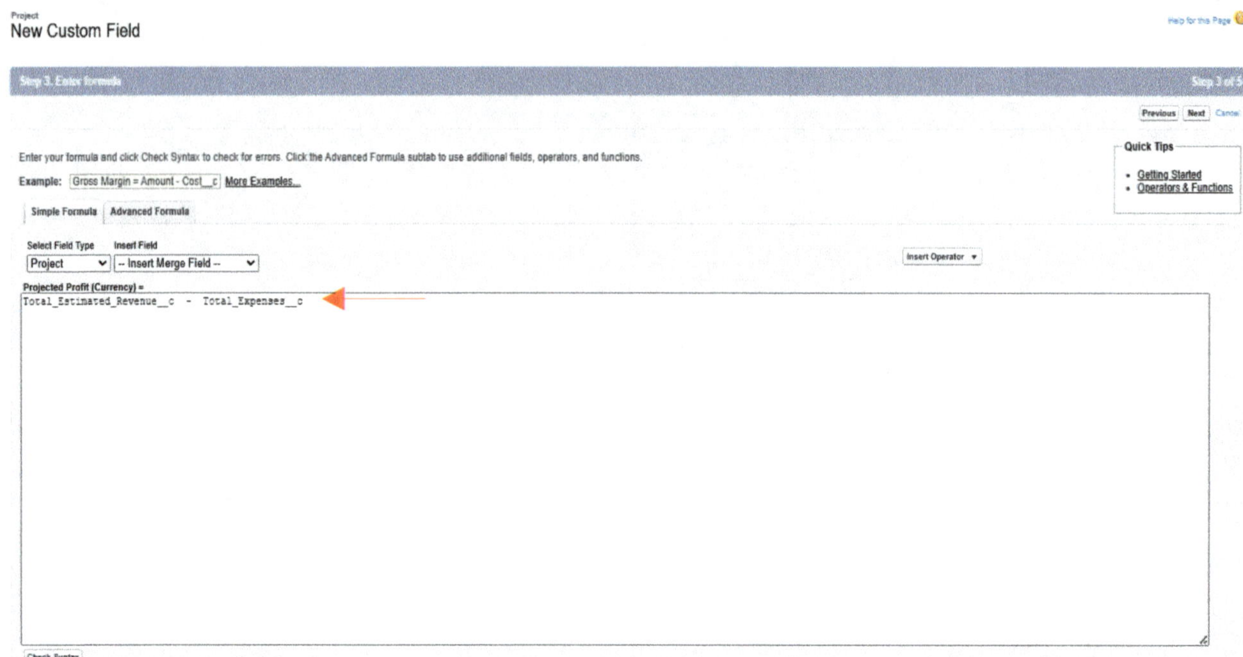

*Select Visible for all profiles and click Next.*

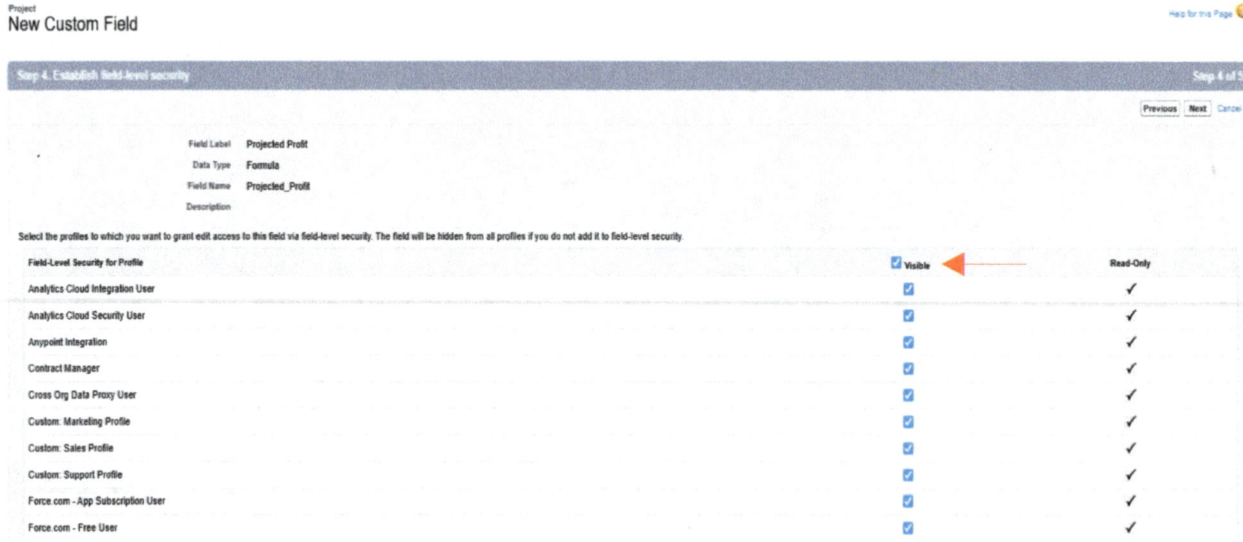

*Click Save.*

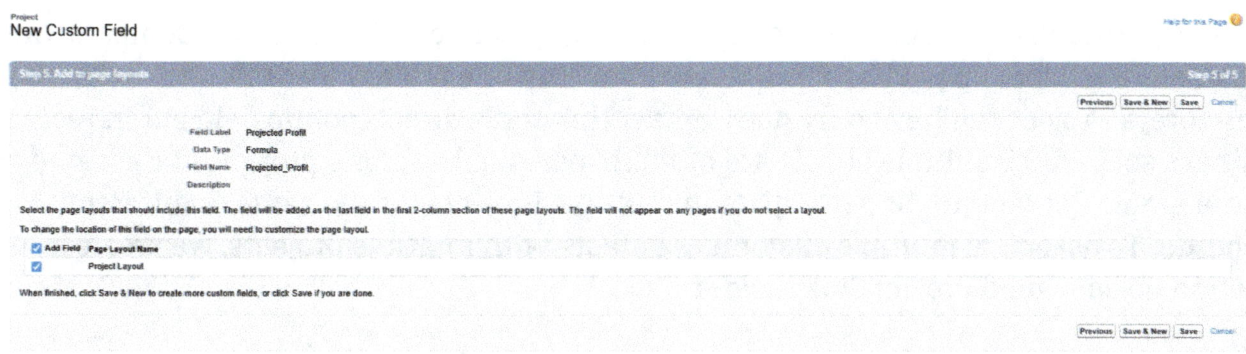

*A new custom Projected Profit formula field is created now.*

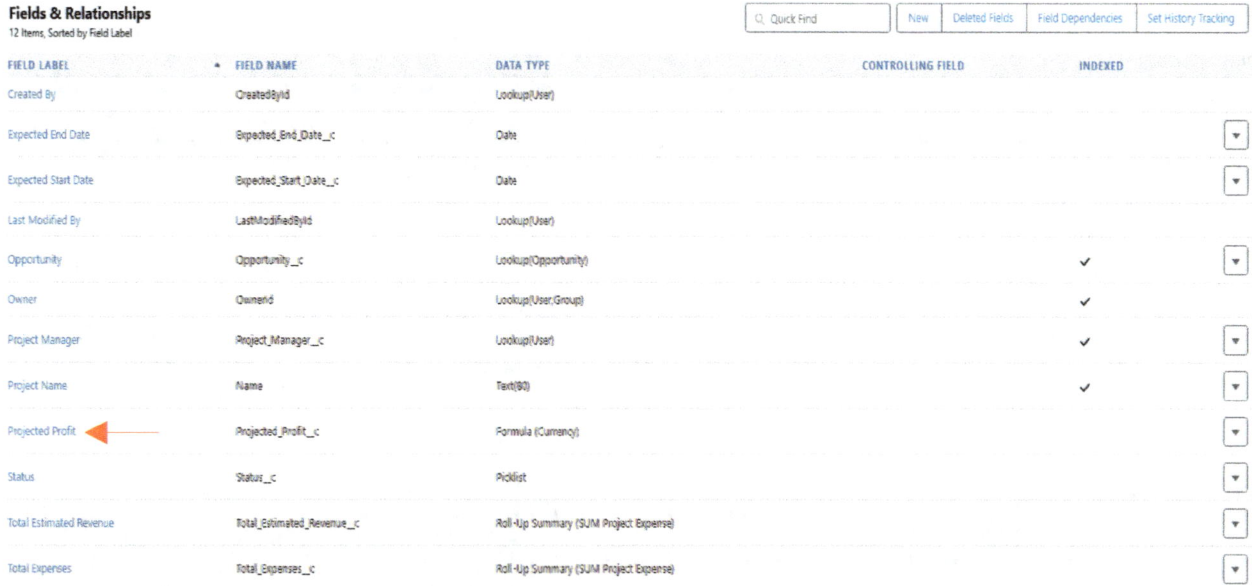

**Fields & Relationships**
12 Items, Sorted by Field Label

| FIELD LABEL | FIELD NAME | DATA TYPE | CONTROLLING FIELD | INDEXED | |
|---|---|---|---|---|---|
| Created By | CreatedById | Lookup(User) | | | |
| Expected End Date | Expected_End_Date__c | Date | | | ▾ |
| Expected Start Date | Expected_Start_Date__c | Date | | | ▾ |
| Last Modified By | LastModifiedById | Lookup(User) | | | |
| Opportunity | Opportunity__c | Lookup(Opportunity) | | ✓ | ▾ |
| Owner | OwnerId | Lookup(User,Group) | | ✓ | |
| Project Manager | Project_Manager__c | Lookup(User) | | ✓ | ▾ |
| Project Name | Name | Text(80) | | ✓ | ▾ |
| Projected Profit | Projected_Profit__c | Formula (Currency) | | | ▾ |
| Status | Status__c | Picklist | | | ▾ |
| Total Estimated Revenue | Total_Estimated_Revenue__c | Roll-Up Summary (SUM Project Expense) | | | ▾ |
| Total Expenses | Total_Expenses__c | Roll-Up Summary (SUM Project Expense) | | | ▾ |

# 10.3 Creating the Junction Object

This object establishes a many-to-many relationship between Projects and Contacts. In Salesforce, each lookup field can link a record to only one related record.
Therefore, a Project can have only one Contact through a direct lookup field but in real business scenarios, multiple people are often involved in the same project. At the same time, a single Contact might participate in multiple Projects for the same or different accounts. To associate multiple customer contacts with multiple projects, we create a junction object called Project Stakeholder.

*Go to Setup → Object Manager → Create → Custom Object*

*Enable the options Allow Reports, Allow Activities, and Track Field History to make the object reportable and auditable and click Save.*

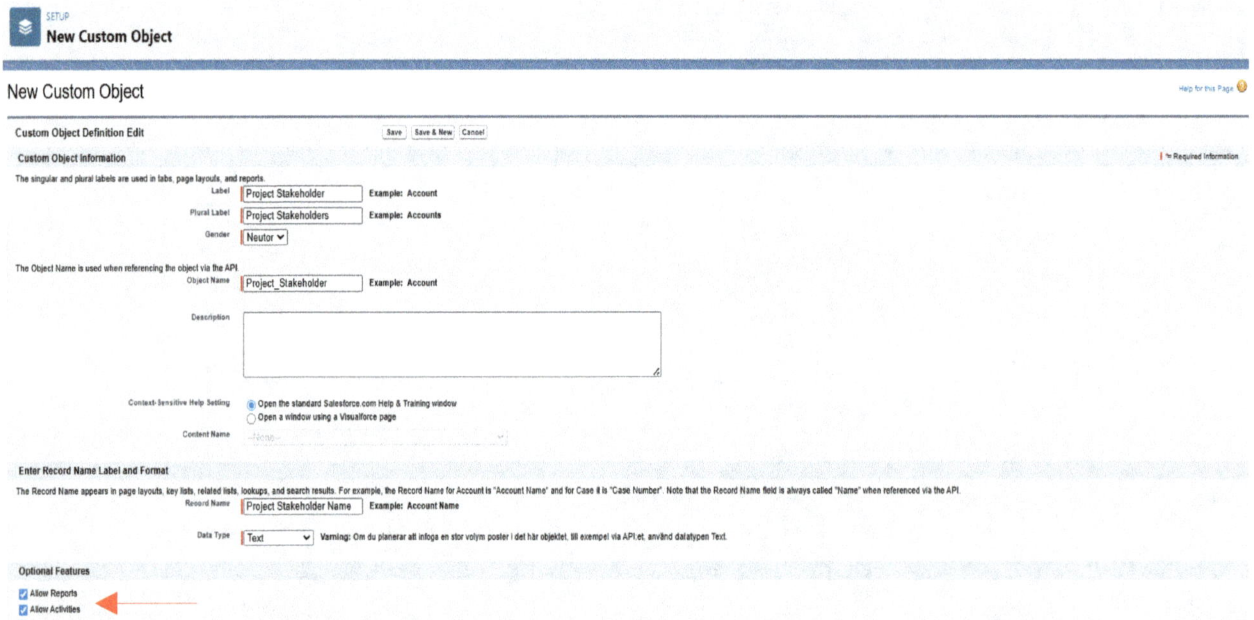

*The custom object Project Stakeholder is created now.*

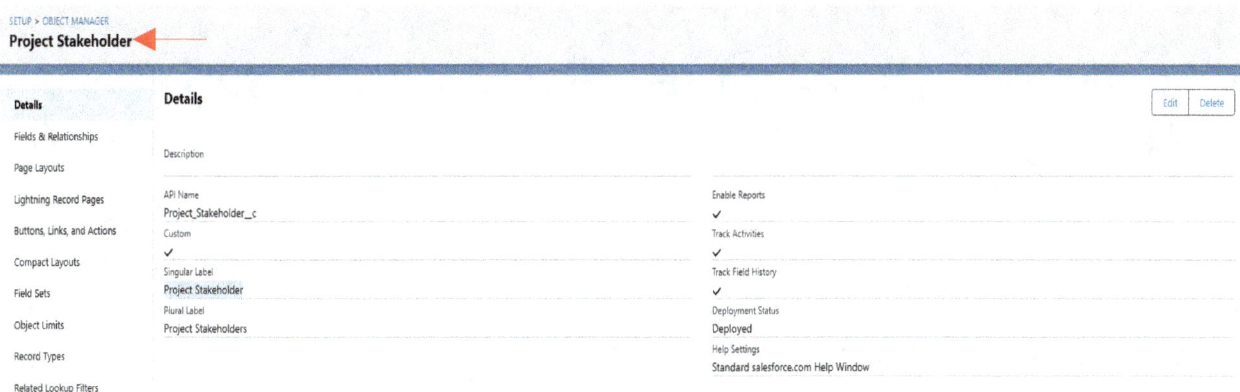

*In this newly created custom object, we will define custom fields to capture essential project information.*

***Project as a Lookup to Project field:*** *Create a Lookup Relationship field to the Project object. This links each stakeholder record to a specific project.*

*Choose Related To Project in the selection list. Click Next.*

*Put the Field Label "Project" and click Next.*

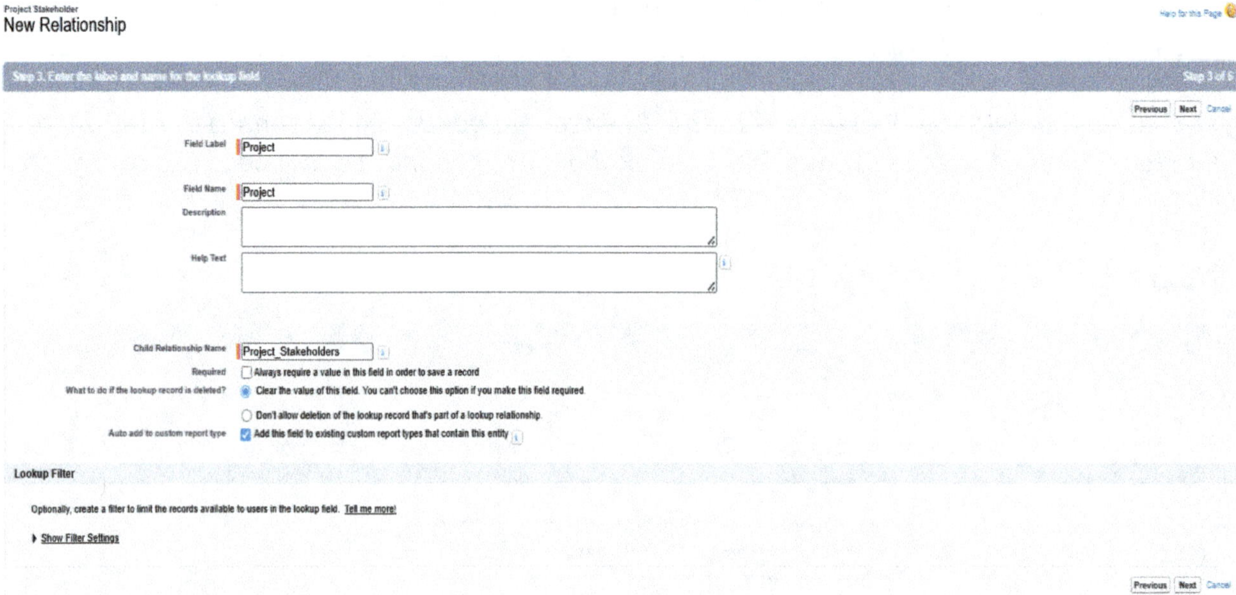

*Select Visible for all profiles and click Next.*

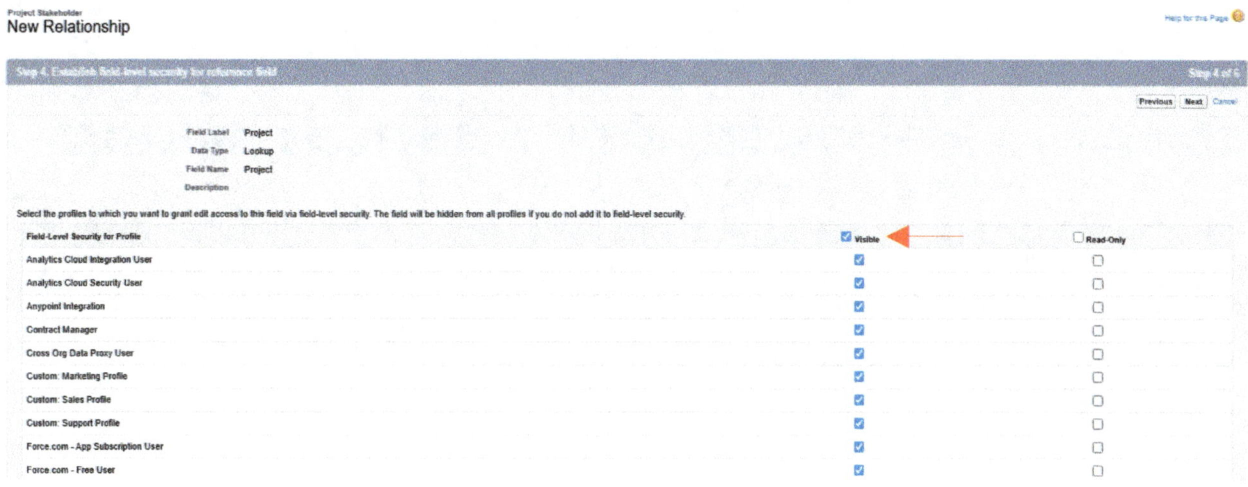

*Check if this field is assigned to the Project Stakeholder Layout and click Next.*

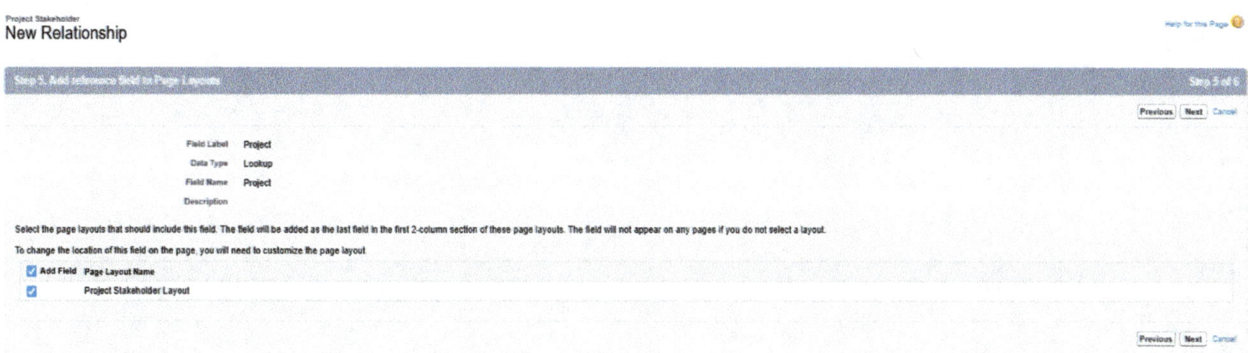

# PART II – Sales Cloud for Product Owners, IT Managers, and  Admins

*Select Project Layout and click Save.*

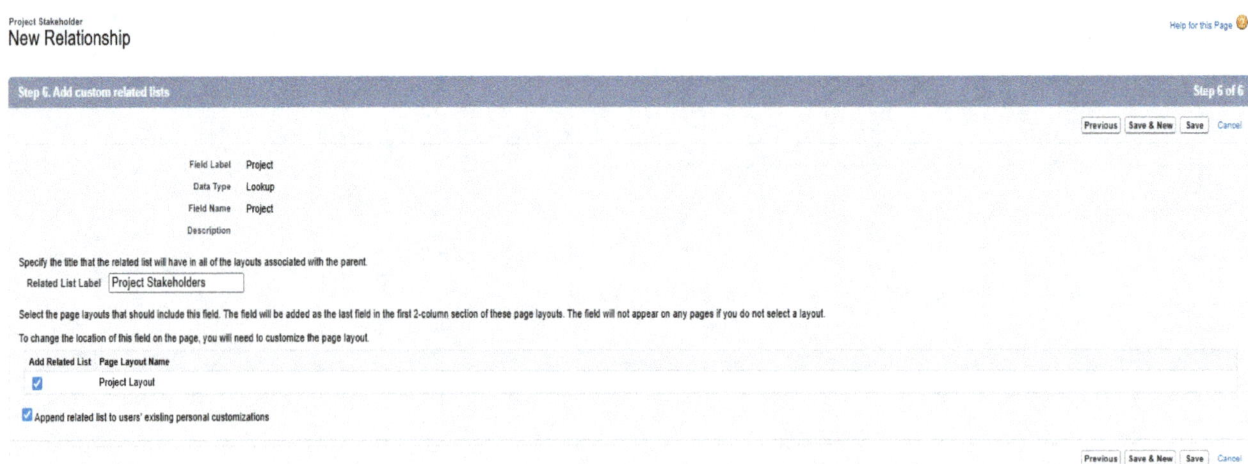

*A new lookup Project custom field is created now.*

**Fields & Relationships**
5 Items, Sorted by Field Label

| FIELD LABEL ▲ | FIELD NAME | DATA TYPE |
| --- | --- | --- |
| Created By | CreatedById | Lookup(User) |
| Last Modified By | LastModifiedById | Lookup(User) |
| Owner | OwnerId | Lookup(User,Group) |
| Project | Project__c | Lookup(Project) |
| Project Stakeholder Name | Name | Text(80) |

**Contact as a Lookup to Contact field:** *Create a Lookup Relationship field to the Contact object. This links each stakeholder record to a specific contact.*

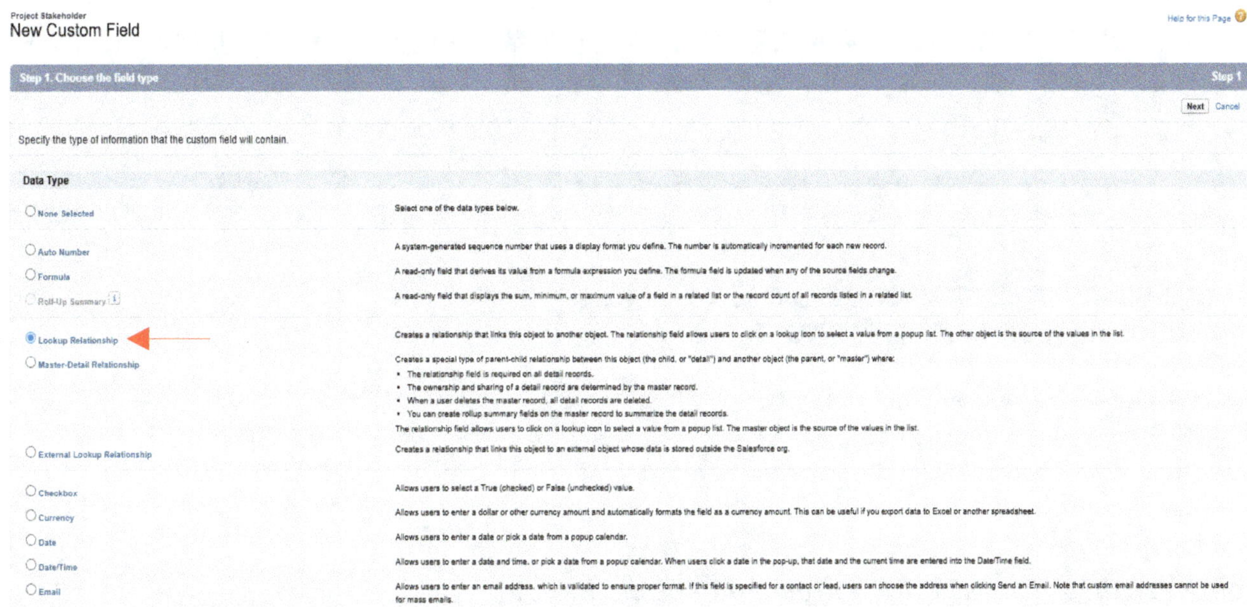

Choose *Related To Contact in the selection list. Click Next.*

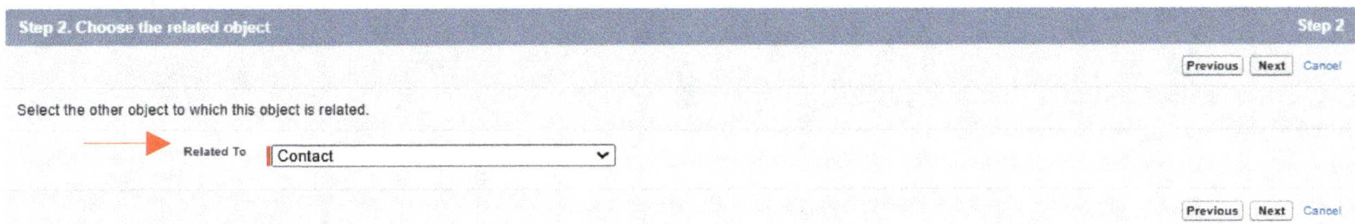

# PART II – Sales Cloud for Product Owners, IT Managers, and Admins

*Put the Field Label "Contact" and click Next.*

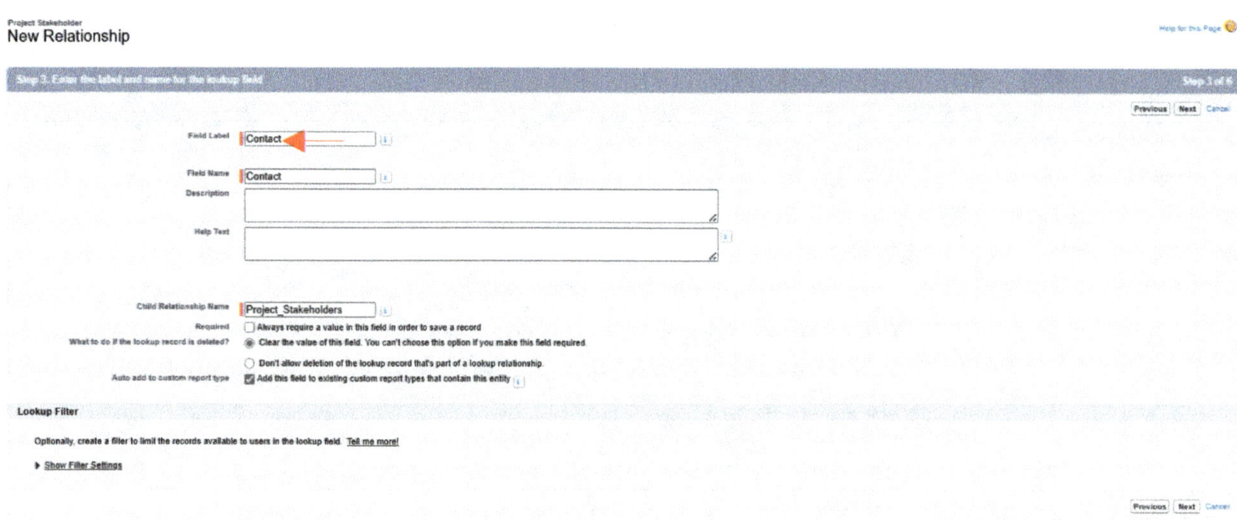

*Select Visible for all profiles and click Next.*

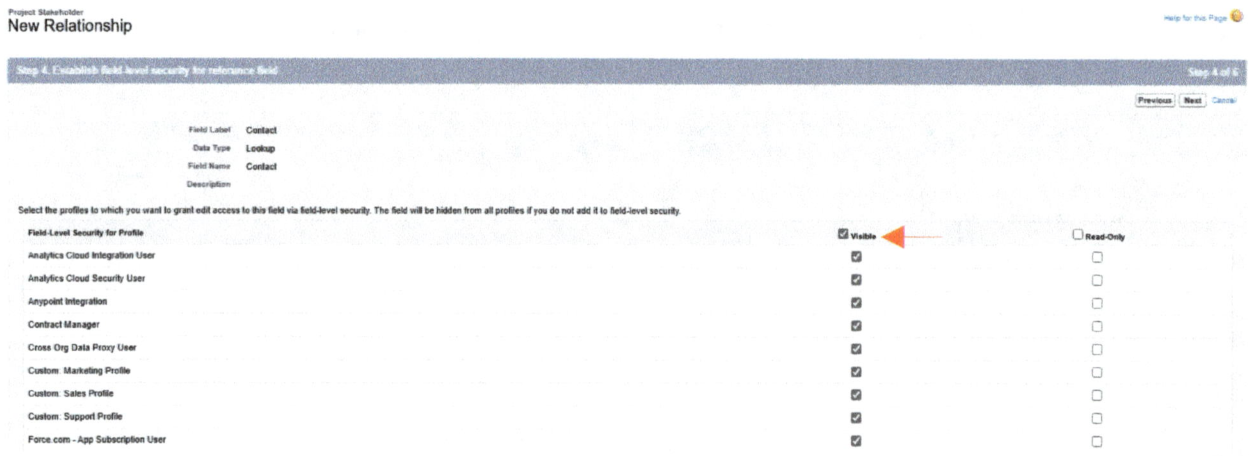

*Check if this field is assigned to the Project Stakeholder Layout and click Next.*

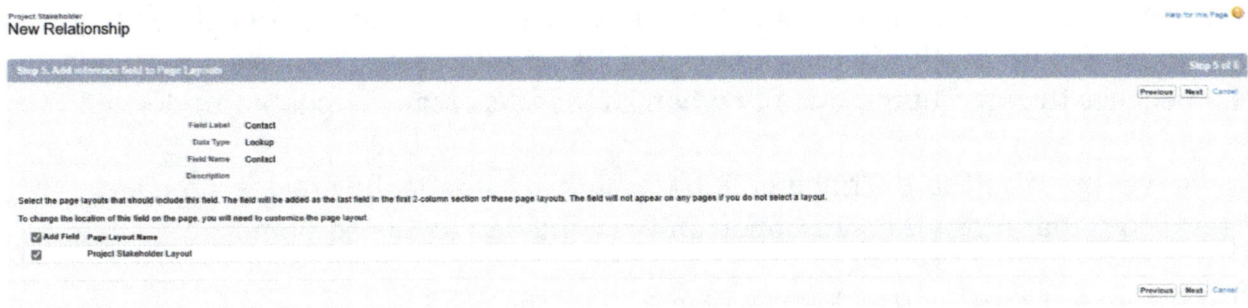

*Select all Contact Layouts and click Save.*

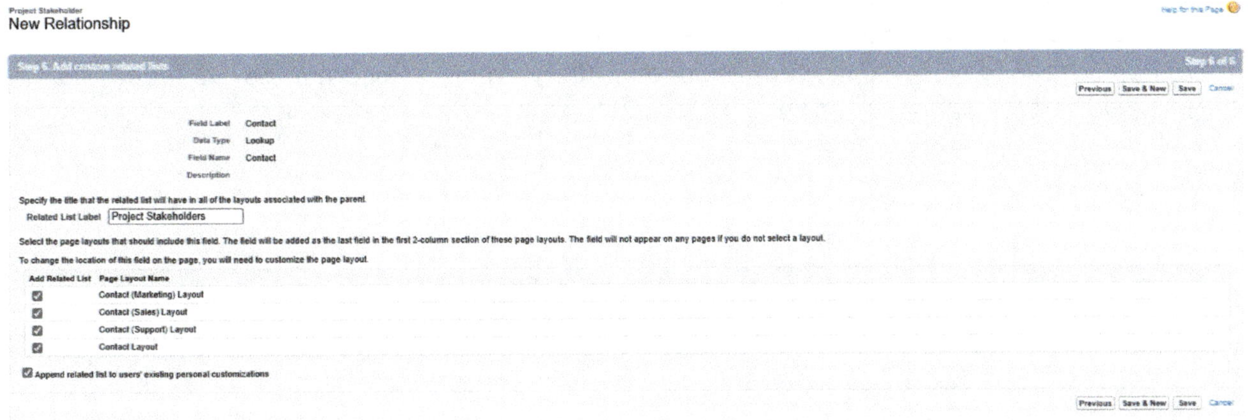

*A new lookup Contact custom field is created now.*

**Fields & Relationships**

6 Items, Sorted by Field Label

| FIELD LABEL | FIELD NAME | DATA TYPE |
|---|---|---|
| Contact | Contact__c | Lookup(Contact) |
| Created By | CreatedById | Lookup(User) |
| Last Modified By | LastModifiedById | Lookup(User) |
| Owner | OwnerId | Lookup(User,Group) |
| Project | Project__c | Lookup(Project) |
| Project Stakeholder Name | Name | Text(80) |

# 10.4 Building a Flow

Flow is Salesforce's powerful declarative automation tool used to perform actions based on defined conditions without writing any code. It can create, update, or delete records and send notifications. Within the Sales Cloud, Record-Triggered Flows are particularly useful because they run automatically when a record is created, updated, or deleted.

Now we will build a Record-Triggered Flow which automatically creates a related Project record that runs when an Opportunity is updated to Closed Won.

*Go to Setup → Flows → New Flow → Record-Triggered Flow*

*Then select Opportunity as the Object and apply the following settings:*

*Configure Trigger: A record is updated*
*Condition Requirements: All Conditions Are Met (AND)*
*Field: Stage, Operator: Equals, Value: Closed Won*
*When to Run the Flow for Updated Records: Only when a record is updated to meet the condition requirements*

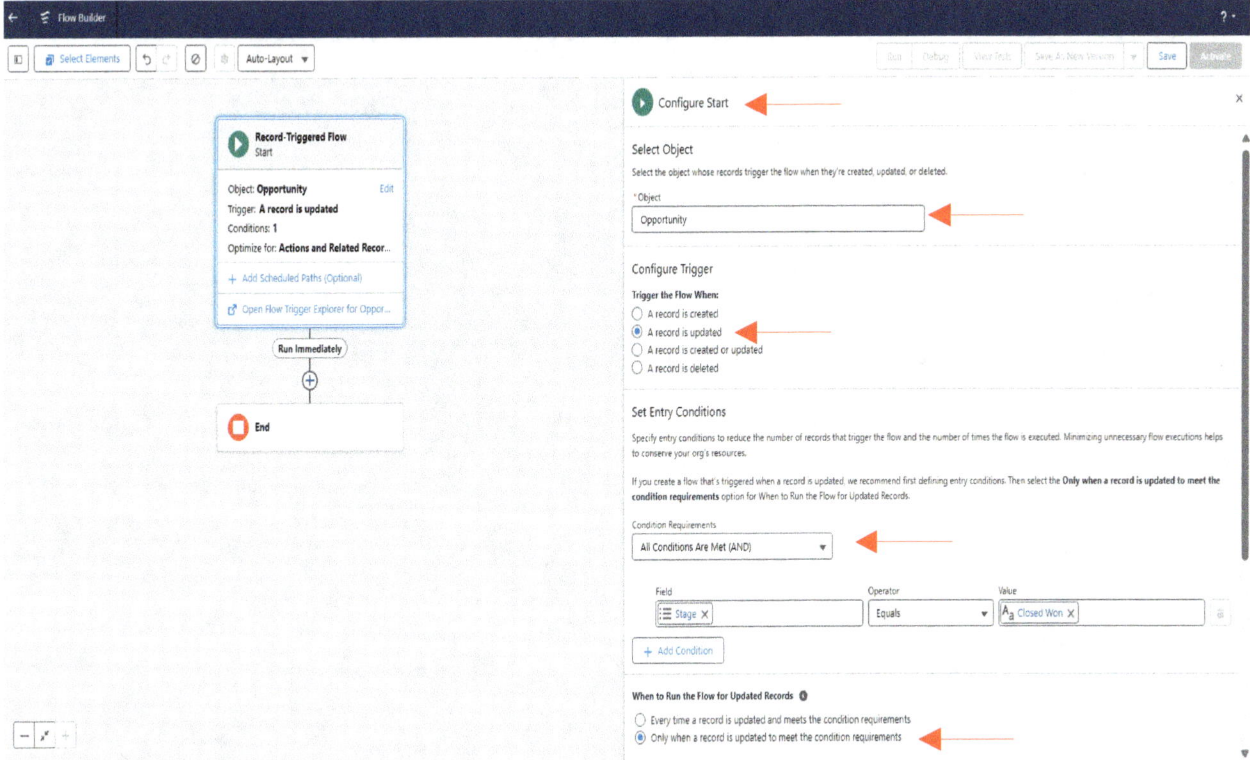

Next, click the plus button as illustrated below.

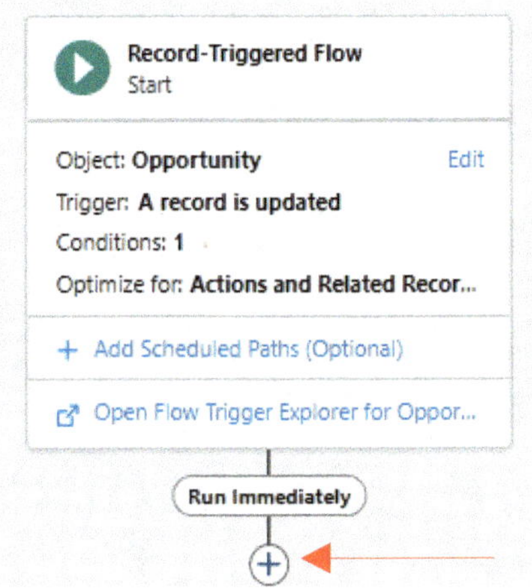

*Type "Create" in the searching field and select Create Records.*

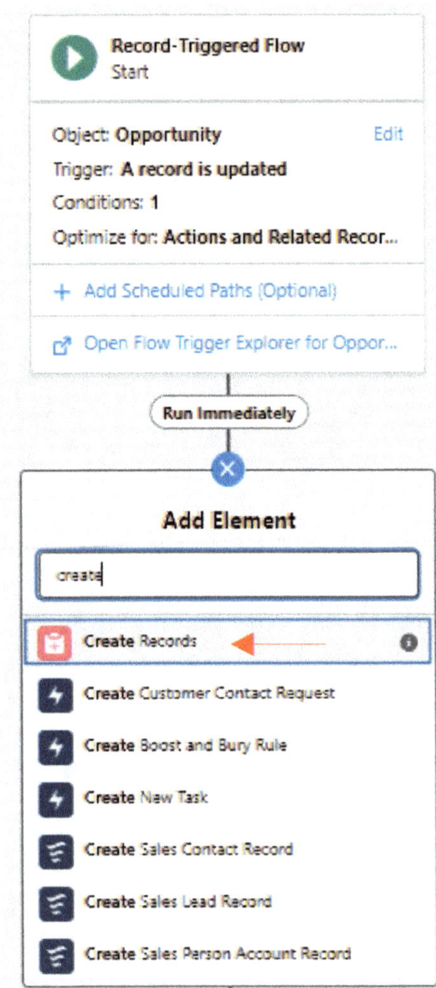

*Put the Label "Create Project", select Manually and Project Object to create automatically records.*

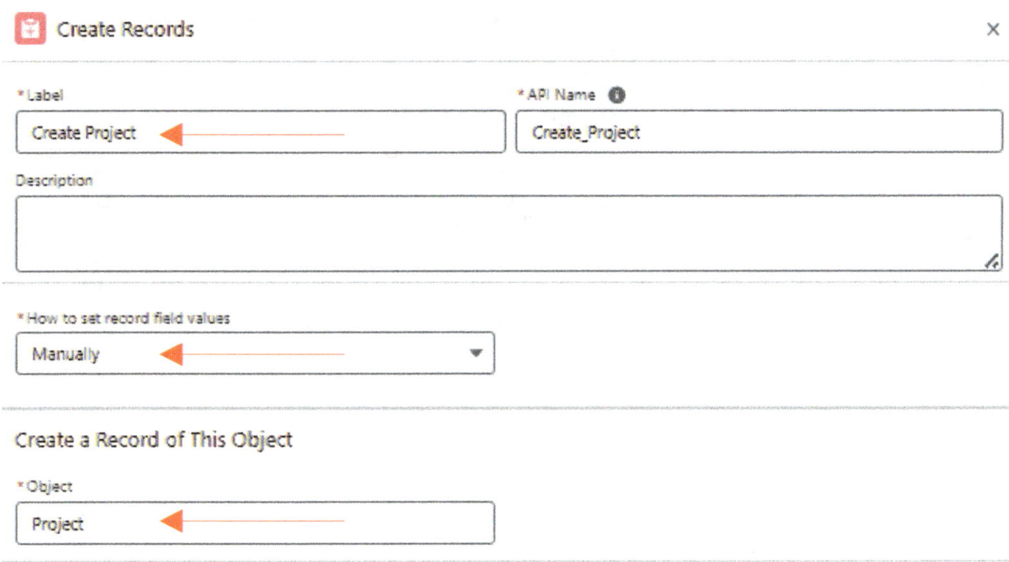

*Set the Project object values as follows: select the Expected Start Date field and assign it the value of the Created Date.*

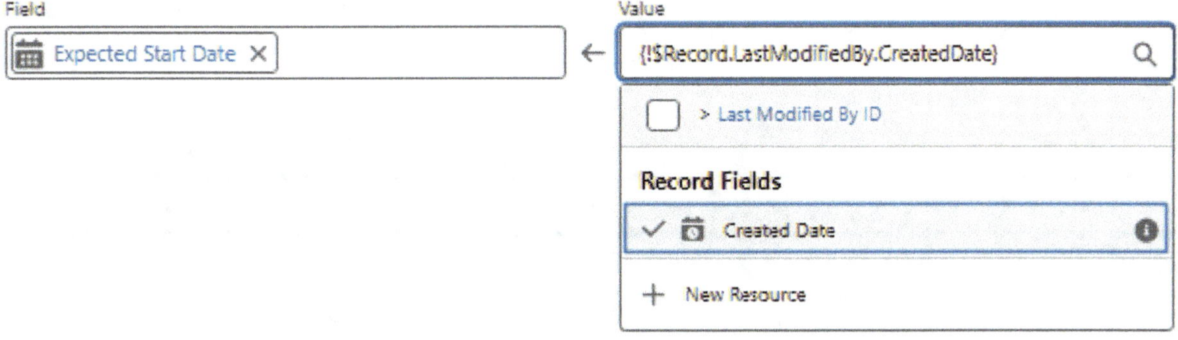

*Select Expected End Date field and New Resource.*

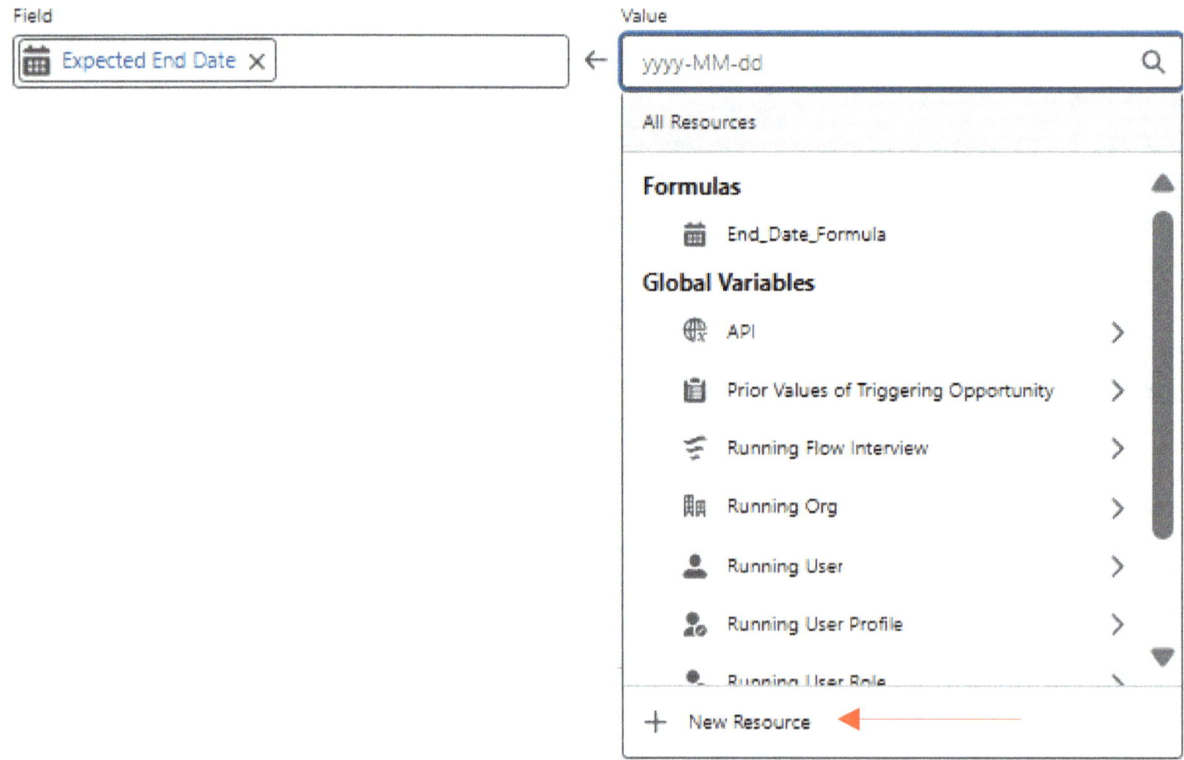

*Then, create a new formula for Resource Type.*

## New Resource

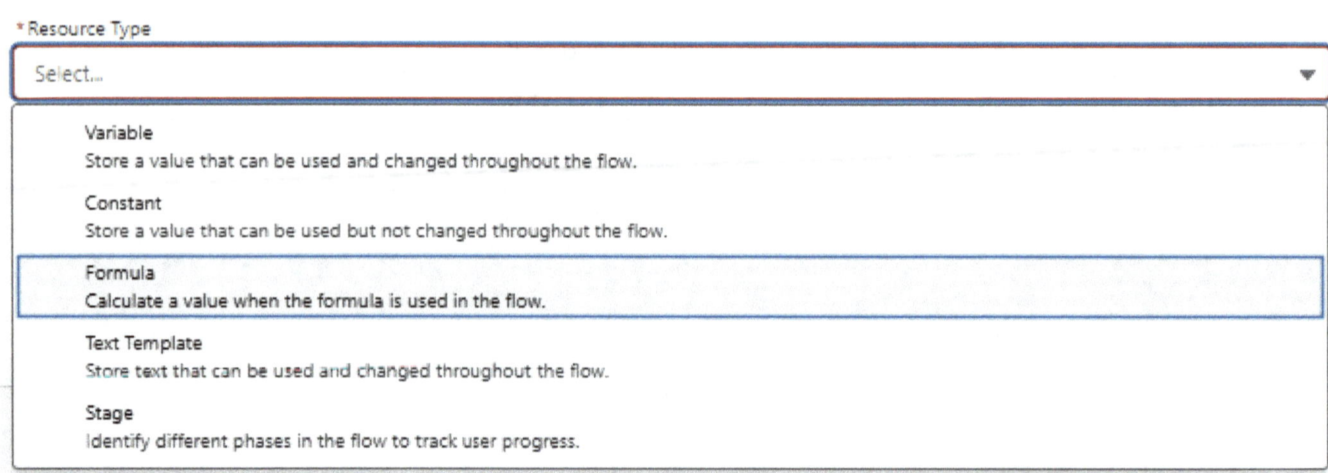

*Please enter the values in the required fields to calculate the Expected End Date as {!$Record.CloseDate} + 45, and then click Done.*

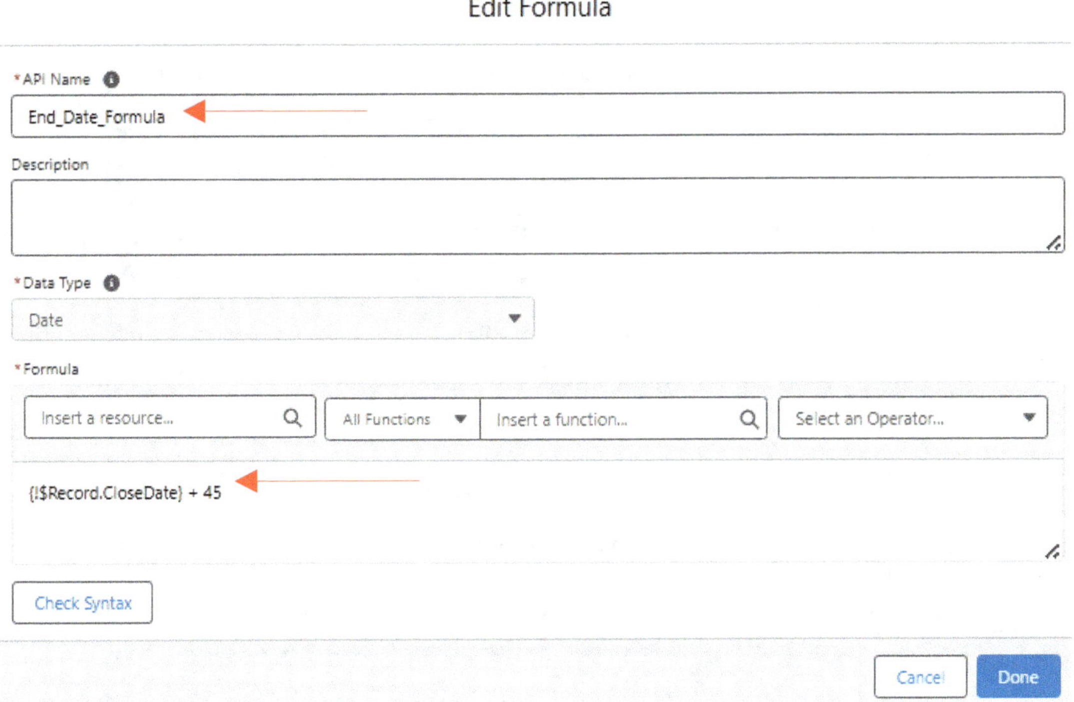

*Select Project Name field and new resource.*

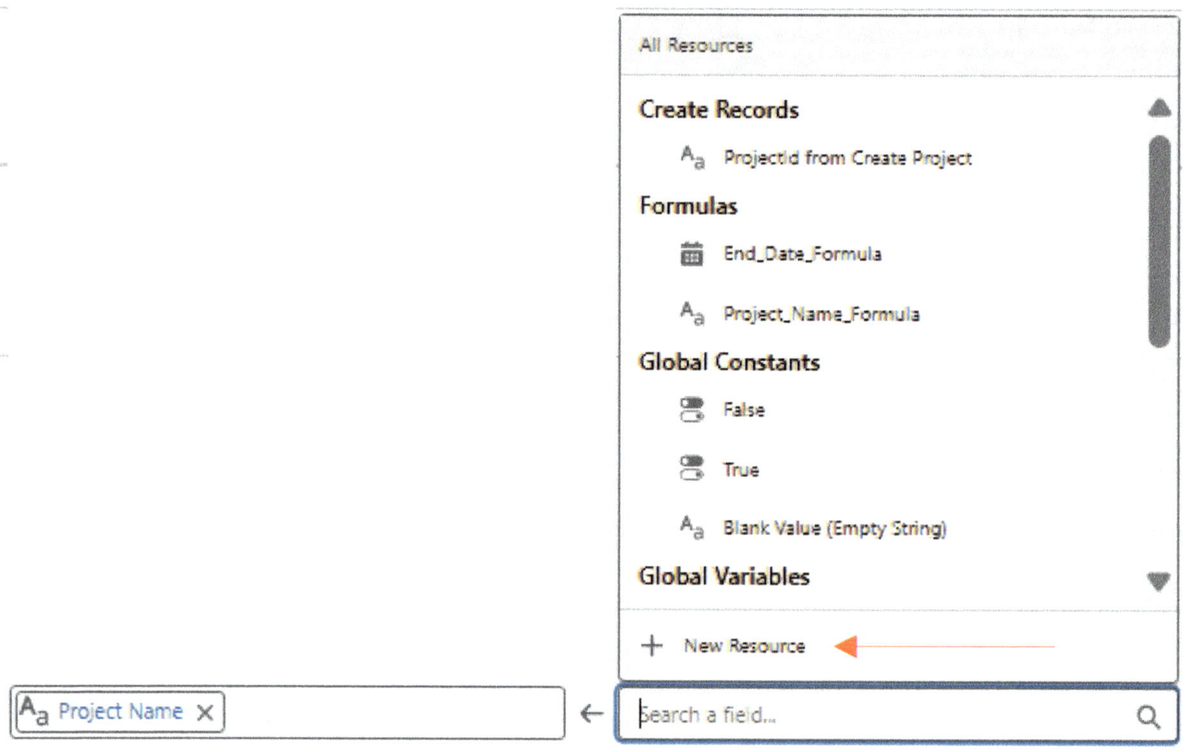

*Create a new formula resource.*

## New Resource

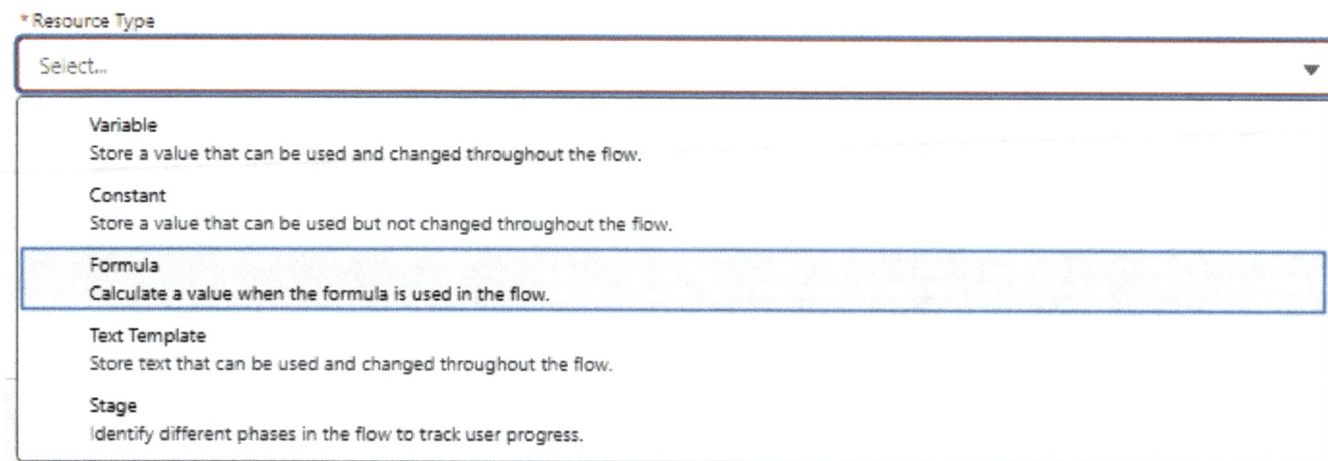

*Put the values in required fields to set up the Project name as:*
*{!$Record.Name} & "Project" and click Done.*

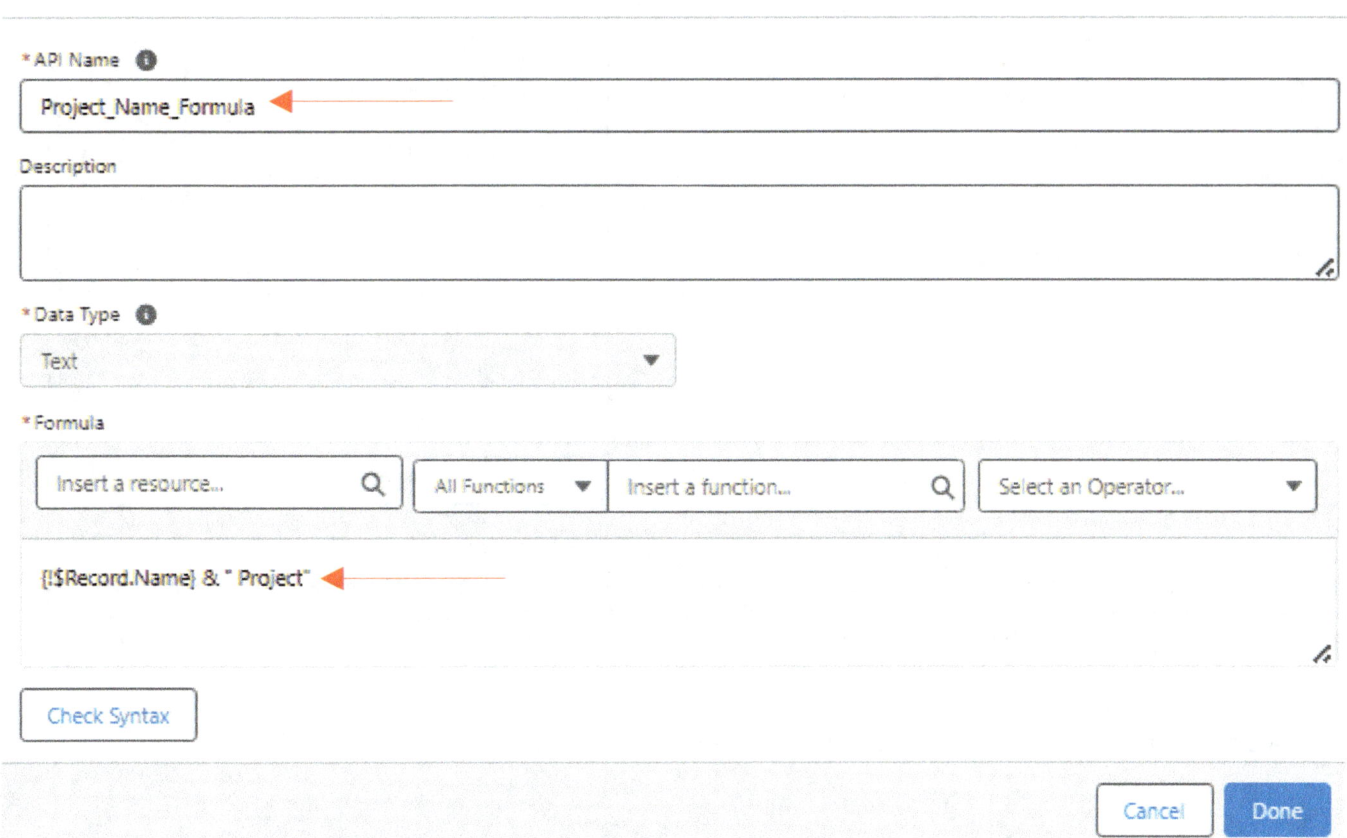

*Select the Opportunity field and set up the value as Opportunity ID.*

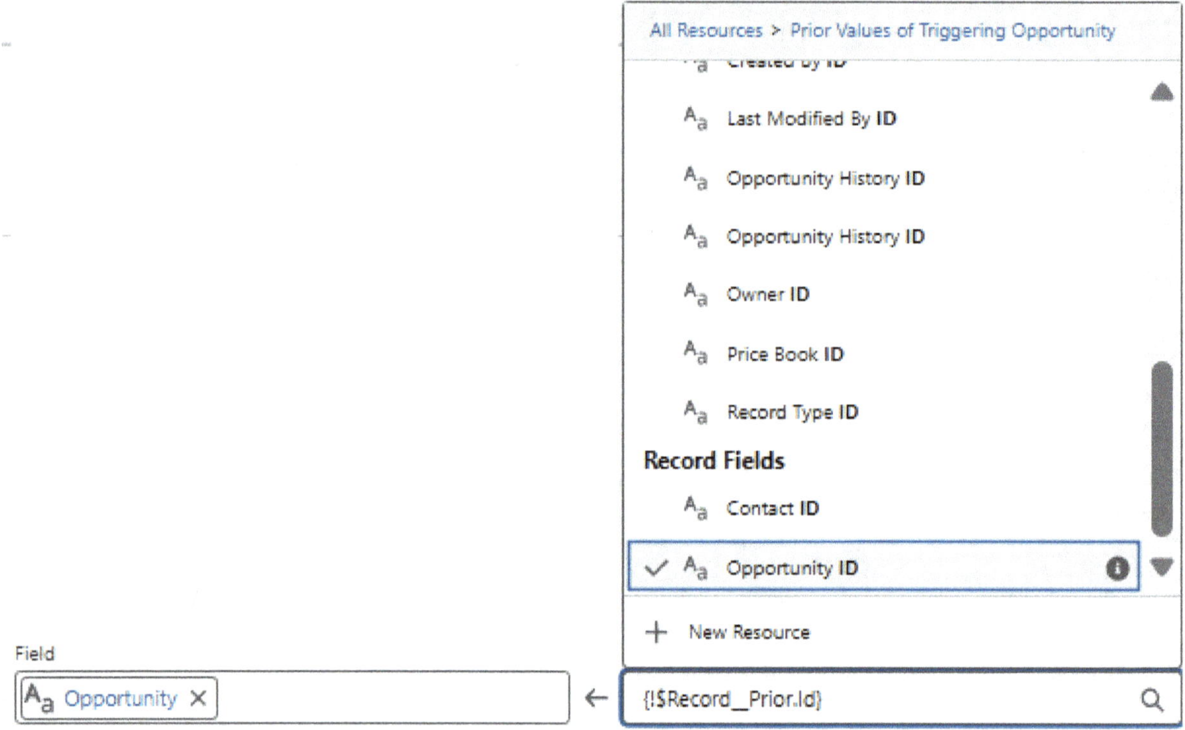

*Select Project Manager field and set up the value as Owner ID.*

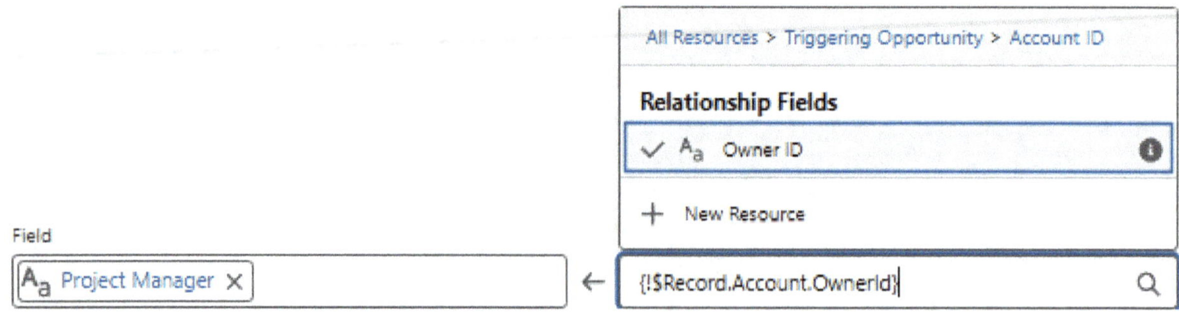

*Save the newly created Flow.*

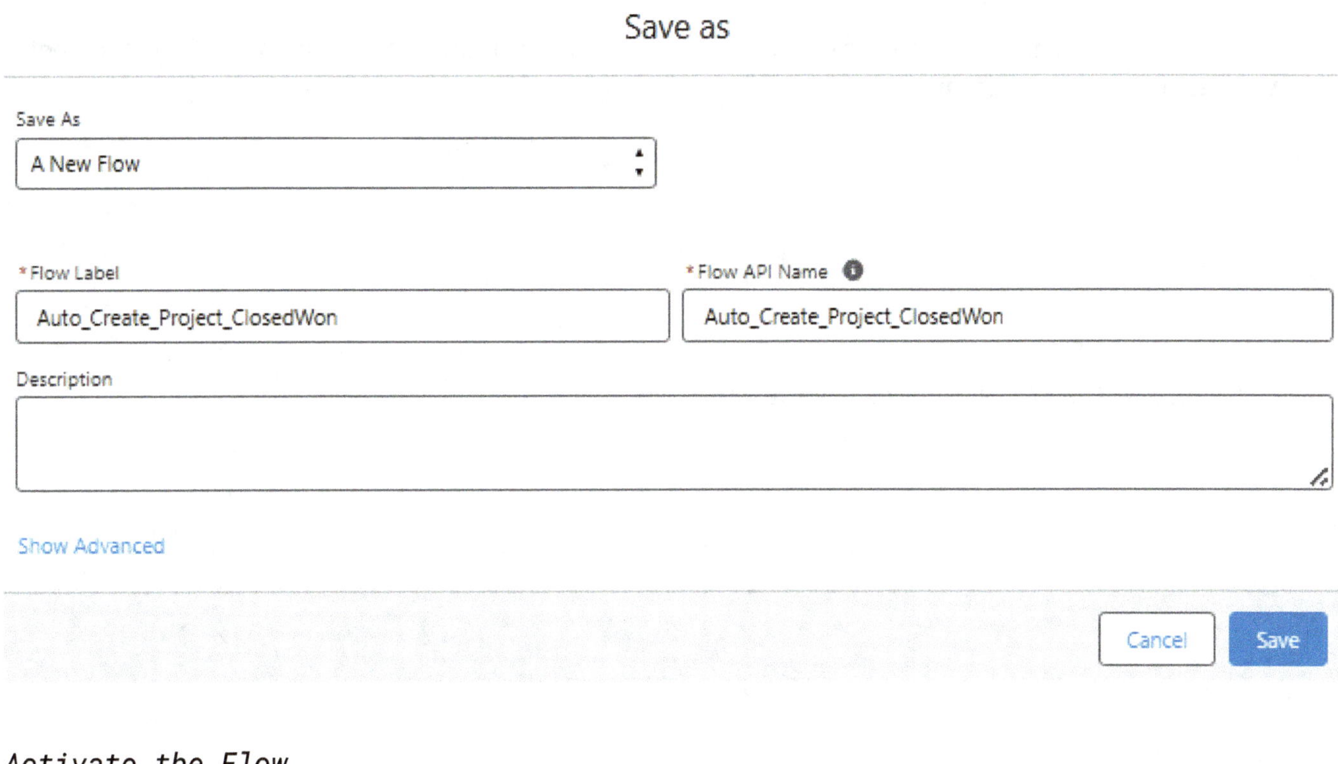



*Activate the Flow.*

# 10.5 Testing

Now we will test the calculation functions and flow implemented for our custom Project object by creating a new opportunity.

*Go to Opportunities and click New.*

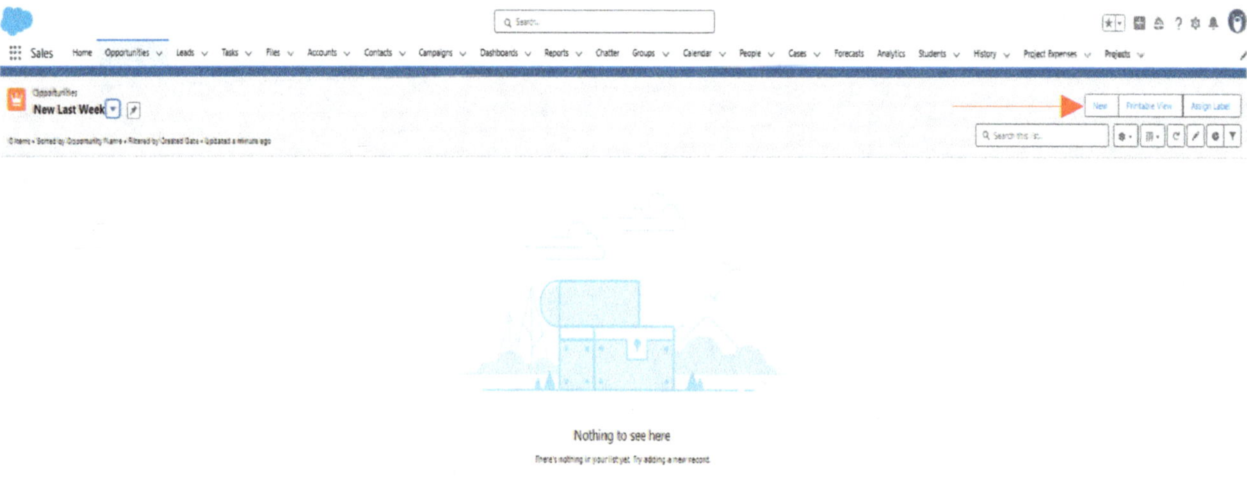

*Put the values in the required fields and click Save.*

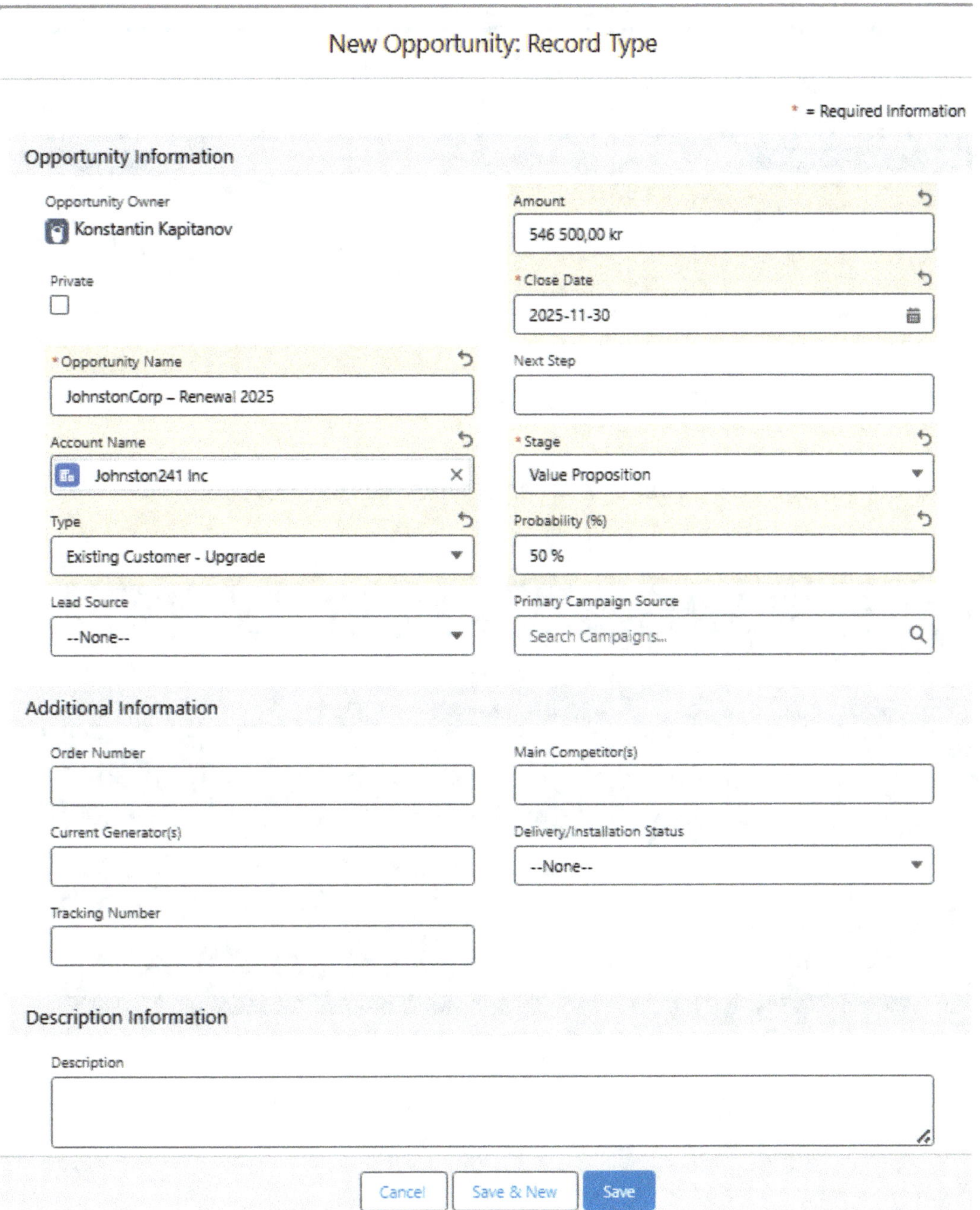

# PART II – Sales Cloud for Product Owners, IT Managers, and  Admins

*A new opportunity is created now.*

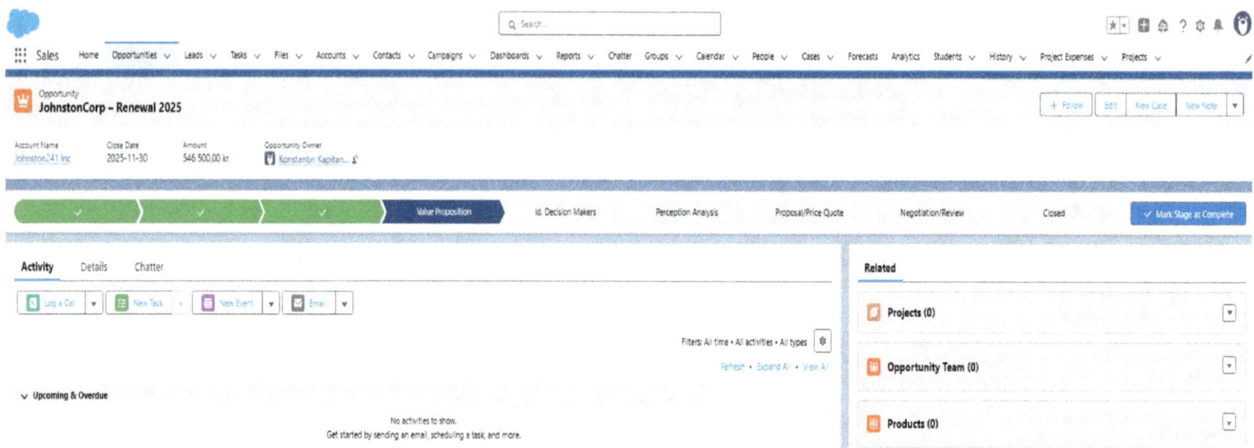

*Change the opportunity stage to Closed-Won and then click Save.*

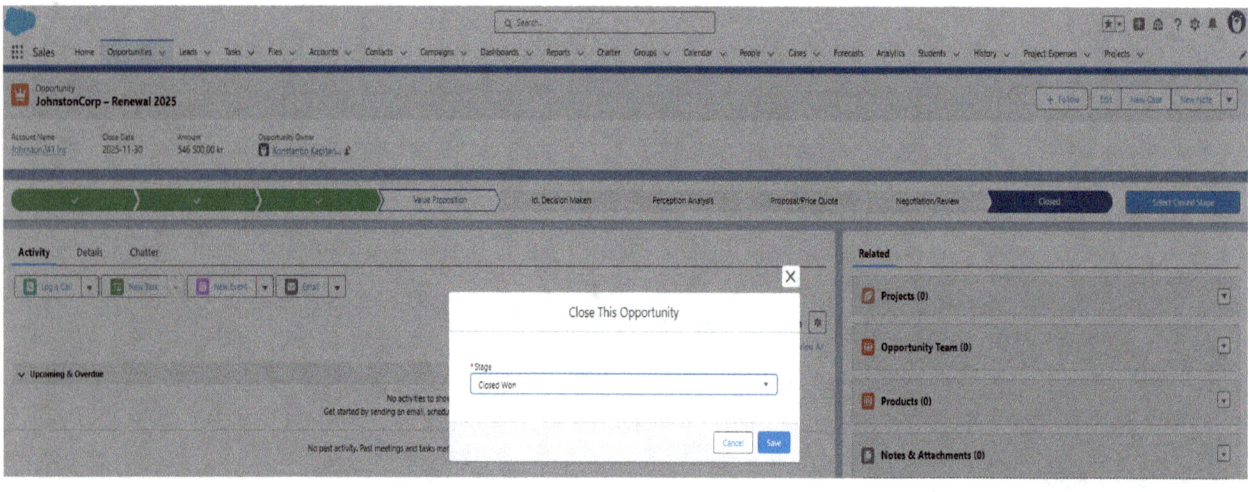

*A new project is automatically created now.*

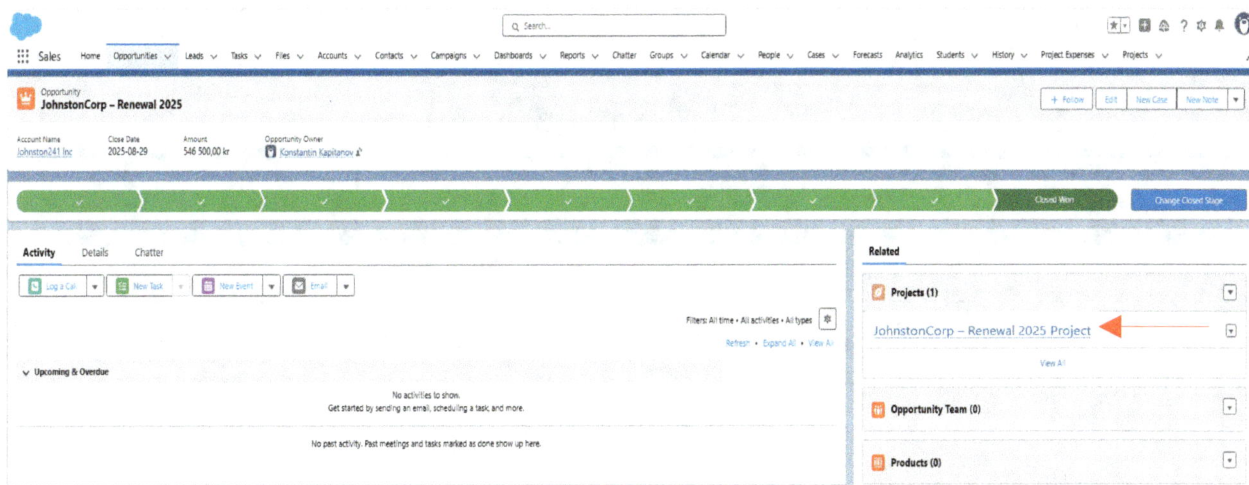

*Open a newly created project and click Related.*

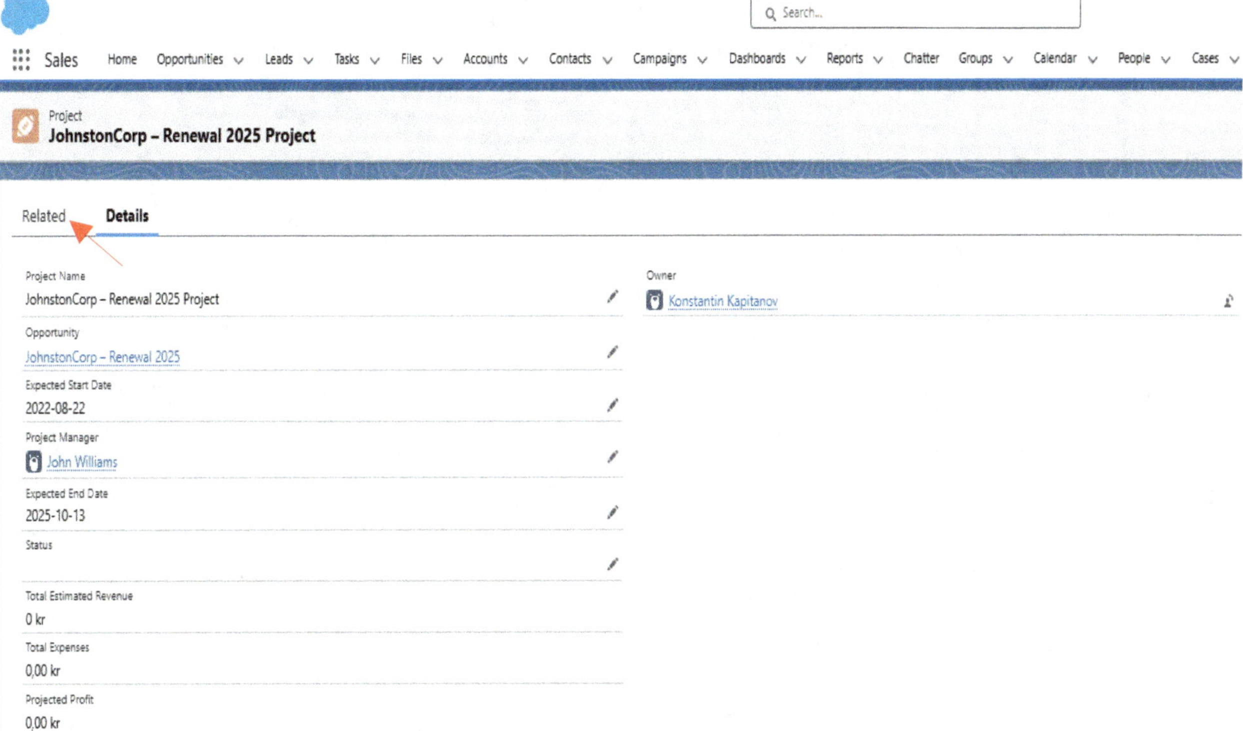

*Click New to create Project Expenses.*

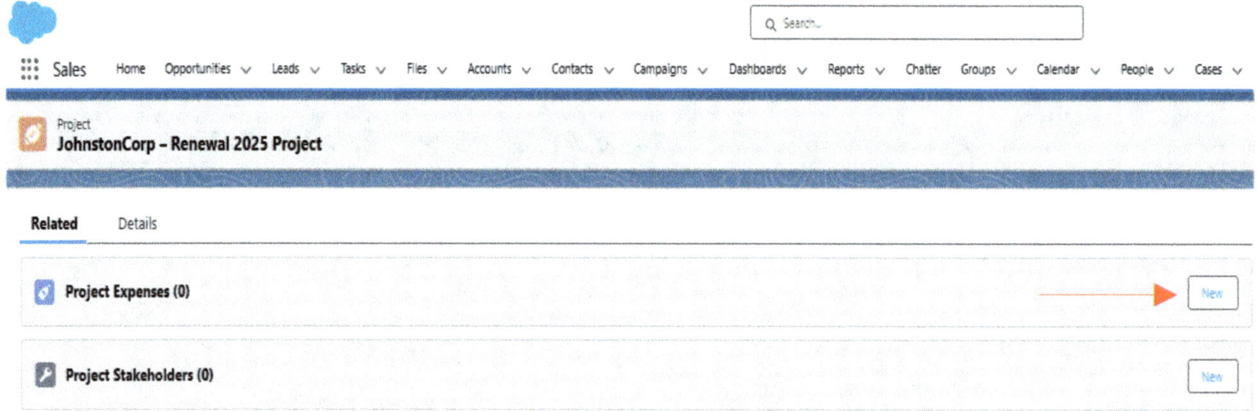

*Create a New Project Expense Internal Type and Save.*

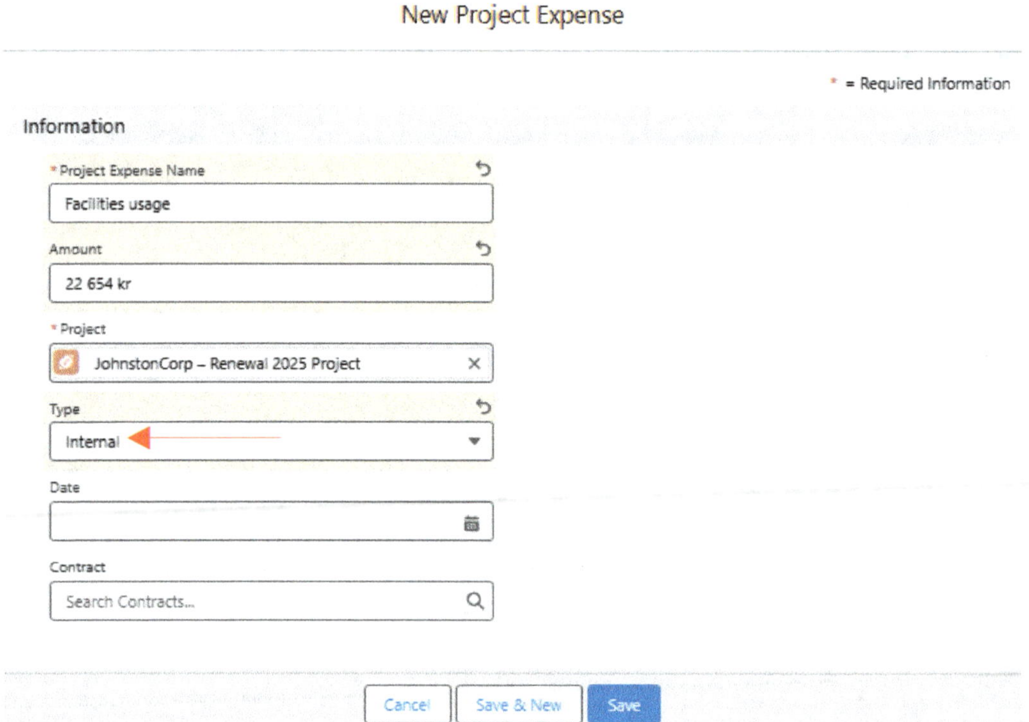

*Create a New Project Expense External Type and Save.*

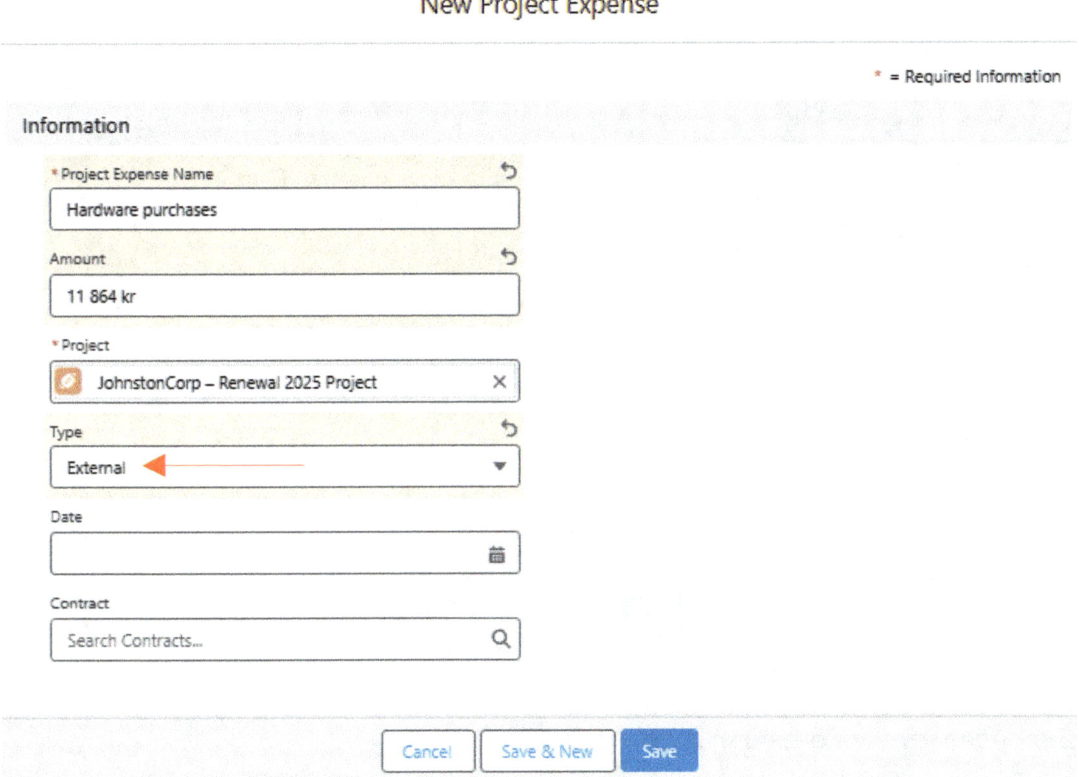



*Create a New Project Billing Type and Save.*

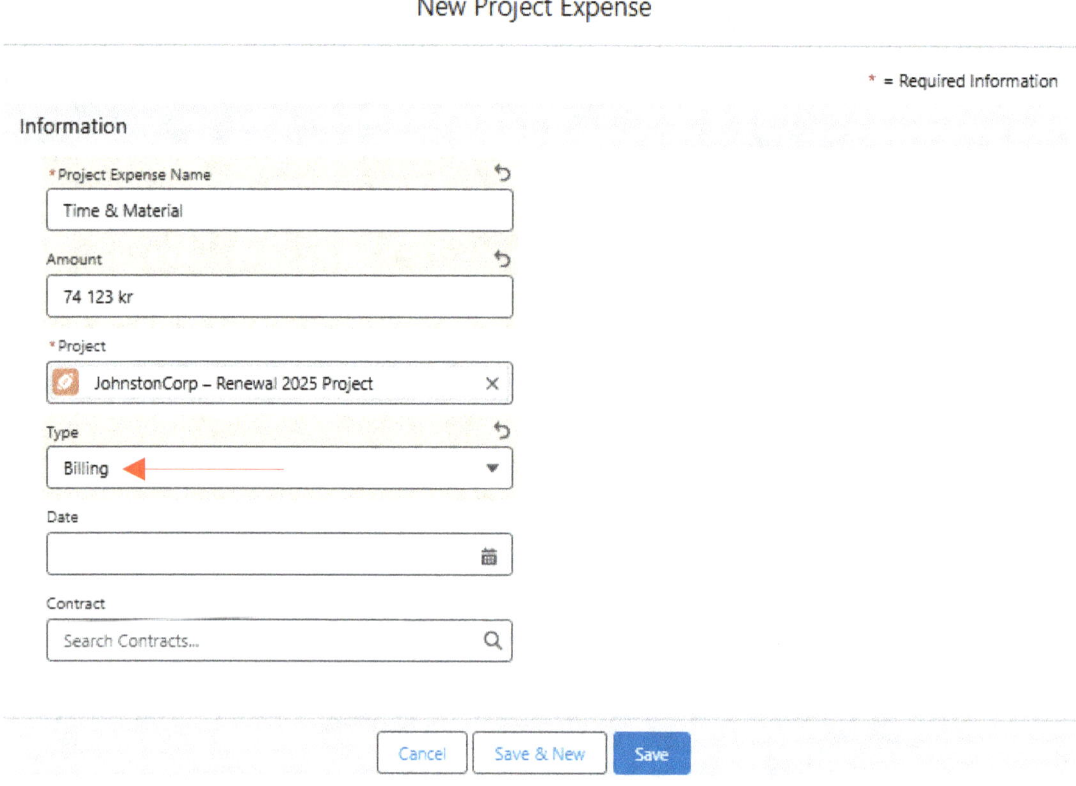



Then Project Expenses are created click Details.

See the calculation details on the newly created project.

246

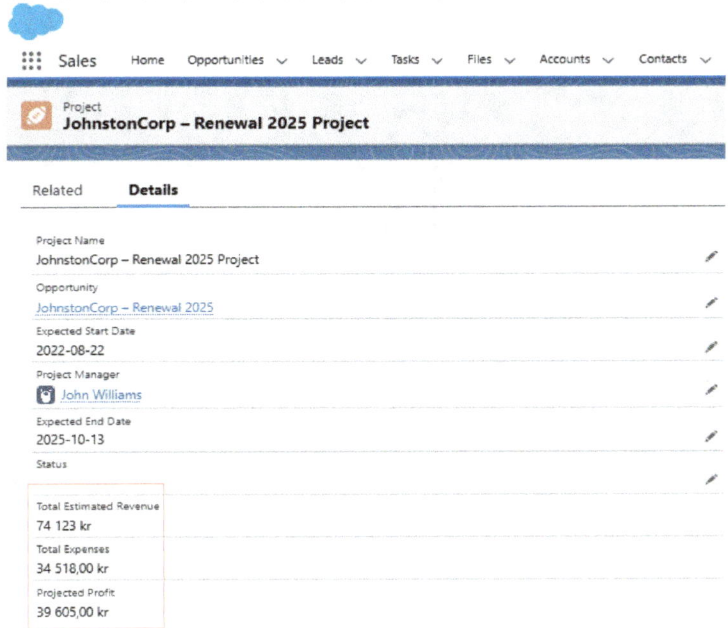

# 10.6 Summary

By the end of this book, you will have a grasp of the fundamentals and practical applications within the Salesforce Sales Cloud platform. This knowledge gives you the tools to advance your career, drive business success, and innovate within your organization. Let this book serve as your starting point in the dynamic world of Salesforce. Embrace opportunities to expand your skills, engage with the Salesforce community, and continue your journey toward mastery and ongoing professional growth.

While this book offers detailed explanations and hands-on instructions, you can build even greater confidence by supplementing your learning with Trailhead Trailmixes:

https://trailhead.salesforce.com/users/strailhead/trailmixes/prepare-for-your-salesforce-certified-associate-credential

https://trailhead.salesforce.com/users/strailhead/trailmixes/prepare-for-your-salesforce-administrator-credential

These resources provide interactive exercises and additional perspectives, helping you deepen your expertise.

# Index


## A, B

Account, 13
Account Access Level, 176
Account-Contact Relationship
    adding new relationships, 26
    confirmation of multiple account
connections, 28
    selecting accounts and roles, 27
Account List View
    creation and customization, 19
    filtering and saving, 21
    visibility settings, 20
Account object, 11
Accounts as Campaign Members, 55
Account Settings, 25
Account Types, 13
Activity Management
    creating and managing tasks, 51
    overview and importance, 50
    using events to schedule meetings and
calls, 52
Adding leads and contacts to campaigns, 59
Adding products to opportunity, 41
App Launcher, 6
Assistant component, 5
Associating Price Book with opportunity, 40
Bulk Data Load Jobs, 167
Business Accounts, 11
Business Processes, 135

## C

Campaign hierarchy, 56
Campaigns, 55
Case Access Level, 176
Cases, 18

Chatter
    Poll feature for quick team decisions, 46
    Post feature for team updates, 45
    Question feature for clarifications and
guidance, 49
    real-time collaboration features, 45
Closed stage, 36
Company Information
    configuration process, 130
    overview, 129
Conditional formatting
    application in reports, 84
    overview, 83
    rules creation and application, 85
Contacts, 18
Creating a campaign, 57
CSV file format, 163
Customer Priority, 23
Custom fields, 190
Custom Object, 183
Custom object features, 184
Custom Profiles, 148
Custom report types
    definition and creation, 69
    linking opportunities to projects, 70
Custom tab wizard   185

## D

Dashboard activation, 112
Dashboard components
    adding and arranging components on
pages, 110
    composition and examples, 99
Dashboard customization, 99
Dashboard folders, 106

Dashboards
    adding reports and widgets, 104
    definition and purpose, 99
    embedded components on Home page, 114
    favorite dashboards and reports, 115
    overview, 103, 113
    saving and managing multiple reports, 105
    subscription feature, 115
Dashboard sharing, 108
Dashboard use cases, 99
Data Compliance, 162
Data Export Tool, 167
Data Import Wizard
    features and limitations, 162
    usage and process overview, 163
Data Integration, 162
Data Management, 161
Donut chart, 97
Duplicate Management, 18
Dynamic dashboards
    dashboard viewer permissions, 106
    definition and user perspective switching, 105

# E, F

Editing product quantities, 42
Email feature, 54
Embedding dashboards, 108
Embedding reports, 108
Exporting reports
    export options and formats, 78
    purpose and process, 78
Field-level Security
    regulation of field visibility and edit permissions, 147
    setting access for Opportunity lookup field, 192
    setting access permissions for custom fields, 195
    setting visibility and access for custom fields, 204
    setting visibility and read-only status, 214
    setting visibility for lookup fields, 225
Field mapping
    editing and auto-mapping in import process, 165
    linking Opportunity and Project fields, 238
Fiscal Year
    custom fiscal year feature, 131
    custom fiscal year templates, 132
    implications of enabling custom fiscal years, 131
    standard fiscal year configuration, 130
Flow automation, 239
Formula Field
    Amount_Internal_External calculation, 209
    Projected Profit calculation, 219
Formula resources, 234

# G, H, I, J

Global Actions, 6
Global Search, 7
Identify Decision Makers, 35
Inline editing
    editing fields directly in reports, 77
    limitations and usage, 77
Joined reports
    application to sales and support data, 92
    creation process, 90
    overview and purpose, 89
    selecting joined report format and adding blocks, 91
Junction object, 222

# K, L, M

Kanban board, 36
Lead, 29
Lead conversion, 33
Lead Information, 31

Lead Management, 30
Lead Qualification, 32
Lead Status, 32
Lightning Home Page, 5
Log a Call, 53
Lookup relationship
    definition and application in Salesforce, 193
    definition and usage in custom fields, 223
    linking Project to Opportunity, 191
Manually Assigned Accounts, 178
Master-detail relationship
    characteristics and use cases, 196
    creation process in Project Expense object,
        203
    definition and properties, 213
Matrix reports
    definition and use cases, 86
    example of sales stage by date analysis, 89

# N, O

Navigation Bar, 5
Needs Analysis, 35
Negotiation/Review, 36
Object Manager, 190
Object Permissions, 147
Opportunities, 18
Opportunities report
    example data and structure, 83
    example data with stages and amounts, 86
Opportunity
    definition and management, 29
    linkage to projects and sales data, 243
    status changes and campaign impact, 63
    use in Record-Triggered Flow, 230,
Opportunity creation, 33
Opportunity object, 240

Opportunity Record Types, 142
Opportunity stage, 242
Opportunity stages
    customizing picklist values, 136
    definition and importance, 34
Opportunity Team
    adding and managing members, 44
role definition and collaboration, 43

# P

Page layouts
    adding custom fields, 215
    adding custom fields and related lists, 193
    adding custom fields and relationships to
layouts, 205
    adding lookup fields and related lists, 225
Parent-child account relationships
    benefits for complex organizations, 12
    hierarchical account structure, 12
Password Reset, 135
Perception Analysis, 35
Permission Sets
    creation and configuration, 153
    flexible extensions to profiles, 147
    user assignment and expiration, 157
Person Accounts, 11
Picklist field
    creation and configuration for project status
tracking, 199
    usage for categorizing Project Expense
types, 206
Price Book entry, 38
Price Book management, 39
Price Books, 37
Primary Account Replacement, 25
Product creation, 37
Product details, 38

Products, 37
Profiles, 147
Project, 243
Project Expense object
    creation and purpose, 202
    custom fields and relationships
configuration, 203
Project Expenses, 244
Project Financials, 246
Project object
    creation and configuration, 183
    custom fields and relationships, 193
    field value assignment, 233
Project Stakeholder, 223
Proposal/Price Quote, 35
Prospecting stage, 35

# Q, R

Qualification stage, 35
Record-Triggered Flow, 230
Record Type, 143
Record Types, 135
Related Tabs, 18
Report charts, 93
Report creation, 87
Report formats, 67
Report grouping, 88
Reports, 67
Report wizard, 69
Resource types in flows, 234
Role Hierarchy, 159
Roles, 158
Roll-Up Summary Field
    Total Estimated Revenue example, 213
    Total Expenses example, 216
    creation process, 213
    total estimated revenue aggregation in
Project object, 212

# S

Sales App Navigation Bar, 187
Salesforce Mobile App
    creating and managing opportunities, 121
    daily tasks and meetings, 119
    getting started and installation, 118
    opportunity and activities management, 125
    overview and features, 117
    task and note creation, 124
Salesforce objects
    definition and types, 8
    relationships between objects, 8
Salesforce Reports, 73
Salesforce Sales Cloud
    analytics and reporting capabilities, 3
    integration with other Salesforce Clouds, 4
    multi-device compatibility, 4
    overview, 3
Salesforce User Access Management, 147
Sales Pipeline
    overview after lead conversion, 34
    overview and purpose, 29
Sales Pipeline Dashboard, 99
Sales Processes, 138
Sales stage analysis, 89
Sales Territory settings, 172
Scheduled Data Export, 168
Sending list emails, 61
Service Level Agreements, 22
Shared folders, 107
Stacked Bar chart, 96
Standard objects, 10
Standard report types, 67
Summary reports
    creating and configuring, 80
    definition and advantages, 80
    example with grouping by account, 80

# T, U

**Tabular reports**
    definition and usage, 73
    example with Opportunities and Projects, 73
Territory, 176
Territory Activation, 182
Territory-based data access, 171
Territory Hierarchy, 175
Territory Management, 171
Territory Model, 173
Territory Type, 175
Upsell Opportunity, 24
User Assignment, 180
**User Management**
    creating and managing users, 133
    overview and responsibilities, 132
Utility Bar, 5

# V, W, X, Y, Z

Value Proposition, 35